The Wizard of Oz
and Philosophy

Popular Culture and Philosophy®
Series Editor: George A. Reisch

Popular Culture and Philosophy®

The Wizard of Oz and Philosophy

Wicked Wisdom of the West

Edited by

RANDALL E. AUXIER
and
PHILLIP S. SENG

OPEN COURT
Chicago and La Salle, Illinois

Volume 37 in the series, Popular Culture and Philosophy®, edited by George A. Reisch

To order books from Open Court, call toll-free 1-800-815-2280, or visit our website at www.opencourtbooks.com.

Open Court Publishing Company is a division of Carus Publishing Company.

The silly poem on page x is the result of Randy Auxier and Luke Dick screwing around.

Printed and bound in the United States of America.

Library of Congress Cataloging-in-Publication Data

The Wizard of Oz and philosophy: wicked wisdom of the west / edited by Randall E. Auxier and Phillip S. Seng

  p. cm.—(Popular culture and philosophy ; v. 37)
  Summary: "Essays explore philosophical themes in the Wizard of Oz saga, comprising the books by L. Frank Baum, the 1939 film, the novel Wicked, and related films and plays"—Provided by publisher.
  Includes bibliographical references and index.
  ISBN 978-0-8126-9657-8 (trade paper : alk. paper)
  1. Baum, L. Frank (Lyman Frank), 1856-1919. Wizard of Oz. 2. Philosophy in literature. 3. Baum, L. Frank (Lyman Frank), 1856-1919—Adaptations. 4. Children's stories, American—History and criticism 5. Fantasy fiction, American—History and criticism 6. Oz (Imaginary place) I. Auxier, Randall E., 1961- II. Seng, Phillip S., 1970-
  PS3503.A923W644 2008
  813'.4—dc22

                 2008039722

Contents

Ideas and Images of Oz

RANDALL E. AUXIER and PHILLIP S. SENG

Just about everyone loves *The Wizard of Oz*. But why? What is it about this tale that inspires agreement, admiration, nostalgia, even joy, among people who couldn't normally agree on what day of the week it is?

Part of it is that everyone likes stories. But we only rarely like the *same* stories—yes, there is the standard list, including everything from Noah's Ark up to *Peter Pan*. The first Oz story makes that distinguished list of universally beloved stories, and it seems to have great staying power. It's difficult to imagine a time when people won't want to hear the story, in one form or another. But why do a few stories captivate every generation while most are ignored? And specifically, why the tales of Oz?

Sometimes it's a good idea to go to the source, to a practitioner of an art. We decided to ask a professional storyteller, Chris Chandler, his opinion. He made the observation that the Oz story shifts for us as our needs, sentiments, and perspectives shift. *Oz* isn't a single story, he said, it's a whole collection of stories organized around a common quest, like the *Iliad* and the *Odyssey*. As in those classic tales, we can understand the whole story from the perspective of *any* of the main characters, depending on where we find ourselves at a given moment. Sometimes we identify with the Lion, see the whole of Oz from his perspective, or later with the Tin Man, or with Dorothy, even Toto the dog or the Wicked Witch (as Gregory Maguire has recently reminded us).

Chandler thinks that the power of a story to shift and show itself to us anew is part of what attracts people to it, at different ages, in different moods, with different concerns. No matter where we are in life, the best stories offer us something to consider, to feel, and to think on. Like the *Iliad* and *Peter Pan*, *The Wizard of Oz* is good for that, a sort of dynamic plurality of tales, all joined by icons and archetypes that we can use on a daily basis, to understand ourselves and others. There are as many Ozzes as there are situations in which it comes to mind.

And there are some philosophical ideas in *The Wizard of Oz* that *everyone* gets right away. "There's no place like home" may seem purely sentimental, but with a little reflection it takes on greater depth. For example, why do we say this in negative terms—*no* place like it? If we think logically enough, it seems to mean that even *home* itself isn't "like home," since *no* place is. But that's too literal, right? Only a philosopher would notice *that*. But hold your balloon down for a minute. One point of the story is that the home Dorothy left isn't *like* the home she returned to, because *she* is different, and she is *part of* what home means. Even if all the other stuff is the same, Kansas has a new Dorothy. Many people have noticed things like this in pondering the Oz stories. This thought about "home" is sort of an "idea," but there are also "images" to consider.

One of the more enduring images of *The Wizard of Oz* is that of the Yellow Brick Road. L. Frank Baum wrote of a "road of yellow brick," but the road really comes to life for most of us in the 1939 movie, where the Yellow Brick Road stands in sharp relief against the green of the forest, red of the poppies, and blue of the sky; all of which counter the drab, sepia-toned Kansas. The Yellow Brick Road provides a valuable metaphor for making sense of Dorothy's saga— it brings to visible awareness the notion of a journey or adventure, and relates the story to all the adventure epics written before. Sometimes we want to go where that road leads and sometimes we don't, but even in rejecting the destination, we need the image.

Contemporary songwriter Kris Delmhorst has said: "I'm not on no yellow brick road / Got a mind and heart and guts of my own," and Bernie Taupin suggests "Goodbye yellow brick road, where the dogs of society howl / You can't lock me in your penthouse, I'm going back to my plow." One assumes the plow is in Kansas somewhere. But the point is that, along with the characters, even the road multiplies its meanings as our needs and moods and perspectives change.

Some ideas and images stand out to the contributors of this volume, probably because they raise questions along the lines of their academic training. We've mentioned "home," but also the moral virtues have obvious philosophical importance, and several authors discuss moral issues that are at the heart (and mind and guts) of the Oz story. Evil is another idea that is difficult to miss in the story. Why does the Wizard ask a young girl to kill the Wicked Witch? Why don't the residents of the Emerald City revolt against the usurping Wizard? Why can't Dorothy's companions figure out that they already possess brains, courage, and heart?

The relationship of Oz to Kansas—to the "real" world as we might say—also raises some fun philosophical discussions. What's the difference between Oz and Kansas (beyond the color of the film)? Why does water melt a witch but not a young girl? What is the nature of fairy tales and why did Baum intend to write these "modern" ones, and not other types of fiction? How do movies help us understand the relationship between the world of Oz and our reality?

And then there are ideas that can't be grouped so easily but are about *The Wizard of Oz*, and to list them here is unnecessary; they're just a couple pages away. What we can't discuss in this volume are *your* particular ideas about Oz, what it means to you and how you've experienced it. Each reader of an *Oz* book or viewer of one of the movies has a unique experience with *Oz*, and, in effect, follows a personal yellow brick road of understanding. Some of your memories of Oz will be engaged in the following pages, but our aim is to bring our Ozzes into contact with your Ozzes, and to think together about what they might mean, for better and for worse.

We're off to see the Wizard now.

Somewhere over the Plato, way up high
There's a Form that I heard of once in a diatribe.
Somewhere over the Plato, all is Good,
Truth reigns over the rainbows, shadows are
    understood.

One day I'll wake up as a Greek and recollect
    geometry, so astutely,
And way before modernity I'll float about with
    Socrates, and he'll refute me.

Somewhere over the Plato, right endures
And the lies that you tell are noble and wholly
    pure.
Somewhere over the Plato, poets sigh.
If Right and Good and Truth can lie beyond the
    Plato, why oh why can't I?

I

Are You a Good Witch or a Bad Witch?

1

Somewhere Over the Rainbow: A Moral Odyssey

LUKE DICK

Following the roar of the MGM lion, Kansas fades into focus as an innocent bastion of greys, occasionally peppered with the purely black and the purely white. Hurl the house over the rainbow, and we discover a vibrant world with colorful, striking differentiations.

As a wide-eyed kid, watching Dorothy open the door was my favorite part of the film, and this once-a-year event really seemed to begin with the crossing of that Technicolor threshold. It is indeed a passing from one world to another. L. Frank Baum and Victor Fleming knew this, so let's take our own trip, there and back again with a new guide.

Ding Dong, She's Dead

Munchkinland is our introduction to the Land of Oz. Right away we realize there's a rigid order to the Munchkin's way of life. This structure is so obviously clear. Look at how clean the streets are. The Munchkins have even devised flower hats to hide from bigger folk. There is a rationality and an incisive Munchkin common sense that seems to reach far back into their history—Munchkin wisdom, perhaps. Their way of life seems prudent and necessary, given that the fifteen or so minutes we see of the Munchkins shows them dealing with three witches, a human, and a house that fell out of the sky. If this is any indication of the terror they experience on a daily basis, it's a wonder they're not a military state. I'll admit, part of me covets their culture, and I think the governors of our own great country could learn a few things about dealing with natural disasters and terrorism from watching the Munchkins in action. Not that I'm condoning flower hats as a respectable means of thwarting or dealing with terror. I do, however, admire Munchkin bureaucratic efficiency.

It's very clear that the little folk had definite plans in place. For instance, when the Munchkin peasants were hasty to declare victory over one of their foes with celebration and song, their mayor stopped them and verified their claims by calling on a piece of the Munchkin bureaucracy, the well-oiled machine that it is:

> As mayor of the Munchkin city, in the county of the land of Oz, I welcome you most regally, but we've got to verify it legally to see (to see) if she (if she) is morally, ethically, spiritually, physically, positively, absolutely, undeniably and reliably DEAD.

So, naturally, he summons the coroner for verification, who promptly appears and answers:

> As coroner, I must aver, I've thoroughly examined her. And she's not only merely dead, she's really most sincerely dead.

Bam! That's how it's done. If only the folks at the Tennessee DMV were as organized, the clouds would be far behind me. Ah, well. You see, the reason the Munchkins are the way they are is because they are essentially German. That's right, hearty, stern folk, ancient Black Forest dwellers, with roots reaching back to a secret hollow in Bavaria. Look at their attire—simply revamped lederhosen, newly crafted in psychedelic fashion. The Munchkin bureaucracy is as efficient as the German public transit system (and that's efficient!).

Now, it may seem as if the mayor is in charge, but that's just an appearance. The *real* person in charge of Munchkinland, as well as the rest of Oz, is Immanuel Kant (1724–1804), known formally as the Supreme Critical Chancellor of Oz. Topping out at just under 5ft, he stood a full head above the tallest Munchkin, which is just one of the many reasons he rose to the top of Munchkinland's hierarchy (his punctuality, dedication to duty, and work ethic are a few others).

It's little known, but Kant actually conceptualized the yellow brick road and oversaw its construction. Becoming Supreme Critical Chancellor of Oz, however, was a matter of being an intellectual juggernaut, not an ethereal aeronaut, like the Wizard. We never see Kant in Baum's book, or in Fleming's motion picture, because Chancellor Kant resides over the rainbows of Oz. Just so you know, to get to the Chancellor's mansion from here on terrestrial Earth, you'd need to hop at least two rainbows, one to get to Oz, then another to get to Kant's place (The punctuality is Kant's doing, too). That's where Kant stays, ruling over Oz and mandating new rules of pure reason and formulating rules for determining moral action.

This description may make Kant sound like some elite ruler who belongs in the sky, not in Kansas or Oz. Let me give you some personal history and get you up to speed philosophically and see if you don't come around to believing he's a mighty fine Munchkin. It wouldn't be an exaggeration to say that when I was a college lad, I saw Kant with the same wide-eyed wonder of my annual amazement at *The Wizard of Oz*.

By now, you're rolling your eyes. Only an egghead could possibly be enamored with some philosopher, right? I'll admit I remember sneering at my physics professor when he teared up at some "beautiful mathematical equation." Such loving talk of numbers usually brought on a bad case of gas for me. Perhaps a few personal roots should be exposed to get you all on my side.

My ninth-grade literature teacher, Mrs. Matthews, assigned each of my classmates a particluar reading chosen specifically for the student. I got Henry David Thoreau. That assignment was the beginning of the dust devil in my brain that grew all the way through high school into an intellectual whirling cyclone. I was dodging the flying debris of literature, science, and religion. I remember my dad heatedly shutting me down on a family vacation when I asked why there aren't dinosaurs in the Bible—all this on a trip to *The Passion Play* in Eureka Springs, Arkansas, mind you.

I was something of a lost country punk on my own odyssey over the rainbow, carried in a house made out of books. The point is, there's a mass of rich information out there for anyone to have, but such academic diversity leads to more good questions than answers. The first time since youth I felt like I was intellectually safe again was when my old professor hipped me to Kant. Levitican mandates? Bah. My house killed all those evil witches when it landed on the quadrangle at college. Don't think I can agree with stoning folks to death—seems a bit *too* old school. But morality and right action based on definitive logic and reason—there's something foolproof, right?

If I Only Had a Brain

So, like many people (up until my experience with Kant), *how well* one lived one's life seemed like a relative issue. I mean, some people equate the goodness of life with how much pleasure they receive. Most of them lived in someplace other than Kansas, because places like California seem to offer more pleasure and fewer cyclones. For these people, better food + better sex + better TV + better channel selection = better life.

On the other hand, some people believe that if they abide by some particular religious doctrine they will live a better life—or receive the blessing of a better afterlife. A lot of those folks *do* live in Kansas and other similar places. I guess we all need some compensation for our sufferings, and Kansas isn't exactly heaven—it isn't even California. But how can Kansas get along with California, let lone the Land of Oz? What I was left with were ways of life that did not adequately address contradictions. After all, hedonism and the religious can't coexist as moral codes, right? According to some hedonists, religious doctrine is man's fabrication. According to some religious observers, the hedonists ignore God's laws in lieu of pleasure. The easy answer as a young man was to say, "To each his own—there is no one right way." But then my house crash-landed, and the little professors all came out to greet me. Relativism wasn't merely dead, it was really most sincerely dead.

Kant actually had a problem with both ways, *and* with the relativist who didn't want to choose sides. In more sophisticated versions of hedonism, namely a philosophy called *utilitarianism,* the general view is that social rules, laws, and "right" are determined by the total pleasure of society as a whole. Killers (apart from those who accidentally land on witches) are not welcome in this society because the human consensus on being killed is that it is not pleasurable. I hope the witch didn't *feel* her legs shriveling up. Makes sense to classify being killed as a pain. However, what if it pleased everyone to be killed?

Wouldn't this make killing right, in a utilitarian framework? It seems so. The main point Kant makes in opposition to utilitarianism is that "pleasure" is not static; pleasure is at the psychological whim of humans—and psychological whims are certainly relative. Therefore, there's an element of relativity to morality in the utilitarian system. After all, one day it may be fun and pleasurable to steal, and the next it may be the opposite. If laws are based on the consensus of "feelings," laws would change with the winds of the emotions—and that certainly implies that laws are not absolute, but rather capricious and temporary mandates issued from capricious individuals. It's like having a wicked witch running your moral life, and who *knows* what she may do, or why?

Have you ever wondered why there's no organized religion in Baum's books or the 1939 movie about Oz? Well, here's why: Muchkins don't really need religion anymore, thanks to the work of their Supreme Critical Chancellor, Kant. Regarding traditionally religious upbringings as bases for morality, there is no doubt that Kant would agree with many of the Ten Commandments, calling the commandments "morally right." Though he was raised in a Pietist Christian home, Kant's ethical doctrine intends to rationally determine moral laws, instead of appealing to a religious book or authority to obtain moral laws.

Most religions teach that our actions are concerned with pleasing God. But the representations of God in various religions can paint different pictures of God, some in black and white, some in Technicolor—it's Kansas and California all over again. And that leaves us with a pretty whimsical entity, and to that extent we may have the same problem as we have in utilitarianism. God apparently can't decide whether we ought to live in Kansas or California, but his press agents seem to tailor the message to the expectations of the crowd that's listening. And when things go wrong, we blame the messengers. Instead of our moral rules being at the whim of capricious humans, for religion, laws can be considered as being at the capricious whim of God—especially when you take into consideration the various rules from the various religions.

But the Supreme Critical Chancellor of Munchkinland isn't interested in justifying our actions as means to please some other entity, or to get better parking in heaven. (Kansas has plenty of parking, by the way. I have often parked there myself.) No, Kant wants moral rules to be as rational, logical, and as absolute as mathematics. 2 + 2 = 4. The sum is self-evident in the connection of the two parts, and this is how Kant wants right action to be defined. Because God says so and promises eternal goodies in a holy book is not a good enough rationalization for moral rules for Kant. After all, there are many holy books with many different (and sometimes contradictory) rules.

Kant's ethics are two-fold, dealing with (1) determining right actions and (2) determining whether or not a moral action is praiseworthy. This second issue has to do with an individual's motivations for doing right actions, and whether or not we have a "good" will in doing dutiful actions. So Kant actually doesn't give Dorothy the credit for killing the Wicked Witch of the East, since it wasn't intentional. But he was off yonder, over another rainbow when Dorothy did the deed, so we can't blame the Mayor of Munchkinland for making such a small mistake. First, let's discuss how Kant determines morally right action.

Kant believes in moral universality and explains *how* a universal morality can be determined. The one thing that you *must* acknowledge in order to become a Kantian Munchkin is that humans (and Munchkins) have inherent dignity. That seems like a faithful stretch. Before we get to what Kant thinks about right and wrong, it's critical to talk about this distinction. I mean, the checker at the grocery store who has a stained shirt, body odor, technical incompetence, AND a generally drooly demeanor seems like a questionable candidate for inherent dignity, right? Not so, says Kant. Inherent dignity doesn't refer to how we dress or smell.

Kant spent the better part of his life thinking about how human consciousness works, and his rationale for his ethics depends on what he thought about consciousness. He believes that humans are distinct from animals in their capacity for reason, and in *The Critique of Pure Reason* (also known as "The First Critique"),[1] Kant's task is to enumerate the ways in which our mind creates our world. As fully functioning adults, we take for granted the fact that objects are formed. I'm looking at my own ruby slippers (okay, they're really just boots), and it doesn't seem all that fantastic that they are objects of my consciousness. They are just there, as other things are, in my room. No big deal. I can paint them red if I want to, I suppose. As adults, the objects of our world are ready-made. The mind has long since organized my visual and tactile sensations to form the object and concept of "boot" and has done so over time.

And right now, we're reading with experienced minds, but in our early development, the mind was forming objects and grouping sensations together to form objects. The way we group and form them is specific to us humans, and maybe certain tin men, scarecrows and at least one talkative lion, Kant believes; it is not

---

[1] *Critique of Pure Reason* (St. Martin's Press, 1956).

the case that bugs, bats, or flying monkeys see the world of objects as we do. The human mind has rules by which it comes to know the world, and for Kant, the mental faculty of "understanding" pertains to those rules through which consciousness organizes raw sense data, and understanding serves "reason." *Reason* is the ghost in the machine of our mind. Our inner world is constituted with objects and people and places, and this constitution is made possible through reason, by which we act on the objects that our understanding has categorized and schematized from the raw sensations that we constantly encounter.

Kant calls these sensations 'the manifold of sense," and that sounds sort of like all the colors and sounds of Oz all mixed together and waiting for someone to make sense of them, or to "understand" them in Kant's language. The main point for our purpose of understanding Kant's ethics is that by virtue of our peculiar mental faculties (understanding, reason), Kant believes we have dignity. That is, humans have dignity because of their rationality. Whether witches get any consideration can still be a problem. If you're going to kill one, it is probably best to do it accidentally.

With me so far? Okay. So what in the world does dignity have to do with morality? Kant believes that *moral action* and one's *moral worth* are directly linked to the fact that humans have dignity.

Follow the Yellow Brick Road

Since all humans are dignified by virtue of rationality, Kant's ethics require that we treat all persons as ends in themselves, and *never* as merely a means to an end. For example, if my inclinations lead me to want a nice pair of ruby slippers instead of these old boots, the slippers are the ultimate end. So, maybe I steal them, not caring about the shop keeper who has paid her honest money to acquire them. I do my best to walk nonchalantly through the shop, lightheartedly whistling "Ding Dong the Witch Is Dead" perhaps, and slip the shoes in my pocket (I suppose they would be too obvious on my feet—and do ruby slippers come in a men's Size 12?). In this scenario, the shopkeeper and her purchase of wholesale slippers were the *means* to my ultimate end, namely, getting shoes for free. I have disregarded her dignity in favor of my own desire for free fashion (or magical characteristics, perhaps). I viewed her as merely an instrument in my desire to adorn my feet.

This action is wrong and immoral, says Kant. Moral action or "right action" is ultimately concerned with the absolute dignity of all humans. Right actions are those which treat all humans as ends and not merely a means to an end. So the right action in this example would have been to pay for or otherwise acquire the slippers in some legitimate way that incorporated the shop keeper and her dignity.

This does lead one to wonder whether Glinda *stole* the ruby slippers in putting them on Dorothy's feet. I mean, surely they have inheritance laws in Oz, and surely the Wicked Witch of the West has a point in demanding the return of the slippers. Is Glinda damaging the dignity of the West Witch, using her as a means only? She tells Dorothy that the shoes must be very powerful or the Witch wouldn't want them so badly, right? Maybe the end is just to prevent someone wicked from becoming too powerful, but it hardly seems Kantian to involve Dorothy in that. Is Dorothy then being used as a mere means to the end of foiling the Wicked Witch? Oh, so many questions. If only Kant had been on the scene to instruct everyone.

Kant also has a more wizardly way of formulating moral absolutes in a fail-safe test of determining an action's morality. And from on high, above the emerald city, the one thunderous decree is boomed out with even more magnificence and power than the man behind the curtain. Kant calls this method the *formula of universalizability* (sometimes it's fun being a philosopher . . . you get to make up words). This formula says, "Act only on those principles by which you can at the same time will that they should become universal laws."[2] In less-wizardly words: never do anything that you couldn't imagine as becoming a universal law.

Let's keep with the stealing example. What would happen if everyone stole—ruby slippers, broomsticks, houses in Kansas, whatever they took a shine to? Would our system of trade work? Nope. If everyone stole, there's no way shopkeepers would display their goods for EVERYONE to steal. There is a contradiction between honest trade and stealing. Society, or the kingdom of dignified ends (that is, people), is made possible through all sorts of universalizable principles. If you hit a contradiction like this, then you can't very well universalize the principles involved in what you're doing, can you?

---

[2] *Groundwork of the Metaphysics of Morals* (Harper and Row, 1956), p. 88.

Take truth as another instance. In Kant's scenario, it's *absolutely* the case that everyone *can* tell the truth and there is no contradiction. Truth is funny that way. It hangs together. Lies slip through the cracks now and again, of course. Lying is actually pretty easy amidst lots of truth-tellers. Makes me wonder why Glinda says to Dorothy that she wouldn't have "believed" her if she had given the heel-tapping instructions right there in Munchkinland.

It looks to me like Dorothy would believe anyone, since she comes from Kansas where things may be grey all the time, but everybody pretty much tells the truth—and that's why you also don't send Dorothy out on the streets of LA alone, since there it's pretty much the opposite of Kansas. But if lies were universally applied, no one would believe anything anyone else ever said, and every place would look like LA, and no place would be like Kansas; it's by virtue of the truth that lies have the possibility of becoming real. It occurs to me that Baum moved to LA, Hollywood in fact, before Hollywood was "Hollywood." But I think people told the truth in Hollywood back then—except maybe Baum, who was fond of making things up.

So, we now have two, clean-cut and golden-bricked ways in which to get to a land of absolute morality. We can figure out our *duty* as humans by (1) the formula of universalizability and by (2) regarding everyone as ends in themselves. We are going to pass right by the Emerald City and glide into the ether of pure, unadulterated rightness. All we have to do is follow the yellow brick road Kant has set out for us. When we're faced with a question regarding another human, we simply "Follow the yellow brick road. Follow the yellow brick road. Follow the, follow the, follow the, follow the, follow the yellow brick road."

Because, Because, Because, Because, Becaaaause . . .

Because of the wonderful things he does? The Wizard is a crackpot charlatan, who tricks folks into ridding Oz of witches, then pays them with yard sale trinkets for their service—which is probably why the song repeats the word "because," because they can't think of reasons why they considered him a whiz of a wiz in the first place. By now, you should have figured out that "because" is not a good enough reason for Kant to consider the Wizard a whiz. On the contrary, Kant means to change the tune to, "If ever, oh, ever a whiz there was, the Wizard of Oz's not one because . . . because of undutiful things he does."

What turns Kant on is purely motivated, absolute right action. In addition to determining right action, Kant also makes a distinction between the action itself and the motivation behind the action. One's moral worth depends upon the motivation behind a right action. You can do morally right actions, but for an action to be "morally praiseworthy," Kant believes you must be motivated strictly by the duty itself, by doing the right thing because it *is* the right thing, not because it makes you feel good or it gains you respect from peers, or happens to suit your fancy. It may be the case that the right thing is the pleasurable, but that fact would be coincidental for Kant (in fact, if you *like* doing the right thing, you'll need to be careful about that, because it might pollute your motives—one almost thinks that Kant wants us to *dislike* doing the right thing, just to be sure we did the right thing for the right reasons). One is morally praiseworthy who does her deed out of reverence for the absolute moral law. That is, one does the right thing *because* it is the right thing, not for the accidental or intended benefits.

For instance, donating time to charity, say the Ladies Aid Guild of Gillikin and Restwater Downs, or LAGGaRD. We all know that getting water to the Emerald City has been an awful problem, and obviously we all want to help, and the peasants near Restwater should be assisted while we help them get water to us. But did you join the LAGGaRDs to help those peasants, or because it's a fashionable charity? The Supreme Chancellor says that your act is only praiseworthy if the rightness of charity motivated you, not the fact that your social-climbing grandmother dragged you to a meeting.

Similarly, not stealing those ruby slippers simply because you did not want to get caught does *not* make you morally praiseworthy for Kant. It would be praiseworthy to want the shoes so badly, having the inclination and opportunity to steal them, and then not stealing them because you know that stealing would be neglecting your fellow dignified shopkeeper's dignity, and just wear something else to the LAGGaRD meetings. Okay?.

When he's found out, and Dorothy confronts him, the Wizard says, "I'm not a bad man, I'm a good man, just a very bad wizard." Kant wouldn't agree. However, let's put him to the test, along with the rest of the bunch. Imagine that we've made it past the Emerald City, the deeds of Fleming's movie are done, and

Dorothy, her three friends, and the Wicked Witch of the West now stand before Supreme Chancellor to await his absolute judgment on their morality.

Somewhere Over the Rainbow

It doesn't matter how shiny the Tin Woodman is made to be, how many ribbons the Lion has in his mane, or how symmetrically the Scarecrow is stuffed; no amount of primping will persuade Chancellor Kant to judge based on any reason other than absolute morality. First up, the Wizard.

What do we know of him? Well, his entire image of a magical man is a façade. Surely his lying forsook the dignity of the heroes, and, we've already seen that lying isn't universalizable. He used the companions as a means only, to the end of upholding his charade and eliminating whatever threatens it. Kant's gavel comes down: "GUILTY. I find you, Wizard, a liar, with not even the possibility of moral worth." But what about the trinkets he gave, and the words of "wisdom" he offered? That was a sweet gesture, wasn't it? Even if it were charitable and morally right, remember that he only gave the gifts after he was found out. It hardly seems that he was motivated by the sheer duty of charity. Morally worthless again.

Now the Lion steps forward. It seems doubtful that the Lion was treating Dorothy with dignity when they met. Perhaps he was defending his territory and protecting his own dignity and the dignity of the woodland creatures when he initially encountered her. Probably not, since he isn't the King of the Forest at all. Regardless, the crucial action that needs judging was his decision to save Dorothy, captured by a witch, unsanctioned by any government authority. This seems to be the clearest case of a morally praiseworthy action, since he had to fight his very strong inclination to run away. Sure he had help, but ultimately, his choice to save Dorothy was of his devotion to his duty to his friend. That sort of thing is universalizable. Verdict: Morally right, morally praiseworthy.

On to the Scarecrow: he's a special case. Since he doesn't have a brain, we needn't even be concerned about him. He does not qualify for judgment, since he doesn't possess rationality in the full, human sense. He is out of Kant's jurisdiction. Make a fire with him, if you like. Oddly, however, he does seem capable of rational thought all along. But he makes a mistake in reciting the Pythagorean theorem, and it there's one thing Kant couldn't stand, it was bad math. That alone would tempt a Kantian to look for a match.

The Tin Woodman, on the other hand, is truly Kant's nemesis. Everyone knows he has a heart from the beginning, by his introductory tune. He wants to "be gentle and awfully sentimental, regarding love and art." Any person who even considers feelings or sentimentality as chief means of happiness is bound for immorality by Kant's lights. We wince in anticipation. Down comes the gavel— BOOM: "I, Immanuel Kant, find you, Tin Woodman, guilty of bad moral philosophy. You are destined for immoral action. I find you pre-emptively immoral. Furthermore any moral action you commit will more than likely be motivated by your heart, rendering you morally worthless, or morally suspect at best. You are henceforth banished. Take your sonnets, and especially your axe, and be gone."

Dorothy and the Wicked Witch of the West are left standing. Dorothy inadvertently killed both Wicked Witches. The Witch of the West acted out of malicious wrath. Sure, Dorothy's milky white skin seems to be an appropriate covering for her innocent demeanor. *But,* look at those shiny things: she's wearing stolen shoes, remember? By most any state law, the property of the deceased goes to the next of kin, or perhaps the state. Dorothy is neither.

Now, she didn't actually take the shoes, they were magically put on her by Glinda. But she refused to take them off. We've been told the Witch is nasty, but the only nastiness we've seen out of her came by virtue of her being pissed off about the shoes. We all know how hairy things can get when it comes to inheritances, so it seems the Witch has some justification for all her actions. She did give the Scarecrow a little fire, but we've already figured out that he lacks rationality, or at least mathematical ability, so we needn't treat him with dignity. That was just a scare tactic, and it is morally passable anyway. Sure, she's green, warty, and probably smelly, but she's human. So, why doesn't she deserve to be treated with dignity? Why shouldn't Dorothy give the shoes back?

And now we've arrived at the crossroads of the yellow brick road. Doesn't it seem like there are cases in life that *require* what Kant would call "immoral" actions? I mean, do *you* want those shoes in the hands of that Witch? Do you want to put nuclear weapons into the hands of rogue states? I heard a story once of a Jewish woman lying to her neurotic mother about her mitzvah

(Jewish good deed). The woman wanted to donate her kidney to a stranger who needed it, but her mother was utterly scared about the operation. The woman ended up lying on several occasions to the mother until the operation was over. The woman forsook the dignity of one person to provide life to another. Tell me she was wholly wrong with a straight face. Human events are much, much more complicated than the individual bolts that hinge them together. I need my moral oil can, because I think our Supreme Chancellor may be rusting in place, with his gavel in the air.

Given the information we know from the movie, tell me Dorothy and Glinda are wholly wrong for keeping the ruby slippers away from the Wicked Witch of the West. The yellow brick road is forked and overgrown with poppies in places. Apparently Kant didn't foresee that when he planned the construction. And that road is busted up and in a state of disrepair in others, and no amount of Munchkins or formulations will ever account for every nuance of life's complicated events. He's a fine Chancellor, but he's also in need of a little scolding, and Dorothy seems to be the right person for the job. I'm afraid Kant would have sent Toto off with Almira Gulch to be "desteroyed." Her claim was lawful, after all.

My grandmother used to cry every time she heard Judy Garland sing "Somewhere Over the Rainbow." I never knew why until I got older. The song is about the dream of a perfect world existing in a place that's well nigh unattainable. But Oz isn't the place, as Dorothy finally learns. A world of absolute morality is truly somewhere over the rainbow, where there are perfect triangles, eternally blue skies, and troubles melt like lemon drops. Here on earth, as in Oz, we have to deal with the multitude of interactions between humans. Luckily, even though the road is in disrepair in places, we can still see it. We have good guides, and in some places, the weeds are trimmed back. But it's not as clean as in Munchkinland, and if moral problems were cars, there's not enough parking for the whole fleet, even in Kansas.

If I Only Had a Heart

This all brings me back to the Tin Woodman. In the movie, the Tin Woodman seems to have all the virtues of the heart. In L. Frank Baum's book, however, the tin man loses his heart because of love.[3] He falls in love with a Munchkin maiden and wishes to marry her. The girl lives with an old woman, and the old woman wants to be taken care of. To that end, she doesn't wish the two to get married. The maiden tells the Tin Woodman that if he makes enough money to build a house, she'll marry him. Secretly, the mother has conspired with the Wicked Witch of the East, who then enchants the Tin Woodman's axe. Every time he works, he cuts off his own limb. To fix his limb, he has the tinsmith fashion him a new one. Eventually, he cuts all his limbs, his head, and eventually his body, so the tinsmith fashions his torso, as well. Except, when the torso is fashioned, he doesn't have a heart anymore, consequently rendering him incapable of feeling his love for the maiden.

This is powerful stuff, and speaks directly to Kant, who most likely was the maiden's older brother, partly responsible for cutting out the Tin Woodman's heart. But there's a hitch: even without his heart, the Tin Woodman knows he wants it back. Perhaps the hole where the heart belongs can speak. No matter how convincing the schema is for Kant's ethics, in my heart of hearts, I don't believe that morality should be wholly devoid of the heart. *Feeling* the good in doing something seems to have *some* sort of place in morality by my lights. But, then again, Kant has a point that morality cannot be placed at the mercy of human emotion and that moral worth has something to do with the purity of our motivations. I think people who give millions of dollars to charities simply as tax shelters are perhaps less morally praiseworthy than the little lady who donates only her free time to the food bank because she wishes to help the world, and it makes her feel good to do so.

It seems to me that it's a good thing for the heart to *like* doing right, that feelings and pleasures are not simply frivolous, and they are not always to be resisted for fear of mixed motives. Sometimes the heart knows what even the most rational mind cannot fathom. Now, to go so far as to say that morality should be wholly based on pleasure seems too radical as well. Kant was responsible for taking the Tin Woodman's heart, and his philosophy won't make practical sense unless head and heart are reconciled. Baum knew this:

---

[3] Frank L. Baum, *The Wonderful Wizard of Oz*, ebook (http://www .gutenberg.org/files/55/55-h/55-h.htm#chap05).

"All the same," said the Scarecrow, "I shall ask for brains instead of a heart; for a fool would not know what to do with a heart if he had one."

"I shall take the heart," returned the Tin Woodman; "for brains do not make one happy, and happiness is the best thing in the world."

There's No Place Like Home

So, at the end of our odyssey, we find ourselves back in Kansas, in the human world, safe and sound. Toto bites the bitchy neighbor lady, good-hearted gypsies read palms for a living, and farm hands dream the dreams of becoming worthy enough for statues in their honor. There are black spots, there are white spots, and there are many shades of grey. Somewhere over the rainbow there is a perfect place for squeaky clean ethics to work. But over the rainbow is no place like home. Here in Kansas, we must hold hands, Kant on one side and the Tin Woodman on the other, and with each step, we simply do our best to navigate through the crossroads and potholes in the road, where the only yellow we find is the occasional lines that warn us when it's unsafe to pass.

2

The Virtues of *The Wizard of Oz*

COREY McCALL and RANDALL E. AUXIER

Dorothy's journey to see the Wizard ends only when she accomplishes the seemingly impossible task he has set for her: to kill the Wicked Witch of the West and return with her broomstick. The primary reason that the Wizard of Oz asks Dorothy and her friends to accomplish this Herculean task is so he will not be found out for the fraud he is. Of course, Dorothy's dog Toto unveils the Wizard as a fraud.

He claims not to be a fraud, for he is "a good man but a bad wizard." What makes this claim plausible? How could one be both good and bad? One of the oldest answers to this question comes from Aristotle and his elaboration of virtue ethics. Although each of us seeks the good, or "to be good men," we are often mistaken about what actions will bring this character about. Furthermore, becoming a good wizard may itself make becoming a good man impossible, for a wizard may be little more than a slick showman who lacks the virtues that make the man good.

Although he can't grant them the virtues they seek, the Wizard can grant the companions external trappings of these virtues that will legitimize them and make them realize that they possessed these virtues all along—by means of the recognition of others. Informing Scarecrow that everyone has a brain, the Wizard tells him that it is how you use it that matters. He provides the Scarecrow with a Diploma, an external and public sign of the virtue of thought, what Aristotle calls "the intellectual virtues." As if to underline the absurdity of this mere piece of paper, he proclaims the Scarecrow a Th.D., a "doctor of thinkology." But Aristotle rightly points out that there is a difference between simply thinking and thinking *well.* The arts of thought have their own *norms,* and that's why we're all aware that some people are *better* at thinking than others. But how else could we recognize that, apart from creating public signs of it, like diplomas?

As for the Cowardly Lion, the Wizard points out that discretion is often the better part of valor, and therefore wisdom is often mistaken for cowardice. But as a virtue, courage is not so easily understood. Aristotle says it is the mean between recklessness and cowardice. Courage is not the total absence of fear in a threatening situation, it's the mastery of fear and the resolution to do what virtue requires in spite of it. Such actions are publicly recognized with medals.

Recalling the scene toward the beginning of the film, the Wizard teaches the Tin Man that hearts are invariably impractical, for no one can find one that cannot be broken. Rather, what is important is recognition; to be loved is more important than to love, and judged according to this principle the Tin Man certainly has a big heart—indeed, he is proclaimed a "Good Deed Doer." The Wizard provides him with a heart watch.

But the issue of love is complicated. In some ways it's easier to love than to be loved, because being loved makes us responsible to those who love us, while loving only makes us vulnerable to the one we love. The virtues associated with the wisdom of the heart are more greatly developed in bearing the responsibility than in allowing the vulnerability.

These absurd tokens demonstrate what most viewers of the film already suspect: the cultivation of virtue is the task of each individual, and no extrinsic goods or tokens of virtue will change this. Yet, the public signification of those virtues is not unimportant.

Dorothy and the friends that she meets on the Yellow Brick Road mistakenly believe that they need the authority of the Wizard to grant them various character traits or virtues that will make them more fully human (in Dorothy's case, the goal is simply to get home again, but "home" is not a simple idea, either). Virtues are the means to the good life, and all of these individuals find themselves lacking in one or more of the characteristics that will make it possible to lead a good life. These tokens of virtue do not virtue make; rather, the development of these virtues takes place on the journeys in Oz.

What Is Virtue?

Theories of moral virtue extend back at least as far as the Greeks. Plato (429–347 B.C.E.) wrote dialgoues in which his hero Socrates often tries to identify and define various virtues, like wisdom, courage, temperance, and justice. Plato held that the several virtues that structure a human life are "ideal essences" that must be *known* before they can be enacted. If you don't *know* what you're doing, you aren't up to anything good. So if you accidentally kill a Wicked Witch, you aren't in a position to claim much credit for doing anything good—or bad.

Plato's student Aristotle (384–322 B.C.E.) doesn't wholly agree with his teacher. Whereas Plato emphasizes knowledge, Aristotle emphasizes habit. Virtues are those character traits that we cultivate so that we can be recognizably human, to others and to ourselves.

A courageous individual (leonine or otherwise) will cultivate this virtue by placing herself in situations which demand a courageous response, or at least not avoiding such situations. The situations which will demand the virtue and hence help her cultivate courage, are, of course, many and varied, though the typical way that one might organize one's life around the virtue of courage involves soldiering. Virtues are habits of character that define the individual, but they are also, according to Aristotle, the means to happiness.

Aristotle thinks that all of us desire happiness; the problem is that we disagree on the nature of happiness. The reason that we study ethics is not to gain *knowledge* of the good; rather, we study ethics because we want to become good people ourselves—the people we want to be and the people that we need to be if society is going to function well. But he is very clear in saying that studying ethics doesn't make anyone ethical—it is performing virtuous actions, and making them a stable part of one's character, that makes a person ethical. Experience and knowledge are required for virtuous action; this means that neither children nor animals can be described as virtuous—not until and unless they know what they are doing and intend to do it, and do what they do from a stable character.

Children who do good things are "practicing for virtue," Aristotle says, but not yet virtuous. One assumes that Dorothy may be in this category, but perhaps her experience in Oz makes the difference—she does, after all, have to recite what she has learned before the ruby slippers will take her home.

Not all philosophers agree that virtue is key to ethics, but in recent years theories of ethics based on virtue have made something of a comeback. Leading this revival is Alasdair MacIntyre, who defines a virtue as *"an acquired human quality the exercise and possession of which tends to enable us to achieve those goods which are internal to practices and the lack of which effectively prevents us from achieving any such goods."*[1] We acquire virtue by living through situations that force us to become either virtuous or vicious, and learning the lessons they teach.

This conception of virtue is at work in *The Wizard of Oz*. Each character is having to learn for himself or herself what virtues are lacking and needed to draw from the situation the right moral lesson. Dorothy, for example, doesn't especially need to develop courage or heart—she has them, and unlike the Lion and the Tin Man, she seems to *know* that she does. We might like to offer her a little more in the way of brains, I suppose. And the dog needs some obedience school. Be that as it may, using this definition of virtue, and examples from the film, we want to show the relationship between virtue ethics and each of the characters in the order that Dorothy encounters them before turning to Dorothy herself.

The Scarecrow: Friendship and the Intellect

After her stormy departure from Kansas and her equally abrupt arrival in Oz, Dorothy embarks on another journey. At Glinda's suggestion, she seeks the Wizard's advice on how to return home. As we all know, she meets the Scarecrow first, and they strike up an immediate friendship.

Aristotle saw that friendship was one of the most important conditions for virtue, and a virtue itself. *The Wizard of Oz* confirms Aristotle's insight. If we're going to have any hope of becoming good, we must first practice the virtues. However, cultivation of the virtues cannot occur in isolation. Our friends become our occasion for practicing virtue, and Aristotle thinks that of all the great things in life, friendship is the "greatest of external goods," by which he means that apart from the internal goods of being wise, just, moderate, intelligent, and the like, friendship "is most necessary for our life. For no one would choose to live without friends even if he had all the other goods." Even if our lives were completely good in every other imaginable way, without friendship and companion-

---

[1] Alasdair MacIntyre, *After Virtue* (University of Notre Dame Pres, 1984), p. 191.

ship, they would be diminished, less than they ought to be. Aristotle does mention that virtuous people are the most self-sufficient, which means they can get along better alone than wicked or vicious people, but the wisest people still choose to have friends and are better for it.

All friendships are not created equal, however. There are certain less than ideal sorts of friendship in which individuals seek only their own advantage or else seek only bodily pleasure (we think you know what he's talking about). Much more significant and lasting are the sorts of rare friendships in which one loves another as one loves oneself. This type of friendship is the kind that each of the characters eventually comes to have for Dorothy, and the sort of love that she feels for them in return.

Initially, the Scarecrow and Dorothy are just useful to one another—the Scarecrow needs some help getting down from the pole, and Dorothy needs directions to the Emerald City. And each needs something and can help the other get it. This is what Aristotle calls a "friendship of utility." But quickly Dorothy and the Scarecrow discover that they would each enjoy having the other around—"If our scarecrow in Kansas could do *that*, the crows would be scared to pieces!" and they dance and skip away. Aristotle calls this a "friendship of pleasure." But in time, the connection between Dorothy and the Scarecrow grows beyond utility and pleasure.

So, the individual Dorothy first encounters on the Yellow Brick Road will eventually become her most trusted friend—the pitiful Scarecrow who lacks the ability to frighten anyone. He associates this lack with his lack of a brain—with a brain, he would be able to deliberate and devise various ways to frighten the crows. But his ambitions are much greater than simply to frighten crows. He doesn't fear anyone or anything (except a lighted match), so we assume he has the makings of courage, and we have mentioned that he's capable of friendship, but he simply can't think, and without this capability, he will never amount to anything more than a failed scarecrow. More importantly, his capacity for other virtues, such as courage and true friendship, is incomplete unless he can think well enough. Thinking will be required to outwit the crows, but more importantly, thinking will be required if he is to alter his current fate as a scarecrow who doesn't scare anyone.

The Scarecrow lacks what Aristotle termed the intellectual virtues. Intellectual virtues are any of the ones that are acquired through learning, while moral virtues are those that are acquired through habituation (of course, one needs habits of learning too, so they aren't completely separate virtues). The intellectual virtues distinguish humans from beasts or mere scarecrows.

For Aristotle, it's the virtues which render us fully human. Although animals certainly feel, imagine and remember, only human beings have the ability to synthesize all of these various factors of experience into a seamless whole upon which they can *reflect*, that is *think*. It's the fact that human beings can reflect on their experience renders them distinct from animals. Animals have distinct purposes and goods that are characteristic for them, such as hunting or grazing or escaping from witches (whether in Kansas or Oz). These characteristics make them typical for their species.

Only human beings can decide to cultivate the various moral virtues that will help them live good and happy lives. Toto may be well trained, but he doesn't do much heavy thinking (if he did, maybe he'd think twice before he gets Dorothy in trouble with Miss Gulch). This capacity to reflect on virtues and order them in a hierarchy that would make an individual's life well-ordered and good Aristotle called *phronesis* (he called it that because he spoke Greek, but in English the word is commonly rendered as either prudence or practical reason). While it's the basic intellectual virtues that Scarecrow believes himself to be lacking, he also lacks the judgment that would either make it possible for him to scare the crows all of the time or even do something more meaningful with his life. If he only had a brain, indeed he might become something more than a solitary failed scarecrow.

The Tin Man: The Heart of a Man

The next individual Dorothy meets on her quest is the Tin Man, whom they encounter while gathering apples. Dorothy exclaims to the Scarecrow, "Why it's a man! A man made out of tin!" The man made out of tin is trying desperately to speak, for he needs Dorothy to lubricate his joints (and who doesn't need a bit of that sometimes?). He has been trapped in the forest since he was caught in the rain "about a year ago." While he seems perfect once Dorothy has greased him down, his chest is hollow: he lacks a heart, although "he's presumin' / that he could be kind of human / if he only had a heart." His lack of a heart stands as a mark of his gross imperfection and lack of humanity. For the Tin Man, this lack indicates a lack of feeling and sentimentality. The Tin Man explicitly links his desire for a heart with becoming human, as he sings that he could be "gentle, sentimental . . . friendly" with a heart. He would have the capacity to feel pain, joy, anger, and every other emotion.

Aristotle sees these and other emotions as an important dimension of moral virtue, but philosophers in the classical Greek tradition are generally suspicious of emotions, for they are often difficult to control and to master. Basically, virtues are states of character that help us to relate and regulate our emotions. In the *Nicomachean Ethics,* Aristotle is trying to describe how the self functions. Since there are only three "conditions arising in the soul—feelings, capacities, and states—virtue must be one of these." Aristotle writes the following with respect to the relationship between feeling and the states of character called virtues:

> By feelings I mean appetite, anger, fear, confidence, envy, joy, love, hate, longing, jealousy, pity, and in general whatever implies pleasure or pain. By capacities I mean what we have when we are said to be capable of these feelings—capable of being angry, for instance, or of being afraid or of feeling pity. By states I mean what we have when we are well or badly off in relation to feelings. If for instance, our feeling is too intense or slack, we are badly off in relation to anger, but if it is intermediate, we are well off; the same is true in the other cases. (*Nicomachean Ethics*, lines 1105b22–28)

In Aristotle's terms, the Tin Man laments the fact that he lacks the capacity for emotion as well as the state of character that would allow him to regulate these emotions, to find the mean between extremes of feeling. If you don't have a capacity, you definitely can't regulate well the thing you can't do at all. Additionally, for the Tin Man, heartlessness indicates a lack of taste and refinement—he mentions he can't appreciate art, even though he has a fine sense of musical pitch, apparently. In order to be truly human, the Tin Man needs to be able to feel, to regulate his feelings, and be cultured. As a Tin Man whose only job is presumably to fell trees, he feels this lack of refinement keenly. Of course, this already indicates that he feels, for he feels that he does not truly have the capacity to feel. Like the Scarecrow and the Cowardly Lion, the Tin Man believes that he does not conform to an ideal type of the good life, and therefore that his existence is hopelessly impoverished.

While the Scarecrow seems to lack what Aristotle called the intellectual virtues, the Tin Man feels himself deficient in Aristotle's moral virtues as well as the feelings regulated by these moral virtues. Cultivation of both sets of virtue is required in order to become fully human. By agreeing to accompany Dorothy to her audience with the Wizard, the Tin Man and Scarecrow are cultivating the virtue of friendship upon which Aristotle places so much emphasis. The Tin Man and Scarecrow will accompany Dorothy to visit The Emerald City and the "wonderful" Wizard of Oz, secure in a friendship born out of opposition to the Wicked Witch of the West and their own desire to be something more than they already are.

Courage: Hearts and Minds

We've seen that the Scarecrow symbolizes our need of intellectual virtues and the Tin Man reminds us of the importance of moral feelings. The Cowardly Lion demonstrates that these have to be brought together in the right proportions in order to make a genuine virtue. Thinking and feeling by themselves won't result in the development of virtue unless they are mixed and moderated. The Greeks had a word, *sophrosyne*, which gets translated as either "moderation" or "temperance," and it is the virtue of striking the right balance and proportion in activities and feelings. "Everything in moderation," we say. Aristotle agrees, although he points out that you don't need just a moderate amount of *virtue*, you need as much as you can get.

The Lion has a brain, and we have no reason to believe he can't think, even if he's a little bit dopey. He also has a heart, but his feelings are immoderate—overly ferocious one moment, crying the next—in short, no moderation. So the Lion's capacities for feeling and thinking are spoiled by his inability to balance them. Aristotle thinks that every single virtue is a "mean" between two extremes—between too much and too little. The main things we have to balance are our feelings, and we do that by thinking well about which feelings to act on and how. That's practical wisdom, *phronesis*, and self-control, self-mastery, which comes from moderation, enables one both to *know* what one ought to do, and to be able to *do it*, while taking the right amount of pleasure from the action. In a word, good people enjoy doing good things. The Lion is capable of doing good things, but he doesn't enjoy it. This is a classic failure of *sophrosyne*, and since all virtues depend on this balanced mixture of thinking and feeling, the Lion can't learn any virtues at all, especially not courage which, as a lion, is the most essential virtue of all.

Whether you're trying to outsmart the crows life sends your way, find your own true feelings, or do the right thing, you need some friends to practice with, and so the saving power of all our characters is that they are capable of friendship. Without that, each would be locked in a prison of ignorance—of not knowing how to get what he lacks. But if you're beginning to suspect that these companions need each other far more than any of them needs a Wizard, well, you're on the right road. But I think you'll agree that Dorothy has the toughest problem of all.

Dorothy: Growing Up in the Land of Oz

According to Aristotle, children and animals lack virtue. Although they may have certain capabilities, and they assuredly feel emotion, desire, pleasure, and pain, they lack the experience that would permit them to regulate these emotions. They are at the mercy of their passions, and they live only in the present moment.

According to Aristotle, children and animals lack the "rational" and "deliberative" powers that would render them fully functioning moral agents, beings who can decide for themselves what is good and what will bring them happiness. "It is not surprising, then, that we regard neither ox, nor horse nor any other kind of animal as happy; for none of them can share in this sort of activity. For the same reason a child is not happy either, since his age prevents him from doing these sorts of actions [i.e. virtuous actions]" (line 1100a1). Of young people, Aristotle famously says:

> They look at the good side rather than the bad, not having yet witnessed much wickedness. They trust others readily, because they have not yet often been cheated. . . . and besides that, they have as yet met with few disappointments. Their lives are mainly spent not in memory but in expectation . . . and youth has a long future before it and a short past behind it. . . .Their hot tempers and hopeful dispositions make them more courageous than their elders. . . . They are shy, accepting the rules of society in which they have been trained, and not yet believing in any other standard of honor. They have exalted notions, because they have not yet been humbled by life or learnt its necessary limitations . . . their lives are more regulated by moral feeling than by

reasoning . . . They are fonder of their friends than are their elders, because they like spending their days in the company of others . . . They are ready to pity others, because they think everyone an honest man, or anyhow better than he is; they judge their neighbors by their own harmless natures, and so cannot think he deserves to be treated that way. . . . Such then, is the character of the young. (lines 1389a1–b12)

Does this sound like anyone you know about, anyone, say, from Kansas? Aristotle thinks that formal lessons in ethics would be wasted on the young. We study ethics in the hope of becoming good, not just to learn about the good in some abstract sense. Sticking young people in a classroom and making them read Aristotle won't do the trick. As Aristotle writes, "our present discussion does not aim, as our others do, at study; for the purpose of our examination is not to know what virtue is, but to become good, since otherwise the inquiry would be of no benefit to us."

What Dorothy needs is *experience.* Oz seems like quite an opportunity for that. Like the other three characters, Dorothy's actual journey along the Yellow Brick Road to the Emerald City is also a metaphorical journey to becoming a moral agent, in a sense, to growing up. Dorothy shares with each of her friends the wish to become more fully human in some way; for Dorothy, the moral journey means leaving her childish ways behind. Oz demands that she become something more than the child she was back in Kansas.

Dorothy's prospects for growing up and for leadership of the friends' quest to the Emerald City, is exemplified by the encounter between herself and the Cowardly Lion. Each of the members of Dorothy's party is frightened by the seemingly ferocious lion until he threatens Toto with harm. Dorothy steps in to defend him; this action contrasts markedly with her initial response to Miss Gulch back in Kansas. There, she felt the only course of action was to run away, while in Oz she defends Toto despite her own fear of this apparently ferocious lion. While the film ostensibly deals with the quest of the Tin Man, Scarecrow, and Cowardly Lion to acquire the various virtues they believe they lack, the film also marks the transformation of Dorothy from a frightened child with no control over events to a mature moral agent who leads her friends along the Yellow Brick Road to seek the counsel of the Wizard of Oz. Dorothy's growth can be seen easily by contrasting the Dorothy we meet in Kansas with the individual she becomes by the end of the film.

The film opens on a hardscrabble farm in the middle of nowhere. This farm provides a glimpse into the lives that transformed this place. We initially meet the avatars of the Cowardly Lion, Tin Woodman, and the Scarecrow, hired hands whose skills help keep the farm running, but they do not reap the benefits of their labor to the same degree as Dorothy's Aunt and Uncle, who own the farm. They also take care of Dorothy, who is portrayed at the beginning of the film as prone to dreamy, childish flights of fancy.

The film begins with twin crises: Dorothy running from Miss Gulch, who has threatened her dog Toto with bodily harm for invading her garden. But Dorothy's Uncle Henry and Aunt Em are in a state of panic themselves, for the incubator that warms the chicks is broken. They have no time for Dorothy and her seemingly childish crisis. It makes one wonder why Dorothy isn't hard at work like everyone else, but apparently that isn't expected of her, at least not on this day. But also, perhaps her status as an orphan has led everyone to be overly solicitous toward her—we really aren't told. All Aunt Em says to clue us in is that "it's no place for Dorothy around a pig sty!"

Failing to get the desired response from her Aunt and Uncle, Dorothy next turns to the three hired men for help, Hunk (The Scarecrow), Zeke (The Cowardly Lion), and Hickory (The Tin Man). They also are too busy to deal with Dorothy's problem, but they at least are able to listen to her. In a bit of foreshadowing, each of the men advises Dorothy that she needs a particular virtue. Hunk advises to use her brains ("you'd think you didn't have any brains at all," he says) and avoid Miss Gulch's house on the way home from school. Of course, he says this just before he stupidly smashes his finger with a hammer. Zeke advises her to get some courage and stand up to Miss Gulch, just as Dorothy falls into the hogs' pen, and Zeke saves her, although he's visibly frightened, causing the other two men to ridicule him for his cowardice. Hickory claims that one day the town will erect a statue in his honor, striking the very pose in which Dorothy later discovers the Tin Man rusted, but the only indication we get of his heart is that he is the first to rush over to Dorothy and ask whether she is alright.

Aside from the obvious foreshadowing, what this early scene shows is that, at least in this world called Kansas, Dorothy is truly the one in need of the right feelings, the right ideas, and the courage to put them together; in short, she lacks the virtues. More simply, in this drab world, Dorothy lacks full agency because she lacks the virtues—she's just a kid.

We also meet Almira Gulch, Dorothy's nemesis in Kansas as well as in Oz. Miss Gulch represents the voice of reason backed up by the authority of the law. She takes Toto away in order to fulfill a sheriff's warrant, but he runs away. This escape is the first of several in the film, for Toto escapes from his appointed destiny with the law; when Toto returns, Dorothy decides that her only option is to flee as well. Dorothy will flee this grey world of grown-up cares and responsibilities, just as she will decide not to cultivate the virtues that would allow her to deal with Miss Gulch. Aristotle knew that children lack virtue, and that moral virtue cannot be taught, although it *can* be learned. Moral virtue comes about as the fruit of experience. Maturity is a result of growing into the virtues. But rather than standing up to Miss Gulch, Dorothy takes her cue from Toto and runs away. She will respond rather differently to the Witch in Oz, as we all know.

And Dorothy soon meets Professor Marvel, an eccentric charlatan. Yet Professor Marvel possesses wisdom of a sort, for he sees that the place that Dorothy belongs, despite what she claims, is at home rather than on the road with him. Obviously, the Wizard has already sent her home once before she encountered him in Oz, and where she was naive enough to believe his silly fortune-telling tricks in Kansas, by the time she has seen more of the world, or at least of Oz, she's in a position to discover that not everyone is honest.

This decision to return home leads Dorothy on to the greatest escape "over the rainbow." This final journey, which comes about either as the result of a head trauma or a tornado, leads to the transfiguration of her self from the childish Dorothy at home on the Kansas plains to the Dorothy who asserts herself as an agent of virtue in the Technicolor Land of Oz. No sooner has she arrived than the crucial question is put to her –is she good or bad? She knows she isn't a witch, but it appears that the other part of the question never quite crossed her mind, until she had to decide whether to accept responsibility for someone's death.

The Munchkins want to know whether they are dealing with someone with the power to kill a witch who uses that power for good or for ill. In short, they want to know what sort of an agent Dorothy is—is she virtuous or is she vicious? Is she Good or is she

Wicked? And she means to be good, but no longer knows whether she is. *That* is what she has to find out, slowly and painfully.

As all of us do, of course. Dorothy had grown accustomed to the role she played back home on her farm in Kansas. Her Aunt and Uncle told her what to do, as did everyone else who worked on the farm. By landing in Oz and inadvertently killing the Wicked Witch of the East, Dorothy has become an actor in a story for which she was not responsible—or so she thinks. She lacked responsibility in Kansas to be sure, but here for the first time she is recognized as a moral agent, and not just a moral agent but a hero as well. She must decide what role to play in this new narrative, which is something a child simply cannot do. As a consequence of this new status as a responsible moral agent (and also due to that messy fact that she killed the Witch's sister), Dorothy also finds herself the mortal enemy of the Wicked Witch of the West who will stop at nothing to avenge the death of her sister. If she wants to find her way home, she will have to confront the Wicked Witch of the West as well as journey to the Emerald City to find the Wizard.

Like Miss Gulch, The Wizard of Oz possesses an aura of public authority without possessing true moral authority. Miss Gulch may own half the county and have the sheriff in her pocket, but as Aunt Em makes clear, that "doesn't mean you have the power to run the rest of us." She's a tyrant who relies on intimidation to get her way, not on any personal virtue. On the other side, the Wizard does everything he can to avoid having to deal with Dorothy and her companions, because he knows that he cannot truly help them. He is incompetent and fearful of being discovered as such, so he uses sleight of hand, intimidates them, sets impossible tasks before them. These are common ways that people who lack virtue try to compensate for it as adults—and they are failing to take full responsibility for the state of their character. Most of us have had bosses that fall into one or both types.

Dorothy realizes that she has to take responsibility for her actions, and that she cannot rely upon the Wizard to get her back home. He hears Dorothy crying and his sentiments get the better of him. He hopes that he can frighten them and get them to flee based upon his "great and powerful" pyrotechnics. It works once, but not twice. But the Wizard has succeeded in bringing Dorothy to face the Witch, who seems to embody not only what she fears, but what she fears she could become. Any of us could. It has to be faced. The Wicked Witch of the West's last moments repeat her sister's, for Dorothy inadvertently kills her while trying to put out the fire that has engulfed Scarecrow's arm.

The Witch's last words are telling: "How could a good little girl like you destroy my beautiful wickedness?" The Wicked Witch has mistaken the good, mature moral agent Dorothy for the well-meaning but dreamy child she was back home, she takes an unintentional act for a deliberate decision—or at least, the effect is the same. And somehow, after all this, the quartet returns to the Wizard, hoping that he will grant them the virtues they still believe they lack. They still don't recognize what they have done or what it has taught them.

Of course, the tokens of virtue that the Wizard confers upon the three friends are really superfluous, for they are tokens of the virtues they have already acquired. But of what value to us are virtues that we don't know we possess? And here we make some progress on the old "paradox of virtue"—whether it's possible to perform a truly virtuous act without knowing one has done it. Whether or not it's knowledge that enables us to act virtuously, it seems assured that getting the benefit of our own experience requires that we recognize which among our own actions do and do not build character.

To possess a virtue without knowing and recognizing it seems to undermine the efforts we made to obtain it. Like Aristotle, the Wizard of Oz knows that virtue cannot be conferred on another nor can it be acquired simply by studying books. This knowledge is what makes him a good man but a bad wizard, for if he were a better wizard he might have been able to say a magic word and grant them all the virtues they seek. But that isn't how life works.

However, as a good man the Wizard of Oz knows that virtue is a state of character that one must cultivate for oneself. This cultivation is what the Scarecrow, Tin Man, and Lion have done: out of a desire to help Dorothy, they have become the sort of (almost) humans they most desired to be. As for Dorothy, the harrowing experience of Oz has taught her what it means to be a true friend and a responsible moral agent. This experience has rendered her an adult. If she isn't a fully developed moral agent yet, she is certainly on the road, and at the very least she should now be equal to the task of facing down Miss Gulch—unless the cyclone already took care of Miss Gulch, as we all secretly hope (and don't pretend you never thought of that).

3

Very Good, but Not So Mysterious: Hegel, Rushdie, and the Dialectics of Oz

GINA ALTAMURA and J.M. FRITZMAN

My great teacher, the blessed Hegel, once said to me: "if one were to write down all the dreams that people in a particular period had, then there would arise out of a reading of these collected dreams a wholly accurate picture of the spirit of that period."[1]

This chapter is about Hegel, Rushdie, and Oz.

Who's Oz?

Well, he's very good, but very mysterious.

Who's Rushdie?

We'll tell you soon.

Okay, who's Hegel?

Thanks for asking. Georg Wilhelm Friedrich Hegel (1770–1831) is one of the most important philosophers ever, influencing people as diverse as Karl Marx (1818–1883) and Martin Luther King, Jr. (1929–1968). Hegel was born in Swabia, in what is now southwestern Germany. He went to school with the poet Johann Christian Friedrich Hölderlin (1770–1843) and the philosopher Friedrich Wilhelm Joseph von Schelling (1775–1854). Hölderlin and Schelling used to tease Hegel, calling him "the old man." He wrote several books, including the *Phenomenology of Spirit* and *Philosophy of History*.[2] He eventually taught philosophy at the

---

[1] Heinrich Heine, *Lutetia*, (Weimar: Volksverlag, 1960), p. 294; translated in Terry Pinkard, "Liberal Rights and Liberal Individualism without Liberalism: Agency and Recognition," *German Idealism: Contemporary Perspectives*, edited by Espen Hammer (Routledge, 2007), p. 223.

[2] Georg W.F. Hegel, *Phenomenology of Spirit* (Clarendon, 1977); *The Philosophy of History* (Dover, 1956).

University of Berlin. He believes that history is the story of progressive realization of human freedom.

So what?

We answer a question with a question. Are there children anywhere who haven't turned to their parents or guardians, at numerous times while watching *The Wizard of Oz*, and pleaded that this movie be explained to them? "We study Hegel's philosophy and that's easy to understand," the children cry, "Why can't *The Wizard of Oz* be just as clear?"

The adults can't follow the movie either, of course, but they lie, telling the children that they'll have to wait until they're older. The children notice the uneasy glances that the adults exchange with each other, though, and so aren't comforted by these promises of a future understanding. "Hegel said that the mysteries of the ancient Egyptian's religion were mysteries to the Egyptians themselves," the children remind the adults, asking, "could this be true of *The Wizard of Oz* too? Maybe no one understands it." Here, the adults repeat the empty promises of a future understanding, while the children continue to raise skeptical doubts about these seemingly unredeemable promissory notes.

Children know about Hegel? Hegel is easier to understand than *The Wizard of Oz*? That's crazy!

"Your theory is crazy," Niels Henrik David Bohr (1885–1962), one of the creators of quantum physics, once said, "but it's not crazy enough to be true."[3] Our theory is crazy enough to be true! We'll prove it. Trust us. All we need to do is to show how *The Wizard of Oz* exemplifies Hegel's philosophy. Once that's done, families everywhere will finally be able to happily watch *The Wizard of Oz* without cognitive dissonance and in tranquility. Shortly after Dorothy arrives in Oz, the Good Witch Glinda describes the Wizard as "very good, but very mysterious." By the end of the film, of course, he's recognized as "a good man, but a bad wizard." And he's not so mysterious, after all. Similarly, by watching the film with Hegel, we'll see that it's very good, but not so mysterious.

We need to introduce Salman Rushdie, since we'll discuss his book on *The Wizard of Oz*. Rushdie was born in Mumbai (Bombay), India, in 1947. In addition to *Midnight's Children*, which

---

[3] Spencer Scoular, *First Philosophy: The Theory of Everything* (Universal Publishers, 2007), p. 89.

won the Booker Prize in 1981 and the Booker of Bookers Prize in 1993, Rushdie has written many other novels and essays. He's best known for his 1988 novel, *The Satanic Verses*, which some Muslims felt insulted their prophet Muhammed. In 1989, Iran's spiritual leader, Ayatollah Ruhollah Khomeini, called for Rushdie's execution. As a consequence, Rushdie had to remain in hiding under police protection for several years. He was knighted by Britain in 2007. *Midnight's Children* is a fabulous story of India's history since its creation and independence on 15th August, 1947. In the novel, the narrator, Saleem Sinai, is born at the same instant when India becomes a nation, and so they have a mystical identity. Sinai plays a role in all of India's important moments.

Midnight's Children, is the literary counterpart of Hegel's *Phenomenology of Spirit*.[4] The narrative structures of the *Phenomenology of Spirit* and *Midnight's Children* are identical, and each text culminates in the recollection and recapitulation of the sojourn of their principle characters (the phenomenological observer and spirit in the *Phenomenology of Spirit*, Saleem Sinai and India in *Midnight's Children*). Indeed, *Midnight's Children* is the continuation of the *Phenomenology of Spirit*.[5]

Rushdie wrote a book about *The Wizard of Oz* called *The Wizard of Oz*.[6] It says "**THE WIZARD OF OZ** RUSHDIE" on the book's spine. Is Rushdie the Wizard? Well, no one has ever seen them together, but probably not. Be that as it may, since Rushdie has brought the *Phenomenology of Spirit* up to date, we can turn to him as we explain *The Wizard of Oz* in terms of Hegel's philosophy. If we occasionally see farther than Rushdie does, it's because we stand on the shoulders of this gigantic successor of Hegel. And we respond in the proper manner—with rancor and envious hatred!

Home Is Where the Heart Will Be: The Material and Spiritual Senses of Home

No matter where, even in Oz, there are always bullies. Here come some now. "You shouldn't explain *The Wizard of Oz* by using

---

[4] Salman Rushdie, *Midnight's Children* (Penguin, 1980).

[5] All of this, and much more, is demonstrated in J.M. Fritzman, "*Geist* in Mumbai: Hegel with Rushdie," *Janus Head* (Summer–Fall 2008).

[6] Salman Rushdie, *The Wizard of Oz* (London: British Film Institute, 1992).

Hegel's philosophy," these malcontents assert, "you should instead talk about Kant. Immanuel Kant (1724–1804) lived in the Prussian city of Königsberg, which is now in Russia. His most famous book is the *Critique of Pure Reason*. Kant argues that persons can *believe* anything that isn't contradictory, but they can only *know* those things that can be experienced by the five senses. People can believe that God exists and they have an immortal soul, but they can't know these things because God and the soul can't be experienced with the senses. Instead of jabbering about Hegel, you should discuss Kant's philosophy."

We could ignore these troublemakers, but let's be generous for a change and hear what they have to say. "You should use Kant's philosophy," they say, "because he clearly distinguishes what we can know (which parallels the parts of the film where Dorothy is in Kansas) from what we can believe (which is comparable to her dream that she's in Oz). Just as Kant claims that what we can really know is like an island surrounded by a sea of dangerous nonsense, Dorothy must learn that Oz was a silly dream and that her life is in Kansas. Oz could still stand for the next world, however, where Dorothy can finally be a wholly good person." Here is the passage from Kant that these grouches have in mind:

> We have now not only traveled through the land of pure understanding, and carefully inspected each part of it, but we have also surveyed it, and determined the place for each thing in it. This land, however, is an island, and enclosed in unalterable boundaries by nature itself. It is the land of truth (a charming name), surrounded by a broad and stormy ocean, the true seat of illusion, where many a fog bank and rapidly melting iceberg pretend to be new lands and, ceaselessly deceiving with empty hopes the voyager looking around for new discoveries, entwine him in adventures from which he can never escape and yet also never bring to an end. But before we venture out on this sea, to search through all its breadth and become certain of whether there is anything to hope for in it, it will be useful first to cast yet another glance at the map of the land that we would now leave, and to ask, first, whether we could not be satisfied with what it contains, or even must be satisfied with it out of necessity, if there is no other ground on which we could build; and second, by what title we occupy even this land, and can hold it securely against all hostile claims.[7]

---

[7] Immanuel Kant, *Critique of Pure Reason* (Cambridge University Press, 2005), pp. 338–39.

Far from showing that we should use Kant instead of Hegel, this passage actually demonstrates why Kant's philosophy isn't suitable. Kant believes that the satisfactions of our moral strivings can occur only after death, in another world. Hegel rejects the idea of there being another world, and so any satisfaction must be in this world. Dorothy's self-understanding when she sings "Over the Rainbow" is Kantian, because she believes that the things she seeks aren't found in Kansas. What she has discovered by the end of the film, however, is that she was always in the place over the rainbow for which she had so yearned, but she didn't yet have the wisdom and maturity to recognize this fact. A place without challenges would be boring and dull, and no sensible person would want that. What Dorothy does have, though she won't realize this until she goes to Oz, is the love of people who care deeply for her.

Rushdie argues that two dreams compete in *The Wizard of Oz*, the dream that "home's best" and the dream of escape, and that the latter dominates. As corroborating evidence, he cites the yearning expressed in "Over the Rainbow." It can't be denied that Dorothy does yearn to leave Kansas when she sings this song. What she doesn't realize, though, is that the leaving that she yearns for in this song would also involve leaving behind the persons whom she loves. Once she arrives in Oz, the land over the rainbow, and recognizes that her family has been left behind, she'll spare no effort to return to Kansas. These two dreams will be combined. Dorothy will realize that what she yearns for, when she dreams of escape, is available at home. It isn't that Dorothy will never leave the farm to go to college or get a job in the city, or even that she'll always stay in Kansas. But (1) she'll always have a home rather than seeking one and (2) the boundaries of her home will expand. Her heart's desire may never be beyond her own backyard, but her backyard may eventually include the world.

When she sings "Over the Rainbow," Dorothy exemplifies what Hegel calls, in the *Phenomenology of Spirit*, "the unhappy consciousness." A person stuck in this form of life believes that everything of true meaning and value isn't in this world, but in the next. As a consequence, the unhappy consciousness isn't at home in this world and yearns to escape it, just as Dorothy wants to leave Kansas for a cloud-cuckoo-land over the rainbow. What the unhappy consciousness and Dorothy must learn is that they've always already been home. As a result, *The Wizard of Oz* is really a story of self-discovery in which Dorothy discovers that her home in Kansas *is* her home, spiritually as well as materially. Rushdie focuses only on the harsh material conditions in Kansas without recognizing its spiritual conditions: love and acceptance.

"'Over the Rainbow' is, or ought to be, the anthem of all the world's migrants," Rushdie writes, "all those who go in search of the place where 'the dreams that you dare to dream really do come true.' It is a celebration of Escape, a grand paean to the Uprooted Self, a hymn—*the* hymn—to Elsewhere."

And here come those bullies again, looking for trouble. "Do you really assert," they demand, "that one's proper home is always wherever one happens to be living?!" No, not at all, we reply, our position is a bit subtler than that, more dialectical. Dorothy does leave Kansas, if only in a dream, and it's only because of leaving that she's then able to realize that her home is in Kansas, after all. It's not only possible but certain that others, living in places where they're not cared for and loved as is Dorothy, would discover that someplace else is their true home. The moment of leaving is necessary in order to find home. In the words of the German poet, Rainer Maria Rilke (1875–1926), "we are born, so to speak, provisionally, it doesn't matter where; it is only gradually that we compose, within ourselves, our true place of origin, so that we may be born there retrospectively."[8] The dream of escaping from home and the dream that home's best aren't ultimately opposed, but receive here their proper synthesis.

In his discussion of *The Wizard of Oz*, Rushdie says that "the film, like the TV soap opera *Dallas*, introduces an element of bad faith when it permits the possibility that everything that follows is a dream" (p. 30). Although his *Midnight's Children* continues Hegel's *Phenomenology of Spirit*, Rushdie seems to be more Kantian when he analyzes the film, wanting a two-worlds metaphysics that is as impossible as it is inappropriate. If Oz were actually real, and Dorothy's journey there were not a dream, then the movie would be invoking Kant's distinction between two levels of reality. There would be the empirical world, experienced through the fives senses. The other would be the *transcendent* world, outside of space and time, and—at least according to Kant—in principle unknowable. Kant's philosophy ties itself into knots, simultaneously declaring that nothing can be known about

---

[8] Rainer Maria Rilke, quoted in Krishenda Ray, *The Migrant's Table: Meals and Memories in Bengali-American Households* (Temple University Press, 2004), p. 137.

the transcendent world, that foggy sea, and yet also claiming that it must somehow affect the empirical world to make freedom possible.

For Hegel, however, there's only one world. So, Oz can't be a place separate from this world, but must instead be contained in it. This relationship is crucial! If Oz is actually in this world, then what Dorothy actually yearns for is in this world too. The problem is that she doesn't yet recognize it. Of course, there's a sense in which she does implicitly understand this point. As soon as she arrives in Oz, and throughout her entire time there, her goal is to return home! To put this point in a paradoxical manner, Dorothy knows that her home is in Kansas, but it's not until she finally clicks her heels and says, "There's no place like home," that she knows that she knows.

Synthesizing Oz: The Tripartite Structure of Dorothy's Journey

The above discussion of Dorothy's material and spiritual homes provides a context to talk about how *The Wizard of Oz* has a narrative structure that matches Hegel's. What Hegel calls the "thesis," our starting place (Dorothy's home is in Kansas, which is wholly defined by its bleak material conditions) represents a partial truth that misunderstands itself as the *whole* truth and nothing but the truth. What he calls the "antithesis" (there's a better place somewhere over the rainbow, where Dorothy would be accepted and loved) opposes the thesis. The antithesis recognizes the error that is contained in the thesis (there's more to life than its material conditions), but fails to perceive that the thesis also contains some truth (Dorothy is accepted and loved in Kansas). The synthesis (Kansas itself is that better place for which Dorothy yearns) combines the thesis with its antithesis, rejecting the error.[9] The synthesis, then, becomes a new thesis and so the process continues (Dorothy might later recognize, perhaps if she goes to college, that

---

[9] To keep things concise, we focus on Dorothy. We don't discuss how Dorothy's family and friends take her for granted at the beginning of the film and only realize how much they love her when they almost lose her after the tornado strikes. So, the Kansas to which Dorothy returns after Oz is different from the one she left. This is why the title of Thomas Wolfe's novel, *You Can't Go Home Again*, is false. Indeed, home (material) only becomes *home* (spiritual) when you go home again.

Kansas isn't her only home). This process finally concludes when we arrive at the final chapter of Hegel's *Phenomenology of Spirit*, "Absolute Knowing" (Dorothy might eventually expand her sense of "home" until it includes the entire world).

For more than fifty years, it's been fashionable among Hegel scholars to pooh-pooh the idea that he thinks in terms of such triads, especially thesis-antithesis-synthesis.[10] These scholars are correct to recognize that Hegel's philosophy is neither that mechanical nor that simple. Nevertheless, it frequently does have a tripartite structure.

So does *The Wizard of Oz*! It begins in Kansas where Dorothy doesn't feel at home, moves to Oz where she recognizes that a place over the rainbow could never be home, and finally returns to Kansas—which she now realizes is her home. Not only that, but Dorothy's time in Oz also has this three-step structure. First, she's "off to see the Wizard" because she believes that he can return her to Kansas. Dorothy wants to go home because she's homesick, but if she went home immediately, she'd still be yearning for someplace over the rainbow. As the fiasco with the hot air balloon near the movie's conclusion suggests, she may never have returned home if she'd gone with the Wizard. What's most crucial here, however, is that Dorothy and her friends believe that what they want is something only the Wizard can give to them, rather than something they'll have to find for themselves. So, although it's false that the Wizard can give them what they want, it's initially necessary that they believe this.

Second, Dorothy goes in quest of the broom of the Wicked Witch of the West, as the Wizard has said that she must get this item before he'll help. It is through this knight's errand that Dorothy implicitly, spiritually, realizes that there's no place like home. And it's by helping Dorothy that Scarecrow, Tin Man, and Lion develop the brain, heart, and courage they'd wanted the Wizard to give them. The Wizard may have demanded that they bring him the broom expecting that they'd become discouraged and go away, but it's by getting the broom that they'll also finally be able to get what they want.

Finally, Dorothy explicitly recognizes that "there's no place like home," clicks together the heels of her ruby slippers, and she's

---

[10] See Gustav E. Mueller, "The Hegel Legend of 'Thesis-Antithesis-Synthesis'," *Journal of the History of Ideas* 19:3 (June 1958), pp. 411–14.

homeward bound. But where is home? What Dorothy realizes is that home isn't a location but a condition: being with those she loves and who love her.

This progression of events nicely illustrates one of Hegel's main points, truth emerges through misrecognition. In a discussion of Jane Austen's novel, *Pride and Prejudice*, the Slovenian philosopher Slavoj Žižek observes that it is only because Darcy and Elizabeth initially misperceive the other as, respectively, full of pride and prejudice, that they can later learn each other's true qualities. Had they married immediately, they would never have learned the other's actual character. As he explains, "if we want to spare ourselves the painful roundabout route through the misrecognition, we miss the Truth itself: only the 'working-through' of the misrecognition allows us to accede to the true nature of the other and at the same time to overcome our own deficiency."[11] In precisely the same way, it's only because Dorothy at first wrongly believes that what she wants is over the rainbow that she can be in a position to discover what she actually wants. Just as *The Wizard of Oz* is the narrative of self-creation of Dorothy and her friends, so Hegel's *Phenomenology of Spirit* is the history of the self-creation of Western consciousness, what Hegel calls "Spirit" or "Mind" ("*Geist*" in German).

Referring to the poem "The Hollow Men" by Thomas Stearns Eliot (1888–1965) about spiritual emptiness and hopelessness, Rushdie says that the Scarecrow, Tin Man, and Lion are hollow men. Perhaps this description is correct when they're first encountered in the film. After all, the Scarecrow lacks a brain, the Tin Man a heart, and the Lion courage. By the end of the film, however, they've become men in full (or, more accurately, two men and a lion in full). Rushdie writes that, together with Dorothy, "they embody one of the film's 'messages'—that we already possess what we most fervently seek." Through their actions they create for themselves the character traits they seek. The Scarecrow has good ideas, the Tin Man deeply empathizes with others, and the Lion acts the part of a courageous hero.

It would be easy to believe that they always had these character traits, and that they only needed to discover that about themselves. This would be a mistake. The Scarecrow, Tin Man, and Lion

---

[11] Slavoj Žižek, *The Sublime Object of Ideology* (Verso, 1989), p. 64.

don't have pre-existing "essences" or "selves." Rather, they become who they are by seeking the Wizard—and subsequently, the Witch's broom—and helping Dorothy. It is these acts that allow them to become worthy of receiving these brains, heart, and courage as gifts from the Wizard. The only gift that they receive, however, is the public recognition of who they are—that is, of who they have become: the Scarecrow has good ideas, Tin Man has compassion and empathy, and Lion acts bravely. Hence, Rushdie is imprecise to say "that we already possess what we most fervently seek" (p. 49). A more accurate way of expressing this point would be that it is through the process of fervently seeking to become a certain kind of person—say, someone with a brain, heart, or courage—that we become what we sought.

So, Rushdie believes that Scarecrow, Tin Man, and Lion were only hollow men in terms of their own self-images, but that they really always already possessed the traits they sought. Whereas Hegel allows us to see that they really were hollow men when they began their journey with Dorothy, and that they actually acquired the traits they sought by helping her. As the Wizard acknowledges, when the journey is accomplished, that he can't give the Scarecrow a brain, the Tin Man a heart, and the Lion courage. But by then he doesn't have to, because they already have them. What the Wizard can do is provide recognition by giving the Scarecrow a diploma, the Tin Man a testimonial, and the Lion a medal.

Further, it's by going to Oz and then trying to return to Kansas that Dorothy learns where her heart's desire really lies. Not somewhere over the rainbow, but in her own back yard. It would be a serious mistake—what Kant calls a "dialectical illusion"—to project this achieved insight back to the time when she sings the famous song. Then she really does believe that she wants to be somewhere over the rainbow. Arriving there, however, she begins the process of realizing that this place isn't where she wants to be. In other words, she'll learn that where she really wants to be is home. Dorothy's growth and realization is why Rushdie is mistaken to believe that the end of the film means that Dorothy never needed to make the trip to Oz (pp. 56–57).

To understand this point more fully, imagine the following hypothetical scenario. In the movie, Glinda explains that Dorothy had to find out for herself the power of the ruby slippers to take her home. Imagine, though, that Glinda had told Dorothy of the slippers' power, what then? Either the slippers wouldn't have been able to take Dorothy back to Kansas because she had not yet discovered that Kansas is her home. Or else she would have returned to Kansas without experiencing it *as* a home—she would still have felt estranged. This scenario answers Rushdie's gripe:

> Glinda's instructions to Dorothy are oddly enigmatic, even contradictory. She tells Dorothy (1) "Their magic must be very powerful or she [the Wicked Witch of the West] wouldn't want them so badly," and, later, (2) "Never let those ruby slippers off your feet or you will be at the mercy of the Wicked Witch of the West." Now, statement (1) suggests that Glinda is unclear about the nature of the ruby slippers, whereas statement (2) suggests that she knows all about their protective power. Nor does either statement hint at the ruby slippers' later role in helping to get Dorothy back to Kansas. It seems probable that these confusions are hangovers from the long, dissension-riddled scripting process, in which the function of the slippers was the subject of considerable debate. But one can also see Glinda's obliquities as proof that a good fairy or a good witch, when she sets out to be of assistance, never gives you everything. Glinda is not so unlike her description of the Wizard of Oz, after all: *Oh, he's very good, but very mysterious.* (p. 43)

There's no need to appeal to squabbling scribblers. Glinda knows exactly what the ruby slippers can do, but—as she later explains—this mystery is something that Dorothy has to find out for herself. This also explains why Glinda can't give Dorothy everything. It's only by not being given everything that Dorothy will be able later to receive everything. This storyline is another exemplary illustration of Hegel's claim that truth emerges through misrecognition.

Creating Oneself and Others Too: How Dorothy Is a World-Historical Individual

As Rushdie says, the Wizard is a hollow man too (p. 50). The mighty Wizard of Oz isn't mighty at all. He proves to be nothing but a good man who is, unfortunately, a bad wizard. Whereas Dorothy and her friends believed that they could obtain their goals only if the Wizard gave them these things, the truth is that he's unable to fulfill their hearts's desires. The Wizard isn't wholly impotent, though, as he can confer public recognition of who they are. In a sense, the Wizard does nothing, but in another sense he accomplishes everything. True, the Wizard can't give brains, hearts, or courage to those who lack them. However, the Wizard, through a performative gesture makes official the Scarecrow's brains, the Tin Man's heart, and the Lion's courage. It's this gesture that allows them to be seen for who they are—that is to say, who they have become.

So far, we've mainly interpreted the personal self-creations and self-understanding of the characters in *The Wizard of Oz* in light of Hegel's *Phenomenology of Spirit*. Now we'll discuss their public political consciousness and liberation in the light of Hegel's *Philosophy of History*. People would rather govern themselves badly, as Gandhi observes, than be governed well by others. Of course, it's only by governing themselves, even if badly, that they can develop the ability to govern themselves well. It's only by acting, moreover, that persons create themselves.

This insight allows an effective response to Rushdie when he writes: "The heretical thought occurs: maybe the Witch of the East *wasn't as bad as all that*—she certainly kept the streets clean, the houses painted and in good repair, and no doubt such trains as there might be, running on time. Moreover, and again unlike her sister, she seems to have ruled without the aid of soldiers, policemen or other regiments of repression. Why, then, was she so hated? I only ask" (p. 42). We only answer: By denying the Munchkins the opportunity to govern and create themselves, the Witch of the East treated them as perpetual children, regardless of how benign or useful her reign might have been when measured against such external criteria as infrastructure, sanitation, the laying of railroads, and running trains on time. Hegel would say that, when measured against the needs of the spirit—be it Munchkin or human—the Witch of the East's reign could be experienced only as a tyranny. The Munchkins aren't free. They haven't bestowed their own laws on themselves, but instead are accountable to laws imposed on them. As such, her laws are also arbitrary in that they're entirely dependent upon the whim of the Witch of the East. Even if the Munchkins can predict, based on previous experience, what they must do to be safe, they can't know that she won't change her mind. If she does, there's no court of appeal. No wonder she's so hated!

Hegel believes that history is the narrative of the progressive realization of freedom. This idea can be described briefly. In *The Philosophy of History*, he argues that the "Oriental World" (which includes the Near East, the Middle East and the Far East) knows only that one individual is free, the "Greco-Roman World" knows that some are free, but the "Germanic World" (that is, modern Europe) knows that all are free.[12] He isn't claiming that all persons are actually free in Europe, of course, but rather that all persons are recognized as entitled to freedom. Hegel thinks that freedom has been decisively advanced by persons he calls "world-historical individuals"—he has in mind such individuals as Julius Caesar and Napoleon—who are intending to pursue their own goals, but inadvertently they set in motion events which result in freedom being advanced. Discussing how uncomfortable many of the characters were in their costumes and various accidents that occurred on the set, Rushdie observes that there's no connection between making the film and pleasure watching it (p. 45). Similarly, there's no connection between the process of making history and philosophical reflection on it. What Hegel calls philosophical history discerns that history is the progressive realization of freedom. This understanding is neither available to those world-historical individuals who introduced decisive changes in history nor to the many unknown persons who suffered because of these changes.

Shortly after Dorothy arrives in Oz—in the process, dropping her house on the Witch of the East—the Munchkins sing "Ding-Dong! The Witch Is Dead." In this song, they tell Dorothy that she'll be history. To be exact, they sing "you'll be hist—you'll be hist—you'll be history, and we will glorify your name, you'll be a bust—be a bust—be a bust—in the hall of fame." These lyrics demand a Hegelian interpretation, according to which Dorothy is what Hegel refers to as a world-historical individual. She'll be history in the sense that she's instrumental in furthering the progress of history while in Oz. Not only does she drop a house on the Witch of the East when she first arrives in Oz, but she later throws water on the Witch of the West, causing her to melt. And so, she frees not only Munchkinland but all of Oz from the tyranny of the Witches. In both cases, though, Dorothy acts unintentionally. It's obvious that she has no idea where or on whom her house would land. And she intends to throw water on the Scarecrow because the Witch of the West set him on fire. Dorothy doesn't know that water will melt the Witch—that'll teach her to leave buckets of water lying around!

---

[12] G.W.F. Hegel, *The Philosophy of History* (Dover, 1956), p. 18.

Dorothy is a world-historical individual in that she has unintentionally furthered freedom's progress.

Rushdie notes that Dorothy runs away when Miss Gulch threatens to take Toto, but that she goes to fight the Witch of the West to get her broom, and she stays to argue with the Wizard after she obtains the broom (pp. 10–11). Rushdie is correct to see that Dorothy becomes more assertive and confident as the film progresses. She's never passive, however, but instead always takes action, even if that action is running away rather than acquiescing to giving Toto to Miss Gulch. Dorothy never passively accepts her fate but acts to alter it—and so transform it. This activity is properly Hegelian as Hegel argues that history is the result of persons taking action, almost always with no understanding of the consequences of their acts.

Rushdie notes that an absence of religion increases the movie's charm, and he emphasizes the importance of its theme that there's nothing more important than the love of people (p. 12). This idea can be expressed in terms of Hegel's philosophy of religion, which involves what he calls a "transcendent-immanence"—or, an "immanent-transcendence"—which means that God becomes most fully manifest in God's embodiment in the worshiping human community. (To put this point in wholly secular terms—but also for Hegel, to distort the point—God becomes the human community which worships God). To return to Oz, not only does Dorothy recognize that she doesn't need the Wizard to give her gifts (because he's just a man, and not a wizard or god), she also gives that knowledge to the people of Oz. The citizens of Emerald City had cowered in awe of "the Great and Powerful Oz" and he ruled over them—as though he had divine authority. The people had taken their freedom and happiness as a gift from Oz, not something they've realized for themselves. (Credit where credit is due: Oz may have been just smoke and curtains, but it was convincing enough to keep the Witch of the West away.)

When Dorothy—with Toto's help, of course—exposes the Wizard for what he is (the stammering, meek, American hot air balloon operator), she grants the people political freedom. By abolishing the dictator, she's progressing Oz (or at least Emerald City) past the "one is free" stage. Granted, this interpretation assumes that the people of Emerald City know, in one of the final scenes when the wizard is leaving on his hot air balloon, what exactly had gone on and that the Wizard never had any great and terrible magical powers. But if they don't know already, they'll find out when they watch the movie! And the Wizard himself confirms their freedom, when he appoints the Scarecrow to rule in his stead, and the Tin Man and Lion to assist him! Given the inherent trajectory of events, can there be any doubt there will soon be free, fair, and democratic elections?

And Your Little Dog Too!

There's one other character who's too often overlooked—Dorothy's dog, Toto. In the book, Toto accidentally knocks over the screen that conceals the Wizard. In the movie, however, Toto deliberately pulls the curtain aside. There's a profound Hegelian lesson here. Acts at the moment of their occurrence are contingent and accidental. When viewed retrospectively, however, they become necessary and purposive. Had things been different in the past, the future (our present) would have been different too. Given that our present (the past's future) is what it is, however, what happened in the past was necessary. So, while Toto accidentally knocks over the screen in the book, when this even is retold, on the big screen, Toto's action becomes necessary and intentional. It's almost as if Toto in the movie had already read the book and so knew what must be done, and so did it intentionally the second time through. Toto also chases a cat so that the Wizard takes off in his balloon without her. This action too is now necessary, as it's only after that, at the prompting of the good witch Glinda, that Dorothy finally explicitly articulates what, in a sense, she always knew: that there's no place like home. Rushdie can't stand Toto, seeing him only as a yapping nuisance and distraction. However, his interventions (Toto's, not Rushdie's) are decisive. Without him, the Wizard wouldn't have been exposed and Dorothy would have returned to Kansas with the Wizard without *fully* recognizing that it really is her home.

This penultimate paragraph is potentially distracting and so may be skipped by bullies who don't appreciate fun that's off-topic: In the Bollywood blockbuster, *Hum Aapke Hain Koun* (*Who Am I to You?*), Tuffy the dog—following the promptings of Lord Krishna—reveals that Nisha (played by Madhuri Dixit) and Prem (Salman Khan) love each other, so that they're married instead of Nisha's marrying Prem's brother, Rajesh (Mohnish Bahl). Let's add that the closest analogue we have to God's unconditional love is the affection that animals have for us. There's a fine sermon to be preached on this theme, but that's for another day.

The children have one last question. Was Dorothy's journey to Oz real or a dream? The father of psychoanalysis, Sigmund Freud (1856–1939), would say that dreams can be more real than what is considered reality. Since this isn't a paper about Freud, let's leave him out of it. We can't ask Dorothy or her family. She maintains that she really was in Oz, and they say that she was unconscious the whole time. They had been hiding from the tornado in the fruit cellar, though, and so they can't know where Dorothy was then. What about the house, the one that took Dorothy to Oz and fell on the Wicked Witch of the East? Surely, it wouldn't be back in Kansas if it'd been in Oz. Not at all. If the ruby slippers can return Dorothy to Kansas, they could have just as well put the house back too. So, whom can we ask? Toto, of course. He'll know! Well, don't be shy, ask. See how he stands on his rear legs, barks, and wags his tail? That settles it![13]

---

[13] Randall E. Auxier, Robbie Roy, and Phil Seng are thanked for their suggestions. Lewis and Clark College provided support through a Collaborative Research Grant.

4

Freeing the Slaves in Oz

JASON BELL and JESSICA BELL

> At first the Witch was tempted to run away from Dorothy; but she happened to look into the child's eyes and saw how simple the soul behind them was, and that the little girl did not know of the wonderful power the Silver Shoes gave her. So the Wicked Witch laughed to herself, and thought, "I can still make her my slave, for she does not know how to use her power."
>
> —L. Frank Baum, *The Wonderful Wizard of Oz*[1]

Prior to the American Civil War, there was, to say the least, widespread *unrest*. Perhaps that description is too mild. But some of the least restful unrest happened between Kansas and Missouri—the newspapers back then described it as "Bleeding Kansas." This is where the Old South met the Wild West, literally, in armed confrontation. It wasn't a picnic.

When L. Frank Baum wrote *The Wonderful Wizard of Oz*, all this strife was still within living memory (as were the Old South and the Wild West), about as far from his readers in time as the Kennedy assassination is from us today. And in some ways, the figure of John Brown held as much fascination for that generation as Kennedy still holds for our own. It isn't easy to say whether John Brown belonged in the Wild West or the Old South, where he was confronting slave holders and defending abolition as a divinely sanctioned reason for struggle. In a way, the question at stake was

---

[1] L. Frank Baum, *15 Books in 1: The Original "Oz" Series* (Shoes and Ships and Sealing Wax, 2005), p. 30. All this chapter's Baum references are to this collection.

whether Kansas would *become* a part of the Old South—to which some Missourians thought the answer should be "yes," and John Brown thought otherwise.

It's true that Baum's youthful readers would not grasp the meaning Kansas had for adults of that generation, though *we* can still get a sense of it. But Kansas leads to Oz, and we should try to think of it as people did in Baum's day—not sunflowers and wholesome Eisenhowers, but Dodge City and bloody raids on Lawrence.

Dead Man's Hand

In a dialogue called the *Phaedo*, Socrates is awaiting his own execution, the verdict of the Athenian assembly for his crimes of "impiety" and "corrupting the youth." His friends are gathered in his cell, and they are discussing, as you might guess, death. Socrates is not afraid, and his friends are pretty impressed. So Socrates warns his friends against fearing death while they struggle for their own loyal cause, cooperative philosophy. It's hard to think of that as a "cause," we know, because philosophy these days doesn't seem like something that could get you in much trouble. But it hasn't always been like that.

So Socrates chides and exhorts the little band of philosophical souls as he awaits his own execution: "You are afraid, as children are, that when the soul emerges from the body the wind may really puff it away and scatter it, especially when a person does not die on a calm day but with a gale blowing . . ." Hmmm. Like a Gale?

Dorothy Gale's adventures begin with just such a problem—there's a deadly gale whippin' up on the Kansas plains (or is that planes? Seems about the same, they're just plain plane). Baum's version of the story differs in places from the more familiar 1939 film, so if you're imagining Judy Garland fleeing the cyclone, that's not quite how Baum's story goes (and in this chapter we're more concerned with the book than with the movie).

In the book, Dorothy, mere child that she is (much younger than Judy Garland), has fear of neither wind nor death: in the middle of a cyclone she risks her life to save Toto rather than retreat to the cellar without him. So the dog is the barking catalyst in both the movie and the book. Knowing Dorothy's relation to *Toto*, (his name means "the all" in Latin, which every schoolchild had to study back in 1900), readers realize that the girl is quite invincible, impervious to storms and stresses. She is Annie Oakley. Later, when the

Good Witch's protective kiss marks Dorothy's forehead, it's really just a symbol of what the children already know—you can't scare Dorothy, and you can't hurt her.

So Socrates's friends want to learn how to overcome their fear of death. Was Socrates Wild Bill Hickok? Well, something like that. He had often faced the witches and wizards, mainly word-wizards called "sophists" (he actually got on with the witches fairly well) without any fear of their threats. And the threats weren't altogether empty, as he eventually found out. But anyway, Socrates tells his friends that they must find a magician to say a spell to charm the fear away, and that to find this magician they must search by "united efforts" through a large country where they will meet "many foreign races." You don't believe that, do you? Seriously, that's what he says. Look it up (*Plato: The Collected Dialogues*, Pantheon, 1961).

Dorothy, too, is ordered to find such a magician. *Now* you believe us, but you cheated. You saw the movie, right? Okay, so in the book, the Good Witch (who is not Glinda, but an old fairy-god-mother type) has a magic slate on which messages appear when she asks it a question. It's sort of like a Ouija Board mixed with an Etch-a-sketch. So anyway, when she asks it what Dorothy must do, the slate commands, "Let Dorothy go to the City of Emeralds" where lives the great Wizard of Oz. To get there, she finds she must indeed encounter many foreign races and unite her efforts with friends she meets along the way, each new friend having some unique qualities that help the group survive and meet their goals. Baum was reading Plato, maybe. Or maybe he just liked Annie Oakley and Wild Bill Hickok. Baum set up shop in the Dakota territory only a dozen years after Wild Bill met his end in those environs. Maybe the grave wasn't fresh, but the legend was, and Baum loved legends.

But in the end, we all get dealt the old Aces and Eights, right? You're holding the same hand, and so is everybody else, and Socrates—well, he's pushing up daisies in some Mediterranean Boot Hill. So the point is that we're all playing a Dead Man's Hand, and there's no way to get the hell out of Dodge, and Bat Masterson isn't coming to the rescue. The Kansas we *all* live in has a dim and scary border, and it's hard to tell whether it's Oz on the other side, or just Oklahoma. So Socrates is saying, look, it's not the hand you're dealt, it's how you bluff the word-wizards and conspire with the good witches that makes all the difference. That's why he says that philosophy is "practicing for death." Dead Man's Hand.

But both Socrates and Dorothy can show us, even though we're going to die, how uniting efforts in a common quest can lead to eternal wisdom. For Socrates, wisdom is a condition of the soul: "when it investigates, by itself, it passes into the realm of the pure and everlasting and immortal and changeless, and being of a kindred nature, when it is once independent and free from interference, consorts with it always and strays no longer, but remains, in that realm of the absolute, constant and invariable, through contact with beings of a similar nature."

Let's translate. When your soul has had a glimpse of Oz, it decides to hang around, because Oz is in color (that is, being wise is like having a Technicolor soul). Fortunately, you don't have to go all by your lonesome. You can bring friends, like the Earps, Doc Holliday, a Scarecrow, Wild Bill, Socrates, Dorothy, anyone you like well enough, no matter how funny looking. The community of inquirers, wisdom seekers (your friends of Tin, Straw, and Fur) makes up for the "illusions of individual perspective," which is the stuff you get wrong because you're just you and not someone smarter. But eventually you have to learn what other people know, just because they are them and not you. See?

Sic Semper Tyrannis

Some wizards like empires—big, shiny ones. But to be the imperialist, to enslave others, doesn't help you out in the long run, doesn't change the cards in your hand. Sure, it seems like a good deal to have others do the work for you, but you end up being lonely, without the benefit of cooperation, without any beloved creative activity, and constantly in fear of your subjects' uprising. You have no friends, and then they kick you out of Oz when you die, if not before. As Socrates tells the slave-owning oligarchs who have commandeered him (for a conversation) in Plato's most famous writing, *The Republic*, the slaves will hate you for enslaving them.

We also see this very clearly in the Land of Oz. After she kills the Wicked Witch of the West, Dorothy's first act was to call all the Winkies together and tell them that they were "no longer slaves." The Winkies hate the witch who had enslaved them, but were "delighted to do all in their power for Dorothy, who had set them free from bondage" (p. 31). So what is this stand that Socrates and Dorothy seem to be taking against empires, slavery, and tyrants?

In Oz, Dorothy is the Great Emancipator, the liberator of the slaves: the Munchkins from the rule of the Wicked Witch of the East; the Scarecrow from his servitude on the pole; then the Tin Woodman from his rust and hence his bondage to the evil witch who had cursed him; then the Winkies from the Wicked Witch of the West who has enslaved them. She even frees herself, and the Cowardly Lion, from slavery to the Wicked Witch of the West— unlike the movie, it appears that Dorothy is actually a slave for some time, weeks at least, before she kills the Witch and liberates herself.

Think about it. Dorothy is liberating people all over the place. Liberating them from what? Well, various forms of slavery. The theme of abolition is found in all the other books of Baum's series as well. This stuff is more serious and more intentional than it appears, and abolition was still as much a *cause célèbre* in 1900 as civil rights remains in our day. It was something people looked back on with a serious feeling of accomplishment. So it's no wonder that Baum chose the state of Kansas as the setting for the beginning of his story, filled with themes of slavery and freedom and starring Dorothy as the Great Emancipator.

As strange as it may sound, Kansas really meant "freedom" in his day and age. As we said, the associations of American readers in 1900 were very different from ours today. In the very same thought as "Kansas," the readers thought about emancipation—and they thought about *John Brown*. Many soldiers marched purposefully to their deaths between 1861 and 1865 with his name on their lips. You know the tune. Today it's called "The Battle Hymn of the Republic," but the soldiers were singing "John Brown's body lies a moulderin' in the grave / His truth is marching on . . ."

In many ways, the fictional Dorothy is like the real-life Great Emancipator John Brown. Abe Lincoln famously reported that he would happily preserve slavery to preserve the union. But for John Brown, there could be no genuine union in which factional slavery was preserved. Likewise, for Dorothy, in the third book of Baum's Oz series, it just isn't an option to let the slaves stay slaves: in one of Baum's later stories, when Dorothy returns to Oz she's determined that she and her friends confront the Nome King and free the Royal Family of Ev who were sold into slavery to him, even though her plan almost certainly means that she and her friends will be lost in the attempt. Better to die than to tolerate slavery.

Both Dorothy and John Brown led campaigns to end slavery against seemingly impossible odds. If you've read the book, you'll remember that as Dorothy, Toto, and their three friends approach the castle of the Wicked Witch of the West, the Witch sends forty wolves to tear them to pieces, forty crows to peck their eyes out, a swarm of black bees to sting them to death, and then a dozen enslaved Winkies with spears to destroy them. The companions are forced to kill all these beasties and to scare away the Winkies just to continue the truth-march. The Witch finally sends a horde of winged monkeys to kill Dorothy, but they realize they cannot harm her due to the sign of the Good Witch's kiss.

Impossible odds are also found in *Ozma of Oz*, the third of Baum's books: Dorothy and a party of thirty-five others (Billina, Tiktok, Ozma, the Hungry Tiger, the Cowardly Lion, the Scarecrow, the Sawhorse, the Tin Woodman, and the twenty-seven-member army of Oz) face an army of thousands of Nomes in the underground kingdom of the Nome King who has enslaved the Royal Family of Ev. It is reminiscent of John Brown's 1859 raid on the Harpers Ferry Armory. He meant to arm slaves so that they might escape to freedom. Nineteen of his men faced off against a much larger company of marines led by the all-star team of the future confederacy, Robert E. Lee and J.E.B. Stuart among them.

Is Oz to be free or slave? Is Kansas to be free or slave? After counting up Dorothy's and John Brown's soldiers, few enough to be named, and then sizing up the hordes of adversaries, the mathematical odds do not at first glance look good for freedom. And indeed, Socrates is for his part an abolitionist too, and if you think Dorothy and John Brown are outnumbered, try getting an anti-slavery movement going in ancient Athens. You could be seriously killed.

John Brown, The Great Emancipator

In 1856, the year of Baum's birth, Kansas was in chaos over the democratic question: is Kansas to be slave or free? The new senators from Kansas might determine the question for the whole nation, and for the world. Why was this so important? The reasons are complex, but slave-picked American cotton was one of the world's premier commodities. It was so important that some European nations nearly intervened on the Southern side to protect their own economic interests.

The election of representatives and senators in Kansas was not quite democratic, however, since it was marred by vote fraud, physical attacks on printing presses, and widespread violence. The abolitionist side was largely peaceful. The pro-slavery raiders from Missouri were not peaceful, and attacked abolitionist settlements in overwhelming numbers. In Washington, D.C., a pro-slavery legislator, Preston Brooks, beat abolitionist Senator Charles Sumner nearly to death on the floor of the Senate with a heavy cane, for having dared to speak out for the victimized abolitionists in Kansas. Sure, all of us have certainly felt like taking a cane to a senator (choose your favorite), but it's one thing to want to and another thing to have your own legislator do it for you. Things were getting ugly.

We've spoken of the Harpers Ferry raid at the end of his life, but John Brown was used to Dorothy-like odds from the beginning. He led a group of thirty-eight men to try to stop over three hundred pro-slavery Missourians from attacking and destroying free state settlements in Osawatomie, Kansas. Despite the overwhelming odds, his forces put up a creditable fight, killing about twenty, and wounding twice as many. (One of Brown's men died.) When it became clear that their Spartan legion's worth of warriors was not enough to frighten their seriously outnumbered opponents, the slave-owners and their allies prepared to send 2,700 troops to crush Lawrence, Kansas.

The conversation at the slave-owners' board meeting went something like this. "Three hundred didn't scare them? Then we'll send ten times as many!" The Secretary-Treasurer did the math: 2,700 new recruits, plus the three hundred that went last time. But sixty couldn't fight any more, and the other 240 didn't want to go back again. "No, not us, not to Kansas; we'll sit this one out on the porch. Weather's pretty nice this time of the year here in Missouri. It's true what they say, there's no place like home."

Still, it was a dangerous assembly that John Brown awaited on the ramparts. We will die for this question of business ownership, both sides pledged. It was guns at high noon on the dusty streets of Dodge. Can you own others and force them to do your work for you, like they did in the Old South, or do you need to work yourself, like in the Wild West? Partisans of each ideal flocked to Kansas, armed with guns and swords, ready to do battle. This was very much in the minds of Baum's readers, in much the same way we still think about the marchers on the Edmund Pettis Bridge leaving Selma for Montgomery.

Socrates, the Great Emancipator

Socrates, too, was an abolitionist, speaking out against slavery in Plato's *Republic*. He also faced tremendous odds. Perhaps because of his advocacy of a society that holds no slaves, or perhaps because he was in the wrong place at the wrong time, Socrates was coerced, practically kidnapped, and dragged to a party in an ostentatious mansion, owned by an arms merchant named Cephalus. The place is filled with slaves and their masters—and fortunately too, Socrates's friends Glaucon and Adeimantus accompanied him (saving him from Senator Sumner's fate).

The merchants who have commanded Socrates there, whose livelihoods and way of life depend on enslaving others, tell Socrates that his poverty must make him miserable, just as life must be miserable for all the working poor who are forced by necessity to cheat each other, and the gods, in contracts. Only the rich man, Cephalus argues, has the means to make all these payments, and so to avoid the deprivations of this life—and the next, since he thinks (as many an entrepreneur would) that the tortures of Hell are especially reserved for those who can't or won't pay their debts. But having declared his convictions, Cephalus must leave the discussion, rushing off to make his payments to the gods! He leaves his son Polemarchus in charge of the argument, but Polemarchus is a bit of a dull edge, and is soon confused. So this guy named Thrasymachus, who is basically a corporate lawyer, takes over Cephalus's argument, on behalf of the slave-owners. One ought to be unjust, Thrasymachus argues, but one must do it on a sufficiently large scale: one must not merely take property, but "kidnap and enslave the citizens as well," because "injustice on a sufficiently large scale is a stronger, freer, and more masterful thing than justice." Good work if you can get it (and Cephalus can get it).

The moral standard for the slave-owner is: "whatever pays." And by this standard, "injustice pays and justice doesn't pay." Stealing purses involves a little profit, but a high risk of detection and punishment, but these slave-owners are interested in stealing an entire group of people, lawfully, so that the law will subject only the slaves to punishment, protecting the slave-owners from the slaves' wrath. And the unjust are intelligent and good, Thrasymachus argues, "if they are capable of complete injustice . . . and are able to subject to themselves cities and tribes of men." This sort of thinking is still around, one supposes, although at least now our lawyers feel obliged to lie about it (is that progress?). Dorothy wouldn't stand for it, and if her weapons use a bit less gunpowder than John Brown's, they are just as effective.

Socrates's Coming Out Ball

How will Socrates respond to this perversion of justice? He has been seized on the street *by* a slave, at the order of Polemarchus, then brought to this spot *as* a slave pro-tem, and commanded to answer this assembly's pro-slavery arguments. Or at least, one can read the dialogue this way by just noticing how much slavery-talk there is. Most scholars today don't notice the slavery theme, but they should, and perhaps Plato's readers in nineteenth-century America, such as L. Frank Baum, were noticing other aspects of the dialogue than we do now.

Let's recast it just a bit, to give it that Antebellum flavor. Socrates lives in Memphis, about 1856, when John Brown is fighting in Kansas and Baum is being born in western New York. Socrates is a stone-cutter, when he works at all, but mostly he hangs out at the corner of Front Street and Adams, talking to anyone and everyone who'll listen about every subject under the Southern sun. So a rumor starts that he's got a problem with the South's "Peculiar Institution" (the word "slavery" was so unseemly as to be banned in some places, such as the floor of Congress). So "Aloysius Cornpone" (name your favorite cotton magnate or merchant of death) sends his boy "Bobby Robert," and his boy's boy "Nat," out to fetch that boy Socrates so's all the boys can talk. When Bobby Robert returns with Socrates there's a pointed question about justice rather than slavery—because Southerners never get directly at what they're really talkin' 'bout—it's downright impolite.

Instead of speaking of such ugly matters as "free states" and "slave states," Socrates engages in a bit of decorous indirection. He talks about just and unjust individuals. Since each person present counts himself among the just, the message about slavery can be smuggled past the sentries of the psyche. The delayed fuse in this approach reaches the gunpowder when it begins to dawn on the group that no one would want the *better* part of his own soul enslaved by the inferior part. Thus, self-knowledge, knowing the order of one's own soul, gradually becomes a symbol of the condition of one's city—and there's a sewer beneath the sidewalks in Memphis. You'll see how it works shortly.

So there he is. Socrates, standin' amongst the slaves and slave-owners, speakin' words of sedition and abolition—and *those* are just the same thing if you're Aloysius, or any kind of true Cornpone, you know. *The Republic* is not just a genteel conversation about the leisurely life of philosophy amongst gentlemen as it is so often portrayed in scholarship. As in an antebellum slave mansion, the pastries are fine, and the servants seem obedient, but the threat of force that undergirds all this politeness and ensures the present obedience is immense, and there is nothing gentle about it. Revolt is always a worry when there are so many more slaves than slave-owners. That's why Socrates cain't be talkin' that way at the corner of Front Street and Adams.

Socrates is here no more genteel in his response than were Dorothy and Ozma of Oz when they were invited to this same type of banquet hosted by slave-owners. In fact his response sounds a bit like what John Brown would have said had he been forcibly invited to tea with the Cornpones. Brown might have had more use for Annie Oakley and Wild Bill than for Dorothy and Socrates, but everyone here is on pretty much the same page, which is that Cornpone is hard to digest.

Fortunately for modern readers, Socrates gives some historical context about how Athens descended from a proud state of free people and hard workers to a state dominated by lazy slave-owners who were "enslaving and subjecting as *perioeci* [non-citizen workers] and serfs their former friends and supporters, of whose freedom they had been the guardians, and occupying themselves with war and keeping watch over their subjects." That is how Socrates says it.

As the desires of the ruling class multiply, the slave-owners become fewer, and the enslaved, greater. But, unlike in the well-functioning republic in which people are doing their work in cooperation with others, the slave owners disdain manual labor and the slaves hate being forced to do the work for *them*. Thus, while desires are multiplying, the willingness to do the work that would satisfy those delicate desires disappears. The city becomes a sewer with a slightly sour perfume to cover the stench. One needs nothing so much as a cyclone. Socrates's description of the psychological and sociological consequences of such an arrangement is a far cry from Thrasymachus's ideal of the (supposed) happily enslaved state:

SOCRATES: Will you call the state governed by a tyrant free or enslaved, speaking of it as a state?

GLAUCON: Utterly enslaved.

SOCRATES: And yet you see in it masters and free men.

GLAUCON: I see a small portion of such, but the entirety, so to speak, and the best part of it, is shamefully and wretchedly enslaved.

SOCRATES: If, then, I said, the man resembles the state, must not the same proportion obtain in him, and his soul teem with boundless servility and illiberality, the best and most reasonable parts of it being enslaved, while a small part, the worst and the most frenzied, plays the despot?

GLAUCON: Inevitably.

SOCRATES: Then will you say that such a soul is enslaved or free?

GLAUCON: Enslaved, I suppose.

For Socrates, the enslaving tyrant and the tyrannical city will be "needy and suffer from unfulfilled desire." The pains of these unfulfilled desires are frightfully immense. This explains why these oligarchs were so scared of Socrates; and why the Southern slave-owners, so full of feigned chivalry, were terrified that Kansas might be admitted as a free state and that John Brown's successful invasion of Missouri might be repeated; and why the wealthy Oz still lives in fear; and why the rich Witch of the West is scared of Dorothy, for, "Must not such a city, as well as such a man, be full of terrors and alarms?" You can't be a truly comfortable slave-owner, no matter how you slice the cornpone. Makes it hard to sleep at night.

As Socrates says to the gathered assemblage:

Individual wealthy private citizens in our states who possess many slaves . . . resemble the tyrant in being rulers over many, only the tyrant's numbers are greater. . . . Now suppose some god should catch up a man who has fifty or more slaves and waft him with his wife and children away from the city and set him down with his other possessions and his slaves in a solitude where no free man could come to his rescue. What and how great would be his fear, do you suppose, lest he and his wife and children should be destroyed by the slaves? (lines 578d–e)

Yes, that's the cyclone we needed. Socrates's command performance is certainly not how you're supposed to behave when
you're a guest, to compare your hosts to tyrants, even petty ones.
And it was the very height of impoliteness to discuss the prospect
of an impending bloodbath at a dinner party, as by saying in mixed
company—slaves and slave-owners—what Socrates then declares
as a natural fact: "god established round about [the slave-owner]
numerous neighbors who would not tolerate the claim of one man
to be master of another, but would inflict the utmost penalties on
any such person on whom they could lay their hands." Toto, I've a
feeling we're in Kansas again. That's about the time John Brown
and Dorothy show up at the Cornpone mansion—or maybe
Socrates doesn't need any help, being as brave as he is. "Socrates's
body lies a moulderin' in the grave . . ."

Although these slave-owners censor the emotions, stories, and
music that might frighten the soldiers who are to do their bidding
and protect their property, and although they forbid these soldiers
all property, lest they become soft and weak like themselves, and
although the slave-owners lie to everyone about their "noble"
ancestry, still, the slaves will hate their slavery and their masters,
and the slave-owners will have to become fawning flatterers, utterly
servile to the government that protects them from their own slaves.

And most of all the slave-owner fears death. Remember
Cephalus rushing off to meet his obligations to make payments on
his divine debts lest the bill collectors come for him and cast him
into Hell? Well Aloysius Cornpone never misses church either.
Tyrants can't really afford to miss church, since no one benefits
more than they from the appearance of religiousness, and no one
needs heaven's mercy more then they do—somewhere deep down,
they know this. All tyrants know it. Since Cephalus is off attending
to sacrifices, he misses Socrates's alternative version of Hell, one
reserved not for debtors but for those who betray humanity and
reduce peoples to slavery.

Dorothy and the Art of War

For Dorothy Gale, John Brown, and Socrates, the numerical odds
of their situations—a few compatriots against hundreds or thousands—look pretty bad. Yet, all three are able to stand up to their
oppressors and win their battles. (Only Dorothy lives to tell the
tale.) In fact, perhaps that is why it's important to recognize a kind

of innocent justice and earned immortality in her character. Socrates went down. John Brown went down. Hundreds of thousands of Civil War soldiers went down. Jesus went down. And Peter, and Paul, and Gandhi, and King, and probably you're next if you open your trap about this sort of thing on the corner of Front Street and Adams. What sort of message does *that* send to children? Well, Dorothy lives.

All three of our heroes turn out to be pretty good at fighting, because really they're so little interested in fighting and instead are so absorbed in the work of life, not in the appearance of justice, but in the living reality of it. Dorothy's sense of justice and fairness is utterly natural to her—but then some children are just like that, until we teach them to be otherwise. That sense of justice is why such people have self-sacrificing friends, the rickety Scarecrows and Tin Men who stand up for them not because they have been paid or coerced or tricked, but because they can see what is right and are not afraid of confronting what's wrong. Their opponents are rather bad at fighting, over the long haul, because they're so interested in luxury and death and killing and subjugation but not in working and friendship and moderate potations. So the slave-owners exhaust themselves while their opponents remain young and vibrant, Socrates says. John Brown didn't fear death any more than Socrates or Dorothy did, and that may be what disturbs a tyrant most of all.

So you may have *heard* that *The Republic* was just a genteel conversation, that John Brown was a madman, and that *The Wonderful Wizard of Oz* is just a childish fantasy. Whose version of history have you been taught? The history of Kansas you know is the Wild West, Dodge City, the righteous sheriff. We don't much think of the struggle to make Kansas a slave state any more. In fact, we look upon the outcome in Kansas as having been inevitable when we think about it now. But that didn't happen all by itself. John Brown created the Kansas Dorothy came from, as Baum knew very well. All of our heroes knew the magic spell that can make just a few friends stronger than hordes of adversaries: the love of wisdom charms away the fear of death, and philosophical cooperation with our neighbors will get us much further than trying to enslave others.

5

When the Wiz Goes Black, Does It Ever Go Back?

TOMMY J. CURRY

> Our greatest fear is not that we are inadequate, but that we are pow-
> erful beyond measure. It is our light, not our darkness that frightens
> us. We ask ourselves, Who am I to be brilliant, gorgeous, handsome,
> talented and fabulous? Actually, who are you not to be?
>
> Your playing small does not serve the world. There is nothing
> enlightened about shrinking so that other people won't feel insecure
> around you . . . as we let our own light shine, we consciously give
> other people permission to do the same. As we are liberated from our
> fear, our presence automatically liberates others.
>
> —Nelson Mandela

Since the late seventies, African Americans have gathered around
the televised version of *The Wiz* and anticipated sharing the stories
and reveling over the novelty of an all Black cast in the remake of
The Wizard of Oz. Often referred to as the "Black Wizard of Oz,"
The Wiz is a wonderful fantasy that literally flips the script on the
1939 screen adaptation of Baum's classic story. The most notable
difference was the skin color of the actors—shockingly they were
all BLACK!

Today our post-integrationist sensibilities would declare the
color of the actors' skin color irrelevant—but an all-Black cast was
certainly shocking to most in 1978,[1] and is probably the reason that

---

[1] The film was made largely as a result of the tremendous success of the
Broadway show that opened on January 5th 1975 at the Majestic Theatre. It wasn't
until 1978 that Motown decided to back the screen adaptation of the project and
include the talents of Dianna Ross, Michael Jackson, Nipsey Russell, Lena Horne,
and Richard Pryor as the characters of the story.

The Wiz did not spark the philosophical curiosity of many of the thinkers encountering philosophy and *The Wizard of Oz*. While whites have fascinated themselves with the idols and themes of Frank Baum's *The Wonderful Wizard of Oz*, African Americans have created and recreated generations of children reared on the promises of triumph, the Soulz of Motown, and the belief in the messages of Black actors that we will emerge within "A Brand New Day."

[The Break-Down]

The rhythms and Soulz / the imagery and molds / the cold harsh truth emerges from the urban Black hole/ and / pushed Dorothy to get on down the Yellow Brick Road / Rather than a symbol of hope / Dorothy's journey revealed her fear of becoming, a cruel joke / Almost as natural as Black girls jump rope / Dorothy found herself in her race's ability to cope / Home did not become a place: / but her belief that that old tyme feeling of race / where knowledge of self was knowledge of people / and the recognition that the virtue of Blackness was that it was not evil / The admission that the courage to look beyond was bound to be scary / but closer to home than we thought, because all along our history could be found in New York's Public Library / The Wiz showed us no matter how cold / the love a people could not erode / And it is in this way that Blackness has become in the minds of a people a worthwhile and cherished virtue to behold.

[And Now Back to Our Regularly Scheduled Program]

In *The Wiz* such effort is made to attend to the racial motifs that its actual narration renders it a very different story all together. Because the change from white actors to Black actors is so totalizing and the imaginings invoked by Black bodies so distinct, *The Wiz* has truly made me wonder if Blackness, beyond a question of racial identity is, in fact, a racial virtue—a habitual acting of behaviors held fast in time by knowledge towards the development of the race. In other words, are there actual lessons of goodness and realizations that particular and specific to the Black condition in America that the movie *The Wiz* appeals to in Blacks and aims to develop in Black people? And if so, does the Blackness that emerges through the cultivation of the lessons from *The Wiz* through knowledge, feeling, courage and admittance constitute a moral excellence in African Americans?

Cook Me Up Some Legacy—Feeling that Old Tyme Racial Virtue

At the beginning of *The Wiz* the viewer is assaulted with the eidetic murals on the brownstones and audacious positive Black images: a world where Black women are married, Black men live to be grandfathers, Black people with children are actually called parents, and three generations of a Black family are present in one room—the youngest of which are rocking dashikis and Afros. From the first scene, *The Wiz* convincingly shows a very different reality to the viewer. Rather than display the over-accentuated stereotypes of Black poverty, and suffering common to the Blax-poitation era, *The Wiz* immerses itself in the possibilities of kinship nourished among multiple generations of a well to do Black family living at 433 Prospect Place, a fictional address in Harlem. The conflict however emerges between the solidity of this family's racial heritage and Dorothy's inability to find her place amongst this sentiment.

Almost as suddenly as the screen is saturated by the ambiance of Blackness, the viewers are pulled into the uplifting tones of "The Feeling that We Have." This song, both in lyrics and the amazing vocals performed by Theresa Merritt (Auntie Em) excites a visceral intuition in Black culture and calls forth the acknowledgement from Blacks that the family, and by extension the race, is interdependent. In an almost familiar religious voice Auntie Em's song reminds us, despite our individuality, that the family and our ancestors before us will remain present in our personal aspirations. While this may appear to be a simplistic and popular cultural motif in the Black community, it should not be taken lightly or mistaken as a hue of an un-philosophical nature. This idea of community is a very common question in Western philosophical thought, but in African American culture it has a distinct character of its own, as it has been and remains fundamentally married to the question of race.

For centuries, the race has been inextricably linked to the analogies of families. Most famously, W.E.B. Du Bois (1868–1963) understood races as "a vast family of human beings, generally of common blood and language, always of common history, traditions and impulses, who are both voluntarily and involuntarily striving together for the accomplishment of certain more or less vividly conceived ideals of life."[2] While this definition of race is on board with the understanding of race invoked by the imagery of *The Wiz*, how do we account for that "Feeling that We Have" and the commandment by the Black matriarch (Auntie Em) that repetitively tells us "Don't Lose the Feeling that We Have."

To most the understanding of a "racial feeling" may seem like a stretch, especially given the "anti-essentialist care ethics" of contemporary philosophical treatments of race. The idea here is that there is no single "essence" of what it means to belong to a race, and so our racial identities come from practices that reflect what we care about most deeply. But ask yourself this question: If these were white bodies on the screen asking the same question, would not this compulsion be taken to be either isolated to Dorothy's immediate family or extended as far as her cosmopolitan humanity? Because Blacks are the main characters of the movie, the messages they convey as well as the reception of these messages by their audience take on fundamentally different meanings. Whereas white characters have the mistakenly assumed the ability to speak for and to a colorless humanity, many Black messages are more humble in their audience—the people that can and do relate to the experience.

For Du Bois and many of the Blacks after him "in order to understand human history and thus be informed in attempting to structure the making of the future through organized effort, the focus of such understanding must be the racial group, the "vast family" of related individuals. While individuals are, of course, necessary components of social groups, and must never be lost sight of when analyzing and assessing human ventures, they are neither sufficient for accounting for social groups, nor self-sufficing and thus able to account for their own existence and well being.[3] The race feeling, however, is much more complicated, because it exists as part of the natural constitution of the self. According to Alexander Crummell (1819–1898),

---

[2] W.E.B DuBois, "The Conservation of Races," in *The American Negro Academy Occasional Papers 1–22* (New York: Arno Press and The New York Times, 1969).

[3] Lucius Outlaw, "Conserve Races? In Defense of W.E.B. DuBois," in *On Race and Culture,* edited by Bernard W. Bell, Emily R. Grosholz, and James B. Stewart (Routledge, 1996), pp.15–37, 31.

Races, like families, are the organisms and the ordinance of God; and race feeling, like the family feeling, is of divine origin. The extinction of race feeling is just as possible as the extinction of family feeling. Indeed, a race is a family. The principle of continuity is as masterful in races as it is in families—as it is in nations. History is filled with the attempts of kings and mighty generals and great statesmen to extinguish this instinct. But their failures are as numerous as their futile attempts; for this sentiment, alike subtle and spontaneous, has both pervaded and stimulated society in every quarter. Indeed, 'race is the key to history.' When once the race type gets fixed as a new variety, then it acts precisely as the family life; for, 1st, it propagates itself by that divine instinct of reproduction, vital in all living creatures, and next, 2nd it has a growth as a 'seed after its own kind and in itself' whereby the race type becomes a perpetuity, with its own distinctive form, constitution, features and structure.[4]

For Dorothy, her family, and many African Americans, this racial feeling is not negotiable. Born within a world with these racial classifications makes them in some sense a permanent social and psychical dichotomy and it is the impulse both to reconcile and thrive in this world that marries Blackness to the humanity of Blacks. The two are simply inseparable. Current theorizations by white philosophers, when they only consider the brief mention of races as families by Du Bois and interpret this relationship as an issue of partiality, when they also without a genealogical understanding of how race functions in Black culture or an historical understanding of how this definition of race functioned amongst Du Bois's peers, are grossly inadequate under a rigorous philosophical light.[5] In contrast, *The Wiz* conveys this conceptualization of race as a family in ways that are much closer to Du Bois's time and highlights. Here, a race's semblance to a family is much more about time and history than partiality. A race needs, just as a family does, time (generations) to develop its legacy, and it is this (much ignored) aspect of racial thinking in philosophy that forms the cornerstone of *The Wiz*, highlighting Dorothy's journey through racial actualization, that makes her role as a teacher all the more significant.

---

[4] Alexander Crummell, "The Race-Problem in America," in *Africa and America* (New York: Negro University Press, 1969), pp. 46–47.

[5] Here I'm thinking of Anna Stubblefield, "Races as Families," *Journal of Social Philosophy* 32:1 (2001), pp. 99–112.

The Crisis of Dorothy and the Problem of One [POWERLESSNESS]

From the very beginning of the movie, the audience is confronted by the uncomfortable distance of Dorothy. She does not seem comfortable with the family and seems to lack the kindred spirit that relatives share. She really just doesn't seem to belong. This suspicion is all too readily confirmed when Dorothy begins singing "Can I Go On," a song that not only announces her lack of self-esteem, but her inability to believe in that Old Tyme racial feeling. "Lose it," she asks. "I don't know the first thing about what they are feeling." At this point in the movie, Dorothy appears surprisingly confused. A Black teacher, living in north Harlem, doesn't know anything about racial feeling. I was shocked, then Auntie Em announces that Dorothy has never been south of 125th street and the dilemma becomes clear— Dorothy lacks knowledge of self,[6] because she lacks the courage to embrace the ideas that brought about Black enlightenment.

This is almost unbearable given that Dorothy is a teacher—an educator—whose job, whose very point of existing, is to cultivate the minds of impressionable Black youth. What does she teach the kids? Here again emerges the conflict. Auntie Em is particularly worried about the inability of Dorothy to leave and find her own home. Instead of taking a job offer that offers her more money teaching high school students ready to confront the world head on, Dorothy prefers to work with kindergarteners and remain safe under the watchful eye of Auntie Em. As with many of us, there's a constant tension between our individuality and group identity. We are constantly worried about being seen by white eyes and viewed through white suspicions; however Dorothy's case is much more severe in that she lacks the foundational understanding of the racial ideals that make her who she is. So instead of being worried about being viewed incorrectly, she lacks to the ability to be seen at all, because she has no position in the world from which she can articulate what and who she is. In short, Dorothy lacks the confidence (the belief in herself) to live a life of racial virtue with full racial commitment.

---

[6] In Black culture, lacking knowledge of self refers to the failure of individuals to know their history and acknowledge their racial duty.

Almost proleptically, as if Auntie Em knew of Dorothy's forthcoming journey to Oz, Auntie Em utters to Dorothy that "whatever your fears are, they'll be defeated just by facing up to them." Moments later we see Dorothy chasing Toto into the wintry night, only to be caught up in a snowy tornado and magically transported to the mystical Land of Oz.

Unlike the white Wizard of Oz, the first Wizard the Black Dorothy meets after killing Evermean is not the Good Witch of the North, but Miss One. Miss One is an interesting character and represents a striking contrast to the characterization of Dorothy and her family which represent plurality and community. Because Miss One is simply one person, her powers don't amount to much. I could only imagine how frustrated Dorothy must have been by the impotence of individuality, but it demonstrates a very important point of racial virtue, namely that *one* can only be empowered through the many. And more importantly race, and more specifically family, are in themselves the origin of power.

In Miss One, Dorothy is confronted by her own reflection; a newly freed individual who is able to go about running her business without direction, without purpose. In Miss One, Dorothy not only meets her limitations but acknowledges her possibility of growth. It's only because Dorothy accepts her limitations that she begins a journey to find friendship, community, and that good ol' racial feeling. So while Miss One is certainly not the personification of the virtue that Dorothy wishes to attain, her presence was necessary to the extent that it showed Dorothy the inadequacy of individuals who by definition are only one and lack the shared constitution of others. However, it cannot be denied that Miss One, while powerless, does send Dorothy on her journey down the Yellow Brick Road to find the Wiz, since Glinda the Good Witch of the South is almost impossible to find, and Evillene, Evermean's sister, probably wouldn't be doing Dorothy any favors.

Before Dorothy is able to find the Yellow Brick Road, she needs to believe in the possibility of her own self improvement. She can no longer ask "can she go on," because now she must. To find home she will have to believe in herself and more importantly the potential she possesses by believing in herself. It is this need of self knowledge that foreshadows her meeting with the Scarecrow, played by the young Michael Jackson.

Damn, that Boy Can Blow—Dropping Knowledge and Elevating a People Away from Negative Thinking. [KNOWLEDGE]

I've always loved little Michael, and his performance in *The Wiz* is so compelling that it seems as if his mantras that "knowledge is power," that "more men are made noble by study than nature," and "don't accept any situation, question, argue, and explore," resonate as novelties. In an interesting twist, the scarecrow in *The Wiz* is not stuffed with hay, but with various newspaper clippings and philosophical literature which he quotes and memorizes constantly. However, the tragic point of the Scarecrow's dilemma is that knowledge is useless without the ability and capacity to utilize it and act on its insights.

The Scarecrow is seemingly trapped on a pole in a cornfield in the middle of a torn down ghetto. (I know the imagery is staggering.) The only objects in the scarecrow's environment are the dilapidated buildings of the ghetto and the four crows who credit themselves with the education of the scarecrow. More than anything, the scarecrow wants to get down from his pole and walk in his garden, but the crows have convinced him that he can't get down. In fact, the crows claim that they are actually taking care of the scarecrow because he can't walk and by keeping him up on his pole they are actually keeping him safe. The crow's message is just as clear as it is disturbing: because of what you are, there are certain things you cannot do, and instead of trying and failing, you're better off accepting things as they are. This type of thinking is so ingrained in the Scarecrow that the crows make him recite the crow commandments, which read: (1) Thou shalt honor all crows, (2) Thou shalt stop reading all bits of paper and literature, (3) Thou shalt never get down from this here pole.

These commandments enslave the mind of the Scarecrow under the presumed authority of the crows and make it impossible for the Scarecrow to apply any of his knowledge towards his own liberation. By getting the Scarecrow to admit to his inability to act against his unfortunate circumstances, the crows convince the Scarecrow that no matter what "You Can't Win." As a testimony of his inferiority, the Scarecrow sings the crow anthem—an anthem that accepts the presumed powerlessness of the Scarecrow to act against any external forces that subjugate him. "You can't win, you can't break even, and you can't get out of the game / People keep sayin' / Things are gonna change / But they look just like they're staying the same. You get in way over your head / and you've only got yourself to blame."

This fatalist tone not only condemned the Scarecrow to his dangling state, but made the knowledge he did acquire by reading useless. In fact, it was not until Dorothy emerged from the ruins of the ghetto and scared the crows away that the Scarecrow was able to accept Dorothy's help and free himself from the pole. Amidst his newly found freedom, the Scarecrow realized that he had the ability to get down the whole time. He realized that the crows had misinformed him, but mistakenly thought that a brain would have protected him from the crows' mis-education. Dorothy, becoming wiser in her journey, showed the Scarecrow that it was not the question of a brain, but rather the type of thinking a brain engages in during thought. In a way, Dorothy drew out of the Scarecrow a virtue he already possessed and called from him a response or action that demonstrated his virtue. Insofar as the Scarecrow revealed this virtue to Dorothy, so too did Dorothy believe in the possibility of knowledge and knowing,. Her choice to act on this knowledge and undertake the process of knowing led her to escape from the ghetto aand began her journey down the Yellow Brick Road.

Dorothy's triumph over the ignorance of the crows is also a triumph over the historical ignorance of racism that continues to convince Blacks that their current amount of progress is acceptable or worse yet, that they are powerless to advance further beyond what they are given. Just as Dorothy's discovery is a personal advance, so too is it a racial one. The need to question the circumstances of poverty, ghettoization, and mis-education is as much an individual lesson that helps Dorothy rise above here particular racial circumstance as a racial lesson because her elevation above negativity simultaneously elevates the race. What is particularly powerful about this question of knowledge is that it is the Scarecrow that finds the Yellow Brick Road and not Dorothy. Unlike the *The Wizard of Oz*, where the Yellow Brick Road was apparent from the beginning of Dorothy's arrival in Oz, *The Wiz* emphasizes the tribulations of racial identity whereby the journey is new and the road much less travelled.

Even Players Can Cry! [FEELING]

Shortly after Dorothy and Scarecrow "ease on down the road," they encounter the Tin-Man trapped under his excessively "thick" fourth wife Tinny. Unlike the Tin-Man of old, the Black Tin-Man's virtue has a specific and compelling function in the achievement of racial advancement. Feeling, understood not as a neutral categorization of emotions affected to varying degrees by pleasure or pain, but as a way through which the world reveals itself to the one who feels, plays a pivotal part in *The Wiz*. In fact, it is feeling that directs knowledge and the feeling—the connection—Dorothy shares with others that will eventually draw her closer to home.

Unfortunately, however, the virtue of feeling seems to be a two-tier process. The first and seemingly most difficult in the cultivation of a racial virtue is the equivocal appreciation of one's self, and secondly the extension of that appreciation of one's self to others. The Tin-Man tells us about feelings in his song entitled "What Would I Do if I Could Feel?"

> What would I do if I could feel?
> What would I do
> If I could reach inside of me
> And to know how it feels
> To say I like what I see?
> Then I'd be more than glad to share
> All that I have inside of here
> And the songs my heart might bring
> You'd be more than glad to sing.
> And if tears should fall from my eyes
> Just think of all the wounds they could mend.

Unlike the other characters, the Tin-man's virtue seems almost natural, almost as if it was simply ignored rather than revealed as in the case of the Scarecrow. Much like the seemingly natural feeling of family, the Tin-Man is without conflict or barrier to his virtue; it is merely a case of exercising his capacity to love, to feel and to embrace others as he does himself. This is further supported by the fact that Dorothy does not announce his virtue to him as she does to the Scarecrow. Hence we're led to believe with even more certainty that the natural affinity for one's racial brethren constitutes a seemingly obvious moral concern.

The Racial Idealism of Fleetwood Coupe De Ville [COURAGE]

After Dorothy acknowledges the power of knowledge to confront reality (the Scarecrow), and the need to feel her (racial) legacy (the

Tin-Man), easing on down the road takes an abrupt stop in front of the New York Public Library. Encountering the cowardly lion in front of the library is easily one of the most powerful and explicit associations with racial progress made in the film. The street lights on the yellow brick road that once read "EASE" immediate read "DON'T EASE" and signal the arduous task that confronts Dorothy in the realization of courage. This scene is only amplified by the historical task that confronts the Black race in remedying its mis-education and learning their nearly forgotten history.

The cowardly lion, a.k.a. Fleetwood Coupe De Ville—so named because his "Mama had high ideals,"—represents a commonly accepted theory of progress after integration. The idea that educa-tion, the cultivation of higher ideals and culture among Blacks would promise a future of acceptance and triumph amidst the racial antipathies at large in America, such an idea was almost uni-versally supported after the Civil Rights Era. Ironically, this attitude was often described by race thinkers as wanting a race of lion-like men who were courageous enough to use their achievements of higher learning for the betterment of the race. One of these men was a philosopher by the name of William H. Ferris (1874–1941) who thought that

> the Negro must acquire culture, polish and refinement, he must acquire aristocratic, high-bred feeling . . . [whereby the racial stock is improved] . . . We must produce a race of bold lion-like men, and aris-tocratic, high bred women, we must make some contribution to civi-lization, must develop the intellectual, moral and aesthetic sides of our nature, —then we will no longer be a despised but an admired race.[7]

Ferris—much like the shining race men of his time and under the same Black enlightenment ideas that were in the background of Auntie Em's push for Dorothy to go south of 125th Street—accepted the idea that race progress could only come from an "educated gentry" (p. 401).

Much like the facade of the "Mean Ole Lion," Ferris claimed that the race is always ready to fight against obstacles or easily identifiable enemies of the race, but lacks the courage to cultivate

---

[7] William H. Ferris, *The African Abroad: His Evolution in Western Civilization—Tracing His Development Under Caucasian Mileu* (New Haven: The Tuttle, Morehouse and Taylor Press, 1913), pp. 401–02.

an educated race of learned men and women capable of sustaining and providing for its own. Combativeness is not courage. Courage would require Blacks to not shrink from the seemingly impossible task of turning whites' racial hatred into admiration. Ferris admits this is no easy task but is convinced that "the Negro must convince a world believing in his inferiority and hostile to his higher aspirations; the Negro must convince a generation that believes he is only fit to be a pack-horse and beast of burden that he is a full-fledged and full-orbed man, with the tastes and desires and hopes and aspirations of other men. How can he do it? He must go out and dazzle the world by his deeds and achievements" (pp. 406–07).

Ferris is almost prophetic in laying out the task of the race, as Dorothy calls forth this courage and commands the lion to act. In her song "Be a Lion," Dorothy serenades the lion, "If on courage you must call / Then just keep on tryin' / And tryin' / And tryin' / You're a lion / In your own way / Be a lion." Dorothy announces the uniqueness of the racial ideal in her melody to Fleetwood. Aspirations to higher ideals do not require the lion to imitate the successes of others but mean that his effort should be unique; he should be a lion (a courageous actor) in his own way. For Ferris, Blacks have been "a critical race, but now we must become a creative race. We have been an imitative race; we must become a productive race" (p. 407). Rather than simply dealing with the conditions set before them, Black persons must have the courage to confront the seemingly natural hostility to their existence in America and find within themselves the courage to act against these hostilities and become—A LION!

What Virtues Must Overcome: The Truth about Black Suffering and the Plague of Racial Realism [ADMITTANCE]

Despite the virtues that we aspire towards, there's an unfortunate reality about life as a Black person living in America that few people, Black or white, are brave enough to accept—namely that racism exists, persists and in some sense, is permanent. The Evil Witch of the West, Evillene, is the epitome of this sad reality. As the slave driver of the sweat shop, Evillene is adamant "Don't Nobody Bring Me No Bad News." Evillene personifies the dominant idea that hard work and suffering through racism is redemptive. As she tells one of her starving workers, "suffering is food for the soul—NOW SUFFER!" Throughout history, Black thinkers have conceded that a level of suffering is needed to achieve a virtuous soul. This belief in the purifying power of tribulation, and the moralizing ethics of hope—the faith in an inevitably better tomorrow –is an all too common idea about race relations in America and has been the Achilles heel of Black racial development.

This virtue however is unattainable under racism as it forces the victim of historical dehumanization and racial debasement to accept this condition as natural and in some sense divine in origin. In popular Black culture it is the belief that "everything happens for a reason," even if that reason is made manifest by the systemic and deliberate tyranny of whites. Evillene's characterization persists even today as most Blacks, under integration, refuse to hear the bad news that integration has failed.[8] Rather than accept the short-sightedness of a half hearted attempt to create equality with whites, many Blacks continue to believe that more time, more patience and more hard work by Blacks can win whites over and create a brighter tomorrow.

Rather than the Wiz himself being a testament against this view of the world, he too is sadly a victim of it. Despite all his efforts to win public office, Herman Smith (played by the young Richard Pryor), could not get elected to any public office. "Not because I didn't try, says Smith, I tried everything. I ran for any and everything: alderman, councilman, assembly leader. I became a laughing stock—I couldn't get on the ticket—in desperation I ran for dog catcher." While some may take the confessions of the Wiz as humorous, they speak to the very real political marginalization of Black people in America. Despite the economic and educational gains of Blacks in the decades since the Civil Rights movement, whites simply don't elect Blacks for at large representation. This was just as true then as it is now. Some readers may take issue with this statement given the recent visibility of Barack Obama.

---

[8] Integration has failed on several fronts. For a brief historical analysis, see Mary Dudziak, "Desegregation as a Cold War Imperative," *Standford Law Review* 41 (1988),p. 61 or her lengthier work entitled *Cold War Civil Rights: Race and the Image of American Democracy* (Princeton University Press, 2002). For a more contemporary treatment of integration and equality, seeTommy J. Curry, "Please Don't Make Touch Em: Towards a Critical Race Fanonianism as a Possible Justification for Violence against Whiteness," *Radical Philosophy Today* 5 (2007).

However race and the debate over whether or not Obama is too Black will remain a question in the minds of white Americans. His leadership, his patriotism, and at a very basic level the willingness of the public to accept him rest on this question.

Blacks are not the governors, mayors, and political representatives of Black interests and causes in most American cities. And even in those cities that have Black representatives, the duties of those public officials are not exclusive to their Black constituents. Simply put, Blacks are the victims of political ostracism and this fact, despite the promises of liberalism, democracy, and equality, remains a barrier to Black social mobility. While it's undeniable that there have been certain changes in American society since the Civil Rights movement (such as that Blacks can now attend the same schools, work in the same jobs, and live in the same neighborhoods as whites), it is likewise just as evident in terms of actual progress—the political and economic advancement of Blacks—that there has been little. Whereas some readers may wince at this reality, *The Wiz* challenges us all to accept that only the promise of a brighter tomorrow is the true standard of racial progress.

What's important about Dorothy's message in regard to the demise of Evillene and the unfortunate fate of the Wizard is that achieving a brighter day does not require Blacks to pretend that the reality before them does not exist. The admission of a dire situation is not the admittance of defeat. Much like the potential had in the Scarecrow's lesson, Dorothy's singing of "A Brand New Day" is not only an acknowledgement of freedom, but announces the transformative power that Blacks have in their power to act contrary to their circumstances.

> Everybody look around
> 'Cause there's a reason to rejoice you see
> Everybody come out
> Everybody look up
> And feel the hope that we've been waiting for
> Everybody's glad
> Because our silent fear and dread is gone.
> Freedom, you see, has got our hearts singing so joyfully
> Can't you feel a brand new day?
> Can't you feel a brand new day?
> Can't you feel a brand new day?
> Can't you feel a brand new day? Hello world
> It's like a different way of living now

And thank you world
We always knew that we'd be free somehow in harmony
And show the world that we've got liberty.

Lessons Learned

Just as the mural painted on the brownstone that opened the movie, Glinda the Good Witch of the South appears surrounded by Black children; infants in some cases. Rather than simply granting Dorothy's wish to go home, Glinda tells Dorothy that her belief in herself is the only power she needs to change the world as she sees fit. This is a profound cultural moment in *The Wiz*. Dorothy's conversation with Glinda, the Good Witch of the South, is a demonstration of the power and racial legacy that Black women command in Black culture. As the mothers of the race, their command of virtue and education of the children of the race is indispensible to racial advancement. It's almost as if Glinda showed Dorothy, the kindergarten teacher, that she got the lil' ones, so now it's up to you to cultivate the minds and nourish the souls of our race's emerging adults. Guided by the words of Glinda, Dorothy believes, not only in herself, but in her reason to be. She believes she can make time stand still from the moment she tries and can now give herself and by extension her race time to grow. As Glinda tells her, "If you believe in yourself, right from the start / You'll have the brains / You'll have heart / You'll have courage / To last your whole life / If you believe in yourself." As the personification of the racial spirit, Glinda's teachings instruct Dorothy in racial mothering. As Dorothy accepts the racial virtues that she now embodies, so too does she recognize that her Black embodiment provides the spiritual nourishment for the race.

By the end of the movie, a very different Dorothy emerges from the inability of "the Wiz" to send her back home. Unlike the Dorothy who landed in Oz without direction, feeling and belief, the new Dorothy identifies the virtues of her friends and more specifically herself. This Dorothy understands the price of freedom and embraces that Old Tyme racial feeling. Just like her Auntie Em before her, Dorothy learned to accept the inevitable historicism of racial development. Because home is concomitantly dislocated and centered, since it exists simultaneously within her and as a place, her belief in herself empowers her to co-author the reality she shares as a member of her racial group. Insofar as Dorothy embodies the ideals of racial advancement, so too does the race embody her. Her Blackness was apparent from the beginning of her journey, but what was concealed was the potential that lay in the simultaneous development of her individual character though the racial ideals of knowledge, feeling, courage, and admittance. By making herself an obstacle to racial stagnation, and facilitating racial advancement, Dorothy fulfills her Auntie's wish and begins the arduous task of authoring the world anew. Just as the women before her, Dorothy now accepts her responsibility to continue the racial legacy of her people.

When Dorothy's ready to return home, she doesn't mention New York as the specific place that she wishes to return to. Instead she describes how she feels about home and commands herself to make that place, the place from which she aspires, a reality. Home is a place "where there's love overflowing, where there are things I been knowing," where there is "love and affection." Evidently for Dorothy home is part of an emotional connection, a feeling that may be new, but one known to her as part of her historical development. Home is now where she can grow and create a "Brand New Day" for all those she can feel.[9]

---

[9] I would like to thank my wife Gwenetta D. Curry for sitting down with me, scene after scene, and talking with me about *The Wiz*, my mother Shirley Mae Curry for forcing me to watch *The Wiz* when I was a small boy in Southern Louisiana and explaining to me the importance of having our people on the big screen, Brittney Chante Cooper for responding to my endless emails asking for feedback, and last but not least, Randy Auxier and my boy Phil Seng for including a piece in this book on "the Black Wizard of Oz."

II

If I Only Had a Mind

6

Oz Never Did Give Nothing to the Tin Man

MICHAEL F. PATTON, Jr.

When I was growing up, my father had a term for certain sorts of children's tales: Mental Violence. So devoted to reason was he that he would prefer for us to watch Sam Peckinpah's *Straw Dogs* than the animated version of *Alice in Wonderland*. He believed that witnessing a movie (or reading a book) in which the laws of logic were turned upside down would scar the reasoning centers of our brains irreparably. And so, we could read certain science fiction, but virtually no fantasy.

To give Dad some credit, perhaps he was merely heeding Plato's advice in the *Republic*. In that book, Plato establishes strict censorship of poetry and the tales that can be told to children. Any literary work that portrays the gods as behaving badly was right out because, as Plato reasoned, if the gods are "better" than us and they run around, for instance, raping people all the time, then kids will begin to associate godliness with the act of rape. (In case you don't remember, the head god Zeus was especially fond of raping human women. He raped Europa while in the form of a god, Leda while in the form of a swan and Danae in the form of a *golden shower!*) Plato thought that children (and citizens in general) should be exposed to stories that portrayed the gods performing only good and noble acts.

Plato had another interesting rule. Poetry that required the reader to assume the identity of the speaker of the lines was to be limited to tales of good things happening and being intended by the character. You weren't supposed to "play-act" at being a villain, in his ideal city. Plato thought that our ways of thinking got fairly settled by custom and practice and that we weren't capable of switching our characters or dispositions. Thus, if you had to play the role of a bad person for too long, you yourself would potentially become bad.

We use the same argument today with video games. And there is some evidence that this may be true or at least that portraying many different characters is harmful to you—just look how crazy the best actors and actresses are. So if dad was just following Plato's lead, I suppose I understand. Still, he has a bit of explaining to do about the time he took me to see *2001: A Space Odyssey* when I was six years old. The music still creeps me out to this day.

Anyway, I never read *The Wizard of Oz* growing up, although I eventually began to watch the movie every year on TV—I guess Dad finally got tired of the fight. Before writing a chapter for this book, my researcher instincts and my curiosity drove me to read *The Wizard of Oz*, making me, as far as I can tell, the only person over thirty who doesn't have kids who remembers the details of the book and not the movie. And believe me, the book makes the movie seem positively mundane in its depictions. Out of all the bizarre happenings and peculiar characters in the book, I have chosen the Tin Woodman to discuss here today.

By the end of this chapter, I bet you'll want to go read the book for yourself, to verify that I am not making this up. *The Wonderful Wizard of Oz* contains Mental Violence aplenty, and I for one am glad I had the resilience of a firm-minded adult before I read it. Unfortunately, I also had the perspective-warping experiences of being a professional philosopher to make the reading kind of problematic.

In addition to reading the book, I also read the introduction to the book (something I've been trained to do). L. Frank Baum explains his goals in writing the book in the introduction:

> Yet the old time fairy tale, having served for generations, may now be classed as "historical" in the children's library; for the time has come for a series of newer "wonder tales" in which the stereotyped genie, dwarf and fairy are eliminated, together with all the horrible and blood-curdling incidents devised by their authors to point a fearsome moral to each tale. Modern education includes morality; therefore the modern child seeks only entertainment in its wonder tales and gladly dispenses with all disagreeable incident.
>
> Having this thought in mind, the story of "The Wonderful Wizard of Oz" was written solely to please children of today. It aspires to being a modernized

fairy tale, in which the wonderment and joy are retained and the heartaches and nightmares are left out.[1]

Oh really, L. Frank? You think you left the nightmares out? I'll let you, the readers of this essay, be the judges of that . . .

Pieces of Me

A cyborg is a cybernetic organism (an organism that has both artificial and natural systems). The term was coined in 1960 when Manfred Clynes and Nathan Kline used it in an article about the advantages of self-regulating human-machine systems in outer space.[2]

Certainly most of us are comfortable with the idea of becoming part-human, part-machine—in short, becoming cyborgs. All of my friends and I took the first step to becoming cyborgs due to our poor brushing habits as kids. That's right, the odds are about eightyt percent that you have parts of your pearly whites that were placed there by science, not nature, according to the 2000 US Surgeon General's Report on Oral Health.[3] Now, that may seem trivial to you, but the number of "artificial systems" that are being incorporated into human bodies is growing by leaps and bounds: artificial limbs, replacement joints, cochlear implants, pacemakers, insulin pumps, internal defibrillators, artificial hearts—the list gets too long to keep up-to-date. At some point, it must occur to one to ask, "Just how much change can a person undergo and still be human?" The desire to ask such a question is even greater if one is a philosopher.

Even the world of sports is having to untangle the question of how much change one can undergo and still be a human, properly speaking, instead of a cyborg. High-tech carbon-fiber blades that some amputees have below the knee allow greater speed in running than do old-fashioned flesh-and-bone legs, in part because they are lighter. Are the possessors of such replacement parts destined to occupy the top of all of the record books? Or do we make these people compete in a different category, as the Olympic

---

[1] L. Frank Baum, *The New Wizard of Oz* (Bobbs-Merrill, 1944), p. 6.

[2] "Cyborgs and Space," in *Astronautics* (September 1960), by Manfred E. Clynes and Nathan S. Kline.

[3] http://www.surgeongeneral.gov/library/oralhealth/

Committee had to do with the East German Women's Swim Teams (the question was whether they were still really "women")? The debate gets more intense as technology marches on.

All of Me, Why Not Take All of Me?

I'll get to the Tin Man in a minute, but let's talk about something more interesting for a bit, like, oh . . . . I don't know, how about *me*. And probably you too, but definitely me. When I sit around and daydream about it, I can convince myself that I am pretty durable. I find it easiest to think about what parts I could live without. I am certain that I would survive if I lost my left little toe. In fact, I could probably be enticed to sell it to you for enough money. Ditto, of course, for my right little toe, or even both at a suitably profitable discount, if you must have them. And while I know that having toes is essential to standing and walking, I could survive without any toes or the ability to walk.

So, I could live without legs and, by similar reasoning, I could get along without my arms (these are not for sale right now, but the legs are headed for the clearance rack before too long). Given modern life support, I could live without a variety of my internal organs. Given some certain-to-be-pending improvements in life-support, I could live without my torso or any of the organs in it. Just hook my head up to a liver/kidney/heart/lung/etc. machine, and I'll be fine. I doubt my colleagues would notice the difference. And from there, I can imagine it being possible in a few decades to replace my eyes with cameras, my ears with microphones and my mouth with a speaker (and whatever we'll call the machine-nose and machine-tongue) and I'll be fine. I'll be the brain-in-a-vat from the B sci-fi movies of the 1950s or one of the replacement heads in Mombi's wardrobe closet (from one of the later Oz books).

I don't mean to imply that I would want any of these things to happen to me, but I do believe I would still be in existence if they happened to me. And I think that if I would survive the loss of these parts of me, it just seems obvious that I could survive the replacement of theses parts. In fact, I actually am waiting for the day I can get my aching knees replaced, but I'm waiting for the recovery from the surgery to be a little less sucky first. Not only will I survive that procedure, I'll be like Steve Austin, the Six-Million Dollar Man. Not the "a man barely alive" Steve, but the "better, stronger, faster" Steve. If I could replace all the parts I just considered losing with better, stronger and faster systems, I'd be willing to pay to have it done. I'm not alone in thinking this upgrade would be a good thing . . .

Stop! In the Name of Love

However, we've reached the limit of what I think I can lose. Suppose we have invented the Memory-Eraser gun. This gun, if fired at the head, leaves your body alive and well but it destroys all of your memories. It's kind of like the neutron bomb of the psyche. And what it induces is not just soap-opera amnesia—where you still remember everything like how to eat, speak English and all of that, but you can't remember the fact that you're about to marry your evil-twin of a long-lost sister—but amnesia that reduces you to the state of a very large and unmanageable newborn baby. If you somehow compel me to choose between shooting myself in the head and using the Memory-Eraser gun, I am not sure it matters to me. I'll just grab the closest one, or the lightest one, or pick one at random. You see, I think if I lose all my memories I cease to exist in any way that matters to me. If there isn't an afterlife, then the blank brain is not me any more than the splattered one is.

Actually, I'd probably choose the gun to leave you a big mess to clean up since you made me kill myself. Ha! Who's laughing now? On the other hand, leaving you with the equivalent of a 250-pound newborn would be quite a handful at feeding time and a little bit later. Decisions, decisions . . .

The Oz Axe Massacre (with apologies to Texas)

Enough about me. This is where *The Wonderful Wizard of Oz* comes in. In Chapter 5, when Dorothy and the Scarecrow rescue the Tin Woodman, he tells them the story of how he came to be stuck in the forest, rusted into motionlessness:

> "My body shone so brightly in the sun that I felt very proud of it and it did not matter now if my axe slipped, for it could not cut me. There was only one danger—that my joints would rust; but I kept an oil-can in my cottage and took care to oil myself whenever I needed it. However, there came a day when I forgot to do this, and, being caught in a rainstorm, before I thought of the danger my joints had rusted, and I was left to stand in the woods until you came to help me." (p. 46)

Okay, fine. I guess a person made of metal needs to know his limitations. But what's more interesting is the tale of how there came to be an axe-wielding creature made of tin in the first place. The dude used to be human like us, and probably more human than the East German women's swim team. Here, in fits and starts, is the whole story:

> "There was one of the Munchkin girls who was so beautiful that I soon grew to love her with all my heart. She, on her part, promised to marry me as soon as I could earn enough money to build a better house for her; so I set to work harder than ever. But the girl lived with an old woman who did not want her to marry anyone, for she was so lazy she wished the girl to remain with her and do the cooking and the housework. So the old woman went to the Wicked Witch of the East, and promised her two sheep and a cow if she would prevent the marriage. Thereupon the Wicked Witch enchanted my axe, and when I was chopping away at my best one day, for I was anxious to get the new house and my wife as soon as possible, the axe slipped all at once and cut off my left leg.
>
> "This at first seemed a great misfortune, for I knew a one-legged man could not do very well as a wood-chopper. So I went to a tinsmith and had him make me a new leg out of tin. The leg worked very well, once I was used to it." (p. 45)

Okay, I'm fine with that. I already said I thought I could survive the loss and replacement of a leg and even though a tin leg doesn't quite rise to the level of the Six Million Dollar Man or the Terminator, it gets the job done well enough so the poor guy can make a living and marry his sweetheart. But the story doesn't end there:

> "But my action angered the Wicked Witch of the East, for she had promised the old woman I should not marry the pretty Munchkin girl. When I began chopping again, my axe slipped and cut off my right leg. Again I went to the tinsmith, and again he made me a leg out of tin. After this the enchanted axe cut off my arms, one after the other; but, nothing daunted, I had them replaced with tin ones." (p. 45)

This much of the story is still fine—I could live like this (except for being a woodman—I don't look good in plaid and I have a soft place in my heart for spotted owls). But now things really get nightmarish:

> "I thought I had beaten the Wicked Witch then, and I worked harder than ever; but I little knew how cruel my enemy could be. She thought

of a new way to kill my love for the beautiful Munchkin maiden, and made my axe slip again, so that it cut right through my body, splitting me into two halves. Once more the tinsmith came to my help and made me a body of tin, fastening my tin arms and legs and head to it, by means of joints, so that I could move around as well as ever. But, alas! I had now no heart, so that I lost all my love for the Munchkin girl, and did not care whether I married her or not. I suppose she is still living with the old woman, waiting for me to come after her." (pp. 45–46)

This story may be the first time the problem of lack of emotion in cyborgs appears in fiction. Somehow, being a mechanism makes one coldly logical like Lieutenant Data from *Star Trek*. However, Baum makes the same mistake the writers for *Star Trek* make at every turn—feelings of regret ("But alas! I now had no heart . . .") *are* emotional states, as are all of the reactions of surprise and yearning and the like are in the aforementioned characters.

Despite these writers' shortcomings, many people intuitively believe that machines, including computers, are categorically incapable of feeling emotions, being creative or some other allegedly paradigmatic human behavior. My own dad thought that a computer could never ask, "Why?" He was not impressed with that very ability by my earliest speech synthesizer program on my computer. You can see why *2001* was so traumatic for me. . . . "Hey Dave, what are you doing?" I'm taking off your head, HAL.

> "The Wicked Witch then made the axe slip and cut off my head, and at first I thought that was the end of me. But the tinsmith happened to come along, and he made me a new head out of tin." (p. 45)

This is the final cut for me. If whatever is responsible for my mental life is destroyed, I think that's it for me. For the purposes of this essay, if we assume all of my mental life takes place in my brain, then that's the only thing for me to hang my hat on, in terms of survival. And the Scarecrow thinks *he* needs a brain? What about the bleedin' Tin Man?

And while we're thinking about this, why doesn't the Tin Man just ask for his old body back? Or at the very least—and I don't want to upset Family Hour here—the Tin Man looks like a Ken doll in certain respects, if you know what I mean, and if you want to keep a Munchkin maiden happy for the long haul, you'll need at least one other bit of working anatomy besides a heart. Why doesn't he at least add *that* to his wish list? I wonder whether I'd include that in my list of replaceable parts. At least I know who I need to ask about it, and it's none of your business.

We'll Meet Again

We've got the Tin man all hacked to bits, so back to me. I'll always be sure I'm dying if you destroy my brain or its contents. That's where I drawn the line. But there's another possibility. What if, although my actual blood-and-guts brain is gone, there is still some mechanism that houses my complete mental life? Could I survive this seeming catastrophe? Could the tinsmith have been good enough a craftsman to make a tin head that had the same mental life as the woodman had previously had? Apparently so. The metal man seems to remember the Munchkin maid.

Of course, philosophers have written quite a lot about this issue (not the Tin Man specifically, but the question of whether we survive when our mental lives continue). In his now-classic discussion of what sorts changes a person could survive, Derek Parfit (a living philosopher who needs to get a life, if his books are any sign) famously separates good, old-fashioned personal identity, complete with its entailments of transitivity, from the a little thing he calls the R-relation (never mind what that is, just memorize it), the relation that matters to us in "survival experiments." His two major examples are teletransportation and brain-splitting surgery. Each of these two cases provides us with the chance to assess what we think we would survive. Consider the case of surgery as described by Parfit:

> *My Division.* My body is fatally injured, as are the brains of my two brothers. My brain is divided, and each half is successfully transplanted into the body of one of my brothers. Each of the resulting people believes that he is me, seems to remember living my life, has my character, and is in every other way psychologically continuous with me. And he has a body that is very like mine.[4]

Parfit argues that brain-splitting surgeries would be the sorts of things we would hypothetically judge that we had survived. "Hypothetically" is the operative term. I would still want to know who gets the Munchkin maid, but that aside, since there is empiri-

---

[4] Derek Parfit, *Reasons and Persons* (Oxford University Press, 1984), pp. 255–56.

cal support for the claim that people survive having essentially half of their brains destroyed, it seems likely that I could survive having half of my brain removed. Parfit argues that it would not matter to me if I found out at a later date that my excised half-brain had been implanted in another body which had not had the same relationship to my unified past that I had. Upon learning of the existence of this "twin," I would not suddenly decide that I had not survived the operation. I would, he argues, decide personal identity did not hold between me and my twin or me and my former, unified self, but I would have nothing but academic interest in this fact, if indeed I had even that much interest. However, these surgeries produce two post-operative patients, and since both could not be strictly identical to the pre-surgery person, personal identity is not preserved. So, these surgeries preserve some other relationship, the R-relationship, which is what matters to us more than personal identity. We're assuming that the surgeons involved will not use axes, but it hardly makes a difference when the surgery succeeds.

Splitting Some Hairs

While I agree with some of Parfit's conclusions, I eschew the first-person methodology. From the first-person perspective, "I" will survive almost any procedure that leaves a conscious entity intact (plus maybe that other thing I wished for, but in this case it appears my wish would be answered two-fold, and I confess I have also wished for two of those). When I awake with severe brain damage, I will still judge that "I" am there, if most reports of such traumas can be trusted. Even the most severe cases of amnesia produce patients who wonder who they are, but not whether they exist (I don't know if they check their other vitals, but I'm sure I would).

Whatever matters to me in survival (memories, dispositions, and so on), those same traits can matter to people who know me. While they might all matter to me, however, different collections of them will matter to varying degrees to the people who know me in various social contexts. After all, when I concern myself with what matters to me in survival, a great number of the things that matter are more or less akin to pieces of luggage I might take on a trip. I rank them in terms of importance: other things being equal, I'd like to arrive with all my bags, but if some have to get lost, I'd prefer to lose some of my memories rather than my sense of humor, my shaving kit rather than my dress suit, my left little toe rather than my . . . well, you know, John-Bobbitt's-bane. In either event, I am arriving at my destination with a depleted luggage selection, until finally none of my luggage arrives and, perhaps, I get lost with it in some travel-related catastrophe. It looks as if I will still be there through a variety of changes even if I can list which changes I would rather not undergo.

I'm a Lumberjack and I'm Okay

Enough about me. How can we describe what matters in all this head-splitting argumentation from a third-person perspective? To retell Parfit's story, suppose my friend Nick Chopper has to have brain surgery. I wonder whether he will survive and anxiously await his awakening in the recovery room. After all, his HMO would only pay for a tinsmith who took a correspondence course in anaesthesia. When I talk to Nick after he has regained consciousness (perhaps over an extended period of time), I decide that he, my friend the woodman, has survived. However, the members of Nick's logrolling league reach a quite different conclusion. The operation has left him with distaste for logrolling (he sinks and rusts at the bottom of the river now, after all) and, as a result, he no longer had much in common with them. They decide that he has not survived the operation, either as a roller or as a friend.

Furthermore, it comes to light at a later date that the quack of a tinsmith put the removed half of Nick's brain into a different body, just as in Parfit's original case. When I find this out, my curiosity leads me to interview this other person, this other "Nick," if Nick he be. His body is made of straw (and this explains much in our story—since in Baum's book, the Scarecrow does get actual brains stuffed into him, but we aren't told whose). I determine that Nick has survived as my friend in this body, as well, and unavoidable experiential differences aside, I judge that there are two equally good candidates for the office of "my friend Nick Chopper." Furthermore, this straw person has retained his love of logrolling and his ability to interact successfully with the team—if not quite the constitution needed for the sport. After they are introduced to this straw person, they judge that Nick has survived the operation, as well.

So there can be different answers to questions of survival from the third-person perspective that are not apparent from the first-person analyses. The third-person analysis does not contradict the first-person data—each half-brained twin judges that it has survived in my scenario as in Parfit's—rather, the third person perspective captures the richness of our social experiences more fully, allowing that some things matter more to some groups than to others and that my surviving from my own perspective is only one matter of concern to the question of personhood. Now it's understandable why the Tin Man and the Scarecrow become such fast friends in subsequent Baum books. It appears that they may be sharing one brain, and more importantly, one identity. This is the untold backstory of the axe massacre in Oz.

Meet Me in Oz, Ozzie

Further troubles caused by Parfit's first-person emphasis can be seen in his analysis of cases of science-fictional teletransportation. He contrasts simple teletransportation, in which a scanner destroys one's body and brain to get data to send to a duplicate-producer at a remote site, with another form of teletransportation in which the scanner gets the data but without destroying me in the process. In the second case, a replica of me gets made in Oz while the original remains in Kansas, with the stipulation added that a scanner failure induced sufficient heart damage to insure my death by heart-attack in a few days. He summarizes the situation thus:

> In Simple Teletransportation, I do not co-exist with my Replica. This makes it easier to believe that this *is* a way of travelling–that my Replica *is* me. At the end of my story, my life and that of my Replica overlap. Call this the *Branch-Line Case*. In this case, I cannot hope to travel on the *Main Line*, waking up [in Oz] with forty years of life ahead. I shall remain on the Branch-Line, [in Kansas], which ends a few days later. Since I can talk to my Replica, it seems clear that he is *not* me. Though he is exactly like me, he is one person, and I am another. When I pinch myself, he feels nothing. When I have my heart attack, he will again feel nothing. And when I am dead, he will live another forty years.
>
> If we believe that my Replica is not me, it seems natural to assume that my prospect on the Branch Line is almost as bad as ordinary death. I shall deny this assumption. As I shall argue later, I ought to regard having a Replica as being about as good as ordinary survival. (p. 201)

To say the least, most people would not regard having a replica as being about as good *for them* as ordinary survival. Would you be consoled in the knowledge that some other "you" was whooping it up with some Emerald-laden lady, drinking green beer, and never calling home? Parfit argues that since we survive brain-division without retaining strict personal identity, it's not personal identity that matters in survival. What matters is the R-relationship, which involves certain psychological connectedness or continuity caused by the right kind of cause, and *that* relationship is preserved in brain-splitting and in the second sort of teletransportation. I don't know about you, but I'm finding it hard to convince my loved ones that only the R-relation counts, and that that Dude over in Oz is not really cheating on *my* wife. Now it seems like everyone wants a piece of me and my fancy R-relation.

There's Gonna Be a Heartache Tonight

To recast the example slightly, let's suppose we have an atom-for-atom person duplicator. If we accept that we *are* our brains and their mental states, for the sake of argument, if you were faced with two identical loved ones after the "original" got into the duplicator, you could have no reason in principle to prefer the one to the other. While each of them would beg to be saved (assuming your original loved one would beg), they are expressing exactly the same sentiments for exactly the same reasons. So it shouldn't matter to you which loved one you went home with. But someone's brains are gonna be scrambled and someone's heart will be broken, won't they?

No matter how clever the arguments for this conclusion may seem, many are left with the uncomfortable position that the survival of a replica is not nearly as good as ordinary survival would have been. They might prefer that their replica remain rather than nothing at all, but this option is clearly second-best at best. The third-person view makes the claim more plausible that the teletransported or duplicated person survives no matter what. My replica will fill all the offices I used to fill as well as I ever did, so having my replica survive *is* as good as my ordinary survival for everyone else who encounters either me or it. One supposes then that the Scarecrow can rule the Winkies as well as the Tin Man can, and that the Tin Man will be an adequate king for the Emerald City. In the book, by the way, the Tin Man gets the castle of the Wicked Witch of the West, and the Winkies are happy to have him—or *them.* In the second book, the Scarecrow and Tin Man pledge never to be parted as they depart the Emerald City to rule the Winkies in tandem: "I shall return with my friend the Tin Woodman," said the stuffed one, seriously. "We have decided never to be parted in the future."[5] Now you know why.

And that social survival should be enough. After all, for all you know, you've been duplicated every year on your birthday and the "original" has been destroyed. You couldn't tell this had been happening, so it is not to be feared, even by a Cowardly Lion (who must be watching all this with some curiosity—he's a cat after all).

Epilog-Rolling

There's a bit of evidence in the text that the tinsmith did miss something in creating the replacement head. It comes up when the group is traveling through the Kingdom of the Field Mice. I'll let Baum tell the story himself:

> The Tin Woodman was about to reply when he heard a low growl, and turning his head (which worked beautifully on hinges) he saw a strange beast come bounding over the grass toward them. It was, indeed, a great yellow Wildcat, and the Woodman thought it must be chasing something, for its ears were lying close to its head and its mouth was wide open, showing two rows of ugly teeth, while its red eyes glowed like balls of fire. As it came nearer the Tin Woodman saw that running before the beast was a little gray field mouse, and although he had no heart he knew it was wrong for the Wildcat to try to kill such a pretty, harmless creature.
>
> So the Woodman raised his axe, and as the Wildcat ran by he gave it a quick blow that cut the beast's head clean off from its body, and it rolled over at his feet in two pieces. (p. 73)

Parfit's experiment? Did the Wildcat survive? We never find out, but it seems not. But clearly, tin is not a malleable enough medium out of which to build a brain capable of *moral* consistency. Maybe the Scarecrow would have favored the Wildcat over the field mouse, but the Tin Man packs a pretty deadly whack if you're unlucky enough to draw the short straw. Thus, even if the tinsmith came close, I'll have to say the original Woodman is gone

---

[5] L. Frank Baum, *The Marvelous Land of Oz* (New York: Dover, 1961), p. 286.

forever. Hard to imagine Nick Chopper, Mister Heart-of-Gold, choosing so arbitrarily, and acting so violently, without any discussion at all.

We shall have to hope that whatever duplicators we design are better equipped to make accurate copies. Or maybe I'm just damaged myself from having to endure a Platonic father—no Oz, too much HAL. "What are you doing with that axe, Dave?"

7

Pay No Attention to That Man Behind the Curtain!

MARK DIETRICH TSCHAEPE

We all know the story. In the beginning of the film, *The Wizard of Oz*, Dorothy runs away with Toto so that he will not be destroyed by Almira Gulch. Not far from her Auntie Em's farm, she and Toto meet Professor Marvel, a travelling huckster. Outside his wagon around the cookfire "the Crowned Heads of Europe" are mentioned, and Dorothy asks if she and Toto can accompany him to see them. The Professor responds by telling Dorothy that he must first look into his crystal ball in order to determine what to do, so they enter the wagon, and he makes her close her eyes. While she has her eyes closed, he rummages through her bag and finds a picture of Dorothy and her aunt in front of their farm. Professor Marvel uses this information to convince Dorothy to return home without telling her to go back to the farm. It's a nice moment.

Rather than offering her a logical or scientific explanation of why she should return home, the Professor gives her a "folk explanation" which works in convincing her to return to the farm. At least, some philosophers would call it a "folk explanation," by which they mean that it short-circuits the scientific processes that they think *determine* our behavior and substitute for it a different kind of explanation. The Professor paints an emotional image of Dorothy's aunt crying, holding her hand to her heart, and falling onto her bed. Dorothy responds by saying, "Oh, you . . . you don't suppose she could really be sick, do you? Oh! Oh, I've got to go home right away!" She then begins to return to the farm, where she is knocked out by the power of the cyclone, which carries her to Oz. Through the representation of Auntie Em having a certain psy-

95

chological attitude caused by Dorothy's running away, Dorothy was convinced that she must return to the farm.

Professor Marvel's explanation of what he sees in his crystal ball foreshadows the folk explanations the Wizard will give to the Scarecrow, the Tin Man, and the Lion after they have killed the Wicked Witch of the West—that they already possessed the desired virtues. Why does the Professor/Wizard give these explanations, which are folksy and emotive, rather than the type of explanation that supposedly gives us the truth: logical or scientific explanation? Because his explanations work! Not only do they work, but they work because they have an important relation to those whom he is addressing. In each case, he's explaining something to someone who does not *want* a scientific explanation. They want to receive something—to go home, to have brains, or heart, or courage. What the Professor-Wizard does in each case is give a folk explanation that convinces each individual that he or she does not want what they *think* they want because they already have something equivalent (or even better).

Couldn't the Professor just give Dorothy a logical explanation for why she should go back to the farm? He could have said that running away was impractical: she has no money; Kansas does not offer much respectable work for a girl in her early adolescence; she has no contacts or network that she can utilize; he really does not have any connection with the Crowned Heads of Europe. All of this could have been packaged in a nice, neat, logical argument consisting of hypothetical syllogisms: "Dorothy, if you actually run away from home, then . . ." However, this type of explanation concerning why she should not run away would most likely be ineffective, or at least less effective, than the folksy approach the Professor takes. In his explanation to Dorothy, and in the explanations that the Wizard gives to the Scarecrow, the Tin Man, and the Lion, the person being addressed is taken into account. Each person has a problem, and the Professor/Wizard takes into account what we will call *pragmatic considerations* in coming up with a convincing explanation that solves the problem.

"Who's Them? Who's Them?"

When we account for the speakers involved in an explanation, we acknowledge the pragmatics of the explanatory situation. When the Professor's gazing into his crystal ball and telling Dorothy what he "sees," he accounts for the fact that he is speaking to a girl who is in her early teens and should probably not run away from home. Generally, pragmatic considerations of an explanatory situation are specific factors within the situation that determine what is problematic or what is desirable about an issue at hand. Pragmatic considerations include acknowledging that we are constrained by the problem we're trying to explain and solve. Specific factors that are part of the pragmatic considerations of an explanatory situation include the speakers' backgrounds, their knowledge, assertions, and beliefs. Of course, someone giving an explanation never knows exactly what someone's background is in any complete sort of sense; however, we can often be successful at surmising what the appropriate level of explanation is for a given audience when we know just a little about them.

For instance, the Professor bases his explanation, in part, on the photograph of Dorothy and Auntie Em that he finds in Dorothy's bag. The explanation the Professor gives to Dorothy is a folk explanation. Folk explanations are usually understood as answers to why-questions that connect mental behavior to physical behavior. They're based on the claim that psychological states, such as mourning or desiring, have important content and cause us to behave in some ways and not others. Such explanations are dependent upon terms such as "desire," "belief," and "want." But it's difficult to explain scientifically or logically what anyone desires or believes or wants.

Here I'm expanding the notion of folk explanation in contrast to logical or scientific explanation, which many scientists and philosophers regard as "better" explanations. Specifically, folk explanations are often contrasted to "mechanistic explanations," which are answers to why-questions that consist of the parts and operations that cause whatever behavior is being asked about. For example, if the Professor was to give a mechanistic explanation of why Dorothy should return to the farm instead of running away, he could give hypothetical answers to the why-question by breaking each hypothetical situation into its parts and the operations of those parts. If Dorothy was to run away, she would have to find a way in which to nourish herself and Toto. If she did not nourish herself and Toto, her body (and Toto's) would begin the process of starvation. If her body began the process of starvation, then . . . (I guess that's why she brought a basket of food). And the explanation would go on and on. It would include as many details as possible of each part and operation that were relevant to the processes Dorothy would go through if she ran away. It's boring and may never reach an end. So many details have to be considered.

Instead of an arduous and overly detailed explanation of why Dorothy should not run away, the Professor simply says that he "sees" a house with a white picket fence, a barn with a weather vane, a running horse, and a woman wearing a polka dot dress who is crying. He goes on to say that the woman has cared for someone who is very sick, and she collapses on a bed with her hand to her heart. That's all Dorothy needs to hear to convince her that she must go back home to Auntie Em.

The Professor successfully inferred from knowing Dorothy had run away and what he saw in the picture from Dorothy's basket what would work as an explanation to convince her to return home. Although there could be a more logical or a more scientific explanation for why she should not run away, the Professor's explanation is the one that works. Dorothy's convinced that her aunt is crying, holding her hand to heart, and falling onto the bed, and this makes Dorothy return home even without her photo.

When the motley crew that has accompanied Dorothy along the Yellow Brick Road finally meets the Wizard of Oz, he too provides them with folk explanations that work much better than explanations that are more logical or more scientific. In each case the Wizard correctly infers enough about the character making a request—the pragmatics of the explanatory situation—to provide a folk explanation that works in solving the problem that led to the request. The Scarecrow, the Tin Man, and the Lion all think that they are missing something that the Wizard can give to them, but, as the Wizard explains, none of them really needs what they think they need. Instead, they just need the Wizard's folk explanations— along with a symbolic token—to convince them that they have won their deepest desires.

"If the Wizard Is a Wizard Who Will Serve, then I'm Sure to Get a Brain, a Heart, a Home, the Nerve"

The Scarecrow wants a brain because he wants to think "deep thoughts." As he sings after he meets Dorothy, "And my head I'd be scratchin' while my thoughts were busy hatchin' if I only had a brain." The Scarecrow is one of the most logical, thoughtful characters in the film. This is evident almost immediately after Dorothy meets him. When she's trying to remove him from the pole upon which he is hung, he says, "Of course, I'm not too bright about things, but if you'll just bend the nail down in back, maybe I'll slip off and . . ." Here the Scarecrow shows that he understands causal relationships. Not only that, but he can think hypothetically: if you bend the nail down, then I will probably slip off of the pole. He has also thought of the following hypothetical, which is strangely materialistic and non-folksy (especially for a talking Scarecrow who claims to have a heart, which makes him feel): if I have a brain, then I can think deep thoughts. In order to think deep thoughts, the Scarecrow is convinced that he must have a brain, even though he is obviously thinking without one.

The Tin Man wants a heart because he desires to feel emotions. He sings to Dorothy and the Scarecrow, "I'd be tender—I'd be gentle and awful sentimental if I only had a heart." He goes on to sing, "Just to register emotion, jealousy—devotion, and really feel the part" in order to convey that he desires to feel emotion. In other words, he *feels* the desire to feel. Just as the Scarecrow *thinks* that he must have a brain in order to think, the Tin Man *feels* that he needs a heart in order to feel. During the film, the Tin Man actually acts as one of the most emotional and devoted characters, especially towards Dorothy, on his way to request a heart from the Wizard so that he can feel emotion and be devoted.

The Lion is slightly more complex than the Scarecrow and the Tin Man. In his case, he desires courage so that he can fulfill his role as "King of the Forest." Initially he attempts to scare the group, especially the two male characters, the Scarecrow and the Tin Man. "Put 'em up! Put 'em up!" is his fighting mantra to them, exclaiming, "Which one of you first? I'll fight you both together, if you want. I'll fight ya with one paw tied behind my back! I'll fight ya standin' on one foot! I'll fight ya with my eyes closed!" (During this scene the Tin Man is scared of the Lion, thus showing one of his emotional sides). When Toto (who, by the way, often seems to be the most cunning of the group) bites the Lion, his cowardice is revealed. While he is crying, Dorothy diagnoses him as "nothing but a great big coward."

Unlike the thinking Scarecrow and the feeling Tin Man, the Lion actually does seem to be a coward. He seems to need courage if he is going to be a non-coward, and he seems not to have it already. However, as the group travels down the Yellow Brick Road and eventually encounters the Witch, the Lion does seem to display courage when he is not convincing himself that he is not courageous. In his case, he accords himself one psychological state—cowardice—because he denies himself another psychological state—being courageous. So there's a disconnect between his actual choices, when the heat is on, and the way he thinks about and feels about himself.

"Because, Because, Because, Because, Because— Because of the Wonderful Things He Does"

After the group destroys the Witch and returns to the Wizard to receive their gifts, Toto unmasks the fact that the Wizard is really only a man (a huckster, so to speak, just like Professor Marvel). However, the Wizard actually does deliver to the Scarecrow, the Tin Man, and the Lion explanations that fulfill their requests. Of course, his folk explanations include why what each has requested is really what each does not need, followed by tokens symbolizing what each believes he has lacked. But the Wizard can do wonderful things. Here are three.

A Dualist?

When the Tin Man and the Lion ask whether or not the Wizard is going to give the Scarecrow a brain, the Wizard first responds with an explanation of why the Scarecrow really doesn't need a brain:

> Why, anybody can have a brain. That's a very mediocre commodity. Every pusillanimous creature that crawls on the Earth, or slinks through slimy seas has a brain! Back where I come from we have universities—seats of great learning—where men go to become great thinkers. And when they come out, they think deep thoughts, and with no more brains than you have.

It seems that the Wizard has visited some universities, and he remains curiously silent about the value of those "deep thoughts." The proximity of the slinking pusillanimous creatures to great thinkers may suggest something about his opinion on that matter. Perhaps he was denied tenure in Omaha and that's why he took his show on the road. In his explanation, the Wizard notes that the amount of brains that deep thinkers have is unimportant—a brain is not a mind. Philosophers call this "mind-body dualism."

The Scarecrow doesn't care about such niceties or remnants of French philosophical thought. Rather, what is important is what signifies the recognition of being able to think deep thoughts: a university diploma. Seeing the situation, the Wizard then confers upon the Scarecrow an honorary degree of Th.D. (Doctor of Thinkology). Immediately after the Scarecrow receives the degree from the Wizard, he gives an incorrect version of the Pythagorean Theorem: "The sum of tin square roots of any two sides of an isosceles triangle is equal to the square root of the remaining side." Although the Scarecrow may think deep thoughts, his thoughts about mathematics may not necessarily be correct, since the theorem applies to right triangles, not isoceles triangles, and to the squares of the sides, not their square roots. How many college graduates catch these errors, and are the scriptwriters mocking us?

The Wizard's conferring an "honorary degree" upon the Scarecrow successfully convinces the Scarecrow that he can, in fact, think deep thoughts. In this case, the Wizard has pragmatically considered who the Scarecrow is and what he really needs: recognition of the fact that he can actually think deep thoughts. The Scarecrow has been in isolation in the middle of a corn field, so even though he has had the ability of thinking deep thoughts, he hasn't had anyone available to acknowledge this fact. The Wizard has indicated that, through his belief that the Scarecrow can think deep thoughts, the Scarecrow actually *can* think deep thoughts. It's pragmatic. The bad geometry helps us understand that the science doesn't matter.

On the other hand, a *mechanistic* explanation of why the Scarecrow can think deep thoughts would most likely be useless in this particular explanatory situation. Would the Scarecrow be convinced that he could think deep thoughts if the Wizard localized and decomposed the parts and operations of the straw in order to explain how these caused thought? Such a scientific explanation might work, but the Wizard's folk explanation really does work. At least for what the Scarecrow desires. Note that he is by no means qualified to be an engineer.

A Stoic?

The Tin Man is a harder sell than the Scarecrow. At first the Wizard tries to explain to the Tin Man that hearts are impractical. "Hearts will never be practical until they can be unbreakable." The Tin Man responds, "But I—I still want one." At this the Wizard shifts explanatory tactics.

Stoic philosophers think that the best life is one without emotional upheavals –that a restful state called "ataraxy" is the best way to avoid trouble and pain. The Wizard tries out this line on the Tin Man. He's unable to convince the Tin Man by an abbreviated stoical argument that a heart is unnecessary and not even to be desired, so he focuses upon the actions motivated by emotions, referring to philanthropists ("good-deed-doers"), claiming that the only difference between them and the Tin Man is a testimonial that signifies others' "esteem and affection." The Wizard presents the Tin Man with a heart-shaped clock for the Tin Man's kindness, claiming "that a heart is not judged by how much you love, but by how much you are loved by others." That's probably a frightening thought for some people. Better get a testimonial if you're in doubt whether anyone really loves you.

Just as the Scarecrow had existed in isolation, never having received recognition of his ability to think deep thoughts (it's called "graduate school" in our world), the Tin Man had existed in isolation in the woods, completely unloved as far as he could know (also a bit like graduate school). No one came looking for the dude, at any rate. Would anyone come looking for you? One hopes so. Try it. Go away without a word and see who comes looking. Then ask that person for a testimonial. In addition, the Tin Man had been rusted, which had caused him to be unable to engage in behavior of any kind (emotional or otherwise). In this case the Wizard explains that others possess the psychological states of "esteem and affection" regarding the Tin Man. This indication solves the Tin Man's problem: his heart is constituted by the love others have for him.

A mechanistic explanation would be pretty silly in this case, unless the Tin Man's heart could literally be a metal mechanism, complete with watch-works and flywheels. One imagines the Wizard saying "Well, my fine man, you have no blood as far as I can see, so what would a heart do if you had one, except dry up and decompose?" Everyone concerned is taking "heart" in the folk sense —the center of the emotional life, not the muscle in the middle.

Courage Is Really Just Wisdom

Regarding the Lion, the Wizard is blunt about the mistaken notion that running away from danger equals cowardice. The Wizard also explains that the Lion has been confusing courage with wisdom: at times it is wise to run away from danger. This is an abbreviated version of Aristotle's argument that wisdom trumps lesser virtues, such as courage. So the Lion is wise (perhaps wiser than he is courageous, but who's counting). Because the Lion has the psychological state of wisdom, he runs away from danger. The Lion isn't buying it yet and he still feels inadequate. Philosophy fails again. As far as courage is concerned, the behavior marked as courageous is recognized as such by the Triple Cross, with which the Wizard awards the Lion for his "meritorious conduct, extraordinary valor, conspicuous bravery against wicked witches." The Wizard declares to the Lion, "You are now a member of the Legion of Courage!" That does the trick. It no longer matters about the complex relationship between courage and wisdom.

What would a mechanistic explanation look like? The Wizard says "there is an epinephrine deficiency here, dear Lion. Let us try a little hormone therapy to see if we can coax your 'fight or flight' response into a little more fight and a little less flight—I think some testosterone might do you some good." And off the Lion goes for some injections. I know what you're thinking: let's not go there.

Successful Inquiry Means Solving the Problem at Hand

In all three of these cases, *recognition* for already having what has mistakenly been desired is necessary, and the Wizard provides such recognition through folk explanations—or at least, he resorts to folk explanations when the more logical ones don't impress. He suggests to the Scarecrow that brains aren't required for thinking—philosophers would call this "mind-body dualism," the mind is something apart from the physical brain—but that doesn't work. So, rather than persisting logical or scientific explanations for why the Scarecrow really does not need a brain, he goes folk.

Similarly, the Tin Man is unimpressed by the impracticality of a heart, so the Wizard shifts ground. And the Lion can't be impressed by the analogy to others who have run away (discretion is the better part of valor), so the Wizard just inducts him into an organization of brave people. We don't learn how many in the Legion ran away when the chips were down. Never mind the contradiction, it's a folk explanation.

The Wizard successfully surmises that explanations concerning belief in each of the companions will work in fulfilling their desires. And he learns this as any good investigator would: he tries logic, common sense, even dualism, but to no avail. The Wizard's explanations signify a focus on inferences he has made based upon the pragmatic considerations of each person's problem, rather than a neglect of the particularity of each situation. The Scarecrow, the Tin Man, and the Lion don't want logical or scientific truths, all else being equal. And the mechanistic explanation is simply out of the picture. They each want the Wizard to give them something that works for the particular problem, and in each case he does provide a workable solution with the use of folk explanations that pertain to psychological states. Through the Wizard's recognition, each no longer feels the need for what he had requested.

"There's No Place Like Home"

The Scarecrow, the Tin Man, and the Lion aren't the only characters with requests for the Wizard. The driving force of their journey to see the Wizard is Dorothy and her desire to return home. In this case, a folk explanation from the Wizard will not work in delivering what she wants, and she is not mistaken about her desire. He can't say "Home is where the heart is, and your heart happens to be here," or explain to her that the whole idea of "home" is really somewhat vague. Her desire to return home is not unnecessary: she really wants to return home because she is not actually there. (There's an interesting question that arises here about whether or not she's mistaken. Perhaps her actual desire is to wake up, since her return to the farm from Oz consists of waking up in her own bed, but the Wizard has no knowledge of her that would elicit this explanation to solve her problem.)

The solution to Dorothy's problem consists of two explanations: one that fails because of Toto's exit from the hot air balloon, followed by the Wizard floating off without Dorothy, and the other one that succeeds. We don't know whether or not Dorothy and Toto could have actually returned to Kansas in the hot air balloon with the Wizard. This suggestion implies that Oz and Kansas are within the hot-air-balloon-distance from one another (although the

Wizard does state, "I, your Wizard, par adua outer, am about to embark on a hazardous and technically unexplainable journey into the outer stratosphere"). If Dorothy had returned to Kansas in the hot air balloon, would she have found herself lying in bed? Would the Wizard have met the Professor?

We'll never know the answers to these questions, although they do pose interesting problems concerning where Oz is in respect to Kansas, as well as whether or not there are doubles of each character (for instance, are Hickory and the Tin Man actually two separate entities, or are they the same? Could they meet one another?). We see in this a mechanistic explanation of how to get home –get in a balloon and travel until you get there. We just don't know if it would work, but we know it's "unexplainable" even if it does. There's no point in asking directions to Kansas from Oz.

The explanation of how to return to Kansas, for Dorothy, is not a folk explanation from someone else, but rather a combination of a basic instruction for Dorothy to perform specific actions and a folk explanation that Dorothy must realize on her own. The basic instruction is: "Close your eyes and tap your heels together three times." Along with this action comes Dorothy's realization that she must *desire* to return home and represent that desire as a psychological proposition. As she says, "It wasn't enough just to want to see Uncle Henry and Auntie Em, and that it's that—if I ever go looking for my heart's desire again, I won't look any further than my own backyard, because if it isn't there, I never really lost it to begin with." Don't even try to work out the logic of this. It doesn't work. Logic doesn't get Dorothy home.

Not only must Dorothy tap her heels together three times while her eyes are closed, but she must desire to return home, which is conveyed through the psychological, propositional state of thinking, "There's no place like home." Logically this is insane. There is *no* place "like" any other place at all, if you press the differences far enough—even "over here" is utterly different from "over there." If Dorothy wanted to be someplace that no place if like, why didn't she just take a step to the left? No, this is a case of the "psychological content of thought," combined with the actions performed with the slippers, having a direct effect on the physical location of Dorothy. In the end, a folk explanation provides Dorothy with a solution to her problem, which is wholly dependent upon the pragmatic considerations of the situation.

"Here, Here, What's All This Jabber-wapping When There's Work to Be Done?"

Regarding explanations, the Wizard of Oz reveals that sometimes folk explanations—explanations that are dependent upon the notion that individual psychological states have content and causal capabilities—work better than logical or scientific explanations. Often we act as if the "best" explanation is one that is "true," meaning that it reflects the way that the world is. However, what we find in the explanations of Professor Marvel and the Wizard of Oz is that folk explanations can, at times, be the best pragmatic explanations, meaning that they work in solving our difficulties.

What determine whether a folk explanation is better than a mechanistic explanation, or a generally scientific or logical explanation, are the pragmatic considerations within the explanatory situation. Perhaps if the Scarecrow was a neuroscientist, or the Tin Man was a cardiologist, or the Lion was a psychologist, then scientific explanations would benefit them in solving their problems. However, given the characteristics of each, folk explanations pragmatically succeed where scientific explanations most likely could not.

The Wizard of Oz reminds us that it's important to account for the speakers and their problems when we formulate explanations to solve problems. The problems of a Scarecrow are not necessarily the problems of a philosopher, regardless of the fact that both wish to think deep thoughts, and sometimes an explanation given to one will simply not work as well when given to another. Sometimes the most mechanistic, scientific, or logical words don't matter—some people just need a good story to get things to work the way they want them to.

III

I've a Feeling
We're Not
in Kansas Anymore

8

"I'm Melting! Melting!"

RANDALL E. AUXIER

Something has been bugging me for a long time. Maybe you've wondered about it too. *Why* did water melt the Wicked Witch of the West? All the writers who have dealt with the Oz stories have had to include this crucial "element" of the story in some way (pun intended!). But no one explains it very clearly.

There are various suggestions made by the authors and script writers, but they don't want to take a firm stand on it. In some ways, the "water thing" adds a bit of mystery to the Witch, and a sort of pathos—I mean, what's life without water? What does she drink, powdered Jack Daniels? I would call the Witch's situation "sad," but if we cry, well, there's water again. Maybe the Witch is grouchy because she can't wash down her pizza with a beer. That would make *me* pretty irritable. Maybe those hideous shoes would protect her while she swims. Anyway, I have a theory, actually three theories in one, about the water thing. It's an odd theory, but who knows?

Growing a Character (Just Don't Add Water)

It's easy to forget that the Witch of the West was just a minor character in Baum's first book about Oz. She makes one real appearance, we learn little about her, then she gets melted, all between pages 139 and 155, and that's about it. Instead of a broom, she carries an umbrella—which makes a fair amount of sense when you can't survive a light rain shower. She has one eye that can see anywhere in Oz, not a crystal ball (the film) or an odd looking-glass (as with Elphaba in *Wicked*). From Baum we don't learn why water harms her, but we do learn that she is dry even on the *inside*—when Toto bites her (man, that dog annoys me), she doesn't bleed because even her blood has dried up. This, Baum writes, is because she was so very wicked. So be nice unless you want all your blood to coagulate. And from Baum there's no suggestion that the Wicked Witches of East and West are sisters. Dorothy's shoes are silver rather than ruby, and the Witch wants them for their magic power, not because she has any, well, inheritance rights. And in the first book, the Witch actually *gets* one of the shoes, for a few moments. It's good to remember such things.

We get a lot more development of the Witch's character in the 1939 movie, but we still never learn why water is such a problem. In 1939 she has a bigger part, although she still lacks a proper name. The Witch is now able to fly on her broom and shows up in several places (not just her castle), and by 1939 the Eastern Witch is her sister, the desired shoes are ruby instead of silver, and her issues with Dorothy are a little more complex—revenge for her sister's death, a desire for the power in the shoes, hatred of the Wizard, general spite towards anything good or innocent. But why is water such a problem?

Along with countless others, I think Gregory Maguire succeeded in the heroic effort to bring Oz to us in such a surprising light that people are likely, on a wide scale, to allow his story to become "the truth about Oz" in their imaginations, replacing the version of Oz found in the 1939 film, which had itself succeeded in replacing the Oz of Baum's beloved series of books (which are not as widely read as they once were). That "replacement" of the film with Maguire's book is what has occurred in my own imagination, which feels simultaneously like losing one's innocence and gaining a whole world for the effort. For most of my life, Oz just *was* the technicolor masterpiece I saw on TV, and Judy Garland just was Dorothy, and so on. Now I can't watch the film or read the old books without noticing some of what Maguire must have noticed, and following him where he takes it. For me, the Wizard is no longer the well-meaning displaced Midwesterner of Baum's book, nor is he the dream residue of Professor Marvel; now the Wizard is some sort of misplaced Nietzschean overman, living beyond good and evil, and wanting nothing better than to find the strength to commit suicide—succeeding in the end, perhaps. And so it is with many other characters and events from the earlier book and the film. It goes without saying that the Wicked Witch of the West is Maguire's special focus, and now she has a name, a history, a complex set of motives, strengths, and weaknesses. And there are some tantalizing suggestions about her relationship to water. Not quite an explanation, however, unless we work through it ourselves.

Fairytales, Dreams, and Other Worlds

Let's start with a simple question: What is *water* in fairy tales, dreams, and other worlds? Is it the same thing? Does switching from one sort of "imagined world" to another sort make a difference to how we think about water? I think it does. I mean, water is one thing in a fairy tale, something else in a dream, and a third thing in a "possible world," but they must all be connected somehow. I mean, water is water, right? I can take you there, I think, with the help of a few philosophers, and I want to trace the transformations of Oz in our imaginations through those three stages: the *fairytale*, the *dream*, and the *possible world*.

The *fairytale* is Baum's creation, and he explicitly warns against treating it as allegory or social commentary (which has not prevented some people from doing so). Baum says that "folk lore, legends, myths and fairy tales have followed childhood through the ages, for every healthy youngster has a wholesome and instinctive love for stories fantastic, marvelous, and manifestly unreal." He denies that the Oz books have any "moral," because "modern education includes morality; therefore the modern child seeks only entertainment," and thus, the Oz books are "written solely to pleasure children of today. It aspires to being a modernized fairy tale, in which the wonderment and joy are retained and the heartaches and nightmares are left out."[1] Most folks now would disagree that Baum left out all the violence and nightmares—heck, no story *ever* gave me more nightmares, except maybe *The Exorcist*, and I'll bet I'm not alone. But I guess what looks like violence after Gandhi and King, and Hitler and Stalin, has changed a bit since Baum's time. It's good to remember that when Baum wrote his first Oz book, there had been no significant war in the Western world for almost thirty years, and in the USA for thirty-five years (although we were beginning to behave nastily toward Spain). But a lot of

---

[1] Frank L. Baum, *The Wonderful Wizard of Oz* (Chicago: Geo. M. Hill Co., 1900), Introduction.

people thought perpetual peace was a real possibility, and they began to forget what war was really like. They were reminded rather harshly in 1914, of course.

The *dream* belongs to the numerous script-writers of the 1939 film, as we all know. The script, credited to Noel Langley and Florence Ryerson, was committee work of about fifteen people (committees don't *always* do inferior work), so I'll call that group the "Committee." One difference between 1900 and 1939 is that the ideas of Sigmund Freud and Carl Gustav Jung had come into the popular consciousness during the intervening years, their popularity fueled in part by the shock of the "Great War," as they then called the First World War. People were astonished at their own savagery and looked to psychology for explanations. Just as Baum was looking at the Brothers Grimm and Hans Christian Andersen and "modernizing" the fairy tale, the Committee was drawing on a popular understanding of Freud and Jung to modernize *dream* interpretation.

For example, the Committee created the characters of Zeke, Hickory, Hunk, Professor Marvel, and Almira Gulch to be "day residue" to explain the appearance in Dorothy's "dream" of the Scarecrow, Tin Woodman, Cowardly Lion, Wizard, and Wicked Witch of the West. The transformation of these people in Dorothy's life into dream symbols is something the 1939 audience understands, more or less, but it would have been a mystery to Baum's original readers. They didn't understand dreams in this way in 1900. Sure, sometimes a dream is only a dream, but sometimes it's the outlet for unconscious desires and unacceptable impulses, "wish fulfillment," as Freud called it. No doubt, one may have endless wicked fun doing Freudian analysis on Dorothy. But I will save that for another day. For now let's look at dreams in philosophy rather than psychology.

The *possible world* of Oz belongs to Maguire's *Wicked*. I will also look at the "metaphysics of possible worlds" in another chapter, but here I only want to introduce the idea of a possible world, and its relation to fairy tales and dreams, and imagination, in another way, through the contemporary philosophy of language. These days philosophers worry about language a lot because it has a great effect on *how* we know the things we know (the questions that belong to the field of epistemology). Some philosophers even say that *everything* we truly "know" depends on language. I don't think that's quite right, but I can see why some people think so. In any case, language is certainly important to knowing many things, and the question is whether our language really allows us to know things without distorting or changing them. The argument is about how language "mediates" between our physical experience of the world and our efforts to formulate that experience into statements (like scientific principles) and equations (like Newton's or Einstein's), since most philosophers think that scientific knowledge is the best kind of knowledge we have. There is a lot of science, especially biology, in Maguire's Oz, and his story is adapted in many ways to the sensibilities of a culture (namely, ours) that trusts science and wants scientific explanations.

It's Just Your Imagination

All three versions of Oz have in common that they are, among other things, "imagined possibilities." Now imagination is pretty mysterious. Possibility is even more so. And somehow the two are related. But mysterious as they are, there are some things we can say about them that will light the path to the possible world of Oz—and to Narnia, Middle Earth, Dune, and so many other fully developed possible worlds we love in books and movies. When we "imagine," we place before our minds events and ideas that are not presently in our senses, at least not directly. Imagine Dorothy. Well, you can do it, right? (I *know* you're picturing Judy Garland). But she's not in front of you. How'd you do that anyway? The things we imagine may be past events, future events, new ideas, or images we have pieced together from different experiences. The point is that whatever we are imagining, it isn't actually in front of us at the present moment. And so, rather than being *actual,* the stuff we are imagining is "virtual" or "possible"—perhaps even "impossible" in some ways. Our *act* of imagining is real enough, but the *stuff* we're imagining often can't even be found anywhere in our familiar world.

So we have this power of forming images of what is not present right now, and may never be present to us at all, and it looks like language is a powerful way of organizing all those ideas and images—just look at the stories of Oz, all organized in language— and it's a bit of a problem to explain how and why we can tell the difference between language that really counts as "knowledge," and language that we just sort of "made up." That's not just true for stories; even in scientific language we have a hard time telling the difference between what we just "made up" and what's "out there" in the actual world. For example, it's hard to say exactly what "gravity" is. Sure, we see its *effects*, but gravity *itself*, if there is any such thing, seems to elude our direct observation. Simply *naming* it, calling it a "force" or making lists of things we *do* observe and then chalking it all up to "gravity" is not the same thing as having a look-see at "gravity itself." So how do we know it really exists, that we didn't just imagine a word to name all those effects?

It wouldn't be the first time we named something that didn't really exist. For instance, there were a couple of centuries when scientists were puzzled by why some things burn easily and others don't. And they supposed that there was something in everything that was burning, and some things had more of it (like wood) while others had less (iron), and they called this flammable stuff "phlogiston" (ugly name, huh? sounds like something that gets stuck in your sinuses). For a long time scientists talked as if phlogiston really existed and they tried to get a look at it, isolate it, study it, measure it. As we came to understand the process of combustion better, it became clear in time that there wasn't any such thing as phlogiston. We made it up. So what about gravity, or curved space-time or quarks? Did we make that stuff up? Just imagine them? How do we know?

So these days philosophers like to talk about "possible worlds," as a way of sorting out possibilities they have imagined, and asking whether there would be, for instance, a possible world where there was no gravity, or where phlogiston really does exist, although they almost never have in mind something like Oz when they do this. Oz is too complicated. But there are certain philosophical puzzles philosophers can't leave alone, and they have developed some pretty arcane methods for discussing such problems in terms of "possible worlds." As I said, I'll show you some of what they do with that in a later chapter –it has the look of science fiction—but for now let's just see if we can figure out why they think that imagining and defining possible worlds helps to talk about stuff like that.

The Dream Scheme

There was a philosopher named Susanne Langer (1895–1985), probably the most influential woman philosopher of her generation in the United States, who wrote a lot about the relationship between dreams, fairy tales and myths. She thought that the best way to explain the mysterious relationship between what we imagine and what we experience was by looking at "symbols." And here's a weird thing she noticed. When you look at a symbol, you are seeing something physical, something in your senses, something that really exists right in front of you, but you aren't taking it for just what it is, just a mark on a piece of paper. You're actively reading it as *standing for* something else, and to *do that*, you have to use your imagination. So she thought that if we pay attention to symbols, we can learn something about imagination, and about how physical things come to have *meaning* for us. And this also deals with possibility, because symbols don't always mean just one thing, they can mean many things at the same time, so to read them, we have to sort through the possibilities of what all they *might* mean, and then sort of suppose what they *do* mean.

Symbols come in lots of shapes and shades, but one place we get them is in our dreams. We would all have to admit that if the 1939 script is just Dorothy's dream, that's one hell of a dream. Of course, we know it isn't a dream at all, it's a *script* in which the Committee invites us to see Oz as *Dorothy's* dream, not our own. Most of us are plenty willing to go along with that, since we've all had vivid dreams, and we would privately like to have a dream as wonderful as Dorothy's. It doesn't seem to bother us that we can't *really* see into another person's actual dream. We just set that aside and peer into Dorothy's dreams shamelessly, to see what's going on with the girl. This benign voyeurism touches on a desire most people feel, at times, to really see into the private mental lives of others, and that's a great part of the psychological attraction in the 1939 film. It feels forbidden, impossible, and adventurous to be shown another person's inner imaginings.

But there are certain other inconsistencies we have to ignore. Langer reminds us that real dreams are very disorderly. Everything is liable to morph into something else without warning, characters become other characters or even inanimate things, and there seem to be no fixed rules about it. Even animals seem to have dreams, and wouldn't it be wonderful to *see* what they're dreaming about? Are the images before their minds anything like our own? Who knows, maybe we'll find a way to do that someday (or maybe it would be too scary to have such a power). Anyway, Langer's point is that dreams are primal and fluid images. Dorothy's dream may tap into some primal stuff, but it is more orderly than most of our dreams. Her dream stays on its track, characters don't suddenly morph into other characters, and above all, we remain within the general order of Oz itself. Movies have been made that imitate more closely the tendencies of actual dreams. The 1990 Adrian Lyne film *Jacob's Ladder* comes to mind, among many others. But the Committee preserves at least some of the dream features. For example, in their Oz, water can unexpectedly burn you like acid, if you're a witch. The mixing of the primal elements of water and fire, giving one the effects of the other, is a classic reversal we do find in dreams and other visions.

Langer doesn't say much more about dreams, but an earlier philosopher, Henri Bergson (1859–1941), made some powerful suggestions about what they are and how they work (and Freud and Jung drew on some of what Bergson said for their own theories). Bergson thought that dreams were the link between present sensation and memory. Even when we're asleep, we're still having sensations, but mainly these are sensations of stuff going on *inside* our own bodies. As Bergson says, "these deep-seated sensations come from every organ and especially from the viscera. One would hardly suspect that these internal sensations could become so acute during sleep."[2] But it's not like we're dreaming *about* our viscera. We use those sensations to form images of other things, like Oz. Makes you wonder what Dorothy had been eating. What *was* in that basket? Must've been something hard to digest, like cheese on pickled herring. But how do we transform our indigestion into images of Oz and suchlike?

Bergson says that we're actually *more* perceptive, in some ways, when we are asleep than when we are awake. He says:

> Our faculty of sensory perception, far from shrinking in every respect when we are asleep, broadens its field of operations. It is true that it often loses in energy and *tension* what it gains in *extension*, for it rarely brings us anything other than vague impressions. These impressions are the materials with which we build our dreams. But they are only the materials; by themselves they could never yield dreams. (Bergson, pp. 32–33).

This is just a fancy way of saying that dreams are less focused than waking perception, but they take in more stuff. What makes

---

[2] Henri Bergson, *The World of Dreams* (New York: Philosophical Library, 1958), p. 31.

the perceptual material into dreams? The *order* of our dreams comes from our remembrances, Bergson thinks. Dreaming is a kind of memory. He says:

> In true sleep—in sleep that involves our whole being [like Dorothy's in the 1939 film, since she is apparently unconscious due to a blow on the head, not just dozing]—remembrances are the warp and woof of our dreams. But we often fail to recognize them. They may be very old remembrances of which we were oblivious during the waking state— remembrances drawn from the darkest depths of our past. . . . Or again, they may be fragments of shattered remembrances which we have collected piecemeal and woven haphazardly into an unrecognizable and incoherent fabric. (Bergson, p. 35)

Others who got excited about Bergson's idea that dreams are memories have gone so far as to suggest that such memories may not even have to be connected to the personal experience of the dreamer—that it is possible to recollect the experience of the whole human species, of which we are just transient examples. Such is Jung's idea of a collective unconscious of the human race. When we dream for ourselves, we *may* be dreaming the dream of our entire race, the memories implanted in our very cell tissue and DNA, transmuting the order and activity of mitosis into a kind of remembering of what we were in the primal soup. All of a sudden, Oz isn't looking so very improbable, whether it is my own past, or the past of the human race, or of all life, fragmented and reassembled using my present perception. Dorothy is pulling off quite a feat, but it's nothing you couldn't do yourself.

So, Explanation Number One as to why water melts the witch goes like this: In a dream, the relationship between what is solid (such as witch bodies) and what is fluid (witches when they melt) is itself a transformation we have seen many, many times. We watch ice melt when it's heated, and we see sugar "melt" when it's soaked in water. We "remember" that in our dreams. This memory creates a very understandable relation between water and fire— that they both melt things—which enables them to trade effects without any great effort. We're remembering "melting," and whether fire or water is the active agent is of no ultimate consequence. Of course witches can melt in the dream of Oz. *Anything* can melt in a dream. Just add water. You're simply "remembering" that. You can melt Dorothy if you like. I'd rather melt Toto. I think I shall, later tonight. I don't know what bugs me more, the dog or the way Dorothy dotes on the mangy, yapping little thing. I'm with Almira Gulch on this one.

Once upon a Time

The "dream" explanation of why water melts a witch is actually the easiest and the most intuitive one. But Oz isn't just a dream (or even a dream within a well-structured movie script), it's also a *fairytale*, and those don't work quite like dreams. Good Professor Langer has more to say about fairytales and how *they* work. She says that the difference between a dream and a fairytale is that fairytales have to possess more structure. When we move from the dream-story to the fairytale:

> it undergoes various modifications, in the interests of coherence and public appeal. Its purely personal symbols are replaced by more universal ones; animals, ghosts and witches take the place of [inanimate things] in the villain's role . . . the development and integration of story-action makes symbols and fantasy take on more and more reasonable outward form to fit the role in which they are cast. A higher mode of fiction emerges . . . Often the theme is quite ephemeral –merely the homecoming of a strayed person . . . but such simple plots grow, with the advancing arts of life and social organization, into the well-known *genre* of fairytale.[3]

Hmmm. That sounds a *lot* like Oz. But here's the unexpected twist: the *more* "coherence" and structure we bring to Oz, the *harder* it is to explain *why* things happen as they do. We expect more plausible explanations for the events as they approach more closely our waking experience. So Baum's task in the fairytale of Oz is actually tougher to pull off than the explanation in the 1939 script. Why does water melt the witch, in a fairytale? The idea is familiar enough, that things like that *happen* in fairytales, but Langer is right. We want them to make a higher kind of "sense" to us.

For example, in a dream we have no problem with one character just morphing into something else, but in a fairytale, characters are supposed to maintain their basic identities. And if a character should change, say, a good witch becomes a bad witch,

---

[3] Susanne K. Langer, *Philosophy in a New Key*, revised edition (New York: Mentor, 1951), pp. 150–51.

we will say that this character was *disguised*, and was really a bad witch all along, but the other characters didn't know it. In fairytales we rigidly avoid the idea that a good character just turns bad, whether over time or suddenly. It messes up the tale.

What Langer says is that fairytales are more "literal" than dreams. Things get restricted so that the symbols will sit still, and the way we restrict them is by isolating the place and time of the fairytale from our own world, and placing all the action in a more limited world. So, "once upon a time in a faraway land" is a phrase we use to separate and isolate the fairyland from our own, and in that land, we can designate consistently what is fixed and what can change. Langer says that the fairytale "is frankly imaginary—and its purpose is to gratify [waking] wishes, 'as a dream doth flatter.' . . . The end of the story is always satisfying, though by no means always moral" (p. 151).

This agrees nicely with what Baum says of his fairytale. So Oz is sort of an isolated place, more literal than a dream, but it's hard to get there. The listener needs to be discouraged about his or her own prospects for making such a trip, and cyclones and balloons are pretty discouraging to people in the year 1900—pretty scary ways of flying over the rainbow. (Orville and Wilbur were hard at work in their bicycle shop over in Dayton, but no one would have believed what they were piecing together and how it would change everything.) The world was still a very big place in the imaginations of children in 1900, still concealing regions largely unknown to their Eurocentric imaginations, like darkest Africa, the jungles of Asia, the interiors of China and India and Australia, the mountains of Tibet, the polar regions. Oz might be over there, somewhere, in the middle of Australia with deserts on all sides.

But as our world has become more familiar to us, and as we have come to know the features of every land and clime, it has become harder to frame a fairytale that way. We travel everywhere, and we expect to find roughly the same world wherever we go, not someplace where water melts witches and magic reigns over science. These days it doesn't require months or years to arrive in even the most exotic places, and there will be Coca-Cola and McDonald's and a Walmart when you get there. Even young children take on this mantle of realism by the age of seven or eight. That may be why fairytales have gone into decline and children's books are now dominated by little tracts on saving the environment or accepting other races. It's more about *this* world.

The effort to isolate the setting of the fairytale, like Baum does, has a certain advantage, so long as we are consistent about it, we can alter some of the features of the place, such as the effect of water on witches, but the alterations in a fairytale now require some sort of more plausible explanation than those in a dream. In the case of Baum's fairytale, well, he says the witch is dry. Very, very dry. She doesn't even have any blood. Dry things often melt (or dissolve) when you throw water on them. That's pretty close to science. You've seen it with your own eyes, in your own place and time. A key feature of Baum's story is that ugly umbrella the witch carries. How practical and reasonable of her, and Baum, to protect herself from water that way. It rains in Oz—just like our world, which is why things grow there. More science. If you have to stay dry all the time in a place where it rains, you'll have a fair struggle on your hands. Why didn't Baum just put the witch's castle in a place where it never rains? But that would make it too strange, and our troop of companions would die of thirst. See how much scientific sense this is all making? The analogies to our world are pretty rigid in *some* ways so as to open up a certain space for alteration, for the fantastic elements of the tale.

So water melts the Witch because she's very dry, not because fire and water can morph into one another and trade effects. And the Witch is wicked and miserable because she is dry. Or maybe she is dry because she is miserable and wicked. It works either way, but the image or *meaning* is that water is *good*, it is life and joy and even justice rolling down like a mighty stream. Of course, dry is *bad*; it is punishment, death, drought and thirst. We grasp this meaning as an arrangement of symbols, even though we know that too much water and not enough dry can be just as bad (like in Noah's flood and its rainbow covenant). But we get the connection. The moral meaning of the symbols is clearer to us than even the physical process of melting, so we quickly respond to the meaning of the symbols, approvingly, and substitute that for the weaker physical meaning, that water dissolves some things that are very dry.

Baum may claim that his fairytale has no "moral," but he surely draws upon our familiar moral judgments and symbols in order to explain the melting of the Witch. And in fact, the moral of the whole story, "there's no place like home," is fairly important to making the whole tale hold together. Granted, Baum describes Kansas as a grey place and makes it perplexing as to why *anyone* would prefer it to Oz, as does the 1939 Committee. But that just strengthens the moral: no matter how grey and awful and lonely home is, there is still no place like it. We *get* this. Obviously. So water melts witches because it has that effect on many dry things, but more importantly, water is life itself and goodness. So the fairy-tale hangs together physically and morally.

Possible Ozzes

That brings us to philosophy, of a sort. Those same symbols we find in dreams and fairytales (and myths and legends), what Langer calls "presentational symbols," can be flattened, disambiguated, pressed harder and harder to line up with our waking perceptual experience until, as Langer says, the images, the presentational symbols we imagine, are "superseded by a discursive and more literal form of thought, namely philosophy" (p. 173). What she means by "discursive" is that we no longer pay so much attention to the rich images before our imaginations, we attend more to their abstract and linguistic structure—logic, grammar, that sort of thing. But the images still have to be there. We never get away from them entirely. It's "only where experience is already presented—through some other formative medium [like an image], some vehicle of apprehension and memory—that the canons of literal thought [like logic] have any application. We must have ideas before we can make literal analyses of them" (Langer, p. 173).

The result of this move toward abstraction is that satisfying explanations of our experience are hardest to get when we try to make language conform to the exact order and conditions of our waking experience. Scientists still have to *imagine* the world, but their challenge is to imagine it in ways that will be sustained by further action in the world itself, in prediction and control of the outcome. They test their imagined theoretical models with measuring and mathematics. Philosophers, on the other hand, test their imagined worlds with logic, with very structured types of reasoning. They try to eliminate every logical possibility except one, and *that* one is supposed to be the "real world." Philosophers and scientists also tend to ignore the work of imagination in helping them come up with a theory, and for good reason. Imagination is quite unruly. It just likes to fly off in any old direction, and so it is more often the source of problems than a help. Philosophers try to accept as little imagined stuff as they can manage, and to work with exactly the same images, and very few of them, over long boring treatises.

This is how they try to hold the imagination still long enough to reason about it. It's hard to do.

And such is the character of the "possible worlds" that philosophers talk about, worlds that are exactly like ours except for small variations that will supposedly help us understand what's impossible and what's possible in our own world. In order to explain how this works, and why water really melts a witch, I have to tell you a tale. It's sort of a fairytale, but it happens in our world, in the recent history of philosophy. You can't get back there, into history, so it is an inaccessible world, but it is continuous with our present world, so it isn't quite a fairytale. Still, it seems surreal, to me at least.

In Munchkinland

So here's where the water hits the witch, so to speak, or the melting point of language. You can imagine and talk about all sorts of things that just can't be found in your everyday experience, like talking lions and the mayor of Munchkinland. And then, you can imagine and talk about things that definitely are in your experience, like your very own copy of *The Wizard of Oz, Restored and Remastered: The Definitive Three-disc Collector's Edition on DVD* (there's one sitting on my desk right now; it's very nice). And you can also imagine and talk about some things that might or might not ever exist, like Gregory Maguire's sequel to *A Lion among Men*. But it's hard to know, in some important cases, whether the things you're imagining and talking about do or don't exist, and even if they don't exist now, whether they ever have existed or ever could. We use (almost) the same sorts of language for all of these things, and all of it derives from those images we've been discussing, but if we want to be able to tell the difference between what we really *know* and what is just fanciful, or an error, we need some good way of sorting it all out. We need some logic.

Once upon a time there was this mathematician with a name that gives him away as a Munchkin, Gottlob Frege (1848–1925). He noticed a lot of things about language, and probably the most famous thing he noticed is that there's a difference between what a word *means* (its "sense"), and what it *refers to* in the world (its "reference"). So Frege issued a Mayoral Proclamation called "On Sense and Reference." This Proclamation became very famous, which is why the Munchkins made him Mayor. The Munchkins still don't agree on how to work out what Frege was talking about, which seems ironic and fitting, but most Munchkins agree he was onto something, at least.

I for one am not very impressed by the Proclamation, but anyone would have to be impressed with the logic that Funny Old Frege invented, because it's pretty much the basis for all computer languages (he got some help from another mathematician named George Boole, sort of the Prince of Quadling Country). The logic is very useful, no question about it, but it's the explanation of *why* it works that is less clear, and that's what the Proclamation is all about; it's Frege's story about *why* this logic works.[4]

For our purposes the theory boils down to this: you can imagine and talk sensibly about things that don't actually exist, and at one level, you can even be wrong or right in what you say. For example, it's true to say "Dorothy melts the Witch," even though it never actually happened anywhere (even in the interior of Australia), and neither Dorothy nor the Witch ever really existed. On the other hand, it's false to say "Dorothy *tried* to melt the Witch," because in all the stories, she didn't know the Witch would melt, so she couldn't have been *trying* to do it.

Now that's kind of weird. You can apparently "tell the truth" about stuff that never happened, maybe even about things that couldn't *possibly* happen. The Mayor put on his pointy thinking cap and suggested that . . . hold onto your houses . . . *meaning* is in some ways independent of *reference*. I know, that's not very exciting, but it was a cyclone through the Kansas of philosophy. Meaning and reference should be considered separately, with different kinds of analysis, even though they *do* have to meet up somewhere down the Yellow Brick Road, in an Emerald City that Frege called "The True." So what? Look, philosophers don't need a good excuse for a party, so on the basis of this one idea they had themselves a party called "Analytic Philosophy" that lasted about a hundred years. Frege's idea killed an imperious wicked witch called "idealism," which had enslaved all the Munchkins for quite a long time. After a hundred years of partying about all this, the Munchkins got bored and went away, but at first they got very excited, started dancing all over the place and singing. There were several reasons, but I'll just give you a couple.

---

[4] You can find Frege's proclamations here: http://en.wikisource.org/wiki/On_Sense_and_Reference.

A lot of philosophers secretly envy mathematicians and physicists, but they aren't good enough at math to do such heady stuff for real, so they feel like mental Munchkins. They compensate for their height by talking big about math and science without ever really having to do any. I'm no exception, by the way, so I'm not bashing Munchkins here. Remember that even our Munchkin problems are *real* problems, but our parties aren't much fun for anyone else (and not even for us, most of the time). The parties are well choreographed, though. Just go to a meeting of "professional philosophers." We have our uniforms: threadbare tweed, with shabby shoes, disheveled hair and untrimmed beards. It's easy to spot us on the streets of Chicago or New York, or whatever city is plagued by us in a given year. We have our own Lollipop Guild, called Analytic Philosophy, which is very juvenile and boyish; they like to brawl and fight. We also have our own Lullabye League, called Continental Philosophy, folks who would rather dance and tell stories than fight. You'd have to see it to believe it. And you wouldn't want to stay long.

Anyway, some folks got excited about the Proclamation when they figured that science can be separated from science fiction because the stuff scientists talk about always has *both* a *meaning* and a *reference*, and they meet up in the True, and that's why science is the best kind of knowledge. They tend to forget that Frege was a mathematician, not a philosopher. They made him Mayor even though he wasn't (I'm sorry to say) *really* a Munchkin at all. This all turned out to be a bad idea a little later, because it's hard to get *direct* experience of some of the stuff scientists talk about. It's hard to get a look at electrons, and black holes, and quarks. We just see *effects*. So what exactly do these words *refer* to? It's like the phlogiston stuff I described earlier. How do we know we aren't talking about nothing? But that's a different problem than we find in Oz. It's called the "problem of reference," and it isn't worth your time to learn about it now. It's over. Nobody cares anymore. We never worked it out, just sort of got bored with it, and the scientists weren't listening to us anyway. (Who can blame them? We were worried about whether *they* were talking about "nothing" when really *we* were the ones doing that.)

The problem with Oz is how can something be *meaningful* when it doesn't *refer* to anything in the literal world? You might say, "Well, Dorothy throwing water on the witch *does* refer to something *in the world*—books in which the act is *described*, movies in which the act is *depicted*, that sort of thing." Yes, of course, but the books and movies didn't *have to* follow that pattern—water melting a witch—and we would have understood the meaning no matter *what* the books and movies said, right? Even if you knew nothing about the Wizard of Oz, and I said to you "water melts witches," you would still know what I mean, even if there aren't any real witches, and even if water doesn't really melt them. So how does it happen that we can give anything a meaning, regardless of whether it can really happen or not? This is called the "problem of meaning" by analytic philosophers, and they are deeply vexed by it. They want a satisfying "theory of meaning," which is a very literal story about how it happens, and a very logical story at that.

One bunch of noisy philosophers, a chapter of the Lollipop Guild called "the Vienna Circle," started insisting that meanings come from the *intentions* of the speaker or imaginer or thinker, or whoever is licking the lollipop at the moment. References are in the world, they said, but meanings, like the taste of a lollipop, are subjective, infused with emotions and all sorts of other sugary stuff that'll rot your brain. So we don't need to study meaning, they claimed, we should just study reference. And this Vienna bunch was so loud and rowdy that eventually the law had to be called to break up their party. But that comes later in the story. For now, just remember that the noisiest Munchkins were saying that *meanings are made by intentions*. Meanings are in our heads, not in the world. Lots of philosophers bought this story, even after the police had hauled away the Vienna Circle.

Where Is Oz?

Back to our story: Remember that Oz is hard to reach, and harder for Baum than for the Committee. In Baum's first book, Dorothy reaches Oz by traveling in a house, lifted above a cyclone. In transit, she does fall asleep, but Baum makes it plain that Oz is no dream. It's a place, and it's supposed to share the same space and time as Kansas. The suggestion is that you could get from Kansas to Oz if you just knew the way. No one happens to know, but it's out there, a part of our own actual world. Oz is bounded by uncrossable deserts on all sides, and its residents know little of the world beyond their enclosed region, only rumors.

It's true that things work a bit differently in Oz. There a scarecrow can talk, or a tin woodman can be alive even though, one by

one, all of his limbs and his vital organs have been hacked off and
then replaced with hollow prosthetics. There are other such devia-
tions from what we assume to be the order of things here in
Kansas. But we are asked to accept the differences without skepticism because our imaginations present them to us as variations of
the familiar ways in Kansas (where you *will* find scarecrows and
you *could* make a man of tin). Baum is saying, in effect: "You've
encountered differences in other lands before, or at least you *know*
things are different in other places. Now, aren't some of those differences shocking? Wouldn't you have said that some were even
impossible, until you saw it for yourself?" So, for example, I know
how to get from Kansas to Australia, but if I didn't, and someone
showed me drawings of Platypuses and Kangaroos, would I not be
tempted to think of Australia as a mythic place and its inhabitants
as fantastical beasts? Baum is suggesting, I think, that Oz is to be
thought of as sort of "Down Under" our Kansas.

There are reasons to present Oz this way. Baum denies that his
books are allegories of our actual world, and insists that Oz really
is created for the edification of children. Now children have a
somewhat hazy picture of what Kansas does contain and can contain. As we grow up and become more familiar with how the world
works, we adults tend to constrict our grasp of what is possible in
terms of what is probable from our past experience. But children
don't have enough experience to use "the probable" as a hickory
switch for punishing the possible, the switch we adults use to keep
our imaginations on the straight and narrow path to reality. Baum,
however, instead of wanting a way of narrowing the possibilities
for practical purposes, gives children a vehicle that flies to places
like Oz. That's what children like, even if philosophers don't. And
almost any vehicle will do—the house atop the cyclone is a pretty
exciting way to fly, when you haven't got much experience of what
it does to people on the ground in Kansas.

So growing up is like narrowing imagined *meanings* into settled
references, and where we cannot do that, we tend to dismiss the
meanings themselves. That's what a lot of analytic philosophers
did. They said that meanings are made by our subjective intentions
about the world, whereas *knowledge* is made by the world itself—
"truth-makers" and "truth conditions," they call this. What a bunch
of killjoys. They said we can ignore or demote the "problem of
meaning" and leave it to psychologists to explain. But other
philosophers, even some analytic philosophers, said "No, meaning

is more than just our private intentions about words and images, meaning is in the world too—or maybe even *all* meaning comes from the world." So people started having an argument at the Munchkin party, and it got ugly. Dorothy left to look for better companions.

A Good Place to Visit, but Don't Drink the Water

I'm sure you remember that when a world starts to get more like *our* world, it gets harder to explain things. Gregory Maguire's Oz is more like our world than any other Oz (at least so far). His whole first book on Oz, *Wicked*, aims to explain why the Witch was so wicked. He gives her a personal history and a whole set of motives, and retells the story so that she is pretty much like us. We can sympathize with her motives, and from that point of view, Dorothy becomes a kind of a simpleton and not a very interesting character at all. In a way, Maguire takes those moral meanings that lurk just beneath the surface of Baum's story and pumps them up with his imagination until they look just like the political, ethical, and religious problems of our own world. And in a world *that* complicated, the Wicked Witch of the West is one of the good guys, sort of a cross between an animal rights activist and a secular humanist. Who would've thunk it? This is not a children's story. Maguire's second book on Oz, *Son of a Witch*, is even less fantastical than the first.

So the explanations of what happens in Maguire's Oz have to be more scientific and more plausible than in Baum's story. And they are. He does an awful lot of thinking about why water melts the Witch. I'll try not to spoil anything here, in case you haven't read the story (although my later chapter on "The Possible World of Oz" does have some spoilers), but in general, the Witch has a peculiar standing in Oz. She sort of belongs and sort of doesn't belong there, because she has one foot in our own world and one foot in theirs, and they aren't the same world. They are similar, but they exist alongside one another, with some differences. And the difference comes to be symbolized by water, its physical effects and its moral meaning. Maguire suggests that the water of *Oz* is deadly to the Witch, but not the water of Nebraska or California (you'll find out why it's Nebraska or California when you read the book). But the point is that some water from our world has made its way to Oz, and it's *probably* ocean water from the coast of

California, although Maguire doesn't make that entirely clear. The water from our world is powerful stuff in Oz, but not deadly.

Dissent in the Lollipop Guild

Now there is a famous philosopher named Hilary Putnam (born in 1926), recently retired from a grand career at Harvard. And he didn't like the idea that *meanings* are just in our heads—subjective, private, unexplainable. Putnam was so good at math and science that he didn't act like a Munchkin either, so other analytic philosophers listened to him even though he was saying some things they really didn't want to hear, like "y'all are wasting your time with your silly separation of meaning and reference, and your ridiculous theories of reference are no better than believing in magic." And he was right, which is part of the reason the party ended. So he developed a new theory of meaning with a very fancy name "The Causal Theory of Reference with Semantic Externalism." Never mind what all that means; it was enough to get him elected Coroner of Munchkinland, and he soon presided over the autopsy of the Mayor, with the assistance of a Munchkin named Richard Rorty (1931–2007), although they never could agree on the cause of death with poor old Frege.

The first thing Putnam did was to reinstate "images" as indispensable to our thinking. He says this because he has some common sense. Of course, people like Susanne Langer and Henri Bergson had been saying this all along, but the Lollipop Guild didn't read their books. In fact, the Lollipop Guild didn't like to read much at all. The Guild had conceded long ago "that *images* don't *necessarily* refer"[5] to things that really exist in our world, which is why we can't trust them, but they insisted that concepts *do* refer to reality, at least when they're *true* (formulated properly in mathematical or logical ways). But Putnam asks them:

> What are concepts? When we introspect we do not perceive 'concepts' flowing through our minds as such. Stop the stream of thought when or where we will, what we catch are words, images, sensations, feelings. When I speak my thoughts out loud I do not think them twice . . . but I can imagine without difficulty someone thinking just these

---

[5] Hilary Putnam, *Reason, Truth, and History* (Cambridge University Press, 1981), p. 17.

words . . . that I do, and realizing a minute later . . . that he did not understand what had just passed through his mind at all, that he did not even understand the language these words are in. (p. 17)

So he says that "concepts are signs used in a certain way," and their meanings are not necessarily subjective. He basically rediscovered what Langer was on about, without reading her book: Imagination counts, that is, Oz counts. It's both meaningful and has some sort of reference to *our* world, with differences created by possibilities we can imagine. It isn't nonsense. The Lollipop Guild was scandalized.

Putnam then argued for his theory with what is called a "thought experiment," one that uses "modal logic." I'll talk more about that in a later chapter, but for now all you need to know is that this involves imagining a possible world just like our own, identical in every respect, except one. The exception is, lo and behold, *water*. Here's how he describes it:

Let [us] imagine a Twin Earth . . . very much like Earth, in fact . . . the reader can suppose Twin Earth is exactly like Earth. Suppose I have a *Doppelganger* on Twin Earth who is molecule for molecule identical with me (in the sense that two neckties can be 'identical'). . . . It is absurd to think that his psychological state [that is, subjective intentions] is one bit different from mine. . . . [But] if the 'water' on Twin Earth is a different liquid—say, XYZ instead of H_2O—then 'water' represents a different liquid when used on Twin Earth and used on Earth. Contrary to the doctrine that has been with us since the seventeenth century, *meanings just aren't in the head.* (pp. 18–19)

The Loneliest Witch

So there! Hummph. Let's see if we can get Gregory Maguire out of his conundrum about the water and the Witch *now*. If he hadn't tried to make his Oz so real, we wouldn't have this problem . . . but he couldn't resist. 'Water' in Kansas is H_2O, but 'water' in Oz is XYZ, same word, same meaning in the head, but different stuff. Apparently Dorothy and the Wizard, who come from our world can drink XYZ, no problem. Apparently, however, H_2O has some drastic effects on the people of Oz. I won't provide the details, but take my word, Earth water is powerful stuff in Oz. And here is where the Witch, Elphaba, comes in. There are two things to notice.

First, if I understand Maguire's view rightly, when Elphaba says "water" she *means* XYZ, and it's deadly to her. She doesn't use the word "water" for H_2O—she doesn't know what the stuff is and never finds out, but drinking it causes her to dream of oceans. There are no oceans in Maguire's Oz, and hardly anyone even believes in them. They seem to Elphaba to be a *fairytale*, isolated, pure fancy, until she drinks a little H_2O and *dreams* of them. Now the relationship between the dream and the fairytale is back upon us. The fairytale doesn't frighten her, but the dream of all that water is so horrifying as to motivate her to create potions to keep herself awake and never dream again. You can see why it would be scary. Elphaba doesn't *know* she's dreaming of H_2O. And she doesn't know that only XYZ is deadly to her. So Putnam is right, meanings aren't entirely in the head. If they were, Elaphaba could take a nap.

A dream grips us viscerally precisely because we can't quite share its meaning with others—we are alone with it. When we turn it into a story, it's not a dream anymore. And fairytales are less threatening just because by their very nature, they conform to the public requirements of a narrative, and we tend to set the feelings aside or minimize them. But notice, that not *knowing* the external meaning of what she is dreaming about, that the H_2O is perhaps a good thing, life not death, is what makes Elphaba so terrified. When I read the book I wanted to *tell* Elphaba that H_2O is nothing to fear. In fact, it is the symbol of *possibility*. But I couldn't get through to her, and probably Putnam and Langer and Bergson couldn't either. She is very hard-headed.

The second thing about Putnam's argument is that we discover the importance of even a tiny difference between one world and the next, like the difference between XYZ and H_2O. That little over-sight on our part can make a massive difference in meaning, and if (like Elphaba) we don't know there's a difference between XYZ and H_2O, we could get it screwed up, we could say and think a lot of things that are just wrong. We could end up ignorantly talking about something like phlogiston for a couple of centuries.

But here's the rub, and this is why Putnam is so very right, although he never thought of this. Elphaba's situation is unique in Maguire's book. It isn't giving away too much if I tell you that Elphaba is the *only* being of her kind in Oz, and the same would be true if she could get to *our* world. She would be unique here too. And because everyone in both worlds uses the word 'water' to describe the stuff that's really different (XYZ and H_2O), the only way Elphaba could ever discover that they are different would be to consult the *different* effects they have *only on her*. Oddly enough, this reinforces what Putnam argues for in that book I've been telling you about. It's called functionalism, with a causal theory of reference and semantic externalism. So I'm saying that, thanks to Gregory Maguire, it is actually easier to make *Putnam's* argument by imagining one unique being straddling two worlds than imagining two identical beings using the same *word* in different worlds.

But we don't need a being as exotic as Elphaba straddling two worlds to make the point, and we don't even need two worlds. All we need is the idea that there's something in our own world, like reading Chaucer, that has a unique effect on any one of us, say, my sister. Discovering that effect is possible for her, but she won't be able to learn it by forming an intention in her head, or by learning how to use the words "Chaucer" or "Canterbury Tales." The only way to find out that she (and only she) is allergic to reading Chaucer, would be to read some, get sick, notice the connection, wonder about it, try a different edition, get sick again, and then confirm it by asking people to supply her with both Chaucer and non-Chaucer texts (say, some Edmund Spenser, some John Donne, and a bit of *Beowulf*) in a double-blind controlled experiment, and then see if she throws up only after the Chaucer, or whether it's really all pre-Elizabethan English writers that make her ill. Bit by bit she learns that part of what Chaucer *means* to her is "that nauseating author." What Putnam really means to show with his argument is not so much that *no* meanings are in our heads, but rather that you can't *reduce* the "meaning of meaning" to the private mental intentions of individual people, whether it's Elphaba or my sister (and I'm not suggesting any resemblance here).

This leaves only one question. Why does XYZ melt the Witch when H_2O doesn't? Hell, I don't know, it just *does*. All the witches I know come from this world and they all like water. I can't get my hands on any XYZ to run an experiment. That's the trouble when you propose something unique in some respect, like Elphaba. You give up the idea of explaining it. XYZ melts the Witch because that's how the story goes. Use your own imagination.

9

Off to See the Wizard: The Romantic Eschatology of *The Wizard of Oz*

JAMES McLACHLAN

The Wizard of Oz is probably the most famous journey story around. It's a story of a wanderer who travels through strange lands and then returns home. But it's not like some of those other famous journey stories.

It's not the *Odyssey*; Odysseus isn't really changed by his travel, Dorothy doesn't just go away and come back twenty years later; her journey changes her and she develops real relationships with the people (and Lions, Tin Men, Scarecrows, and witches) she meets. Dorothy's not like those Christian wanderers either. Not like Pilgrim in John Bunyan's *Pilgrim's Progress*, or Dante in *The Divine Comedy* or those other children who head off to Narnia. Although in the movie version Dorothy wants to go "over the rainbow" and escape Kansas (like Pilgrim wants to escape the world), once she gets over the rainbow she wants to go back to Kansas and Aunt Em. Pilgrim runs away from his family with his hands over his ears crying "eternal life, eternal life."

All's Well that Ends Well

Usually "eschatology" is considered a theological term. It's the study of "the last things," the "end time," the end of the road, the end of the journey. Today the word could evoke apocalyptic visions of the "end times;" we could read *Left Behind* books or get on the internet and check out "The Rapure Index" to get an idea of how close we are to the end of the world as we know it.

But there are other theological, philosophical, and even secular ways to think about eschatology. Marxism has an eschatology

Page 134, James McLachlan

where history moves to an end in the communist utopia. Or, Disney and 1950s America had an eschatology of eternal progress toward the consumer utopia with spotless malls and beautiful cloverleaf freeways. Of course, the end of the world doesn't always have to be nice, either, as in John Boorman's 1970s *Wizard of Oz* inspired dystopic movie *Zardoz*, where the utopia is a nightmare.

Eschatology as the doctrine of the "end" of the world is a theory of the "end" and "ending." In some usages, especially in ancient Greek, the "end" was not merely the conclusion or termination, but also the *purpose* of the whole process. The purpose of everything that happens is clearest in hindsight. One way to distinguish different eschatologies from one another is to see how they respond to the question, "Is God plus the world greater than God alone?" Dorothy was not the first girl to steal an apple. Think of the old story of the first apple thieves, Adam and Eve. The question you would ask about the story is whether or not it was a good thing that they ate the apple. Has the whole history of the world been a bad detour or a great experience? Is it a good thing that Dorothy went to Oz or would she have been better off just staying home? If you answer "bad detour" to this question you basically pit an eternally perfect reality against the illusion of a temporal and imperfect world of appearances. There are two possibilities here:

1. This world's end is a termination and is without purpose; no aim, no goal of its own. It's a valley of tears, a training ground of virtue, a pilgrimage or waiting room to eternity. Thus in *Pilgrim's Progress* Pilgrim seeks to escape this world to the eternal city. Or for the philosopher Plato the goal of this life is to escape to the real world of which this one is only a shadow.

2. This world has a goal assigned by God, and that's good; but that goal which the world itself may attain is not the true purpose or end of the world; the world must first end and be destroyed in order to accomplish the true purpose, the Kingdom of God.

In the movie, Oz might only be a dream but at least it's a dream that changes Dorothy and the way she looks at Kansas. In the books, Oz is a real place to which Dorothy returns and eventually brings Auntie Em and Uncle Henry along.

(1) and (2) are pretty much comprehensive of traditional eschatologies. Notice that both these types of eschatology suppose a

relation of eternity to time and history in which eternity is not affected by time. Notice also that this isn't just true of Christian, Jewish, or Islamic theism, where God is a perfection that is beyond space and time. This perfection of God or eternity is a feature of any philosophical, religious, or scientific system where what happens in history is unimportant or predetermined. Whether one is the Idealist Plato, the Christian Augustine, the atheist Spinoza, or the Hindu non-dualist Shankara, the relation of the world to God, Nature, or absolute Brahman is ultimately the same. One is real (God) while the other is an appearance (the human world); its time and history are ultimately less real or not real at all. The eternalists think that the sooner we get done with all this illusory stuff and on to something real and eternal the better.

The eschatology of *The Wizard of Oz* is different than either of these. God doesn't save the world at the end of the Oz books but there is a kind of utopia—it's built out of love and kindness. In the film, Dorothy leaves Oz and returns to Kansas but Oz has changed her, she learned something there. The Eschatology of the Wizard of Oz is *romantic*. But what's that mean?

Romantic Eschatology

In *The Wizard of Oz* the journey through the world is all important. I mentioned that the journey changes Dorothy, but actually it changes everything, even God. There was a German romantic philosopher Friedrich Wilhelm Josef von Schelling (1770–1854). He can help us. He wrote a book called *Of Human Freedom* and several other books that set out the pattern of this kind of journey, the romantic eschatology. This sort of story emphasizes the importance of individuals and the battle between good and evil. There are basically three moments in the journey.[1]

1. Unconscious Unity: At the beginning everything is "one" but it is a vague and meaningless unity.

2. Alienation, Egoism, and Diversity: The unity of the first moment is shattered by the self-assertion of individuals. This disruption

---

[1] The classic book for all this is M.H. Abrams, *Natural Supernaturalism* (Ithaca: Cornell University Press, 1971). Abrams sees the Romantic philosopher G.W.F Hegel's fabulous *The Phenomenology of Spirit* as the pattern text for thinking of the romantic eschatology.

usually occurs as an egoistic act but it makes possible the development of personal relations. It is a fall from unity but a fall towards something better.

3. Return to unity: The alienation caused by self assertion opens two possibilities: continued egoistic individualism and competition which is the source of evil and suffering, or love which is a return to unity that retains diversity. Love demands real others.

The unity aimed at with the fulfillment of the journey includes the conflict and risk of a world with real beings and differences. The path of *The Wizard of Oz* is a circuitous journey from a dull and dead unity, through the strangeness of a strange land with its even stranger inhabitants, to the creation of friendships and community, culminating in a return to Kansas. Dorothy leaves the gray nothingness of Kansas and with her friends departs on a journey where, as Salman Rushdie writes, the characters "embody one of the film's 'messages' that we already possess what we seek most fervently."[2] *The Wizard of Oz* is a great secular and democratic fairy tale. The weak overcome the strong, becoming strong themselves but retaining their weakness. Good triumphs over evil, liberation over slavery, and color over black and white.

It Doesn't Take a Hero

Salman Rushdie said that one of the great qualities of the "heroes" of the film is their apparent lack of great qualities. The Scarecrow, The Tin Man, and the Cowardly Lion are anything but superheroes. That's why we love them—they are sort of like us. Rushdie calls them "hollow men." The Tin Woodman really has a nice echo, the Scarecrow is literally a straw man, and the Lion roars so that the other creatures won't know he is afraid. But, of course, they really aren't hollow. The Scarecrow is always coming up with great ideas despite his lack of brains, the Tin Woodman weeps about Dorothy and, in the book, cries so much that he rusts when he steps on a beetle.

When, in the book, he encounters the truly frightening Kalidahs who are literally the tigers and bears of the movie's famous "lions, and tigers, and bears" chant, the Cowardly Lion tells Dorothy "We

---

[2] Salman Rushdie, *The Wizard of Oz* (British Film Institute, 1992), pp. 49–50.

are lost, for they will surely tear us to pieces with their sharp claws. But stand close behind me, and I will fight them as long as I am alive."[3] In the movie there is that famous scene where, even though he wants the other two to "talk him out of it," the Lion will enter the Witch's palace for Dorothy. And of course it's the Scarecrow's *idea* that the Tin Woodsman cut down the tree that sends the terrifying Kalidahs tumbling into the abyss. These little hollow men are smart, caring, and brave and these are not gifts from that humbug, the Wizard. They are qualities that emerge in each character along the journey. And it is Dorothy "the small and meek" who leads them all. They have this "divine" potential within themselves.

But what is that "humbug" the Wizard? Obviously he seems to be a kind of "eschaton," a final end that pulls everything towards itself. The Wizard's presence at the end of the Yellow Brick Road brings the companions to full realization of how much they already have and how much they've learned. You might say that "God was *in* them" and not in a separate or transcendent realm. But in another sense "God is outside them" in the journey itself and in the bonds of friendship, connection, and loyalty that they create along the way. Rushdie thinks it's a good thing that there's no religion in the film, but there is a sort of divinity or deity implicit in these characters.

Unconscious Unity: Kansas and the "Ungrund"

Schelling thinks that in the beginning there is no-thing, no history, but there is unity and oneness, pure boredom. Dorothy is at home in black and white Kansas but the conflict with Miss Gulch and Dorothy's desire to go over the rainbow leads her to the point of leaving that will plunge her into the color and fear of Oz. For Schelling that "unconscious unity," that undifferentiated grey mass, is the potentially fertile but actually meaningless abyss or freedom that has yet to express itself. He borrowed a term from the German mystic Jacob Boehme to describe it: "the *Ungrund*," the groundless. If one called such a being as the *Ungrund* "perfect" it would have to be the perfection of perfect vagueness, perfectly boring, per-fectly empty (like the vague platitudes of politicians, we can agree with any of them because they're not saying anything). For God to

---

[3] L. Frank Baum, *The Wonderful Wizard of Oz* (Ballantine, 1956), p. 64.

really "be," to become actual, God requires determination, finitude, a self and another. This is a wordy way of saying that even God has limits and needs them. The boring oneness, of course, is also bliss, since nothing is going wrong for anyone—no witches, no ruby slippers, no cylcones, and no fun. This absolute beginning, absolute unity, is not something to which we would wish to return. Schelling thought that to be a person is to be in some sense finite, to be limited by and related to another real person; but in the *Ungrund* there are no others, only unity. This kind of oneness is both boring and meaningless. It's like driving across Kansas at night and trying to pick out the black cows.

The first description of Kansas in the book is like the *Ungrund*. It is the chaotic though boring bliss of oneness, q total gray unity. Baum uses the word "gray" over and over to describe the land and its people. Dorothy might be there united with Auntie Em and Uncle Henry but everything is no-thing. Everything is gray, including Auntie Em and Uncle Henry. Only Toto isn't gray, only he breaks the monotony of Dorothy's world. One could say that Auntie Em and Uncle Henry are "one" with the land but being "one" is not such a great thing.

> When Dorothy stood in the doorway and looked around, she could see nothing but the great gray prairie on every side. Not a tree nor a house broke the broad sweep of flat country that reached the edge of the sky in all directions. The sun had baked the plowed land into a gray mass, with little cracks running through it. Even the grass was not green, for the sun had burned the tops of the long blades until they were the same gray color to be seen elsewhere. Once the house had been painted, but the sun blistered the paint and the rains washed it away, and now the house was as dull and gray as everything else. (*The Wonderful Wizard of Oz*, p. 2)

The film captures this grayness wonderfully in the different shades of gray we find in black and white photography. One can only imagine the impact on 1939 audiences when Dorothy steps through her doorway into Oz, and BAM, COLOR!!

Alienation: The Tornado and Falling Up to Oz

But let's not get ahead of the story. In both the film and the book the tornado changes everything. In one famous example of the romantic journey, *The Rime of the Ancient Mariner*, the Mariner's quest is initiated by his alienation from the other members of the crew. His realization is the result of his willful assertion of himself in shooting an albatross, a symbol of good luck to all sailors. We never know why he does it, he just does. But afterwards everything changes. It is an act of self-assertion but as such it alienates the Mariner from the rest of the crew. It is chaotic and is the source both of evil and of the story.

Dorothy is torn from Kansas not by any act of her own but by a cyclone—an act of nature. Thus she doesn't fall away from unity with nature/Kansas, rather, nature picks her up and deposits her in Oz. Of the film Rushdie writes that Dorothy herself is a tornado. This interpretation makes her much more like the Mariner, she upsets the order of the world. But unlike the Mariner she does it for Toto.

There is, however, one other way of understanding the tornado. As Rushdie points out, Dorothy has the surname of Gale. And in many ways Dorothy is the gale blowing through this little corner of nowhere, demanding justice for her little dog while the adults give in meekly to the powerful Miss Gulch; Dorothy who is prepared to break the grey inevitability of her life by running away, and who is so tender-hearted that she then runs back again when told by Professor Marvel that Auntie Em will be sad that she has fled. Dorothy is the life-force of Kansas, just as Miss Gulch is the force of Death; and perhaps it is Dorothy's feelings, or the cyclone of feelings unleashed between Dorothy and Miss Gulch, that are made actual in the great dark snake of cloud that wriggles across the prairie, eating the world.

Rushdie describes the grayness of Kansas in Baum's book in ways similar to Jacob Boehme's description of the birth of desire in the *Ungrund*. According to Rushdie,

> It is out of this greyness—the gathering, calculative greyness of that bleak world—that calamity comes. The tornado is the greyness gathered together and whirled about and unleashed, so to speak, against itself. And to all this the film is astonishingly faithful, shooting the Kansas scenes in what we call black and white but what is in reality a multiplicity of shades of grey, and darkening its images until the whirlwind sucks them up and rips them into pieces. (p. 17)

This conflict of order and chaos, good and evil, runs throughout the film. Usually we see order as good and chaos as evil, for example, the little Kansas farm and home are ordered while the tornado that snakes through the plains brings chaos. Oz and Munchkinland are geometrically ordered while the forest around the castle of the Wicked Witch of the West, with all its gnarly trees, is chaotic. But too much order is also a problem. Almira Gulch wants to be totally in charge; she can't even bear little dogs stepping out of line. She wants to run the country. She already is the wicked witch. The efforts of Auntie Em and Uncle Henry to create order on their little farm on the huge plain seem as tenuous and unsure as the America that sat on the tremendous chaos of the close of the Great Depression in 1939 and the eve of the Second World War.

In one of the film's deleted scenes, Joe, who will be the Tin Man in Oz, has created a wind machine that will protect the farm from tornados. The machine failed miserably of course. Our human attempts at order are always delicate and our attempts to protect ourselves from chaos ultimately fail. But chaos is also important for everything that will happen. Rushdie sees Dorothy herself as a force of chaos that demands a reordering of the world. She is Dorothy *Gale*, a little tornado herself. The chickens that Auntie Em and Uncle Henry are trying to count will shortly be blown away by the tornado. Dorothy dives in among them demanding justice for her Toto. What's great about this scene is that it's Dorothy's demands to set the world right in relation to her dog that upsets the unjust, monotonous order set down by Almira Gulch. But it also upsets the delicate order that just allows Auntie Em and Uncle Henry to get by.

In the book it seems that Dorothy's visit to Oz is completely accidental because she tries to save Toto and doesn't get into the storm cellar located in the center of the house. Toto, who is pretty much a force of chance in the book (his unmasking of the Wizard as the great humbug is accidental whereas in the film he purposely pulls back the curtain to expose Frank Morgan) hides under the bed. Dorothy doesn't make it to the cellar and is whisked off to Oz. Later, Toto will run after a cat, and, just as he kept Dorothy from getting to the cellar with Auntie Em, keeps Dorothy from riding off in the balloon with the Wizard. It is only after this seeming disaster that she discovers that she has the power herself to return to Oz. Dorothy's attachment to Toto seems to be what causes her to forsake the adults and become herself.

As her fear and desire break up this tenuous monotony, Judy Garland lifts her face to the sky and sings her desire to go "somewhere over the rainbow." She longs to escape, to become someone free of the farm and Kansas. Salman Rushdie called it "a hymn—the hymn—to elsewhere" (p. 23). But this conflict that takes her to a new world also places her in alienation and danger.

This way of understanding Dorothy's experience really resembles the Romantic Journey. Like the Ancient Mariner, all the characters in such a journey start from a position of naive egoism that separates them from the unconscious unity, the *Ungrund*. Once Dorothy gets to Oz she can think of nothing but returning to Kansas. In the book, when the Tin Man and the Scarecrow are arguing about which is better, a heart or a brain, Dorothy listens to them and can't make up her mind who's right. She finally decides she doesn't care and doesn't even care about them—she just wants to accomplish her dream of returning to Kansas.

> Dorothy did not say anything, for she was puzzled to know which of her two friends was right, and she decided if she could only get back to Kansas and Aunt Em it did not matter so much whether the Woodman had no brains and the Scarecrow no heart, or each got what he wanted. (*The Wonderful Wizard of Oz*, p. 48)

This self-absorption is true of all the characters at the beginning of the romantic journey; each is so bound up in his or her own quest that at first none really thinks of the others. The Scarecrow, Tin Man, and Lion are all absorbed in their own problems, and each sets out with Dorothy from a motive of self-interest.

If I Only Had a Mind

The Scarecrow, though he has no brains, is a philosopher if ever oh ever there was one. Being made of straw he is the almost the perfect Platonist already: almost disembodied, living in a world of pure ideas and pure contemplation that Plato regarded as the true source of all genuine knowledge. But the Scarecrow is actually *too* cerebral—all mind, no physical brains. He is an idealist living in pure thought. His body lacks weight. The real problem is not that he has no brain but that all he does is think. In the book he sits in his the doorway of his beautiful room in the Emerald City all night and never notices the room but spends all of his time watching a spider. There are famous stories about another philosopher who lived too much in his mind, Baruch Spinoza (1632–1677). He was completely absorbed in his little room, watching spiders, just like the Scarecrow (one wonders if Baum knew these stories). But Spinoza loved to feed the spiders bugs and could even be heard laughing as they tore up their prey.

The fact that the Scarcrow (or Baum) doesn't go this far is important for the differences that distinguish the Scarecrow from Spinoza. For Spinoza admired the Epicurean philosopher Lucretius (99–55 B.C.E.) who wrote that living in the mind was like being in a fortress on a mountain above a battle. One observed the battle but did not become involved in it for it was not ultimately real. The eternal truths of reason are real, these heady philosophers believe. But the Scarecrow wants down from his pole, wants to join life and battle. The Wizard will later say to the Scarecrow that he doesn't need brains, he just needs experience. It sounds like what is necessary is real-world, empirical observation and involvement. The experience that Scarecrow receives is not simply the empirical experience of watching spiders it is the moral experience of being tied to the others in the group, of leaving the egotism of his own woes and taking on the burdens of others.

When the Wizard, in the false form of the beautiful woman (in the book, of course), tells Scarecrow that he will have to kill the wicked witch of the West before he can get some brains, the Scarecrow protests that this is Dorothy's job, not his. He's still an egoist. But as they pursue the journey the Scarecrow gains weight through his experience and loyalty to the others. He involves himself in the battle. He struggles with the wolves, crows, and bees; the Scarecrow and the Tin Woodman defend the others and help in the final victory over the Wicked Witch of the West. But his "end," his "eschaton," is foreshadowed by his egocentric quest for a brain, and that is what sets him in motion.

If I Only Had a Cardiopulmonary Muscle

In the book the Tin Woodman's journey also develops from egoism to love for the others. When he was human he loved the beautiful Munchkin Maiden but lost his love for her once he lost his heart and he says he did not care for her anymore. But he is still absorbed by self-love. The Wicked Witch of the East has enchanted his axe so that it cuts off his own limbs one by one, and a tinsmith repairs him, little by little, until all his limbs are gone, but still loves the Munchkin Maid. He explains the final blow this way:

I thought I had beaten the wicked Witch then, and I worked harder than ever; but I little knew how cruel my enemy could be. She thought of a new way to kill my love for the beautiful Munchkin maiden, and made my axe slip again, so that it cut right through my body, splitting me into two halves. Once more the tinner came to my help and made me a body of tin, fastening my tin arms and legs and head to it by means of joints, so that I could move around as well as ever. But, alas! I had now no heart, so that I lost all my love for the Munchkin girl, and did not care whether I married her or not. I suppose she is still living with the old woman, waiting for me to come after her. (p. 47)

As he becomes impervious to physical pain he also stops caring for his true love. Like Lucretius he cannot be touched by events in the world about him, he is in love with his own beauty. (He even has himself nickel-plated in Baum's second book so that he will shine more brightly.) The last move of the Wicked Witch of the East could be to turn him into something like her.

The Tin Woodman becomes absorbed with himself and his own power and beauty. "My body shone so brightly in the sun that I felt very proud of it and it did not matter now if my axe slipped, for it could not cut me" (p. 47). The only danger was that he could rust. Is there a relation between the Tin Woodman's self-love and fear of water? He's not vulnerable to the pain of love. These drawbacks make him resemble the Wicked Witch of the West. But contrary to the evil witches he feels this privation as a terrible lack, the most unfortunate thing that could happen to a person.

As water will destroy the evil Witch of the West, it is water that really saves the Tin Woodman. After he speaks of being so proud of his shining body he tells of how he forgot his oilcan and is caught in the rainstorm. He stands in the woods for a year suffering and thinking.

It was a terrible thing to undergo, but during the year I stood there I had time to think that the greatest loss I had known was the loss of my heart. While I was in love I was the happiest man on earth; but no one can love who has not a heart, and so I am resolved to ask Oz to give me one. If he does, I will go back to the Munchkin maiden and marry her. (pp. 47–48)

Unlike the witches who literally "dry up" inside, the Tin Man uses his stationary suffering to feel the absence of the love he had once felt when he was flesh. He resolves to find it again. But in a conversation with the Scarecrow we learn that he only wants a heart so he can be happy, "for brains do not make one happy and happiness is the best thing in the world" (p. 48). Thus, the Tin Woodman's "end," his "eschaton" is also self-seeking at the beginning of his journey. A similar story can be told of the Lion and his desire to be King of the forest, but I'm sure you see the pattern by now.

Alienation: Wandering in the Woods

For Schelling, alienation is the split between the natural or unconscious realm of the natural world and the conscious realm of the individual subject. The Scarecrow is conscious of his lack of brains, but unconscious of his overactive mind. The Tin Woodman has confused his lack of a heart, of which he is conscious, with the presence of his ability to love (at least to love himself), of which he is unconscious. Each is alienated. This split is a false rupture that can only be healed by the imagination. Alienation can be seen as a series of false images or projections of the self and its relation to the world.

Schelling thinks that two forms of evil or despair arise from this condition. The first evil is to be swallowed up in chaos or a complete loss of the individual. For example all our heroes, Dorothy, the Scarecrow, the Tin Woodman, and the Lion, imagine they are nothing, that they have no power. The second evil is to create such a stultifying order as to do away with freedom. It is to think that "I" am everything. In the 1939 film, the Wicked Witch–Miss Gulch imposes her order on a world of free beings in order to turn them into things that she controls. Almira Gulch controls the county in Kansas and wants to control every part of it, even little dogs. The Wicked Witch of the East enslaved the Munchkins, and the Wicked Witch of the West enslaved the Winkies. The Wizard hides in his palace for fear his people will discover he is the "great humbug." These are examples of the second evil Schelling sees arising from the alienation of unconscious nature from individualized conscious self.

The Wicked Witch–Miss Gulch seeks to introduce a single order in the world-Oz that will eliminate the freedom of all others. Notice that this depiction is how we often think of God, the great and powerful being who is in control of everything. This conception is how the friends think of the Wizard. He is "Oz, the Great and Powerful Wizard" who controls everything and can solve all problems. The Scarecrow thinks he lacks brains, the Tin Man thinks he lacks a heart, the Lion thinks he lacks courage, and Dorothy "the small and meek" lacks a home. The friends all think they will be powerful when they get what they want. It's only as the friends become as concerned with each other as with their own quests that they are able to differentiate themselves from the evil beings of Oz. From that point of view, the all-powerful Wizard no longer looks so intimidating or even interesting.

What's the message here? Like the friends we don't have complete control over our chaotic condition. If we think that such control would solve all our problems, we remain alienated and arrested in our own egotism. What is interesting for Schelling and in Oz, is that Evil is actually the fantastic attempt to exert such control. We assert ourselves to be God, to attempt to control everything. But the order that is created by good is quite different; it's the desire to create an order that allows for the creativity, our own and that of others, of the chaos. It is an order that cares for the others as much as for the self.

Conscious Unity: "There's No Place Like Home"

For Schelling even God is socially related and it is through the choice for relations to others, for creation, that God leaves eternity, enters time and becomes a personal being. God is also changed, for the better, in the process. Dorothy leaves the unchanging vagueness of Kansas, enters time, and also comes into being—becomes more personal—through her relation to the friends. She can return to Kansas, and with a higher love for her people there, only after she has learned how to enact such love.

For Plato, and other traditional eschatologists, the world in which we live, including all the beings within it, is an imperfect copy of the ideal beauty that alone we should love. When we love something finite or someone here we fall into the unreal, so the old story goes. This pattern is echoed in all negative versions of the Fall in the Christian tradition. The desire to be an independent being, to be free, and to love other beings than God, or independently of God, is impious. In *Pilgrim's Progress* Pilgrim begins his journey by forsaking his family and running toward the eternal city.

Then said the *Evangelist,* If this be thy condition, why standest thou still? He answered, because I know not wither to go. Then he gave him a *Parchment Roll,* and there was written within, *Fly from the wrath to come.*

So I saw in my Dream, that the Man began to run; now he had not run far from his own door, but his Wife and children perceiving it, began to cry after him to return: but the Man put his Fingers in his Ears, and ran on crying, Life, Life, Eternal Life: so he looked not behind him, but fled towards the middle of the Plain.[4]

No earthly love can compare with the glories of the perfect heavenly realm, from the traditional point of view. Dante, at the end of his journey, arrives in paradise and is greeted by his early love Beatrice. But when he gets to the highest point in paradise he turns from her as she turns from him and contemplates the perfect beauty of God. Dante, enraptured by the beatific vision proclaims: "O light eternal, who alone abidest in Thyself, alone knowest Thyself, and, known to Thyself and knowing, lovest and smilest on Thyself!"[5] God's eternal perfection is the only thing of ultimate worth. This is the view we inherited in the Western world, and still the most common eschatology.

But Schelling thought "we have to 'penetrate above the general to personality.' For 'reason and law do not love, only the person can love" (Schelling, *Werke*, XI, pp. 566, 569–570). Schelling's point is that it's easy to love the general, the concept, the perfect idea. It's easy to love "God" or "humanity," as long as they are abstractions, but loving concrete persons who are other than us, and who limit our fantasies is more difficult. Dorothy becomes who she is through her love of the others.

In a neglected part of Baum's book the friends travel through the Dainty China Country where Dorothy tries to capture the pretty China Princess, telling her that she would love her and she would take her back to Kansas and stand her on Aunt Em's mantel. The princess objects to being turned into a pretty object for Dorothy's admiration.

"That would make me very unhappy" answered the china princess. "You see, here in our own country we live contentedly, and can talk and move around as we please. But whenever any of us are taken

---

[4] John Bunyan, *The Pilgrim's Progress* (Oxford University Press, 1962), pp. 13–14.

[5] Dante Alighieri, *The Divine Comedy, III Paradiso* (Princeton University Press, 1975), Canto XXXIII: 123, p. 379.

away our joints at once stiffen, and we can only stand straight and look pretty. Of course that is all that is expected of us when we are on mantel-shelves and cabinets and drawing-room tables, but out lives are much pleasanter here in our own country." (p. 196)

Dorothy tells the little China Princess that she would not make her unhappy for all the world. Our powers are and should be limited by others. This constraint is what the evil characters in Oz do not understand. To love another is not to see her as a beautiful ornament but as a person. Limitation and finitude are essential to personality and to love. We are limited by others and the existence of the other is what creates the possibility of love.

In a maddeningly obscure passage Schelling writes that true unity is only attained in love.

> But, as has been shown, it cannot be this in any other way than by dividing into two equally eternal beginnings, not that it is both at the same time but that it is both in the same way, as the whole in each, or a unique essence. *But the groundless divides itself into the two equally eternal beginnings only in order that the two which could not be in it as groundless at the same time or there be one, should become one through love; that is, it divides itself only that there may be life and love and personal existence.* (my emphasis)[6]

The oneness of the *Ungrund*, Kansas in our story, is neither love nor true unity. Its oneness is just nothing. Only by standing out and becoming someone does Dorothy become Dorothy, and when Dorothy is really Dorothy, we're not in Kansas anymore –or more precisely, only afterwards is Kansas any place like home at all. And it's because she stands out as an individual amongst others that she can love home and love others.

In the film Dorothy decides she doesn't want to run away over the rainbow or go see the crowned heads of Europe when Professor Marvel tells her that Aunt Em misses her and is ill. Dorothy's love for Aunt Em trumps everything and the journey is the quest to get home. In the book, when Dorothy goes to Oz and sees its beautiful colors she says to the Scarecrow that she wants to return to Kansas because there is "no place like home." She can

---

[6] F.W.J. von Schelling, *Philosophical Investigations into the Nature of Human Freedom and Related Matters* (Open Court, 1936), pp. 88–89.

make this claim because she is intelligent and has brains. The Scarecrow agrees and says that it is good that there are people smarter than he in the world, otherwise no one would live in Kansas. This exchange is interesting because there is the irony that most of us would agree with the Scarecrow that Oz is infinitely preferable to Kansas but it is also a matter of love that makes Dorothy want to return there.

> "I cannot understand why you should wish to leave this beautiful country and go back to the dry, gray, place you call Kansas."
> "That is because you have no brains," answered the girl. "No matter how dreary and gray our homes are, we people of flesh and blood would rather live there than in any other country, be it ever so beautiful. There is no place like home." (p. 34)

She returns home but it is not a return to the innocence of phase one of her journey; her consciousness is at a higher and more intense level. Dorothy has slain two witches, liberated the Mucnkins and the Winkies, and helped her friends attain their heart's desires. She has grown, become independent, and now can love more fully.

In romantic visions this termination of the quest was usually thought of as social and was represented by love and marriage. Schelling writes: "This is the secret of love, that it unites such beings as could each exist in itself, and nonetheless neither is nor can be without the other." He continues: "This is the secret of eternal Love—that which would fain be absolute in itself nonetheless does not regard it as a deprivation to be so in itself but is so only in and with another" (p. 89). Schelling was not known for being an especially clear writer. But here is the gist of it. When Dorothy Gale gets home to Kansas it's a different Kansas than the gray nothing she left. There's no place like home because the people there are more than ideas of perfection. They're really real. So there really is "No place like home."

10

The Wonderful Smallness of Evil in Oz

GEORGE A. DUNN

Those who know *The Wizard of Oz* only from its most famous movie adaptation, the 1939 MGM musical, might be surprised to read L. Frank Baum's children's book, *The Wonderful Wizard of Oz*, on which the movie was based.

In his introduction to the first edition of the book, published in 1900, he explained that he deliberately left out the grim and frightful elements found in traditional fairy tales in order to fashion "a modernized fairy tale, in which the wonderment and joy are retained and the heartaches and nightmares are left out." Tender minds should be spared the terrors instilled by those old-fashioned fright-fests and nourished instead on

> a series of newer "wonder tales" in which the stereotyped genie, dwarf and fairy are eliminated, together with all the horrible and bloodcurdling incident devised by their author to point a fearsome moral to each tale. Modern education includes morality; therefore the modern child seeks only entertainment in its wonder-tales and gladly dispenses with all disagreeable incident. (*The Annotated Wizard of Oz*, Norton, 2000, p. 4)

According to Baum, the frightening elements of the traditional fairy tale are typically in the service of some moral lesson that can be imparted better through more enlightened forms of moral instruction that don't induce nightmares. A few years later, in 1909, he reiterated these sentiments in an interview with *The Advance*, the journal of the Congregationalist churches, telling a reporter that children's stories should exclude "the tragic and the dreadful."

And in an essay on "Modern Fairy Tales," published a month later in the same journal, he advised parents to choose stories for their children that are "not marred by murders or cruelties, by terrifying characters."[1]

Needless to say, the makers of the 1939 musical version didn't hew too closely to Baum's philosophy of fairy tales—and most of us are probably grateful for that. Okay, maybe we could have done without the heavy-handed moral about how there's "no place like home," however tempting it may be to search for happiness "over the rainbow." Such patent moralizing would certainly have annoyed Baum, especially since it's through the terrible ordeal of being afraid and forlorn that Dorothy learns her lesson.

But forget the clumsy pedantry for a moment. What would the movie have been without the shudder-inducing sight of the cruel, green-faced Witch tormenting Dorothy or the nightmarish image of the Winged Monkeys swooping in for their attack? The "heartaches and nightmares" that menace Dorothy and her companions at every turn are precisely what make the movie so thrilling. Moreover, they can't be separated from the elation we feel when, thanks to unexpected good fortune, the band of adventurers just barely dodges death at the hands of the Wicked Witch. At the very least, we have to admit that Baum's philosophy of fairy tales may not offer the most entertaining recipe for a movie.

Gonna Sweep That Evil Right Out the Door

While Baum's *The Wonderful Wizard of Oz* does contain a few scenes of outright gore that the movie-makers wisely chose to omit—the Cowardly Lion decapitates a giant spider and the Tin Woodman gives us a blow-by-blow (literally!) account of how he was dismembered by an enchanted axe back when he was still a flesh-and-blood human—it does a pretty good job of keeping the sad and scary parts to a minimum. When Dorothy is a captive in the Witch's castle, we learn that she's never in any genuine peril because she's protected by a mark placed on her forehead by the kiss of the Witch of the North. The Wicked Witch longs to get her hands on Dorothy's Silver Shoes (which become Ruby Slippers in the movie), but she's too afraid of the dark to sneak into the child's

---

[1] Quoted in Katherine M. Rogers, *L. Frank Baum: Creator of Oz* (New York: St. Martin's Press, 2002), p. 92.

room and steal them when she's sleeping. While her counterpart in the movie is prepared to kill Dorothy to get the slippers, the Wicked Witch of the book merely puts the girl to work as a scullery maid in the kitchen until she can devise some trick to part Dorothy from her shoes. Adventures in Oz become even less perilous in later books, when we learn that residents of this fairyland never age, get sick, or die—an exception evidently having been made for the Wicked Witches of the first book.

Despite Baum's distaste for moralizing children's tales, *The Wonderful Wizard of Oz* does seem to be guided by a moral outlook that pervades the story from start to finish even if it's not the sort of thing that can be summed up in a pithy adage tacked on at the end. It comes to light when we consider how the story depicts the nature of evil and our prospects for overcoming it. Baum's fairy tale world may assail his protagonists with a steady barrage of obstacles, dangers and hardships, but in the end they never meet up with any difficulties that their ample supply of good sense, heart and courage can't surmount. Evil may at the moment *seem* to have the upper hand, but that's never really the case, for, as the leader of the Winged Monkeys observes, "the Power of Good . . . is greater than the Power of Evil" (*Annotated Wizard*, pp. 215–16).

Now, of course, if Baum's moral outlook consisted only of this platitude, it would be nothing special. For, as he readily acknowledged, "never has a fairy tale lived, if one has been told or written, wherein the good did not conquer evil and virtue finally reign supreme."[2] The remarkable thing about the adventures Baum crafted, especially compared to more traditional fairy tales, is *how* good conquers evil—and, more importantly, how *easily*, as if evil was never that big to begin with.

Let's compare the book and the movie again. In both versions, the Wicked Witch of the West is destroyed when Dorothy douses her with water. But in the movie, this dousing occurs in a terrifying scene that reaches its climax with Dorothy shrieking in panic as she tosses a bucket of water on the burning Scarecrow and only accidentally splashes it on the Witch. Good triumphs through a stroke of luck, not through its inherently superior power. But in the book, Dorothy douses the Witch in an outburst of anger at her refusal to return one of the Silver Shoes she has just stolen. The

---

[2] Quoted in *Annotated Wizard*, p. 217.

moment Dorothy stands up for herself and refuses to play the role
of a docile and timid slave, her oppressor literally melts away to
nothing. The Witch is able to enslave her in the first place only
because Dorothy "doesn't know how to use her power" (p. 218).
The Winkies, on the other hand, were enslaved because they "were
not a brave people" (p. 211). The lesson seems to be that evil has
only as much power as we grant it due to our own ignorance or
timidity. On its own it's a relatively small thing, easily swept out the
door like the melted remains of the Wicked Witch of the West, once
its (or her) insubstantial nature has been exposed.

The optimistic outlook of *The Wonderful Wizard of Oz* teaches
that evil isn't that powerful once you muster up enough nerve to
face it down. Moreover, as we'll see shortly, it teaches that your
virtues will always reward you with success and that human nature
is fundamentally good. But first, so we can put Baum's outlook in
perspective, let's consider some influential philosophical views on
the nature of evil and our prospects for overcoming it.

Wicked Witches, Deadly Poppies, and Fighting Trees

It's hard to come up with a concise definition of evil, but not hard
at all to produce examples. Arguing that the evils of this world far
outweigh its pleasures, philosopher David Hume (1711–1776) compiled the following list, meant to be merely representative and by
no means exhaustive:

> Were a stranger to drop on a sudden into this world, I would show
> him, as a specimen of its ills, an hospital full of diseases, a prison
> crowded with malefactors and debtors, a field of battle strewed with
> carcasses, a fleet foundering in the ocean, a nation languishing under
> tyranny, famine, or pestilence.[3]

In short, evil encompasses everything we experience as malign,
harmful, painful, repellent, crippling and destructive, everything we
despise, blame or lament—all of our "heartaches and nightmares."

With such a wide variety of evils, philosophers have often found
it helpful to sort them into two broad categories—*moral evils* and

---

[3] *Dialogue Concerning Natural Religion and Other Writings* (Cambridge
University Press, 2007), p. 71.

natural evils—both regularly encountered by Dorothy in the course of her adventure. Moral evils, as the name suggests, originate in the voluntary choices of persons or "moral agents," as philosophers like to say. The class of moral agents has traditionally been restricted to human beings but nothing stops us from ascribing moral agency to intelligent scarecrows, mechanical men, talking animals, and even animated china figurines, as long as these creatures can be guided in their actions by an understanding of the difference between right and wrong. When the Wicked Witch enslaves Dorothy, imprisons the Lion, and has her Winged Monkeys tear the stuffing out of the Scarecrow and crash the Tin Woodman against sharp rocks, the harms they suffer stem from her evil will. Much less heinous but still morally evil are the scores of deceptions practiced by the Wizard, such as his fraudulent presentation of himself as a "Great and Terrible" wizard and his false promises to Dorothy and her companions.

Natural evils include all those sources of woe that don't depend directly on the actions of moral agents, especially when they result from the ordinary workings of the natural world. We could cite the unremitting grayness of the Kansas prairie, which *The Wonderful Wizard of Oz* tells us had seeped into the weathered faces Dorothy's Uncle Henry and Aunt Em, as a specimen of this type of evil. But Dorothy's first encounter with natural evil in a big way occurs when the cyclone tears her house from its foundations and deposits her far from Kansas in the Land of Oz. We could also include under this heading many of the obstacles the landscape of Oz sets in her path to the Emerald City, such as the Deadly Poppy Field and the swift currents that sweep her and her travelling companions downstream as they attempt to raft across a wide river.

Still, certain features of the landscape of Oz pose a challenge to this tidy classification of evils as either moral or natural. How, for example, should we label the Fighting Trees that block Dorothy and her companion's path through Quadling Country on their way to Glinda the Good? "The Trees seem to have made up their minds to fight us," the Lion conjectures—and if it's true that the trees actually have minds to make up, an argument could be made for placing their unprovoked assault on innocent commuters in the category of moral evil. On the other hand, tossing intruders may just be a reflex over which they have no control and for which they therefore can't be blamed.

Wickedness and Woe

The distinction between moral and natural evils focuses on their causes, drawing a line between harms that arise from conscious intentions and those that result from blind natural forces. But there's another way to classify evils that cuts across this classification. One of the most influential traditional views holds that evil, however it may be caused, always involves a *privation* (absence, loss, diminution or destruction) of something good that ought to be there. Sickness is an evil because it's the privation of health. Severe poverty is an evil because it's the privation of the material resources needed to survive.[4]

On this theory, there could be as many evils as there are vulnerable goods susceptible to harm. But philosophers have often argued that, for rational beings like us, all the genuinely valuable goods can be gathered under two headings, those that pertain to our material well-being (our happiness) or to our moral perfection (our virtue). Consequently, there are two kinds of evil: the evil we *suffer*, diminishing our happiness, and the evil we *do*, compromising our virtue. We can call these two evils *vice* and *unhappiness* or, if you're fond of alliteration, *wickedness* and *woe*. When one person's wickedness results in another's woe—as when the Witch imprisons and torments Dorothy—both virtue and happiness are casualties, a double privation of the good.

But the deplorable character of this situation goes beyond the mere doing of wickedness and the suffering of woe. Most people feel that when wickedness causes woe, they both ought to occur in the same person. In other words, if anyone should suffer on account of the Witch's wickedness, it should be the Witch herself. Likewise, virtue and happiness should meet in the same individuals, preferably with happiness resulting as a direct causal consequence of their virtue. Alas, outside of the Land of Oz we can't always count on this to happen.

The philosopher Immanuel Kant (1724–1804) thought that since morally sensitive people must find it unacceptable that virtue often goes unrewarded, it is both necessary and legitimate to posit the existence of a supernatural power (God) and a supernatural realm (the afterlife) that crowns virtue with happiness and punishes vice

---

[4] A classic statement of the theory of evil as privation is found in Augustine, *Confessions* (Hackett, 1993), Book Seven, especially pp. 111–12 and 118–120.

with misery. However, part of Baum's optimistic outlook is his belief that no supernatural or magical intervention is needed to engineer the coincidence of virtue and happiness, at least not for Dorothy and her companions.

Who Needs Magic when You Got Virtue?

In Baum's fairy tale, if you refuse to be cowed, never lose heart, and trust your native good sense and ingenuity to pull you through, success is assured. The hurdles you encounter along the way are just opportunities to discover and exercise your natural abilities and virtues. Dorothy and her companions face a host of difficult and dangerous obstacles in their journeys—they escape ferocious Kalidahs only to have their path blocked by a raging river, which they raft across only to find themselves waylaid by the Deadly Poppy Field—but they can always find creative solutions to their problems.

The virtues that guarantee their success fall into two categories. In the first place, they manage to triumph over difficulties by drawing on their ample store of *personal* virtues, such as good sense, bravery, determination, cheerfulness and self-confidence. But they're also indirectly aided by generous *social* virtues that pertain to their conduct toward others. Our heroes are kind, loyal and always ready to help others in a pinch—and these virtues also contribute to their success. The field mice who help rescue Dorothy and the Lion from their poisonous sleep among the Deadly Poppies are directed to do so by their Queen, who feels gratitude toward the Tin Woodman for saving her from a hungry wildcat. Kindness is invariably repaid with kindness in Oz. Instead of a "fearsome moral" like the ones Baum believed the traditional fairy tale attempted to browbeat into young minds, incidents like this convey the salutary lesson that helping others will benefit you because they will usually be happy to repay the favor. In Baum's world, good deeds are always rewarded and bad deeds are always punished—dependably and usually as a direct consequence of the person's good or bad will.

Dorothy and her companions only rarely require any supernatural or magical assistance. The notable exception is when Dorothy finds a way to get back to Kansas through the magic of the Silver Shoes. But since she had been wearing them all along without any awareness of their power, it's natural to read even this instance as a metaphor for our ability to solve our problems using resources we already possess. Like her companions, Dorothy discovers that what she set out to find—in her case, a way home—was something she already had. But unlike the Ruby Slippers of the movie, which work only after Dorothy learns her lesson that "there's no place like home," the Silver Shoes have a power she can tap at any time, once she learns the rules for commanding them. While in the movie the charm is activated by repeating the words that sum up the lesson she's learned, the Silver Shoes, designed to take orders from whoever wears them, respond straightaway to Dorothy's command, "Take me home to Aunt Em!" *Annotated Wizard*, p. 353). In the movie, Dorothy informs her family and friends that during her stay in Oz, "all I kept saying to everybody was, I want to go home. And *they* (emphasis added) sent me home." In the book, however, it's clearly Dorothy's own resourcefulness and tenacity that finally gets her home, not some mysterious *they* pulling levers from behind a curtain or waving a magic wand.

It's All for the Best

The moral and natural evils that complicate Dorothy's efforts to return home become the occasion for her, and especially for her three companions, to discover their talents and to cultivate their virtues. The Scarecrow would never have discovered his brains, the Tin Woodman his heart, and the Lion his courage were it not for the evils that forced them to bring to put those latent capacities to work. If Dorothy doesn't derive a comparable benefit from her hardships, it may be because she's already abundantly supplied with all the virtues her companions are seeking. Does she gain nothing from the difficulties she's forced to surmount? After all, if she had only understood the power of the Silver Shoes, she could have returned home the very day she arrived in Oz. But her hardships have brought benefits—if not necessarily to her, then to her friends, as they remind her before she leaves them for Kansas. Had her return home not been delayed,

> then I should not have had my wonderful brains!" cried the Scarecrow.
> . . . "And I should not have had my lovely heart," said the Tin Woodman. . . . "And I should have lived a coward in the forest forever," declared the Lion, "and no beast in all the forest would have had a good word to say to me." (p. 351)

Dorothy replies, "I am glad I was of use to these good friends," granting that she agrees her troubles were indeed all for the best.

The benefits Dorothy and her companions derive from their adversity brings to mind the response of contemporary philosopher John Hick to those who argue that a world such as ours, plagued with so many moral and natural evils, couldn't possibly have been designed by a benevolent God. If whiling away our days in ease and comfort is our idea of the good life, then Hick concedes that we're bound to find fault with the world's design for making suffering and hardship so much more the norm. But he dismisses this complaint as misguided, since it assumes that God's purpose in creating the world was simply to keep us all pleasantly entertained. To the contrary, he argues, God designed the world not as a garden of delights but as "a vale of soul-making," supplying it with enough pain and suffering so that our personal misfortunes can become opportunities for developing virtues like courage and self-control, while the suffering of others can help us to open our hearts to the less fortunate and teach us compassion. The "soul-making" values this world was designed to foster include

> compassion, unselfishness, courage, and determination [and] these all presuppose for their emergence and for their development something like the world in which we live. They are values of personal existence that would have no point, and therefore no place, in a ready-made Utopia. And therefore, if the purpose for which this world exists (so far as that purpose concerns mankind) is to be a sphere within which such personal qualities are born, to purge it of all suffering would be a sterile reform. (*Evil and the God of Love*, Harper and Row, p. 326)

The only problem with this explanation of the existence of evil is the presence of so much suffering that doesn't contribute to "soul-making." All too often, the encounter with evil is *soul-destroying*, crippling its victims in ways that prevent them from ever developing the moral traits Hick believes this "vale of soul-making" was designed to nurture. *The Wonderful Wizard of Oz* shares Hick's faith that all our troubles are really in the service of something wonderful enough to make them all seem worthwhile, but with this difference—the Land of Oz actually delivers on that promise in a more dependable and straightforward manner than our world ever does.

Dorothy . . . and Her Little Dog Too

But the crowning jewel of Baum's optimistic outlook is the character of Dorothy herself.

Judging from the illustrations that accompanied the first edition of *The Wonderful Wizard of Oz*, Dorothy is a very young child, possibly five or six years of age, far too young for her considerable fund of virtue to have been the product of her education or life experience. When we consider the circumstances of her young life, her abundance of good sense, kindness and determination seems even more astonishing. She's an orphan, raised on the bleak Kansas prairie by a joyless Aunt and a taciturn Uncle who never smile and never laugh, having as her only friend and playmate her dog Toto (pp. 18–20). Lacking role models or mentors, she could only have come by her virtues as natural gifts. Her virtues appear to be as innate as the indomitably cheerful disposition that helps her endure with aplomb the worst hardships fortune sends her way. When, for instance, the cyclone rips her from the Kansas prairie, she's able to calm herself enough to take a nap while her house is in transit to the Land of Oz. And even during the sad days of her imprisonment by the Witch, she never lets despair swallow her last bit of hope, consoling herself with the thought that the Witch at least hadn't killed her and never ceasing to look for some means of escape.

The ancient Greek philosopher Aristotle (384–322 B.C.E.), whose account of virtue and happiness set the terms for most of the subsequent discussions in Western philosophy, would have scoffed at the idea of virtue in a child like Dorothy. Virtue and happiness, he believed, could be attained only through long disciplined practice that gradually habituates us to think, act and feel in ways that are not only admired by others but a source of pleasure to ourselves. (Even then, we must still hope that we don't fall prey to some terrible misfortune that drains all the joy from our lives.) A five year old child—and a *girl* child at that!—could be neither happy nor virtuous, according to Aristotle. At most, he thought a fortunate youngster might be "pronounced blessed on account of our hope" that her potential will someday reach fruition in her adult life.[5]

Baum was obviously operating with a very different set of assumptions about the sources of virtue and happiness when he

---

[5] Aristotle, *Nicomachean Ethics* (Focus, 2002), Book I, 1100a, p. 15.

created Dorothy. Consider that, when she takes up permanent residence in Oz in later books,[6] she's consigned to an eternal childhood due to the immunity from aging and death that all inhabitants of Oz enjoy. Now, if Aristotle is right, this is a lamentable move that deprives her of the chance to grow into someone capable of a full and happy life. But for Dorothy, remaining a child doesn't seem like a misfortune, since she's already a lot more sensible, virtuous, and happy than most of the grownups she encounters in and outside of Oz. In a world full of corrupt, miserable, and foolish adults, Dorothy's arrested development begins to look like it could be a blessing.

She's definitely not an Aristotelian. Dorothy reminds us more of philosopher Jean-Jacques Rousseau's (1712–1778) ideal of someone whose natural goodness and decency hasn't been sullied by the corrupting influences of civilization. In his classic *Émile*, a philosophical novel about how to cultivate and safeguard just such a naturally good moral disposition, he wrote, "Everything is good as it leaves the hands of the Author of things; everything degenerates in the hands of man."[7] Like Rousseau, Baum presents joy and goodness as the natural or default condition of human beings, a birthright that we must not let the harsh necessities of grinding out a living or the deceitful lures of superficial refinement steal from us. Dorothy, a wholly natural creature, still too young and socially isolated to have been corrupted by society, is as wholesome and happy as can be. Compare Dorothy to her nemesis, the Wicked Witch, an almost wholly unnatural and dried up creature, destroyed by the same natural substance that gives life to the rest of us. Significantly, the liberation of Oz from the tyranny of the two evil Witches and the rule of the fraudulent Wizard is accomplished by someone uncorrupted by civilization, whose only close companion until very recently has been a small black dog.

Okay, on One Condition

There's something undeniably appealing about Baum's rosy outlook, however much we may doubt whether it reflects reality very well. Katherine M. Rogers, in her biography of Baum, reports that

---

[6] This happens in *The Emerald City of Oz* (HarperCollins, 1993), originally published in 1910.

[7] Jean-Jacques Rousseau, *Émile: Or, On Education* (Basic Books, 1979), p. 37.

he wanted to create fairy tales with a distinctively American flavor (pp. 77, 93)—and what could be more American than the belief you can accomplish just about anything once you put your mind to it (as critic Terry Eagleton puts it, "'Challenge' is Americanese for an utterly irreparable disaster"[8]) and that deep down inside people are basically good? So the allure of Baum's worldview isn't hard to understand. But its genial optimism is a striking contrast to the views of two other prominent twentieth-century fantasy writers who reflected on the philosophy of fairy tales: G.K. Chesterton (1874–1936) and J.R.R. Tolkien (1892–1973). Both devout Christians and both British (products of "the Old World"), they each ascribed a moral and metaphysical significance to fairy tales that departs significantly from the outlook that guided Baum in his writings.

In "The Ethics of Elfland," Chesterton declared, "My first and last philosophy, that which I believe in with unbroken certainty, I learnt in the nursery. . . . The things that I believed most then, the things that I believe most now, are the things called fairy tales."[9] Needless to say, the fairy tales that supplied Chesterton with his philosophy were of the traditional sort that Baum was eager to replace, stories fraught with peril and the prospect of grief, set in a world where happiness is a fragile thing dangling from a slender thread. Chesterton thought it was significant that, more often than not, this thread was some seemingly arbitrary prohibition—Don't open that box! Don't stay at the ball past midnight! Don't eat that apple—that would bring your joy crashing down around your ears if you were reckless enough to disregard it. "In the fairy tale," he wrote, "an incomprehensible happiness rests on an incomprehensible condition" (p. 53).

The traditional fairy tale that Chesterton describes bears little resemblance to *The Wonderful Wizard of Oz*. While Dorothy comes across lots of people and situations that are incomprehensible at first blush, "she is," as Rogers observes, "able to make sense of the confusing world she is plunged into and to influence it . . . she can act effectively and resist unreasonable authority" (p. 91). Of course! Isn't that just how Americans are? As Chesterton construes the traditional fairy tale, authority must be heeded however unreasonable its demands. Dorothy, on the other hand, remains true to her own

---

[8] *Holy Terror* (Oxford University Press, 2005), p. 103.

[9] "The Ethics of Elfland," in *Orthodoxy* (Doubleday, 2001), p. 46.

ideals, even going so far as to lecture an imposing authority figure on the responsibilities of power. When asked by the Wizard why he should help her get back to Kansas, she tersely replies, "Because you are strong and I am weak; because you are a Great Wizard and I am a helpless little girl" (p. 188). In the end, of course, Dorothy is no damsel-in-distress but an endlessly resourceful girl who succeeds against all odds due to her good sense and other virtues.

For Chesterton, the conditions attached to happiness in the traditional fairy tale were meant to convey a fundamental truth about the human condition. "We are in this fairyland on sufferance," he wrote, summing up what he took to be the moral of these tales; "it is not for us to quarrel with the conditions under which we enjoy this wild vision of the world."[10] The fairy tale teaches that happiness comes to us as a gift, not as something we have any right to expect or demand. It's a godsend (literally) that comes with conditions attached in order to remind us that it's an undeserved bounty for which we should feel gratitude rather than complacency. Indulging in a bit of self-mocking pedantry, Chesterton calls this the Doctrine of Conditional Joy. Something like this doctrine can be inferred from the movie version of *The Wizard of Oz*. Dorothy runs away from home because, as Professor Marvel discerns in a decidedly unremarkable feat of "clairvoyance," "they don't appreciate you at home" and "you want to see other lands, big cities, big mountains, big oceans." When she finds herself trapped in a perilous and often hostile world far from her home, we can imagine Chesterton sermonizing that this is the price of violating the condition that had been set for her happiness, namely, not to seek her "heart's desire" outside her own backyard. But whatever the movie may be trying to teach, Conditional Joy is far from the message of Baum's version of the story.

Consider Dorothy's three deluded traveling companions, the Scarecrow, the Tin Woodman, and the Lion, each hoping to receive as a boon from the Wizard something they already possess or are in the process of getting on their own. It's almost as though their mental horizons had been shaped in Chesterton's nursery, his Doctrine of Conditional Joy such an article of faith for them that each can't imagine receiving his "heart's desire" as anything other than a gift from some external, quasi-divine agency. Part of the

---

[10] *All Things Considered* (BiblioBazaar, 2008), p. 137.

comedy of the *Wizard* is that they never recognize the truth, so obvious to the reader, that what they want can only be cultivated inside themselves through their own efforts (and perhaps it's this self-recognition that Baum considers necessary for real moral maturity). Even after the Wizard has been unmasked as a humbug, they still demand that he grant their requests. So he stuffs bran, along with pins and needles, in the Scarecrow's head, surgically implants a silk-and-sawdust heart in the Woodman's chest, and has the Lion down a draught of "liquid courage."

"How can I help being a humbug," the Wizard reflects after performing these entirely symbolic operations that his literal-minded patients believe will actually work, "when all these people make me do things that everyone knows can't be done?" (p. 283). Could Baum be poking fun at sacramental religions that believe intangible realities are actually present in physical objects and expect symbolic actions to produce real changes in someone's condition? Even if it seems like a stretch to attribute that much whimsical irreverence to Baum, he's clearly rejecting a notion dear to many religions when he lampoons those who turn to a higher power to satisfy their deepest desires. The irreligious implications of his story haven't gone unnoticed. In 1986 a federal judge ruled that requiring children from Christian fundamentalist households to read *The Wonderful Wizard of Oz* in school offended their religious beliefs and violated their First Amendment rights, since it teaches that intelligence, love, and courage can be acquired through human effort rather than being received as gifts graciously bestowed by God (p. 42).

Old World Magic and New World Technology

Baum's presentation of the Wizard as a humbug also runs afoul of an important stricture about magic laid down in J.R.R. Tolkien's famous essay "On Fairy-Stories."[11] One of the defining features of a fairy tale, according to Tolkien, is the presence of "real" magic,

---

[11] *Tree and Leaf* (Houghton Mifflin, 1965). The essay is currently available in J.R.R. Tolkien, *The Tolkien Reader* (Del Rey, 1986). John J. Davenport draws on the themes of Tolkien's essay to probe the religious significance of Tolkien's *The Lord of the Rings* trilogy in "Happy Endings and Religious Hope," in *The Lord of the Ring and Philosophy: One Book to Rule Them All*, edited by Gregory Bassham and Eric Bronson (Open Court, 2003).

which he distinguishes from various counterfeits, such as dreams, illusions and technological marvels. The magic of the fairy tale may serve any number of narrative purposes—"satire, adventure, morality, fantasy"—but it must always remain

> magic of a peculiar mood and power, at the furthest pole from the vulgar devices of the laborious, scientific magician. There is one proviso: if there is any satire present in the tale, one thing must not be made fun of, the magic itself. That must in the story be taken seriously, neither laughed at nor explained away. (p. 10)

Tolkien believed that the magic of fairy tales helps us recover "a freshness of vision" so that things can be seen "freed from the drab blur of triteness or familiarity" that blinds us to their wonder (pp. 57–58). Magic answers to "certain primordial human desires," including the desire "to survey the depths of space and time" and "to hold communion with other living things" (p. 13), giving the realm of fantasy the "arresting strangeness" that accounts for so much of its appeal.

But for magic to arrest us in this way it's imperative not to confuse it with anything as prosaic as exotic scientific technologies or, worse still, carnival tricks of the sort the Wizard uses to manufacture the spectacles Dorothy and her companions witness on their initial visits to his throne room. (As it turns out, one of the more remarkable "spectacles" in the Emerald City is an illusion created by the simple expedient of donning the spectacles given to them by the Guardian of the Gate, which cause a sparkling green glow to appear to emanate from everything in the city. The spectacles of magic are presented as optical illusions that trade on our desire to be dazzled. Baum's debunking of the Wizard's magic and the gentle fun he pokes at those gullible enough to believe in it are both violations of Tolkien's stricture that the magic in a fairy tale is never to be "laughed at nor explained away."

Admittedly, there are many other displays of magic in the Land of Oz that aren't outright chicanery, such as the magical charms employed by the Witches. And, in later installments of the series, even the fraudulent Wizard himself masters some "real" magic, after returning to Oz and becoming an apprentice to Glinda.[12] But even

---

[12] *Dorothy and the Wizard in Oz* (HarperCollins, 1990), first published in 1908.

after the humbug becomes a real Wizard, it's often his skill as an inventor that offers the greatest service to his friends, rather than the little bit of magic at his command. Even in *The Wonderful Wizard of Oz*, most of the "real" magic involves nothing more than manipulating magical equipment—such as the Silver Shoes that take Dorothy home and the Magical Cap that summons the Winged Monkeys—that can be operated like any other technology by anyone who's been properly instructed.

The line separating magic and technology in Oz becomes so blurred that it's not at all clear how to distinguish them. According to Rogers, "Magic in Oz, particularly in the later books, usually operates in accordance with natural (if hidden) laws. Glinda in her laboratory and the Wizard with his bag of tools conduct their business like scientists." One of the characters in the later books remarks, "There's lots of magic in nature . . . is anything more wonderful than to see a flower grow and blossom, or to get light out of the electricity in the air?"[13] Magic in Oz turns out to be just another way to harness the laws of nature, involving nothing otherworldly or divine In short, Baum thoroughly demystifies magic, allowing it to exist in Oz only as a technology or a hoax. Tolkien wouldn't call that magic at all, but then he's pretty "Old World."

Eucatastrophe to the Rescue

Also absent from *The Wonderful Wizard of Oz* is what Tolkien calls the *eucatastrophe*, literally the "good catastrophe," an abrupt and unanticipated "turn" at the climax of the story that resolves the plot in the hero's favor just as events seem to be rushing headlong toward a tragic conclusion. An example of this from Tolkien's own *Lord of the Rings* is when Gollum suddenly appears at the Crack of Doom and, despite his intention to steal the Ring from Frodo, accidentally helps to bring the hobbit's mission to a successful conclusion just as Frodo's will is faltering. Tolkien describes such a *eucatastrophe* as

> a sudden and miraculous grace, never to be counted on to recur. It does not deny the existence of *dyscatastrophe*, of sorrow and failure: the possibility of these is necessary to the joy of deliverance; it denies (in the face of much evidence, if you will) universal final defeat, and

---

[13] *L. Frank Baum*, p. 52.

in so far is *evangelion*, giving a fleeting glimpse of Joy, Joy beyond the walls of the world, poignant as grief. (p. 68)

The movie version of *The Wizard of Oz* resolves the quest to destroy the Witch and retrieve her broom through such a *eucatastrophe*, when, as we discussed earlier, Dorothy douses and destroys the Witch accidentally, while trying to extinguish the fire on the Scarecrow's arm.

Apart from the *eucatastrophe*, Tolkien thinks the world of the fairytale is largely a tragic affair. Heroes are unevenly matched against the malevolent forces they battle, virtue doesn't automatically prevail, and sometimes just remaining virtuous can be a daunting challenge. The *eucatastrophe* signifies that while the triumph over evil may demand costly sacrifices of us, our own efforts may still require a supernatural supplement given the magnitude of the evil we must fight. This supplement can perhaps be viewed as the fairy tale equivalent of the supernatural God that Kant believes we're entitled to posit as the guarantor of a happy ending—virtue crowned with happiness—that neither our own efforts nor natural causality can be counted on to produce. Like that God, the *eucatastrophe* compensates for our moral failings and the cruel vicissitudes of fortune through a miraculous stroke of luck that we could never engineer on our own. Hinting at what Davenport calls "an eternal source of hope beyond darkness and despair," it awakens feelings of joy—hence the elation we feel when in the movie fate steps in to save Dorothy and her companions. But that joy is inseparable from our acute awareness of the terrible power of those "heartaches and nightmares" from which they've been miraculously saved.

Let's remember that Baum said he wanted to retain the "wonderment and joy" in his modernized fairy tale. As readers of *The Wonderful Wizard of Oz*, is our joy diminished by the fact that its evil is so small and its "heartaches and nightmares" can be defeated without any eucatastrophic intercession? If so, do we gain anything in return? Explaining that Baum's intention was to write stories that would "develop the best side of child nature," Rogers contends that his "fantasy of an idealized world reassures children that they can solve puzzles and overcome difficulties" (pp. 92–93). This undoubtedly valuable lesson is precisely the opposite of what Tolkien believed fairy tales had to teach us. But it's well to remember that Tolkien was in the trenches in the First World War, and Baum most definitely was *not*. This sort of experience can re-orient a person's expectations and cast a pall over one's optimism about technology.

While Tolkien may have wanted to nourish our hope that a power greater than us can defeat the evils against which we feel helpless, Baum preferred to defeat that sense of helplessness with good old fashioned elbow grease. At the end of the day, we might doubt whether the sort of optimism Baum sought to inspire in his young readers, based on the conviction that evil is no match for what's best in us, is all that realistic. Place these young people at the Battle of the Somme and all their courage, compassion, and brains might not be enough. Ironically, the old-fashioned fairy tale in which eucatastrophic magic saves the day may actually turn out to be more realistic than Baum's "modernized fairy tale," inasmuch as it admits our all-too-human frailty and fallibility in the face of evil.

Roll Credits

As we noted at the outset, the 1939 movie version of *The Wizard of Oz* doesn't stay faithful to Baum's philosophy of fairy tales, choosing instead to spice things up with a heaping helping of those "heartaches and nightmares" that he wanted to purge from children's literature. In the process, the movie-makers produced a story much closer in spirit to Chesterton and Tolkien, replete with conditional joy, "real" magic, and a eucatastrophic ending. This imparts a certain irony to the words that appear in the opening credits of the movie:

> For nearly forty years this story has given faithful service to the Young in Heart; and Time has been powerless to put its kindly philosophy out of fashion.

Whether or not Baum's philosophy is immune to shifts of fashion, that's definitely not *his* "timeless" philosophy being dramatized up on the screen.

11

The Possible World of Oz

RANDALL E. AUXIER

Oz has sparked our imaginations. Why? What is it about the Land of Oz that won't leave us alone?

I don't think there's any single answer to such a question, but we can still have some fun thinking about Oz if we just ease on down a Yellow Brick Road of the mind, and perhaps we will stumble across ideas about Oz (and other imaginary lands) that may fan a spark into a flame ("How about a little fire, Scarecrow . . .").

In *Wicked: The Life and Times of the Wicked Witch of the West*, Gregory Maguire made Oz grow into a place as detailed and interesting as Middle Earth or Narnia. This was an ambitious thing to attempt. Since we loved Oz already, we would hold to a very high standard any author so audacious as to infiltrate our settled and beloved images and memories saying, "I have a better idea . . . no, really, hear me out." The new story must not only *match* our imaginative expectations, but *exceed* them. We have to see unexpected creative twists that delight us, and we enjoy them because we somehow know the twists were there all along, *as possibilities*, at the vague edges of our consciousness, but we hadn't quite noticed them. But if a writer or a filmmaker introduces ideas or characters that feel arbitrary or out of place, well, we just return to our own private pictures of Oz and ignore the new ones.

Such was the fate of the earlier movie versions of *The Wizard of Oz*, with scripts departing so much from the basic idea of the book, and following other quirky narrative agendas, as to make them barely recognizable as versions of the original stories. Our grandparents and great grandparents received those early movies with approval, but succeeding generations do so with a collective

yawn or a puzzled countenance. Success in capturing an established audience is not even under the control of the original creator. The 1910 film version of *The Wizard of Oz* was done
collaboratively with L. Frank Baum, and based on the script of the
stage play he had written himself. The play had been successful,
but why it succeeded is a little hard to grasp at this historical distance. I mean, for heaven's sake Baum substituted a *cow* for Toto
in the play and the 1910 film. Yes, a *cow*. I think it was the same
cow that flew by Dorothy's window in 1939. I'm sorry but that's just
a bad idea. We all eventually opted for the annoying little dog, no
matter what Salman Rushdie thinks about Toto.

Everyone's a Critic

So adapting and rewriting and elaborating upon a story like *Oz* is
sort of like making a new recording of a Beatles song. One either
has to do it exactly like the Beatles, in which case we don't need
or want the new recording, or one must introduce some new ideas
that dazzle us because we would never have quite imagined them
clearly on our own. For example, you could make "I Wanna Hold
Your Hand" into a lament, as the creators did in the film "Across
the Universe." Nice idea. I hadn't noticed that the lament was
buried in the song, but then, there it was, no doubt about it.
Similarly, the stage and movie adaptations of *Oz* in "The Wiz"
worked well because, surprisingly, Dorothy really *can* be a kindergarten teacher from Harlem, and it isn't too great a stretch to see
New York City as Oz. And the music is a *tour de force* of Broadway
meets Motown pop, which we also love. That sort of artistic insight
and re-interpretation is very difficult to do, or at least to do *well*.
The latent imaginings of an entire culture are hard to perceive and
still more troublesome to express. But we all have *opinions* about
people who try such adaptations, and we judge their accomplishments or failures pretty sharply.

We express these opinions in what philosophers like to call
"normative judgments," which are statements both about (1) how
things *can* be done (that is, what is genuinely possible to enact),
and (2) how they *ought* to be done (which, among the genuine
possibilities available for action, are better, or which is the very
best, and how do we show what is better or best?). For the last two
hundred years or so, the way many philosophers have expressed
this point about what we *can* do and what we *should* do is with

the catch-phrase "Ought implies can." This bit of philosophical short-hand means that *before* you insist that anyone ought to do something, you must be reasonably confident that the deed is genuinely possible for that individual; and secondly, just because she *can* do something does not, by itself, mean she *ought* to. It only means that if she *can't* do something, it is meaningless to say she *ought* to. You wouldn't want to be told, by someone who is serious about it, that you really *should* try to be a few years younger than you are, or that you *should* sprout wings and fly to Omaha.

Ding Dong!

So, to take a mildly troubling example—and I'm sure you have been troubled by this along the way—the (allegedly "Wonderful") Wizard insists in about every version of the story that the Companions have to kill the Wicked Witch of the West (fondly, we'll call her WWW), as a barter for having their deepest wishes granted. A little reflection on what the Wizard is doing can be disturbing, morally speaking. He's holding a little girl hostage to the demand that she commit murder.

Dorothy's protests against this barter involve mainly ambiguous uses of the word "can" and "can't" because this is a nice way to melt together the conditions of action (what we *can* do) with their moral implications (what, among the choices, we *should* do). If someone says "You must kill the witch," and I respond that "I *can't,*" I may mean that the deed is impossible, or I may mean that even if it is physically possible, it is morally impossible for me; that is, what I really mean is "I absolutely won't do it, never mind why."

As we all know, Dorothy sort of won't and sort of will kill the witch, if she can figure out *how* and can be satisfied as to *why* it is justified, or if she can just bumble her way into the right sort of accident. Baum and his successors establish that it is *possible* to kill a witch, since the first event that happens when Dorothy arrives in Oz is that she manages to snuff out the Wicked Witch of the East. So Witches *can* be killed, and apparently, they can be killed *by* Dorothy. Further, since the WWW is the sister of the witch Dorothy already killed, we can suppose that the two witches are made of similar stuff, and even if no one *else* in Oz can off a witch, including the Wizard himself, it seems to be in Dorothy's power to do so.

So it's at least probable that the WWW *can* be killed, and that Dorothy *can* do it. But of course, we don't know for certain. The "falling house strategy" worked once, but a repeat performance would be difficult to contrive—perhaps impossible, or so very improbable as to relieve Dorothy of any obligation even to try. But when we ponder the *how*, and the question of whether Dorothy really *can* kill the WWW, we tend to lose sight of the other part of the question. It's true that ought implies can, but it is difficult to convince anyone that *can* implies *ought*. If we really *ought* to do everything we genuinely *can* do, then we will all be very busy doing good 24/7 (or at least 16/7, when we're awake, but then, maybe we ought to sleep less so we can do more good). Anyway, none of us fares very well in the world of moral accomplishments if we really ought to do everything good that we can do. Even Gandhi and Mother Theresa would be slackers by that standard. And certainly there are plenty of things we *can* do that we ought not. For example, if you happen to be a Wizard, you ought not send little girls off to kill people, and you ought not lie about whether you have the power to grant wishes, even though you *can*.

The point is that most philosophers these days like to make a pretty clear separation between discussions about what *can* be done, the genuine possibilities for individual and collective action, both bad and good, on one side, and what *ought* to be done, the field of ethics and values, on the other side. The two sorts of discussions are really very different. I want to set aside (for now), the issue of whether Dorothy *ought* to kill the Wicked Witch of the West, and whether the Wizard is a moral monster for demanding such a trade, and whether Dorothy does anything wrong in carrying out the demand, or even in *setting out* to do the deed (I mean, what are her intentions, and she seems to have a choice, after all, which is to remain in Oz).

Right now I want to talk about the *can* side of the matter. This discussion of *possibility*, of what *can* be done and what *can* happen, is what philosophers classify as matters of "metaphysics" and of "logic." We use logic because want to organize what we know about possibilities, and about the order of the universe, so as to know what *can* be done, in principle, and only then do we have the needed information to ask which, among the genuine possibilities, we *ought* to do, and why. So when we say that "ought implies can," we are also saying that ethics depends in part on metaphysics and logic.

A Haunted Forest

Metaphysics and logic suck. What I mean is that learning how to do them sucks, and then even if you are very smart, very disciplined, and you spent (wasted?) half a lifetime learning how to do them well, chances are fairly high that you will still suck at it, because it is all so very abstract, vague, and difficult. Some of the best philosophers in history still made huge mistakes in metaphysics and logic. Granted, a few philosophers who did a pretty good job, such as Plato and Aristotle and Immanuel Kant, do still have folds of enthusiastic followers bleating their pet doctrines like a bunch of sheep. Let them shear one another; it *all* looks pretty pathetic to me, and I certainly have little prospect of doing half as well as Kant or Plato did.

One of my favorite philosophers, Charles Sanders Peirce (1839–1914) once described the whole history of metaphysics as "rickety, puny and scrufulous." Ha. Scrufulous. Like Toto. Metaphysics and logic may just be too difficult for human thinking at this stage of our cosmic evolution. So we have lame metaphysics and questionable logic flying around like so many snow monkeys. It's hard to avoid the feeling that it is pointless to learn them at all. So, many (perhaps most) professional philosophers learn only as much metaphysics and logic as they must (for their other purposes), and leave the rest alone.

Now, the flying monkeys always frightened me as a kid, far more than the witch, and I think I know why. I felt that I understood the witch and knew what she would do, but the monkeys might do anything at all.[1] I couldn't know. Spooky, eh? Like metaphysics and logic. (Not to mention that scene where for all the world the flying monkeys filling the sky look like the pictures of the Luftwaffe over London in ominous clouds, dropping death and fire, and us without any way of knowing exactly where the bombs will fall.) Dwelling in the unknown is difficult to bear, portentous, and worrisome, whether it's monkeys or Messerschmitts or metaphysics. A person could go a bit crackers pondering such questions as, "Can God create a rock so heavy that He can't lift it?" Or, "why doesn't Glinda just *tell* Dorothy from the first how to dance the Kansas Soft-shoe, and save us all a lot of hassle?" (I mean, Judy

---

[1] For ever so much more on flying monkeys, see Chapter 13 in this volume.

Garland could dance, right?) Labor as we might to sort out the possibilities, we'll still never know the answers. But metaphysics is also
sort of like music—people just do it anyway, especially when
they're lost in a haunted forest. It's a part of being human to ponder and fret, but it doesn't have to be so very depressing. It can be
funny too.

Dweebs, Nerds, Dorks, and Geeks

Philosophers in general are a pretty geeky lot. Attend a meeting
of philosophers and you may sigh, and think to yourself, "So
many people, so *few* social skills." But just as in the domain of,
say, Trekkies, or *Dungeons and Dragons* enthusiasts, there are
geeks and then there are *geeks*. The dweebiest, nerdiest, dorkiest
geeks of philosophy (let's call them "Geeks" for short), when they
aren't surfing the internet for formulas, spend their days and
nights trying to achieve Level 42 in the video game of "Being and
Thinking."[2]

Okay, it isn't actually a video game, but it might as well be a
game on the video-screen of the mind, which we call the imagination. And Geeks sort of like *not* knowing what comes next; that is,
they don't mind flying monkeys (or at least they don't *admit* to
being afraid of them). Instead, they work very hard at . . . well . .
. not much, and for their trouble they achieve slumped shoulders,
flabby bodies, carpal tunnel, poor eyesight, and no life.

I won't ask you to play Being and Thinking, I'll just describe
some of the typical features of the game. And there are lots of different ways to play at B&T, but it comes down to about three main
options, depending on what the Geek decides is the nature of *possibility*. Some Geeks think possibility is *greater* (bigger, broader,
includes more stuff) than actuality (what really happens). These
Geeks say that some things are genuinely possible, but never actually happen. So possibilities are real, and they still exist, even
when they don't actually happen. I'm that sort of Geek, I'm afraid.
Geeks-such-as-I go under a number of names: process philosophers, relationalists, possibilists, temporalists, and the like. Some
like me are even called "libertarians," not because of our political
views, but because such Geeks generally defend the idea that real

---

[2] See Douglas Adams's *Hitch-hiker's Guide to the Galaxy* for an explanation of
why the game stops at Level 42.

freedom exists *because* there are *more* genuine possibilities available to us than we can ever act on, and that's what *gives* us a choice about what to do. Probably the most famous Geek of this sort was a guy named Alfred North Whitehead (1862–1947). He was one of the first among the temporalist Geeks to achieve Level 42 in B&T. He wrote a book called *Process and Reality* that is sort of like the *Dungeon Master's Manual* for temporalist B&T. Very geeky. I love it.

Other prominent Geeks think that whatever actually *is* exhausts *all* the genuine possibilities. So they think nothing is genuinely possible except what actually happens, and the rest is illusion, or error, or doesn't really exist. These Geeks have a number of names too: determinists, eternalists, necessitarians, Platonists, Spinozists, Hegelians, and suchlike (they don't all get on with each other very well either). A historian named Arthur O. Lovejoy (1873–1962) did a whole history of these Geeks from Plato to the present (well, until 1962, when Lovejoy disappeared in a balloon headed for somewhere else). His book was called *The Great Chain of Being*. It's boring, but there are several Level 42 players discussed in it, so you might want to give it a glance. I think of it as *The Monster Manual* of B&T (since Lovejoy was a temporalist and was critical of all the characters in his book).

A New Kind of Geek?

For a long time, people thought these were the only two options for serious B&T, and maybe there *are* only two. But in the twentieth century, a guy came along and pointed out what seemed to be a third option. He was a Geek named David Kellogg Lewis (1941–2001). If you want to *see* a Geek, just check out his picture on Wikipedia (and then try to tell me he doesn't look like the Wizard of Oz). His idea had been suggested before by any number of geeks, but no one had ever taken it seriously until Lewis defended it (basically because Lewis got at least to Level 36 in B&T, which isn't half bad). He wasn't Whitehead or Spinoza, but no one had ever even cracked Level 10 on this version of the game before. What's the idea? Well, brace yourself. This is going to sound silly. Lewis said that possibility is indeed the biggest idea, but *every* possibility *is* actual, in its own separate world. In short, every genuinely possible world *actually exists*, infinitely many such worlds, and they are all "causally independent" of one another.

In case you're not quite getting the gist of this yet, let me provide an example. I first saw *The Wizard of Oz* when I was eight years old, and it was a Sunday evening in October (they would air the movie every year close to Halloween). I don't remember what television network it was on, but let's say CBS. Now, I think we would all agree that it *might have been* (in those halcyon days when we had *three* networks) on NBC instead. This was a "genuine possibility," if certain negotiations and bids had gone differently. Lewis is saying, well, Oz actually *was* on NBC, but in a *different* possible world than ours, and that other world *actually* exists. But that other world has no effect on our world.

But he doesn't stop there. There is also a possible world in which Oz was on CBS, but my TV was broken, so I didn't see it. And that world exists too. And there was a possible world in which it was on CBS but I watched Lassie instead, and yet another world in which it was on CBS, and I watched it, but the flying monkeys didn't scare me . . . and so on, to infinity. All of it really happened. Lewis is serious about this. Think of a possibility. If it's genuinely possible, then it's just as real as anything you've ever actually experienced. In short, this means that David Lewis believes that even Oz is a real place. Or at least, he would be willing to believe it if we can show that it is genuinely *possible*. Believe it or not, Lewis wasn't crazy (in this world at least). Everyone says he was as gentle as Professor Marvel, and much nicer than the Crowned Heads of Europe.

Oh, the Possibilities!

Well, how do we show that anything is genuinely possible? How can we show that Oz is a genuine possibility? I'm not sure that I could have done it, but I think maybe Gregory Maguire managed to in *Wicked*. Check out this snippet of dialogue below, and then I will tell you what David Lewis might say about it (in the possible world in which he isn't dead yet). Elphaba, the Wicked Witch of the West, is having a discussion with Sarima, who is the Dowager Princess of the Arjikis, about a book discovered in the library of Kiamo Ko (the place that will eventually become the castle of the WWW). Sarima tells of a strange old man who visited the castle and left the odd book. Sarima says::

> "He told me a fabulous tale and persuaded me to take this thing from him. He said that it was a book of knowledge, and that it belonged in another world . . ."

"What a load of tripe," said Elphie. "If it came from another world I shouldn't be able to read any of it. And I can make out a little." . . .

"But you know, I believed him," [Sarima said]. "He said there is more congress between worlds than anyone would credit, that our world has attributes of his, and his of ours, a kind of leakage effect, or an infection maybe." . . . "He said [the book] was too powerful to be destroyed, but too threatening—to that other place—to be preserved. So he made a magic trip or something and came here." . . .

"Can you really say you thought the man who brought this here was a sorcerer?" said Elphie. "And that this book comes from another world? Do you even believe in other worlds?"

"I find it a great effort to believe in this one," said Sarima, "yet it seems to be here, so why should I trust my skepticism about other worlds?"[3]

One suspects Maguire of being a closet Geek. This is a clever argument, about a Level 20 argument in B&T. He doesn't follow David Lewis exactly, since he suggests that, as a genuine possibility, *travel* from one possible world to another can occur, which means that things in one possible world *can* cause things in another. Lewis argues vehemently against this, and does so effectively. But the last statement made by Sarima is a sucker punch to both of the other kinds of Geeks (and all people who don't believe other possible worlds are real). Sarima is saying that if you can find a way to believe that *any* world is actual, then you have *already* mistrusted your skepticism about *one* world. Having reined in your skepticism *once*, and being satisfied that you should not give in to it in this one instance, regarding *this* world (with all its errors and illusions and unknowns), what would justify you in *trusting* your skepticism when it comes to other worlds? I mean, be consistent, unless you don't have a brain or something, she is saying. Why not trust your imagination instead, or as in Lewis's case, why not trust logic? Lewis is able to show pretty clearly that the most important characteristics of "possibility" are the *logical* aspects. He was motivated by a simple little logical puzzle that you should consider. I will adapt it to our topic.

---

[3] Gregory Maguire, *Wicked: The Life and Times of the Wicked Witch of the West* (HarperCollins, 1995), pp. 266–67.

You Can't Get There from Here

Here is a sentence: "If everything else was the same, but my TV was on a different channel that Sunday long ago, I would have watched something other than 'The Wizard of Oz.'" We want to say that this statement is *true*. But what *makes* it true? I mean, it didn't *happen*, right? We're saying it was *possible* for me to watch another channel, and that option carries certain consequences, one of which is that I would have seen a different show. But I didn't do it. I watched CBS. So where is the proof that it was genuinely possible for me to have watched something else on another channel? And what makes it necessary that *if* I had watched another channel, I'd have seen a different show? This kind of sentence has a fancy name. It's called a "counter-factual." That's just making a statement about something that might have happened but didn't, so it's counter to the facts.

Some statements contrary to fact seem *true*, like the one I gave above, while others seem *false*. For example, this is a counter-factual we probably want to call false: "If I had watched a different channel that night, the Witch wouldn't have died in the story." But we want to say, "that's not right, she'd have died anyway." So surely there is some sort of difference between the two counter-factual sentences, since one feels true and the other feels false –and we are pretty sure about it, even though none of it ever happened. Why do we feel in our bones that the first one is true and the second one is false when we can't really prove either one, or how do we know that they are even *different*? Lewis is saying that we should believe in other possible worlds so that we have a basis for determining which counter-factuals are true and which are false. And he says that there is *some* possible world in which almost every sentence is true. For instance, the sentence I said "felt false," about the witch not dying, *could* be true in the possible world in which stories change depending on who is watching them on TV. That's pretty different from our world, and would require some interesting advances in technology, but it isn't *impossible*.

So what *is* possible? In fact, whatever isn't a flat contradiction is *logically* possible, and that's what Lewis means. The other worlds are connected to our world not by physical causes and effects, but by obeying the same *logical* laws. The logical laws have to be operating before we can even make sense of causes and effects. So, to *doubt* the reality of what is logically possible actually requires *more* effort and a *greater* leap of faith than simply to *believe* in the reality of the possible world in which any statement is true. Just avoid flat contradictions and save yourself all the effort of trusting your own skepticism. I mean, you are sitting here thinking of Oz, and you aren't continually vexed by contradictions, only intrigued by the differences and similarities with Kansas. So why waste time and effort investing your trust in a skepticism that has been unreliable in the past? Indulge. Oz really and actually exists. You just can't quite get there from here.

The Tik-Tok Diagram

So we want to know what's true and what's false, and we also want to know what is possible and what's really impossible. So why not put these ideas together and create a kind of logic that tells us what we want to know? Logicians did this. Actually, it was another guy named "Lewis" who invented it, Clarence Irving Lewis (1883–1964), no relation to David (except a logical one). I'll shorten the story because it's boring. They say that things we can *really* know *are* true would *be* true in *every possible world*, while the rest of our sentences are just true in *some* possible worlds, or in at least one. But if the other possible worlds don't really exist, then there is nothing that *makes* counter-factuals true in *this* world. And also, more importantly, we couldn't tell the difference between what just *happens* to be true in this world, and what *must* be true in any and every genuinely possible world.

David Lewis wants to be able to tell the difference between events that might not have happened (contingent events) and events that couldn't possibly be otherwise (necessary events). If you can't tell the difference, then the only way to go is to say all events are contingent, as far as we can know; or you can say all events are necessary and couldn't have been otherwise. In the first case, the process Geeks like me win the argument, since they say you really can't tell the difference between contingent and necessary events, but freedom is real. In the second case, the determinist Geeks win, since they say that everything real had to happen just as it did. Neither group believes in possible worlds.

Lewis says, in effect, that if you don't believe in Oz, you can't tell whether you just happened to skip breakfast this morning, or whether you had no choice about it. But for him it's not about winning the argument between the two sets of Geeks, the problem is that currently there is no way to settle the argument at all, or even to have a very good discussion about it. So, Lewis thinks, it may be helpful to believe in Oz –but he doesn't say he believes in *Oz*, specifically, just that all genuinely possible worlds are real. Is Oz a genuinely possible world? It's a pretty weird world to believe in, frankly, although I guess it isn't any stranger than the sorts of heavens and hells that so many people profess to believe in. And David Lewis doesn't shrink from granting that dragons and unicorns exist in some possible world, and that donkeys talk in some worlds, so why not Oz?

Don't Contradict Me!

But here we hit upon the test for whether Lewis would have to believe that Oz really exists. Does Oz contain a logical impossibility, a flat contradiction? Recalling that, like L. Frank Baum, Gregory Maguire says we can *get to* Oz, that old farmhouse is floating atop some pretty rough air and it will probably land us in an ugly contradiction. We all know what a mess we get into when we try to think through the meaning and implications of time travel (and actually Lewis is willing to allow that time travel is logically possible in a sense, that it isn't a contradictory idea), but it's even worse when we try to work out traveling from one possible world to another. But what if we back down a little bit, for the moment, from Maguire's (and Baum's) claim that Oz is a place you and I can *get to*. What if we just look at the place by itself and ask whether it contradicts itself? If it doesn't, then David Lewis will grant us it is *real*, and I mean just as real as the world we inhabit, and that we should *believe* that.

Searching for contradictions in Oz is going to be tricky, even perilous. Because we aren't looking for things that are improbable, and we aren't quite looking for things we would judge impossible in *our* world. Nor are we looking for characters who happen to say or believe inconsistent things, or who act contrary to habit. Heck, that stuff happens in our own world, and we think this place is real enough. We are looking for things that would be impossible in *any* world. It is hard to find criteria for that, unless we assume that the logic (not the laws of physics, not the habits of action, not the scientifically unquestioned facts, but the *logic*) of every possible world is *the same*. And we also need to know what that logic is and how to work with it.

There is a kind of logic Lewis uses called "quantified modal logic," which is more complicated than almost any Geek can stand or understand. Listening to a discussion of it is almost like a visit to Oz, but a fair analogy is that it's about as interesting as listening to two computer geeks discussing in highly technical terms the flaws of the Microsoft operating system. For those who haven't heard that particular discussion, I'm sure you can invent your own ultra-geeky equivalent from some past experience. Anyway, the point is, we won't go into what quantified modal logic is. You can look it up if you have time to waste.

But here is, in my opinion, the bottom line on it: in all logic (especially quantified modal logic), a contradiction is very difficult to prove beyond all questioning. The reason is simple. All it takes is a tiny, tiny modification of one or the other term in a supposed contradiction, and the contradiction disappears. For example, in Baum's first Oz book, Dorothy's magic slippers are silver. In the 1939 film, they're ruby. The silver slippers didn't work well with the new Technicolor processing, so the filmmakers needed some other idea for the slippers. They made them ruby. Is this a contradiction? Some would say "look, the real shoes are either silver or ruby, but not both." We can avoid that conflict in a bunch of ways, but let me give the sort of thing you'd say if you were Lewis. We can say, "no, the Oz of the first book is one possible world, the one in which Dorothy has silver slippers, and the Oz of the 1939 film is a different possible world, in which she has ruby slippers." You get the game, I'm sure.

If you ask what color the slippers *must* be in all possible worlds, we can squirm out of that by pointing out that questions like the color of slippers are not fully determined by logic alone. In a world in which we suppose that *all* slippers *must be* ruby, logically, it would be a contradiction to say that Dorothy's slippers "are silver" in that world. And so on. But nothing forces us to say that such a world is the only world. There could be worlds with no slippers of any kind. Further, we can do as Maguire did, and make the slippers shine and shimmer in such a way as to look silver sometimes, ruby sometimes, and make it difficult for anyone to say exactly what color they are. There is no flat contradiction here.

So how do we find a flat contradiction in Oz, or anywhere else, for that matter? One needs to say that the slippers both are and are *not* ruby, in exactly the same respect, at exactly the same time, and in exactly the same sense – it is not that Dorothy *sees* them as ruby

and the WWW *sees* them as silver, or some such. No, we are saying that Dorothy sees the shoes, in every possible way, as *both*
ruby and *not* ruby, at the same time and in the same respects. Now,
I have not thought through every single assertion made in every
version of Oz, but I cannot recall either author ever being quite so
precise as to generate a contradiction this strong. Lewis Carroll, on
the other hand, likes to do this sort of thing in Wonderland, so
please don't generalize these conclusions about Oz through the
looking glass or down any rabbit holes.[4] The point is that there
aren't any logical contradictions in Oz that couldn't be removed
with a slight qualification. Bible scholars have, for example, shown
great ingenuity in this regard, in *their* favorite possible world (call
it Holyland). They have even given a name to this art of removing
contradictions: "exegesis." And when the contradictions are moral
in nature, rather than logical, they call the art of reconciling them
"casuistry." Casuistry depends on exegesis just as closely as *ought*
depends on *can*.

Getting to Oz

Have we then bewitched David Lewis and taken his slippers? Is Oz
real, *really* real? There are no contradictions to throw water on us.
Or so it would seem. There is still a problem, one Maguire brings
to our attention in *Wicked*. If you haven't read the book yet, what
comes next is a spoiler, I'm afraid. So be warned, and heed a piece
of advice. Maguire's book is ever so much better if you do not
know where it is going when you read it. Maguire cleverly conceals
the clues about who the witch is and why she is wicked until late
in the story, and he has done the right thing, I believe. I did not
know what was coming when I read it, and I believe I would have
enjoyed the story far less if I had known (this is a *true* counterfac-
tual). I do not want to be responsible for reducing your enjoyment,
if you haven't read it. So do yourself a favor and set this essay

---

[4] Beginning with Baum's second book, *The Marvelous Land of Oz*, in 1904,
Baum starts inserting little comments, bits of dialogue, and scenarios that sound a
lot like Lewis Carroll. There's a scene between the Scarecrow and Jack the
Pumpkinhead in which a translator is summoned because the two don't realize
they speak the same language, even though they have been speaking to each other
already. There are numerous other little things like this after the first book, and I
don't know it for a fact, but I'll bet a ruby slipper that Baum read the *Alice* books
between his first and second Oz books.

(maybe this whole book) aside, now. Resume reading this when you have finished *Wicked.* I have asked the publishers to place a gratuitous page break right at this spot so that your eyes won't wander down to what is below.

Alright, I assume that I now count among my readers only the weak-willed, the lazy, the dangerously curious, other assorted fools, and people who have finished *Wicked*.

It's easy to notice that people *do* travel from our actual world to Oz—in balloons, in cyclones, magically by way of certain shoes, or even by the pure power of belief. The story really depends on it. In *Wicked*, Elphaba, our WWW, is the offspring of the Wizard from Omaha, and a Munchkin from Oz named Melena. Elphie is, without knowing it, a half-breed, half of our world and half of Oz. This is a difficult mode of being, with one foot in either world. Indeed, it may be *im*possible, in the sense of contradictory. She lives nearly her whole life not knowing why she is so misplaced and miserable, and she is not quite able to believe the truth about herself when she finally learns it.

Elphie's situation leads her to suspect that she has no soul, and in a self revealing moment, when pondering what she would ask for from the Wizard if she could have anything at all, she wishes for a soul. Maguire is suggesting, in a literary way, that to have a soul, that is, a strong sense of belonging and self-identity in the world, one needs to belong wholly to one and only one world (although that alone is no guarantee you won't feel like an alien, it's a sure bet that you'll feel like an alien if you try to straddle more than one world).[5]

Anyway, our beloved WWW, being a hybrid, and under the influence of a potion that apparently came from Omaha with the Wizard, has dreams of the other world, *our* world. I have a feeling, from internal clues Maguire provides, that the "potion" is nothing more than sea water, from our world, which is not deadly to Elphaba (see my essay in this volume about why water from Oz melts her). Here is how Maguire describes the scene:

> The Witch had taken the green glass bottle, whose label still read MIR-ACLE ELI-, and placed it on her bedside table. She took a spoonful of the ancient elixir before sleeping, hoping for miracles, seeking some version of the fabulous alibi Dorothy was unwinding, that she had come from someplace other —not the real states across the desert, but

---

[5] You might pick up the Walter Tevis novel *The Man Who Fell to Earth* for a Level 35 exploration of this point, or just rent the spooky 1976 movie of the same title, in which David Bowie proves that he actually *is* an alien, by being so convincingly weird.

a whole separate geophysical existence. Even metaphysical. The Wizard had made such a claim for himself, and if the dwarf [who told Elfie the Wizard was her father] was right, the Witch had this ancestry too. At night she tried to train herself to look on the periphery of her dreams, to note the details. It was a little like trying to see around the edges of a mirror, but, she found, more rewarding. (p. 383)

After drinking the potion, the Witch dreams of our world that night, and it is to her, a nightmare so severe and intense that she vows never to sleep again and sets about creating potions to insure she will stay awake. But in this dream, she sees the Wizard, her father, failing in a suicide attempt. He swims out into the ocean and is spat back up on shore again and again by the tide. Perhaps the Witch has no soul because she fails to belong wholly to any world, and is therefore "no one," a metaphysical wanderer, or perhaps, on the moral side, she thinks she has no soul because her father could not bear his own world and also could not end life, and so ended up a sojourner in a land he could never endure, one called Oz, which was, to him, hell, a punishment for his impiety. Maybe Elphie is trapped in the Wizard's dying vision or dream. In any case, when Dorothy arrives on her appointed mission from the Wizard, Elphie is sleep-deprived, paranoid, and excitable. In the climactic scene, Elphie shrieks at Dorothy "You're my soul come scavenging for me, I can feel it . . . I won't have it. I won't have a soul; with a soul there is everlastingness, and life has tortured me enough" (p. 400).

In his own way, Maguire has posed a problem that Geeks call the problem of "trans-world identity." It is part of a larger geeky problem called the problem of personal identity—what makes us just who we are, and not someone else. In this case, the question is what makes the "me" in some other possible world the same "me" as the one I know in this world? David Lewis doesn't believe in trans-world identities, he believes in what he calls "counterparts." But he does allow that trans-world individuals may exist as "oddities." Is Dorothy Elphaba's "soul"—that is, are they the same person being manifest differently in Oz and in Kansas, but meeting in some larger cosmic "place" that can hold both of them? Lewis doesn't rule it out. But he says, "after all, we're talking about something that doesn't really ever happen to people except in science fiction stories and philosophy examples, so is it really so very bad that peculiar cases have to get described in peculiar ways?" (p. 219).

So, here's the Witch dreaming of our world, and maybe of her odd identity in it, as Dorothy (of all things!—Gregory Maguire's so playfully wicked). Setting aside the literary niceties of this, the point for us is that, just as the Witch is thinking and dreaming of *our* world from a physical existence in Oz (and finding it a "metaphysical" problem), *we* are thinking (or dreaming) of Oz from the confines of Omaha, or Kansas, or in my case at the moment, Texas. And here is the question: How could I ever know that the logic of my thinking here and now is the *same* as the logic of other possible worlds, like Oz? When I make judgments about what *can* be, and later what *ought* to be, in this game of B&T, am I not just exporting the *laws* of Texas, logical, physical, and moral, to *Oz*, and then pretending it doesn't matter?

In fact, the nature of logic itself, and its relation to the world, is something fairly mysterious, as even David Lewis admits. We can't be altogether certain that *our* logic is binding in other worlds. And if our logic isn't binding, then neither are our physical and moral laws. As Lewis puts it, in terms uncannily similar to the report of Sarima I quoted above:

> The other worlds are of a kind with this world of ours. To be sure, there are differences of kind between things that are parts of different worlds –one world has electrons, and another has none, one has spirits and another has none—but these differences of kind are no more than sometimes arise between things that are parts of a single world . . . . Nor would this world differ from the others in its manner of existing. I do not have the slightest idea what a difference in manner of existing is supposed to be. . . .Why believe in a plurality of worlds?—Because the hypothesis is serviceable, and that is a reason to think it is true.[6]

Maybe David Lewis was *the visitor* to Sarima, and maybe the magic book was *On the Plurality of Worlds*, except that Lewis hardly seems to have written something dangerous to anything in this world, except the order of our thinking. Common sense informs us that, for whatever else it may be, logic at least reflects some features of the order of our *thinking*—it may also provide a link to the order of our *world*, or even to the order of *other* worlds, but we don't know that. We just suppose it. All we can be sure about is

---

[6] David Lewis, *On the Plurality of Worlds* (Blackwell, 1986), pp. 2–3.

that logic seems to depict one aspect of human thinking. Further, as some very famous logicians, George Boole and Charles Sanders Peirce, once argued, logic actually doesn't describe the way we usually *do* think, but rather how we *can* think and *ought* to think. That is, logic is a collection of norms for thinking well, a mental hygiene course. Whether logic does any more than that is difficult to prove. In this case, just because we can believe in the reality of other possible worlds, like Oz, does not mean we *should* –not if doing what Lewis recommends screws up our thinking and makes us too geeky to function.

Yet, Lewis and Maguire have complementary views, and I have to admit that it is Maguire who has rescued Lewis, for me at least, since I wasn't taking Lewis seriously before I read *Wicked*. Lewis says that believing in a plurality of worlds is *helpful* –something Maguire also suggests later in the dialogue I quoted. But Maguire also made the stronger point that got my attention, which is that if my *skepticism* should be mistaken once, concerning my very own world, how much less should I give my trust to it when it tries to reach its tentacles into another world? It is true that I can't really think of Oz except from Omaha, or Texas, or wherever I am in this world. But I also can't *doubt* Oz from any more privileged place. Lewis makes the very same case in different language (see pp. 116-117). Well, can you justify *your* skepticism about the reality of Oz? Surely at least it's an open question.

Granted, we can't step out of our actual world and into Oz. We think about Oz, imagine it, even feel it, from our own world. Are we then converted to this odd doctrine of Lewis or Maguire, modal realism? I am not. It looks to me like what Lewis means by saying that Oz (or other worlds) are real, is that we *really* think about them, and that this thinking is susceptible to logical analysis, and that the norms for thinking about it well or poorly are available to us. And *we* are real. I am conceding we *can* do this. I am not conceding that we ought to believe the hypothesis that Oz is real, because it isn't clear to me that such belief has any effect on whether we improve our logic or not. On the other hand, Lewis and Maguire are both saying that to relegate Oz to the dust bin of non-Being is to undermine, in a way, our hold on *our own actual world*, which, as Sarima points out, is hard enough to believe in.

We commonly indulge our little skeptical turn without recognizing that skepticism requires as much or more faith as does belief. Belief is easy, skepticism is a lot of work. At the very least, you *can* hold on to Oz as the actual creation of human imagination and thinking, without contradiction, and you *ought* to respect that this is something real. Baum and Maguire believe in Oz in a way that you probably do not –and that belief may have been the key to inventing Oz. It was a possibility, and they tracked it down and expressed it so well that the rest of us, well, the rest of us wanted to believe them.

Further, you cannot fully explain what you mean when you say "Oz isn't real," and you also cannot prove conclusively, by any logic, that there can't be *more* to Oz than is dreamed of in your philosophies. It might exist in *more* than just our thinking, for all we know. But if you return to the basic options I outlined early on, you will see that this is actually the same view that is taken by those process philosopher Geeks I sympathize with. What is a possibility? At the very least it is something we think of and imagine from our actual standpoint, but it may be more than that, for all we know. You don't need to shock any Geeks with your "modal realism" to say you believe in Oz. Why not just have fun with it. Level 42 in B&T awaits some possible Geek out there.

IV

(Completely)
Over the Rainbow

12

Dude, When Did Pink Floyd Write a Soundtrack for *The Wizard of Oz?*

PHILLIP S. SENG

About eight years ago when I was in graduate school I was at a party (not an uncommon event back then) and at one point in the evening or morning I decided to relax and sit on a sofa. I was facing the TV, and playing on it was *Metropolis*, Fritz Lang's great silent-movie masterpiece from something like 1929. It didn't really matter that it was a silent movie, of course, because I was at a party; and this particular party was hosted by a certain philosophy graduate student who liked music. I mean, he *really* liked music— he had probably well over a thousand CDs on his wall, in cabinets, all over his living room.

Anyway, the point is that there was already music playing (very loudly) so whether the movie had a soundtrack or not was irrelevant to my being able to hear it. In fact, I already knew at the time that the soundtrack put with the VHS (do they still make those?) version of *Metropolis* was pretty shabby (and thankfully when they released it on DVD it was a different orchestral version), so I didn't mind listening to something else. In the spirit of the movie, the host put in some kind of Classical (or Baroque or Romantic—heck, I don't claim to know old stuff) music to accompany the movie. Surprisingly enough, it worked. We watched in fascination as movements in the music corresponded to actions in the movie; rousing speeches gained accompaniment, confrontations were highlighted with staccato beats and sadness was soothed with soft transitions.

At the time I'd only heard of the particular phenomenon of pairing Victor Fleming's *The Wizard of Oz* with Pink Floyd's *Dark Side of the Moon* album, in which synching them up at the beginning in just the right way would result in some surprising conjunctions of

189

the music, lyrics, and movie action. It's known by various names: Dark Side of the Rainbow, The Wizard of Floyd, The Dark Side of Oz, and many others. I hadn't yet tried it out with *The Wizard of Oz*, but I was certainly enjoying the experience with *Metropolis* (did I mention it was a party?).

As a philosopher, or at least a student of philosophy, I naturally wonder how it came about that a chance selection of music could evoke meaningful situations in a movie that was also selected by chance. Fritz Lang certainly didn't intend for that piece of classical music to be paired with his movie—if he had, then wouldn't he have made it the soundtrack for his movie? And the composer of the music could not have predicted that a silent movie many years in the future would synch up so nicely with his score. So, why did they work together as well as they did?

How are we fans of Fleming's *The Wizard of Oz* to make sense of the phenomenon of pairing the Pink Floyd album with Fleming's movie? Are we right to interpret Pink Floyd's musical suggestions as part of Baum's original story or is the experience simply a coincidental novelty? As we'll see, at the root of all these questions is the meaning of the word *meaning*. If we can understand what it is that's going on when we watch a movie, then the novelty created by pairing the movie with a little Pink Floyd will make sense (depending on one's state at the time).

The (106) Hidden Meaning(s) of *Dark Side of the Rainbow* (DSOTR)

The exact date of the origin of the Dark Side of the Rainbow is unknown. It's first mentioned on the World Wide Web in a newsgroup, alt.music.pink-floyd, in 1994, but surely some fan of altered states stumbled over this experience on his way to the remote control before the 1990s. In any event, now there are many, many web sites devoted to explaining and keeping track of the ins and outs of the Dark Side of the Rainbow.[1] The sites offer tutorials on how

---

[1] A couple of the sites I've drawn from for information in this essay are: the Synchronicity Arkive (www.synchronicityarkive.com/) and Dark Side of Oz (www.everwonder.com/david/wizardofoz/). A "definitive" list of moments of conjunction is found at http://members.cox.net/stegokitty/dsotr_pages/dsotr.htm. Doing a simple web search for "dark side of the rainbow" will produce these and many other links to web pages.

best to start the synch (where to begin the album in relation to the movie for the best outcome), provide lists compiled by fellow fans of moments of synchronicity, proffer theories on how it's possible for this phenomenon to work so wondrously and even provide forums for discussion.

As for the theories as to why there are so many synchronous moments with the correct alignment of *The Wizard of Oz* and *Dark Side of the Moon*, these boil down to three (most clearly summed up on one of the web sites listed in the notes): intent, synchronicity, and fluke. I'll take on each of these theories in order.

They Did It on Purpose

The idea of intent, what philosophers call "intention" when speaking about artworks, supposes that the author or creator of a work meant to have the connections and meanings that we find in the work.[2] Now, we can't attribute the intention behind Dark Side of the Rainbow to Victor Fleming or even L. Frank Baum—both of them were deceased by the time Pink Floyd's album was released. They could not have crafted their works to account for the music and lyrics of the album, so intention cannot be attributed to either of them.

The real traction that the idea of intention has for fans of DSOTR is with the band Pink Floyd and its leader at the time, Roger Waters. Fans suspect that either Waters by himself, or the whole band collectively, were fans of Fleming's movie and created songs for the purpose of accompanying the movie as a kind of soundtrack (though just a forty-three minute one). Every single web site that mentions this premise also recounts the repeated denials that band members have made—in public and on record. Bordering on the verge of sounding like conspiracy theorists or *X-Files* fans (if there's a difference) die-hard fans of DSOTR still press that somewhere, deep down inside perhaps, Waters or some of the other band members *must have been* fans of the movie. Well, in the face of absolute denials from Pink Floyd this "theory" of the cause for finding meanings in the combination of two different artworks cannot persist— unless there's something deeper in the connection.

---

[2] A good book providing an overview of several variations of the concept of intention, and rebuttals of it, is Gary Iseminger, ed., *Intention and Interpretation* (Temple University Press, 1992).

It's Synchronicity, Man

"Synchronicity" is a term borrowed from psychologist Carl G. Jung, who's famous for developing the ideas of the collective unconscious and of archetypes recognizable by all participants in the collective. Jung's theory will sound promising, and fulfills all the desperate needs of fans reluctant to give up some notion of design or intention behind the symmetries in DSOTR. But, I think the theory is needlessly complex to answer the questions raised at the beginning of this essay. In a nutshell, Jung supposes that coincidences are not simply purely random occurrences. Events that seem to spring from the same cause and that are meaningful can be attributed to an "acausal" principle of connectivity. That is, there is assumed to exist a principle of connection between two correlated events, but the principle is not open to description in the way we'd normally describe their causes. There's a connection between events deeper than physical causality can explain.

A couple of examples will help understand the idea of synchronicity. Frank Morgan, who played Professor Marvel in *The Wizard of Oz*, received as a part of his wardrobe costume a "tattered" and depreciated, yet "nice-looking," coat which a property assistant had purchased from a second-hand store.[3] One day, when Morgan "turned out the pocket" of the coat the name on the label read "L. Frank Baum." The crew checked on the veracity of the label with Baum's widow and with a tailor in Chicago, and it was indeed Baum's coat, making an appearance on Professor Marvel in *The Wizard of Oz*. Now, that's just weird. It's a pretty amazing coincidence, right? But, can it really be anything more than just a coincidence? Does it mean something greater than just the fact that the original author's coat found a way into the movie? I guess it depends on what you believe as to how far you're willing to take it.

But let's examine another example to gain a better perspective on coincidences. Imagine that there's a very flavorful and filling spread we use to make sandwiches, and also imagine that sometimes in the cold winter months we prepare a hot, sweet drink to warm and soothe our aching backs (after shoveling snow). Now, imagine the spread and the rich, sweet ingredient combined to produce a snack of peanut butter and chocolate. Tasty, right? I don't think we have any problem seeing that the collusion of peanut but-

---

[3] Aljean Harmetz, *The Making of the Wizard of Oz* (New York: Limelight Editions, 1984), pp. 241–42.

ter and chocolate to create a really tasty candy bar is pure coincidence (or brilliant marketing research). However, it's not a spiritual conflagration of some recessed force moving peanut butter and chocolate into sweet, sweet harmony. Of course, foods don't participate in the collective unconscious or recognize the force of archetypes, so Jungians will argue that my counter-example is a bit skewed. But, there's no evidence on either side in the argument about forces beyond our causal explanations, so it's a moot issue in that respect.

Just a Fluke

The final supposition to consider when we watch DSOTR is to simply throw one's hands in the air and exclaim, "You must be joking!" I mean, *so what?* A look at what constitutes some of the magical points of symmetry will reveal the absurdity of the whole phenomenon. I'll list a few examples here:

- **When Dorothy walks along the top of the fence (before falling into the pig pen), the lyrics are, "Balanced on the biggest wave."**

- **Toto wags his tail in time to the clicking sound effect in the song "On the Run."**

- **Almira Gulch points her finger on the bass chord of the song "Time."**

- **The guitar solo in "Time" begins on a scene change.**

- **The drums kick in as a tree is uprooted by force of the wind.**

- **The "cha-ching!" of a cash register at the beginning of the song "Money" is heard as Dorothy steps out into colorful Munchkin Land. Money would be associated with color and better living, as is apparent from Dorothy's reaction.**

- **From the song "Us and Them," the lyrics, "Up and Down": On "up" the Wicked Witch of the West is holding her broomstick upright, and on "down" she lowers it.[4]**

---

[4] Examples adapted from "The Definitive List:" http://members.cox.net/stegokitty/dsotr_pages/printable.htm.

Now, when you watch the movie while listening to the album you can't help noticing some of these instances where things match up. But the extended analysis and interpretation required to make some of these points substantial enough to consider is impressive to say the least. And here's the kicker: *not everyone will see the same points of symmetry.* In preparing to write this chapter I sat through the movie again, with my Pink Floyd in the stereo (took me back a few years, to tell you the truth). I had my laptop opened up to a list of all the things I was supposed to be catching, and I must've missed forty percent of them because they were so insignificant. I even caught one that wasn't listed: When the lyrics sing out, "Forward, they cried, from the rear and the front ranks died," the group pushes Lion forward, and he faints and falls to the ground. Pretty amazing, huh? Maybe Fleming was in touch with the complaint of foot-soldiers everywhere who are sent to become cannon-fodder. More likely, it was the happenstance of my timing in pausing and un-pausing the CD player while the movie began, and then doing it again after the CD finished the first time so as to keep the soundtrack playing.

Oh yeah, did I forget to mention this little detail? *The Dark Side of the Moon* is only about forty-three minutes long, but the movie is about two hours long. Perhaps Pink Floyd also planned it out that their album would have to be played two-and-one-half times to conclude the movie? That would've been very convenient back in the day without CDs or DVDs or even VHS tapes. I think we can agree with the final theory which claims, "You must be joking!" It's a fluke.

But not so fast. All those points of symmetry and interpretations about the interconnected meanings behind the rhythms, lyrics and movie action—they aren't *nothing.* They exist, and people—real people—actually spend their time taking notice of them and find meaning in them. So, while I don't think we can buy into any of the above theories to explain the grand convergence of movie and music, I also don't want to suggest that these experiences don't happen. They are real, and for those who find meaning in them, they *do* have meaning.

Making Meaning: Fleming, Floyd and You

One web site's creator, in response to the implausibility of the above theories, suggests that the occurrence of symmetries is evidence of "relativity of human perception. We all see the world differently, we all create our reality within our minds. And our individual reality does not always match the people around us."[5] This statement is characteristic of the widespread relativism in our culture, and it must be tempered. And, even more egregiously, it's flat out wrong. It's a little bit correct, too, but let's excise the incorrectness first.

Reality is not created by our minds. If that were the case then the explanation for any and all symmetries would be easy and clear: we create them ourselves with our own minds. Furthermore, one would simply have to make a persuasive case for the symmetries and then no one would disagree about their significance. And yet there's widespread disagreement, even lack of concern, about the phenomenon of DSOTR. Just glance back at some of the points of congruence mentioned . . . Do they convince you? While it's true that *in my mind* when I hit "Play" on the DVD remote I expect to see *The Wizard of Oz,* my believing or thinking that fact *in my mind* does not make the circuitry operate. Nor does it establish that the DVD in the DVD deck is in fact *The Wizard of Oz.* There is a physical reality that cares not one bit for what I think about it (or anyone else, for that matter). Need we look any further than the cyclone and its impact on Dorothy's family? The material world exists, and we can think about it, shape it, and act to bend it to our benefit, but we can't make it any more or less real just by thinking.

So, what's right about the above statement? We do, in some ways, see the world differently. But, and this is important to keep in mind, we also see the world in similar ways most of the time. Thank goodness, too. If we didn't agree on a large majority of our perceptions, then communication—and, therefore, the sharing of meanings—would be impossible. And meaning is precisely what we need to be concerned with here. What viewers of DSOTR latch onto are new meanings created by the mingling of Fleming's and Floyd's artworks; the new meanings aren't simply the result of adding meaning A with meaning B, resulting in meaning C. Rather, the new meanings are the result of viewers perceiving something from the movie and something from the music *in their own way.* It's a combination of three factors, not just two. Now, some of you will be wondering: How is this different from saying it's all in the mind?

---

[5] www.synchronicityarkive.com/node/18.

Well, it's different because our present minds don't entirely control the way we interpret many of the things we encounter in our daily lives, at least not consciously. Many of our perceptions occur as the result of habits we've developed during the course of our lives.

The Wicked Witch's "Time"

Let me return to some of the items on the list of symmetries mentioned above. When Miss Gulch wags her finger at the same time a deep, strong bass chord from the song "Time" reverberates from the speakers, a viewer can certainly perceive the combination as a point of symmetry. Why does that action "fit" with that sound? Miss Gulch's accusatory stance is very threatening, and her hunched-over posture makes her all the more threatening. We—most people who've had a fair amount of experience watching movies or TV—tend to associate Miss Gulch's characteristics with threats, with fear. Also, most people viewing DSOTR are already familiar with the basic story, so they know Miss Gulch is an avatar for the wicked witch. Furthermore, it is our common expectation that ominous or threatening soundtracks to movies are deep, loud and in the lower octaves. For example, consider the fear-inducing, two-note leitmotif in *Jaws* (Steven Spielberg, 1975), or the thunderous footsteps of dinosaurs in *Jurassic Park* (Steven Spielberg, 1993).

It's no accident that I've used Spielberg's movies as examples of soundtrack effects on audiences. The composer for both of these movies and many, many others was John Williams. Williams understands and has been awarded for his skill in composing scores to accent and evoke emotional responses to the actions we see on the silver screen.[6] So, the deep, thick bass chord helps us feel the doom Miss Gulch intends for Dorothy and Toto. We don't get this meaning as the result of some overt communication or written sign that tells us, "Loud bass sounds are evil portents, and those actions that synch with them are likewise evil and ominous." Instead, we've come by dint of habit to accept this relationship as a fact, as one of the many possible meanings loud, deep sounds can convey. It's as much *us*, our habits and expectations, as it is the music or the film.

---

[6] Williams has won five Academy Awards and been nominated thirty times for Best Original Score (by my count) according to the Internet Movie Database: http://www.imdb.com/name/nm0002354/awards.

Money, It's a Hit

As another case study let's examine the point of symmetry that seemed to be a bit of an interpretive stretch: the "Cha-ching" of the cash register that marks the beginning of the Pink Floyd song "Money" which happens (for some viewers) to correspond with Dorothy's opening of the door onto a world of color. When I watched the DSOTR I didn't have this exact alignment, but it was close enough that I could understand what the viewers mean. The person who posted this item of symmetry went the further step of explaining what the symmetry means (to him or her). Money means a better standard of living (if I may elaborate a bit on the terse explanation above), and better living cannot occur in the same old sepia-toned black and white cinematography. Thus, color cinematography begins with the appearance of money and higher standards of living. The song "Money," then, is an excellent transition from the gray and plain (or plane) Kansas and the bright and wonderful land of Oz. Everyone, I think, can understand this interpretation. But, does everyone get it when they view DSOTR (without the list in front of them)? Maybe not.

This viewer or viewers see in money and wealth something colorful that isn't necessarily there when others think about money. Simply because of the timing of the song and the movie the interpretation is pushed in this direction. But even with the coincidence of timing, is this interpretation the only one available to us? Not at all. In fact, money is the cost of doing business, and what Dorothy has to do in Oz is suffer the consequences of her childish naïveté. She has to grow up, and the cost is her innocence. In other words, I've just provided an alternate explanation for the exact same coincidence of movie and music, a different meaning that is every bit as plausible as the one in the "definitive list."

This plurality of meanings is one of the reasons why communication is so difficult and also so rewarding for humans. Communication depends on commonly shared meanings of the terms (words, images, sounds) by which we communicate. Were the case any different we'd spend much more time clarifying what our parents, spouses, siblings or students intended us to understand. We do so much of this common clarification work by habit that it seems like we have very little in common with each other. The opposite is the case. We share so many meanings that when someone points a finger, or when we hear a cash register ring up a total, we have many possible ways of understanding these visual or audio cues. On the basis of shared habitual meaning, we can go any number of directions. Some take the cash register and Technicolor Oz to indicate prosperity, others to foreshadow sacrifice.

Come Together, Right Now, Over Me

Now, weave together all that's involved in experiencing the Dark Side of the Rainbow. We have Fleming's *The Wizard of Oz* and all of the possible meanings from the images of the movie (without the soundtrack, of course). Second, we have Pink Floyd's album *The Dark Side of the Moon* and all of the meanings possible for each of the crescendos, lyrics, guitar riffs, percussion beats, and so on. But that's not all that's involved in this equation. *You*, the viewer, are also in the experience. *You* are experiencing it. Each one of us has a certain kind of experience with movies, with seeing images and making sense of them in a particular way. Philosopher and literary theorist Louise Rosenblatt describes how a reader interacts with a book (substitute "movie" for "text" and you get the picture):

> The reader's attention to the text activates certain elements in his past experience—external reference, internal response—that have become linked with the verbal symbols. Meaning will emerge from a network of relationships among the things symbolized *as he senses them*. The symbols point to these sensations, images, objects, ideas, relationships, with the particular, associations or feeling-tones created by his past experiences with them in actual life or in literature. The selection and organization of responses to some degree hinge on the assumptions, the expectations, or sense of possible structures, that he brings out of the stream of life. Thus built into the raw material of the literary process itself is the particular world of the reader.[7]

Perhaps one viewer has seen not only Fleming's movie but all of the various adaptations of Baum's novels, and also the Broadway show *Wicked*. This viewer will bring a wider field of meanings to bear on the conjunction of movie and album than a viewer who has yet to see even Fleming's movie once. Also, consider the importance of having experience with classic rock of the late 1960s

---

[7] Louise Rosenblatt, *The Reader, the Text, the Poem: The Transactional Theory of the Literary Work* (Southern Illinois University Press, 1978).

and early 1970s, or more particularly with the music of Pink Floyd. If we were to ask someone who only listens to Gregorian chants on CD to see DSOTR there would probably be a wide divergence from the "definitive list" of symmetries. I think it is now clear how the experience of DSOTR is not evidence of the "relativity of human perception" as the web site quoted earlier suggests. But, it's also not evidence of the objectivity of human perception either. What it *is* evidence of is the fact that we see things the way we've become accustomed to seeing things; that is, the way we are habituated to seeing them. Whatever we create or discover in our experience is drawn from that background.

Okay, Now This Feels Like It's Cued Up Juuuusssst Right

Dorothy's desire to get back home, made overt in Fleming's movie, makes a lot of sense when we understand that a person feels most at home in her accustomed surroundings. Her desire for comfortable surroundings is in large part the work of her habits, and the fact she acts on them so incessantly (how many times does she tell someone of her desire to return to Kansas?) is evidence of the forcefulness of habits. What Dorothy enacts on the larger scale— her desire to return to a habituated home—is also enacted in *all* of the perceptions we take for granted. When we are not entirely focused on something our habits fill in the gaps for us. We walk around in our daily lives and focus on a small minority of the sensory impressions we actually receive.

How do we incorporate these myriad background impressions without having to dwell on and interpret the meaning and significance of each one? Perceptual habits do the work for us so we can focus on the really important stuff, like the brake lights ahead of us, or the charred smell rising from the unattended pan, or the change from black and white to color film processing. John Dewey (1859–1952) explains how overlooked, and yet how far reaching, the work of habits is in our lives:

> Repeated responses to recurrent stimuli may fix a habit of acting in a certain way. All of us have many habits of whose import we are quite unaware, since they were formed without our knowing what we were about. Consequently they possess us, rather than we them. They move us; they control us. Unless we become aware of what they accomplish,

and pass judgment upon the worth of the result, we do not control them.[8]

Today, it's difficult for us to comprehend the experience of watching *The Wizard of Oz* during its original theatrical release. When the second reel of film introduces the amazing splash of color and the land of Oz. . . . Wow. Talk about sensory overload. But audiences today don't see the movie the same way audiences did in 1939. The reason why should be quite obvious by now—audiences today are used to color film. It's no shock to see color film. The rarity nowadays is black and white, and when it's used for movies now those titles immediately carry the label "art" whether they're any good at all. Spielberg's use of color in *Schindler's List* (1993) stands out because the entire movie was filmed in black and white, except for a little girl's red overcoat (likely added in later via digital effects). This red stands out like a beacon, crying out for interpretation and significance. It *means* something.

The Wizard of Oz is at once not so obvious but also incredibly overt. Dorothy's farmhouse door opens up to reveal a whole world in color. *That* must certainly mean *something*. But then, the whole of Oz is in color, so what could it mean? The overabundance of signification dampens its lasting effect. We sort of don't know what to say about this onslaught of color because there is *too much* to say, too much it might mean. In any case, audiences today are immeasurably more equipped to understand movies than audiences in 1939. The meanings of common editing techniques, of verbal cues, and colors and symbols provide a wealth of resources and background that constitute our perceptual habits. On the other hand, our more sophisticated array of habits can also lead us to overlook important meanings. What is this wider background? For example, consider the various genres of movies like thrillers, action-adventure, westerns, cop dramas, horror, or romantic comedies. When we go see a movie and notice it is falling into one of these genres (or any other), we already have a good idea what to expect from the movie. Do we need a detailed program to follow the plot of, say, *Lethal Weapon 4*? If we've seen the first three installments of the series, we pretty

---

[8] John Dewey, *Democracy and Education* in *The Middle Works of John Dewey Volume 9* (Southern Illinois University Press, 1980), pp. 34–35.

much know what to expect. Or maybe *Rocky 12* will defy our expectations? Hardly.

Caution: This Can Be Habit-forming

The point I'm getting at is this: our way of watching movies (or TV, or of listening to music or of reading books) is the result of the accumulation of all of our experiences in these very activities. The first time a person watches a movie with subtitles can be challenging. But after thirty or so movies with subtitles the skill of reading and watching matures. The same holds true when technological innovations change filmmaking; like the introduction of color film, or of talkies, or computer generated effects (CGI), or that neat little 360-degree camera technique introduced by *The Matrix* (The Wachowski Brothers, 1999). Does that Matrix stunt still leave us in awe anymore? I doubt it impresses anyone who keeps up with the movies. The technique, its uses, and some meanings it opens up are already available as part of our perceptual habits. Rosenblatt explains how these habits operate without our conscious attention:

> Past literary experiences serve as subliminal guides as to the genre to be anticipated, the details to be attended to, the kinds of organizing patterns to be evolved. Each genre, each kind of work . . . makes its own kind of conventional demands on the reader—that is, once he has set up one or another such expectation, his stance, the details he responds to, the way he handles his responses, will differ. Traditional subjects, themes, treatments, may provide the guides to organization and background against which to recognize something new or original in the text. (p. 57)

Rosenblatt identifies the very items I was discussing earlier involved in making meaning. Not only do I, or you, bring a set of interests to bear on whatever movie we watch, but the movie is of a certain kind, made a certain way. It's the product of someone's craft, and thus is not just a random piece of work. There are reasons Dorothy does what she does in the movie, and as we watch the movie we gain clues from the dialogue, the lighting, the costumes, the soundtrack, and everything else *in* the movie. We also have our own dispositions guiding us to find some meanings more reliable than others. For example, we think it is more likely that Dorothy doesn't really *want* to run away from home. She's just an unhappy young girl who actually loves her home. We all see that.

Having her run away is just a plot device to have Professor Marvel trick her into going back home—he sees the truth in Dorothy's feelings as clearly as we do, and this moment foreshadows the whole story when he later becomes the Wizard. We all grasp this.

Now, with the experience of Dark Side of the Rainbow we add another complete system of meanings into the mix of movie and viewer. We are not simply merging two things, but three, when we include ourselves and our habits, and so the meanings may be even more varied, or even more difficult to perceive. This isn't exactly a familiar or habitual genre, it's something novel. Our expectations are opened in ways they wouldn't normally be, we attend to things differently, notice new moments in the music and the movie. There's a sudden influx of new available meanings, sort of like opening the door on a new land in Technicolor. For example, much is made of the vocals during the song "The Great Gig in the Sky" overlapping with the cyclone's attack and the beginning of Dorothy's journey to Oz. The song quiets and slows after Dorothy is struck on the head by the window, and this conjunction is taken by some as evidence that there really is some kind of connection between movie and music. I think it's quite clear now that the connection is created by the viewer who *sees* the connection as an opportunity for making a meaning. I, for one, think a jolt to the head from a window pane is cause for alarm, not soothing and peaceful melodies. But that's just me.

Wait, Did I Hit Pause? Where'd the Remote Get to . . . ?

The force of our habits is so strong that we tend to like the things we like simply because we are used to them. Feels like home, like Kansas. We just like it and we don't think much about why. Sounds pretty ridiculous, I know. *Of course* we like what we like—we like it. But the point is we just go with what our habits tell us, and we like it. Now, take the previous few sentences and insert the word "meaning" for what it is we like, and the issue becomes clearer. The meanings we get out of movies and music arise from our habits, and habits aren't the result of our *thinking* about present circumstances. It's more like not having to think.

So when a viewer finds synchronicity when pairing *The Wizard of Oz* with *Dark Side of the Moon*, she may be basing all her ideas on habituated meanings. Now, that claim doesn't mean that her experience is invalid in any way. It simply means that her habits are likely the result of her longstanding experience with movies, music, or a novel opportunity to look for synchronicities against that background. She can't expect everyone else to agree with her. Experiences like Dark Side of the Rainbow are not experiences that can be judged "Right" or "Wrong." You might "get it" or you might not, as some of the submissions to web sites indicate. But not "getting it" is not a sign that you don't want to or can't possibly understand the concepts involved. Failing to attribute the meanings that arise during DSOTR to some greater collective unconscious or a conspiracy theory means either you don't care to explain where and how meanings develop or that you realize meanings are sometimes very individual and sometimes so public we take them for granted.

For those new to the phenomenon of "synching" movies with music albums, I'll refer you to a recent article in *The Rolling Stone* magazine:

> By now most everybody (stoned or otherwise) knows that watching *The Wizard of Oz* while listening to Pink Floyd's *Dark Side of the Moon* unspools a motherload of eerie synchronicities. But did you know that the same thing happens when you combine *Led Zeppelin IV* and *The Fellowship of the Ring?* Or *The Matrix* and Metallica's "Black Album"? *Fellowship of the IV* and *The Black Matrix* are just two of the 17 full-length DVDs that you can pick up at Syncmovies.com. Other bizarre mash-ups include *The Ozzorcist* (Black Sabbath meets *The Exorcist*) and *Nevermind the Memento* (Nirvana's *Nevermind* with *Memento*).[9]

So, what we have here is not something unique to Fleming's movie and Pink Floyd's album. It's a way of finding something new in something old, and has become a genre of its own in the recent past, although most people are not yet habituated to it. In other words, synching movies with albums can be a way of breaking out of our perceptual rut and learning to see things in a new way, of not taking things for granted. Of course, there's every possibility that those finding all these rockin' synchronicities are simply involved in one binge weekend after another, but that doesn't eliminate the fact that they're seeing things in a new light (if they're still seeing anything at all).

---

[9] Article retrieved on July 3rd, 2008: www.rollingstone.com/rockdaily/index .php/2008/04/18/meet-the-king-of-stoner-rock-movies-just-in-time-for-420/.

13

Lions and Tigers and Bears: A Phenomenology of Scary Stuff

RANDALL E. AUXIER

Delightful little girls. Sadie is seven and Vega is four. They were visiting my home with their parents recently, and they come from Kansas. Hmmm, little girls from Kansas. I should have known better, but I suggested that we watch the *The Wizard of Oz* while I was babysitting the girls.

"No," said their mother, "the monkeys scare them." Well, *yeah*. They scared me too when I was a kid, gave me awful dreams. But some of us sort of *like* the feeling of being frightened, you know? There's something alluring about it. But why does such stuff chill a child? And especially, why do things like flying monkeys give children "bad dreams."

Songs of Innocence, Songs of Experience

There was a gloomy Dane by the name of Søren Kierkegaard (1813–1855). He thought too much. He thought so much that eventually he even thought about the question I just asked (though he never watched *The Wizard of Oz*). He said:

>]Innocence is ignorance. In innocence, man is not qualified as spirit but is psychically qualified in immediate unity with his natural condition. The spirit of man is dreaming. . . . In this state there is peace and repose, but there is simultaneously something else that is not convention and strife, for there is nothing against which to strive. What, then, is it? Nothing. But what effect does nothing have? It begets anxiety. This is the profound secret of innocence, that it is at the same time anxiety. Dreamily the spirit projects its own actuality,

but this actuality is nothing, and innocence always sees this nothing outside itself.[1]

Whew. I warned you about Kierkegaard, right? Let me see if I can translate, and you'll have to strain your memory back to your own childhood to get a feel for this (I realize that's more of a stretch for some of you than for others).

When you're a kid, you sort of live in your body and that's *all* there is *to* you, apparently, just a little collection of physical functions you basically ignore, preferring instead to just experience things innocently. You'll become obsessed with the physical functions when you're old, and you won't talk about much else, but as a kid the world is more like a big picture show and you don't worry too much about the projector, the film, the price of a ticket, and suchlike.

But no, Kierkegaard says, even when you're a kid, there is something inside you already dreaming, your "spirit," the man calls it. What's it dreaming *of?* Well, basically it's your adult self, but you don't know that's what it is. So you innocently take that dream of what you *will* be, or *might* be, and you see it outside yourself, but you don't recognize it as *you*. That's because you're innocent, and you don't realize that the adult you will become has done some ugly and unbearable things.

You will have broken people's hearts, lied, cheated, screwed up royally, perhaps even killed. But it's already there, in your dreaming spirit. Kierkegaard even says this dream of the innocent (ignorant) spirit is "original sin." Geez, man, give the kids a break, huh? Already dreadful sinners dreaming of their sins? Holy cod. People didn't invite Kierkegaard to dinner, and they certainly didn't let him babysit. He's too scary.

So I don't know whether any of this stuff is true. I hope not, but I admit that it makes some sense to me. Poor Sadie and Vega, frightened by the flying monkeys, and if Kierkegaard is right, those monkeys are pretty much just external projections of what they will be and will do, or at least some part of their own hideous future deeds, a symbol in a spirit dream of their own ugly and unworthy souls. Kierkegaard needed to lighten up. Everyone thinks so. But he's right; things that scare us are probably, at least over time, things that come to symbolize something within ourselves. We

---

[1] *The Concept of Anxiety* (Princeton University Press, 1980), p. 41.

scare ourselves far more than the world scares us. That's why the scariest movies have a human "monster."

Kierkegaard also says that the "something" inside us is, apparently, *nothing* at all, and *that's* actually the problem. It's not that we're afraid of "nothing," it's that the nothing inside us, our own ignorance, makes us anxious, and being anxious (as children often are), we readily see in the world things (like flying monkeys) that somehow manifest physically some hint or shade of ourselves, and we fasten onto it, and *then* we feel afraid of *it*, instead of ourselves. Anxiety has no special object, but fear does.

This idea is provocative, and perhaps a bit dubious. You may be inclined to dismiss it. That's what Kierkegaard expects you to do, but not because you're right. He thinks you'll be uncomfortable with this suggestion about the dream of your innocent spirit—or not so much uncomfortable as, well, actually a bit anxious. And that's a reason to think he may be right, your own discomfort. This is subtle stuff, so let's back away from it and come back to it later, see if it's any more plausible then.

So all this set me to thinking (but then again, what doesn't? I'm not as bad about it as Kierkegaard, at least). I remember being frightened or disturbed by a lot of things in *The Wizard of Oz*, and as I got older, different things worried me, and in different ways. It wasn't the flying monkeys anymore so much as the idea of the Wizard demanding that a child commit murder to earn a reward he hasn't even got the power to bestow. That's one of the worst things I could ever imagine. I mean, just think of what a scary movie you could build on such a premise. But it looks to me like that's the very essence of this story, and it's *awful*. Who invents such a twisted idea? I think that now I may be afraid of L. Frank Baum. So I'm still not entirely free of it, fear I mean, and my guess is that lots of people are like me in this regard. So I began to wonder if a more systematic description of what was scary, and how so, might reveal a pattern. Lo and behold, it does.

A Method in the Madness

Philosophers have a number of tricks they can use to sort out experiences, but I think the right one for this question is a method called "phenomenology." Now that's an imposing word. It's really two words: "phenomenon," that is, anything that appears in our experience, and "logos," which means a lot of things, but one of them is "logic," or in this case, the structure and principles of the *ways* that things appear in our experience.

If we can do a phenomenology of scary things in *The Wizard of Oz*, we may find some common ground. We may ask what things create a tension in our common anxiety in such a way as to catapult us out of the dream of spirit and into the world of our sense experience. I'm sure that *The Wizard of Oz*, the 1939 movie I mean, does this very well because it scares lots of kids, most kids, and it's the same things that do it.

In this case, the *experience* I'm after, the "phenomenon" in this phenomenology, is "fear," but that's just a word. It covers millions of different experiences, just like the words "love" or "hope" do. The philosopher Alfred North Whitehead (1862–1947) once observed that human understanding is greatly inhibited by the poverty of our language about subjective feelings. I mean, *one word* for all the experiences that are involved in "love"? If Eskimos can come up with thirty words for "snow," you would think we could all have at least a few dozen for "love." In a sense we do have lots of words, for both love and fear, but the *connection* of such words to all those feelings is vague, indistinct. Phenomenology sort of specializes in creating more distinct connections between our inner lives, including both our feelings and our thought processes, and our *descriptions* of those processes in language. It's an important part of philosophy. But before we do any phenomenology, let's look at something a little more familiar.

Primal Stuff

There are some things that seem universally scary to human beings, immediately, involuntarily, instinctively. The list of such things is not long: sudden loud noises, falling, sudden bright light, the dark, Ozzy Osbourne, and that's about it. Okay, I'm kidding. I know that not *everyone* is afraid of bright light. But since Kierkegaard says that in our innocence we are at one with our bodies (the "immediate unity with our natural condition"), it makes some sense to look at what happens in our bodies, our physiology, when we experience fear. It explains a lot about what happens to us, although it doesn't even begin to explain what it comes to *mean* to our lives (which is what Kierkegaard is more on about).

There are a lot of ways to think about our bodies. For example, we could "know our bodies" the way that athletes or dancers "know" their bodies, knowing what the body will and won't do, mastering and refining its motions. Or we can know our bodies in the sense of knowing how they look and feel. When my clothes get too tight, I "know" it's time to lay off the rich foods, and when I haven't had enough sleep, my body lets me "know." One familiar way to think of our bodies is as objects of science, using concepts of anatomy and physiology. From that point of view, you have a little part of your brain called the amygdalae (that's two amygdalas, one on each side of your brain). Brain scientists say that these little guys process and retain emotional memories, and they sort of take quick snapshots of stuff you see or hear. Then sometimes, if the stuff happening to your senses is severe enough, your amygdalae short circuit the rest of your brain processes and send a message straight to your adrenal gland to release some epinephrine into your blood stream. The result is what's called the "fight or flight" response.

I know you've been there. You'll be minding your own business, and all of a sudden "Crazy Train" starts playing on the sound system, there is an adrenaline rush, and you *know* you either have to smash the radio or get out of there. You can recognize this condition easily: your heart starts beating faster, you feel like you want to run or you can't listen to another excruciating note. This is the onset of primal fear, accompanied by disgust. Do we find this in *The Wizard of Oz*, stuff that sets off the amygdalae? Sure, several things. I'll just look at three. But one thing that makes a big difference to the overall experience is its *duration*, how long it lasts, because the duration affects the amount of "reflection," conscious thought, that accompanies the experience. Some experiences happen too fast for any thinking to occur, but the ones that are most interesting, in my opinion, are the ones that take a bit of time to unfold. But we'll look at three from the movie, increasingly spread out in duration, and see how the effects are different.

Now phenomenologists are not so much interested in brain chemistry. They know it's important, but a question they like better is *how* those emotional memories, the sort of thing scientists say are registered in the amygdalae, come to be saturated with certain kinds of *meanings*. I mean, if you think about it, you'll notice that the same memories can have different meanings and carry different emotions from one person to the next. For instance, not everyone likes *The Wizard of Oz*, even when they're remembering the same movie. Even for a single person, the same image can be experienced differently, take on different qualities, in different situations, and over time. *The Wizard of Oz* just doesn't mean the same thing to me now that it did when I was eight, even though I do remember, sort of, what it meant back then.

So how do the images we perceive come to be experienced in such varied ways, with such varied meanings? Phenomenology is sort of an art (or some say it's sort of a science) of describing that process. And one way that we can get at it is by introducing *variations* in the experience to see what remains constant and what changes. It's called "imaginative variation." Let's do some of that varying with the scary stuff and see what we can see.

Naughty Glinda?

There actually is a good moment in the film that is quite fleeting, a shock to the old amygdalae that we *feel* first, all over our bodies, and have to sort out later because it happens so fast. We've been dancing and singing all around Muchkinland and then without warning the Wicked Witch of the West shows up in a puff of red smoke, scattering the little people to and fro; that sets us on edge to be sure, activates our "fight" response. But the moment that sticks in the amygdalae is when, after confronting Dorothy and Glinda (and since *Glinda* isn't afraid, we aren't so much either), the Witch goes to fetch the ruby slippers from her dead sister's feet. Naughty Glinda apparently waves her wand (it's off-screen) to put the slippers on Dorothy's feet instead. But of course, the image that stays with us is those legs shriveling up and withdrawing under the house. I know you can see it right now. We all cringe. Makes you wonder who came up with that, right?

Well, in a sense, it's in Baum's book, but the *variations* make a difference. In the original book, the Wicked Witch of the West makes no appearance at all in this scene, Dorothy is all distracted with the Munchkins, and with the good Witch of the North, who is not Glinda, but rather a little old woman (and a far cry from the glamorous Billie Burke!). In Baum's tale, Glinda is the Good Witch of the *South* (a detail that was restored to the plot when it became a Broadway musical in *The Wiz*, along with the magic shoes being silver rather than ruby). In the book, Dorothy has to make an *extra* journey to see Glinda after the Wizard fails to get her back home. But in the scene we're examining, this is what Baum says:

Dorothy was going to ask another question [of the Witch of the North], but just then the Munchkins, who had been standing silently by, gave a loud shout and pointed to the corner of the house where the Wicked Witch had been lying.

"What is it?" asked the little old woman; and looked, and began to laugh. The feet of the dead Witch had disappeared entirely and nothing was left but the silver shoes.

"She was so old," explained the Witch of the North, "that she dried up quickly in the sun. That is the end of her. But the silver shoes are yours, and you shall have them to wear." She reached down and picked up the shoes, and after shaking the dust out of them handed them to Dorothy.[2]

Yuck. Shoes filled with witch-dust. I wouldn't want those shoes on *my* feet until they'd had a bit of scrubbing, if even then. So, sort of the same thing happened in the book as in the movie, but we don't "see" it in our imaginations because it is described as having happened just the moment before our attention was drawn to the spot.

The feeling of having just missed something is very different from seeing it happen (as any moviemaker knows). That moment's respite is like arriving at the scene of a car accident while the wheels are still spinning—scary enough, but not as hard on the amygdalae as actually seeing it happen. Among the images we can't erase from our emotional memories is the stuff we see in an instant, before we can even grasp what is happening, that imprints the amygdalae. A strong link has been demonstrated by neuroscientists between these sorts of moments and Post-Traumatic Stress Disorder.

The decision to *show* this shriveling moment in the film is, physiologically speaking, a recipe for PTSD, especially among kids. It lasts only a second, and in the film the Munchkins don't see it because they are cowering some distance away. The main characters do see it, as do we, but they sort of proceed as if it weren't scary. The Wicked Witch of the West, who is only a foot or two away when the shriveling occurs, only reacts to the slippers' disappearance, not to the horrendous shriveling. No one discusses it, and we get no reassurance that we have even seen what we

---

[2] L. Frank Baum, *The Wonderful Wizard of Oz* (Chicago: Geo. M. Hill Co., 1900), pp. 24–25.

thought we saw. As we search our minds for the cause of this awful sight (and this happens only after we've seen it), the inference we all make is that Glinda did it with her wand, or maybe Glinda just took the slippers and the shriveling was a result of the magic in the shoes being taken away from the witch. But it's the image on the screen that imprints in the amygdalae, and our reflection on the cause feels quite secondary. Why? And what is its phenomenological meaning?

The Men behind the Curtain

As we move from physiology to phenomenology, let's start by noticing something about the moment: the music. The moment we are discussing is accompanied by a sudden jump in volume and a highly dissonant blast of brass (this sudden loud noise signals us to be afraid, while the dissonance presses us toward disgust), then in a second or two the music is fading off into the bass instruments, a little like the music from *Jaws* when the shark has done his worst and is swimming away. If you ever doubted that this moment was intended to shock, the music will confirm that it was all well contrived by the filmmakers. As the moment fades, the music recedes again into the background and the visual images come back to the foreground of our perception, and we are being prepared for more dialogue.

I'll say more about what music does in a moment, but for now, just notice how the shocking image is reinforced by a sudden sound. Makes you wonder what your daily life would be like if it were accompanied by a movie score. It can be fun to imagine it: you walk in the door alone and your spouse says, "You forgot to pick up the kids?!?" Is that serious? A sudden dissonant chord. Or is it no big deal, just old forgetful you, backing out the door to get them . . . with a little playful clarinet flourish as in a *Dick van Dyke* episode . . . "whoops."

Similar sorts of effects can be achieved with shadows and light. The same event takes on a different meaning in the shadows than in bright light. Every quality of your perception can be varied to reinforce one effect or another. It's a play of the senses that is fairly delicate and thus, particular effects can be difficult to achieve. Getting something to be scary in a movie is one of the hardest effects to achieve, along with getting something to be funny. For instance, sometimes, depending on context and set-up, showing something in bright light so that you see every detail can be scarier than showing it in shadow. The shriveling shot we are discussing is an example of that.

So the reason the moviemakers show you the feet only for a second, and in bright light, is that any more time or any less light wouldn't be scary, any less time and it wouldn't register in your conscious mind what you just saw. The duration has to be just right. So much for the physical aspect, what about the phenomenological side?

If I Only Had a Brain

There are many things one could say, but I am drawn to some observations that were made by a phenomenologist named Maurice Merleau-Ponty (1908–1961). He said that scientific explanations of what *happens* in the body are actually very different from our *experience* of our own bodies, and that the experience is far more basic and more important than the science. This seems pretty obvious, but people fall in love with science and forget that it isn't the be-all and end-all of their own experience.

You don't need any science to have a good experience, or a bad one. You have no direct experience of your amygdalae, and you may not have even known you *had* any such thing. And the amygdalae aren't really "things," they are clusters of neurons in the center of the brain that have a separate name because they have specialized functions. That's a handy concept for a brain scientist, but not much use to most of us. Even the concept of a "neuron" is less than a hundred years old, so billions of people have lived and died (and still do) without the least clue that they have "neurons," let alone amygdalae.

Science gives us very abstract causal explanations of the body, but there's far more to the body than science can even describe, let alone explain. So Merleau-Ponty reminds us that people had ways of perceiving their bodies that were rich and highly functional long before science ever told us anything about how it all works. The same is true for kids. They don't even know they have something called a brain until you teach it to them, but that doesn't keep them from perceiving and thinking and experiencing. And take the Scarecrow. Why does he think he has no brain? His problem may be that he got some very narrow ideas about what a "brain" is: just the physical mass of, well, I hate to tell you this, but the brain is pretty close to being just fat. So the Scarecrow started getting all worried that he couldn't think without one. He wasn't willing so much as to trust his own *experience* of thinking, which he was obviously good at, because somehow he heard that you can't think without a brain.

Phenomenologists like Merleau-Ponty tell us that with or without science, we still have experience of our bodies, so there is a broader and richer perception of the body from which our science derives. Science is a *genre* of meaning, a sub-field of meaning we created with our language, and it's a bad idea to mistake one part of meaning for the whole of it. Don't be a Scarecrow.

Your Body, Your World

So what is a frightened body, to a phenomenologist? Well, Merleau-Ponty says that basically your living body *as experienced* is your *whole world*: "The body is the vehicle of being in the world, and having a body is, for a living creature, to be intervolved in a definite environment, to identify oneself with certain projects and to be continually committed to them."[3]

That comes down to saying that what we *do* in the world forms our perceptions of our bodies. Athletes and dancers live in a different world than I live in, because the things they do with their bodies are so different from what I do with mine. But our bodies won't *do* just anything and everything, won't reveal to us *everything* about the situation or environment they inhabit. There are limits and gaps, deficiencies.

Yet even the deficiencies are concealed, "silent," Merleau-Ponty says, especially to children. They don't grasp what's missing, because the world *seems* more or less complete. He continues:

> in concealing [the] deficiency from [us], the world cannot fail simultaneously to reveal it to [us]: for if it is true that I am conscious of my body via the world, that it is the unperceived term in the center of the world towards which all objects turn their face, it is true for the same reason that my body is the pivot of the world: I know that objects have several facets because I could make a tour of inspection of them, and

---

[3] *The Phenomenology of Perception* (Routledge, 1962), p. 82.

in that sense, I am conscious of the world through the medium of my body. (p. 82)

If I'm getting his point, he's saying that the world can teach me that my experience has something missing in very simple ways. For instance, you're reading this book (thanks for that, by the way). But you aren't looking at every page right this second, so the book is not *all* before you. You can make a tour of inspection of the pages, but the only reason that makes sense is because the book isn't *all* there right now, even though you're holding the *whole* book in your hands. Your experience is incomplete.

But here we come to an interesting point about movies. They show us "objects" (or pictures of objects) in motion, the sort of stuff we would normally be able to wander around and inspect, but they do so in such a way as to make that "tour of inspection" impossible. My body is no longer the "pivot of the world." Instead, I'm glued to my seat and at the mercy of what the camera shows me. I'm arrested, unable to act on my usual habits of perceiving. The camera has become a substitute for my living body, and presents itself to me as a total world, but one that is in someone *else's* control. I'm already helpless, and then, as I settle in to watch the movie, I sort of forget how much control I have given away—until the feet shrivel, and I don't want to see it, but it's too late. And I can't move around the scene to see what happened, to reassure myself that there is a benign explanation. So part of the reason I'm *afraid* has to do with the fact that I'm helpless, and until that moment, I had forgotten it. I trusted Victor Fleming, and he took advantage of me, using his wicked camera to shove images into my world that I didn't want.

Now we see something about the men behind the curtain, the concealed portion of our living world. In the same way that you're careful about what food you put into your mouth, you have to be careful about the images and sounds your body consumes from the wider perceptual world. It's really the same thing. You *are* what you see and hear as truly as you are what you eat. Think about that next time Ozzy comes on the sound system, and ask yourself, if this were food, what sort of food would it be? Would it be like eating a live bat? And would I really bite its head off? Oh my. So those shriveling legs are scary because you just ate them with your eyes and ears, and now it's too late. That's the chance you take when you trust a moviemaker.

A Great Gig in the Sky

Now, the cyclone surely sets off our amygdalae too, but because the events occupy a longer duration, about five minutes, we do not register the same adrenal reaction, as viewers, that we do when the shriveling occurs. Dorothy, on the other hand, is getting some serious "flight" signals (you don't stand to fight a cyclone) when she's stomping on the door of the storm cellar with her foot.

Notice, by the way, her foot makes *no noise* when she stomps, even though you can hear *other* sounds that wouldn't be as loud. This is the work of the men behind the curtain again, controlling everything you hear. Anyway, I think you'll agree she engaged in adrenaline-assisted behavior, and watching her act out the flight response fills us with some of the same stuff. But there's more. The noiseless stomping actually makes *us* feel more desperate, ineffectual, and powerless, and that isn't just amygdalae stuff. You are getting *signals* to flee but you *can't*. So you try to think and you *can't*. Over the course of a minute or two, you start to feel desperate.

The tornado sequence contains just about everything you need to fire up your amygdalae: especially loud noise, falling, impending darkness. If you've never actually heard a tornado (I've heard one, and I can tell you there's nothing like it) it is so loud that it cancels out the other senses. That's part of why you can't think. I've heard this noise described as sounding like a freight train, but that doesn't do it justice. It's more like sticking your head in a jet engine powering up, or maybe gluing your ear to a speaker at a Black Sabbath concert back when Ozzy used to be able to screech the high notes.

Here's a little thought experiment. This isn't actually imaginative variation, this will be *perceptual* variation, but it'll help you get a handle on imaginative variation. Some of you will have seen "The Dark Side of the Rainbow," which is the synching of Pink Floyd's recording *The Dark Side of the Moon* with the 1939 *The Wizard of Oz*. When this is done, the whole tornado sequence lines up with the song "The Great Gig in the Sky," and I suspect that the near perfection of the timing of this synchronization is what has led some people to think it just possible that Pink Floyd *intended* this synchronicity. It is, after all, Dorothy's great gig in the sky, and here is this woman wailing like a Les Paul guitar, and since that song has no lyrics, why did the band entitle the song so? With no lyrics, they could have called it anything at all. But I'm sure the whole thing is a happy accident. Very happy, for us, as you'll see. Now, I want you to watch the tornado sequence with the Pink Floyd music.[4] Then watch the sequence with no sound at all.

It's very different, isn't it? In 1939, sound technology in theaters was not advanced enough to create quite the experience of sudden loudness that activates the amygdalae,[5] although today it could be done well enough. But people don't *like* the experience of sudden loud noises, and they go to the movies to *enjoy* themselves. So filmmakers more often use music to *suggest* the experience of sudden noise rather than to actually create it (that, and, unlike Ozzy and his crew, they worry about being sued for damaging people's hearing).

For most people, the music in movies is a part of what phenomenologists call the "passive synthesis."[6] This idea is complicated, but basically when you pay specific attention to something, you process *that* actively, but you don't pay attention to *everything* in your perceptual field, just a small part of it. The stuff you aren't actively noticing is still there, as a sort of background awareness. You're "synthesizing" it passively.

The relationship between the active and passive aspects of the perceptual field is slippery and delicate, but manipulating *that* relationship is where *all* the action is. Filmmakers can alter your emotions about anything and everything not only by altering loud and soft, shadow and light, but more essentially they are altering what you're noticing and what you're not, what you synthesize actively and passively. They do all this by first controlling what you actively notice, and then screwing around with the background stuff, and moving your attention around with sound and light and action.

When you alter the background stuff, you alter the total experience. So, if you watch the tornado sequence with the original soundtrack (now that I have called your attention to it), you'll see that there is *no music at all* until the moment when Dorothy is hit

---

[4] Here's where you can find it: www.youtube.com/watch?v=ZMGlGOQJUyw& feature=related. Or just type in "Dark Side of the Rainbow" in any web browser.

[5] The famous "Voice of the Theater" speaker was created by Altec Lansing in 1947. Before that, theater sound was fairly pinched into the mid-range (and of course, Dolby came much later than that, first used in the movies in 1971).

[6] Here's a big book on it, containing far more than you ever wanted to know about the subject: Edmund Husserl, *Analyses Concerning Passive and Active Synthesis* (Kluwer, 2001).

on the head by the dislodged window. The music at that moment is at first characterized by descending tones as she falls unconscious, then by ascending tones as the house is lifted, and then it turns into a sort of overture of themes, both playful and threatening, as various things pass by the window. Then there's more descending orchestration as the house falls into Oz. At the moment the house lands, dead silence. The visual images are such that you really can't give your active attention to anything else but the images (especially on the big screen), because the human eye is drawn by motion and flickering light (as any moviemaker knows), so the music is perceived passively by most people. If you're a filmmaker and you want the music to rise toward active consciousness, you need to hold the visual scene still; when you want the sound to recede into the background, you move the images. The absence of music during the first part of the sequence makes the music more powerful and meaningful when it comes in.

You probably never actively noticed all this, just "synthesized" it passively. But put in the Pink Floyd as a substitute and the whole sequence becomes ethereal, actually sort of calming; you are far more aware of the sequence *as a whole*, there is no real danger (since you know how it comes out), and you feel like floating with Dorothy to Oz. So the same images take on a different overall quality, and thus, a different *meaning*.

I wonder what would happen if you showed the tornado sequence to children before they had ever seen the movie, and used the Pink Floyd music. Or what if you just showed them the images with no sound? Would their amygdalae register different primal emotions? Anyway, the point is that the process by which some scary things come to scare us is dependent on the way we "synthesize" the background stuff, passively, and every moviemaker (and every writer of horror stories) knows this. Do you like to read scary books at night, alone? Why? Is part of the reason that they're not scary enough to be fun when the sun is shining and others are around? And why is *that*?

I think the cyclone images themselves do carry some primal stuff, but it's one thing to see the whirlwind on a screen, and another thing to reap one in 3-D, with sound effects worse than Ozzy's flattest note. So remember this when we get to flying monkeys later on, and when you want to calm down, *Dark Side of the Moon* may be better for that than The Blizzard of Ozz. . . . But I'd love to hear Ozzy's rendition of "The wind began to switch, the house to pitch. . . ."

Okay, maybe not. For now, I do want to point out that you can't easily sustain a "fight or flight reaction" for very long. Your body begins to adjust and equalize itself in just a few seconds, and your reflective powers begin to operate, on high alert. This is no instantaneous reaction, it becomes a heightened response, one that "intervolves" the whole body and its surroundings, and this response is more exhausting than enlivening. As you remain in the situation, you accept more and more responsibility for continuing to watch or wait. You come to be aware that the experience can change you, and you choose to endure the change. It isn't like the shriveling feet.

Damnable Monkeys

So we come to what scared the little girls, Sadie and Vega, and what frightened me the most too. Actually, the worst recurring nightmare I ever had was of the Tin Man, of all things, but in *watching* the movie, it was the monkeys I couldn't bear. So what's the deal with the monkeys? I remembered they bared their teeth, and Charles Darwin (who should know about monkeys if anyone should) says we all have a primal reaction to *that*. But watching the film again, I see there isn't any gnashing of teeth until later. The littlest monkey who has Toto, in the witch's castle, bares his teeth at Dorothy when she reaches for the basket Toto is in. I had imagined teeth earlier, to make things worse than they are.

But there might still be something to thinking of these beasties in Darwinian terms. I have later noticed that the monkeys are played by some of the Munchkins, the same little people all suited up, with blue Mohawk hairdos (perhaps subliminally reminding Anglocentric viewers of "savage" Indians), and in the days before you could get this "do" for yourself at Regis in the local mall. Shocking blue hair, really.

I didn't notice, as a child, that the monkeys were transmogrified Munchkins, but perhaps I was dreaming of distorted little people in my innocent spirit, to return to what Kierkegaard said. Instead of little people with monkey suits on, was I grasping the monkeys as something that lurked within the Munchkins? Am I afraid of little people? And there I was, sort of a Munchkin myself, a little person, fearing the monkey in me? Maybe the human being is the *suit*, and the flying monkey is the essence of a person. There may be something to all this, but I have come to think it isn't the key to the castle.

Following what we have discovered so far, I see that the duration and placement of the monkey scenes probably make a difference. By the time the monkeys show up, which is over an hour and fifteen minutes into the film, the attention and natural defenses of a child (or an adult) have been greatly weakened, the sense of self control much diminished, and the moviemakers take possession of more and more of our psychological space, penetrating more deeply into our consciousness and perception. We have forgotten who we are. And at just this moment, Victor Fleming and his diabolical cronies do something they haven't done before; they've been saving it, but it's also a reprise, a repetition of sorts. They prepare us by *dimming the lights*.

The monkey scene is preceded first by the frightening encounter with the Wizard (nice special effects for 1939). The lights dim as the companions proceed down the endless hallway towards the Wizard's throne room, or whatever it is, where the companions are utterly dwarfed by the scale of the place (which makes *us* feel small, since we have been taught by now to identify with the companions). Then Oz (not Ozzy) speaks in a painfully loud voice and the intermittent music is highly dissonant. Without a break or bright moment, this scene is followed with the companions treading warily through the Haunted Forest, and here *everything* is shot in *shadows*. There had been a bit of contrast in the Wizard's throne room, with isolated lights we could see that were casting the shadows. Now it's all in shadow. This is more powerful and invasive precisely because we can't see any source of light. We had grown accustomed to the brightness of Oz and this would have been even truer for our parents and grandparents in 1939, since *The Wizard of Oz* was the first major motion picture made with Technicolor processing. On the big screen it was stunning to them, I'm sure, so that the contrast of the Haunted Forest in shadows would have had an even greater effect, I suppose.

The shadows had been used before, in an earlier forest where Dorothy, the Tin Man, and the Scarecrow first encounter the Lion, as a sort of self-fulfilling prophecy coming in answer to their chant of "Lions and Tigers and Bears, oh my!" The encounter with the Lion is followed immediately by our first glimpse of the Witch in her castle, and just one small flying monkey, conjuring the poppies for the companions. This is foreshadowing, but also your passive side is being trained to place the Witch and the monkeys after the forest. In a sense, you know what's coming when the companions enter another, even darker, forest. You're being taught to project it, and to take responsibility for projecting it, to become active in the face of the future and be terrified at what you yourself are doing. The slide from passivity to active projection is a central gear in the filmmaker's machinery.

"These Things Must Be Done . . . Delicately . . ."

Now we come to a point about passive synthesis, and I have suggested how delicate the balance is between active and passive synthesis. I will tell you something that may surprise you, even shock you. When Dorothy and the companions are treading through the Haunted Forest, the Tin Man, Lion, and Scarecrow are *armed to the teeth*. Did you ever actively *notice* that the Lion now has a giant mallet and a butterfly net? The Tin Man has not only his trusty axe, but also a giant pipe-wrench. And the Scarecrow, my friends, has not only a big stick, he's actually *packing heat*. That's right, the Scarecrow has a .45 pistol. It isn't concealed at all in several shots, you just don't see it, actively at least. But you *perceive* it anyway, and all the other oversized weapons too. By the time the monkeys show up, all these fine weapons are somehow gone, except the Tin Man's axe (which the monkeys take easily as they swarm around him). So, if you're one of the rare people who noticed all these weapons, congratulations. Most people don't. The weapons tell us, passively, that this situation is more threatening than any other we've yet encountered, and the dim lighting reinforces the message.

But Fleming isn't finished with us. When the monkeys first appear, he uses a well framed shot of the Witch and her crystal ball in the center, her long boney fingers hovering threateningly, greedily, just above the image of the Lion repeating "I do believe in spooks . . ." and there are the monkeys with their hideous wings framing all corners of the shot. We are much too close and we can't get away, monkeys everywhere we look, and one stone raven floating in the upper left taking in the whole wicked scene. No escape.

Then, as if we hadn't had enough, the witch sweeps around a velvet cushioned chair and the camera follows her—the camera movement is too fast and so it's disorienting—and then it closes on her still further, framed by the large window overlooking a precipitous fall. If we were too close before, we are *way* too close now. She barks orders to the monkeys and soon they fill the skies on an awful *sortie* like Messerschmidts headed for London. They are so numerous as to darken the skies to near blackness.

Nightmares

In the monkey air-raid, our devilish filmmakers employ a number of common nightmare images: things swarming around us, being chased through a forest, being unable to move one's leaden body, being scattered and separated from one's companions, fear of heights, in short, complete chaos. And all of this havoc made by those monkeys. Then it all subsides, but the damage is done. "Nightmares for you, my pretty, a lifetime of them . . . and your little dog too!" It has been too much, and we're exhausted. Sure, the director draws us back in and scares us some more, but it's suspense rather than shock from here.

Why is this scene so effective, especially in frightening children? I think I know, or at least here's part of the answer. Obviously a number of things are at work in us, but this is not the effect of our amygdalae ordering up an epinephrine cocktail. This is much more complicated and involves the training and manipulation of the processes of active and passive synthesis, exchanging background for foreground, just as in our earlier examples. Merleau-Ponty makes the point that really we have two bodies, a "habit body" and a "lived body." The lived body is the one you can move easily, but the habit body has coalesced into a less flexible sort of image you carry around with you. He gives the example of a person who has lost a limb, but can't quite remember it isn't there. The habit of feeling it and expecting it to be there is very strong in us, and becomes inflexible.

The same thing happens with our entire body, which is to say that in our perception it becomes overlaid and coated with a whole armor of habit and expectation. We all become Tin Men living inside a habit body. And here is the scary part: Merleau-Ponty says, and he's right, that our habit body is an "impersonal being," not *us* at all, but a sort of trap we're caught in, and one of our own making. This is one reason, for instance, that people suffering from Anorexia nervosa *cannot* see themselves as too thin. No matter how thin they may be, they are at the mercy of a habit body they have created, a hard-shell image, unalterable by living perception, and that body, while only an image, is too fat. Now, the habit bodies of children are less well-formed, and in fact, they are so malleable that children can make for themselves a new one in the course of a single movie, if the filmmaker is sly enough to manipulate the active and passive syntheses well enough to get a child to form and project a habit body from which he or she cannot later escape.

And *that's* what happens in *The Wizard of Oz*. Children build for themselves an image-world while their living bodies are immobile before the screen. They become quickly habituated to what they have projected, and before they know it, they can't get out and can't get away. And then *there* are the monkeys, *inside* the space they have projected, too close, uninvited. You *bet* they want to go home. The effect on adults is smaller because our habit bodies, impersonal and uncomfortable as they may be, are less easily manipulated by our present perceptions. The active and passive syntheses are familiar, routine, patterned for adults. It takes a better moviemaker than Victor Fleming and his crew to penetrate *that* habit body. But still there are the nightmares, aren't there? The memories abide of when we first encountered the impersonal being we would become.

That brings us back to Kierkegaard, I suppose. He spoke of innocence as a dream of the spirit that is moved into existence by nothing at all, a nothing *in* us. That nothing isn't just the projection of the bad things we will eventually do, it is the spiritual torpor from which we will allow ourselves to become a mere habit of existing, impersonal, a shell that cannot remember its own living self. That is living death, which is a fair way of understanding original sin, as far as I can see. To live and allow your projections and habits to dull and blunt all that your living body could bring you— the bright joy and wonder of the world. We build our prisons and then can't find a way out of them; it wouldn't be so bad except for the monkeys. We never counted on the monkeys.

That's the stuff of nightmares, far more than any lions or tigers or bears. In a word, it's the Ozzy in *us* more than the Oz beyond us.

V

No Place Like Home

14

Coloring Kansas: Reality by Way of Appearance

MATTHEW CALEB FLAMM and
JENNIFER A. REA

A lot of nonsense has been circulated about how Dorothy left Oz.
There are some who say that she never did.

—Gregory Maguire, *Wicked: The Life and Times of the Wicked Witch
of the West*

Just think of it—until the present moment of your life you have
coasted in blissful ignorance of the deeper evils of the world. Your
worst foe up to now has been a cranky rich widow named Gulch,
whose sole aim in life has been to convince others of the mortal threat
posed by your "mangy dog," Toto. Home geography only encourages
your insularity, for Kansas includes in its north-central region Smith
County, the exact geographic center of the forty-eight states. This is
hardly a setting befitting a person of "worldly" character.

But what does it mean to be worldly anyway? If one means
something like a cultured or well-traveled person, our Dorothy certainly has her work cut out for her. But there is a deeper worldliness that our heroine lacks before her journey to Oz. The
worldliness eluding Dorothy is the same eluding all young persons
before they've encountered larger realities, experiences occasion-
ing deep loss, such as death and sudden displacement.

Dorothy's life in Kansas is not without its darkness. L. Frank
Baum tells us that Dorothy's Aunt Em, once a "young, pretty wife,"
has lost the "sparkle from her eyes" and "the red from her cheeks
and lips" has come to resemble the "dull and gray" Kansas prairies.[1]

---

[1] *The Wonderful Wizard of Oz* (Everyman's Library, Children's Classics, 1992),
pp. 2–3.

Her Uncle Henry, too, "never laugh[s]," "look[s] stern and solemn, and rarely [speaks]" (p. 3). But Dorothy does not understand the source of depletion in her morose guardians, and she can still laugh and avoid turning gray, in large part due to her beloved Toto with whom she constantly plays. Chances are, if you are like Dorothy Gale, things are going to change for you sometime soon.

What better engine of change in this tenuous setting than a cyclone? Unsubtle as a plot device, perhaps, if one insists by some dogmatic artistic principle that such devices always fail when they take an overtly physical form. But Baum's genius in choosing this device (apart from its attention to the geographic setting which might itself be a justification), is reflected in the range of possibilities an imagined cyclonic transplant provides for drawing parallels between physical and spiritual realities. These realities are central to the human life process in so far as they provide a means of resolving a larger distinction, yet more central to the human sense of things: that between appearance and reality.

Growing into Reality

There are many fascinating ways in which Baum's *The Wonderful Wizard of Oz* and Victor Fleming's 1939 film adaptation encourage us to consider the difference between appearance and reality as a decisive moment in human development. What is appearance, and what is reality? One central aim of the *Oz* story is to convey the adaptive function of imagination as individuals undergo transformations of memory and perspective when they encounter profoundly foreign realities.

Baum's child-heroine Dorothy can be, and has been, understood in political terms.[2] The attempt in such approaches is to understand the primitive attitude towards governing authorities by way of Dorothy and her innocent companions' encounters with the phony Wizard. Is Baum taking a "Madisonian perspective" whereby individuals, represented in the figure of Dorothy and her companions, understand that "enlightened statesmen may not always be at the helm" and strong government is therefore to be avoided?

---

[2] See for example Timothy E. Cook. "Another Perspective on Political Authority in Children's Literature: The Fallible Leader in L. Frank Baum and Dr. Seuss." *Western Political Quarterly* 36:2 (June 1983), pp. 326–336.

There's a sense in which we are asking about our proper "home" when we ask political questions, and while such questions are not unprofitable, they set aside other philosophically meaningful questions that Baum's legendary story raises. Two such questions involve the role of imagination in radically uncertain times and the transformation of one's conception of home across time and place.

What Happened to Dorothy's Parents?

Dorothy's cyclonic journey to Oz typifies the coping function of imagination when a person is faced with realities wholly unknown. In his introduction Baum clues readers into the nature of this imaginative coping. He observes how "every healthy youngster has a wholesome and instinctive love for stories fantastic, marvelous and manifestly unreal." The characterization, *stories manifestly unreal,* is of crucial importance here. It's the very *unreality* of the story that draws the attention of young ones. The young *play:* they make-believe, dress-up, role-play, and so often in unsuspecting, delightfully creative ways. Too frequently adults view such play as reflecting an immaturity of mind, of the inability of the child to distinguish the real from the unreal, appearance from reality. In fact, as Baum well appreciates, children are *pre-eminently* aware of unreality, so much so that children are able to find pleasure in the unreal that eludes most adults.

This realization naturally begs the question: why do so many adults lose delight for the unreal? The accumulation of experiences perhaps accounts for a good part of this diminishment, but one has to be careful here. Perhaps we no longer imagine the unreal because we remember the real instead. Revisiting our pre-cyclonic Dorothy, we might assume a certain lack of experience, but neither Baum's *Oz* series nor Fleming's film adaptation explains what must have been a hugely formative experiential factor for Dorothy: the absence of her biological parents. Did her parents die suddenly? That experience, if she remembers it, would almost certainly make her sad, and she would remember instead of imagine, right? Except for some anecdotal indications of Dorothy's cheerfulness amidst her drab pre-cyclonic surroundings, we are at a loss to know the emotional impact of her orphaned situation. Apparently Baum wanted us to notice other things. He certainly knew we would wonder what happened to her parents, but he directs our attention elsewhere.

A Box of Sixty-Four

Following Baum's lead, we can understand the contrasting imaginative orientations of youth and adulthood apart from appeals to accumulated experience. Of course, delight in the unreal persists in many adults. Perhaps they preoccupy themselves with fantasy reading, or even writing children's stories, or some other occult interest. For that matter, *Oz* is considered one of the very first *American* fantasies. Baum's tale is the first to construct a fairyland out of American material and present it to the American public as a tale of pure wonderment.

In most cases the unreal interest will remain on the margins and any spillover of it into daily social life will be strongly frowned upon, or at the very least limited by the strictures of behavioral etiquette. In *all* similar cases the unreal interest will be viewed from the social perspective as an eccentricity, and a derangement when carried beyond certain social boundaries. These social boundaries delineate behaviors deemed acceptable in the young as opposed to the adult. Imagine a bank teller playing peek-a-boo behind the wall of her stall door as she prepares your withdrawal. If it isn't flirting, it's a problem—and it may be a problem even if it is flirting. We can't quite bring ourselves to believe she is simply playing—not here, not now.

But if we can say that, in general, adulthood carries with it the expectation that excessive love for unrealities should be avoided, then what is the healthy adult to love? Gray realities? As in, those things gathered under the cosmic ledger of hard facts and empirical understanding? Hardly. Prolonged love for such things is seen in only the most rarified of human occupations, such as the homicide detective or the lab scientist, each of whom only upholds the love in service of a science. Even adults want some color in their lives.

It's not mere love of reality that motivates most adult humans, but love of something more. Whence the color? Let's suppose that all adults love, not realities, but *ideals*. It is often and mistakenly assumed that only religious, political, or artistic people live for ideals. In fact, behind every orientation of adult life one can identify some ideals. Even the most opposed adult sensibilities agree in this loyalty. The vilest criminal performs his crimes in service of some degraded ideal (like revenge or wealth) no less than the priest when appealing to his God as he blesses the confessor. We all see with our imaginations what is not available to our senses or to our sense of the "real." When we consider "reality," do we include only what is gray, or do we pull out our own box of Sixty-Four Crayolas and make the present look a bit more lively. Think of that box as your portable set of imagined ideals, and the "real" as your very own coloring book. We are all doing this all the time, we just seem forgetful about how we learned to do what we're doing, and too many of us fear coloring outside the lines.

Be Careful with That China, Little Girl

Baum's appreciation of this important distinction—the adult use of imagination in behalf of ideals versus that of the child's use of it in behalf of unrealities—is displayed on multiple levels in the plot of *Oz*. A key moment near the end of Dorothy's Oz journey poignantly displays it. It occurs in a lesser known part of the book, when Dorothy and her companions encounter "a great stretch of country having a floor as smooth and shining as the bottom of a big platter" (p. 183). In this land reside many colorfully-decorated characters, milkmaids, shepherds and shepherdesses, and they are made of porcelain. The porcelain-constructed characters have to stay in their own land in order to be able to move their bodies. Take them out of their homeland and presto, they're stock still. Dorothy learns this in a conversation with a porcelain Princess:

> ". . . you are so beautiful . . . that I am sure I could love you dearly. Won't you let me carry you back to Kansas, and stand you on Aunt Em's mantel? I could carry you in my basket."
> "That would make me very unhappy," answered the china Princess. "You see, here in our country we live contentedly, and can talk and move around as we please. But whenever any of us are taken away our joints at once stiffen, and we can only stand straight and look pretty. Of course that is all that is expected of us when we are on mantels and cabinets and drawing-room tables, but our lives are much pleasanter here in our own country."
> "I would not make you unhappy for all the world!" exclaimed Dorothy. "So I'll just say good-bye." (p. 188)

Dorothy instinctively wants to remove the beautiful porcelain-Princess into the *unreal,* ideal relation she holds in her Kansas-world understanding. This relation for Dorothy makes sense because it fits what she knows and expects from her Kansas existence: porcelain figures functioning as statuary symbols: cute, little, painted *idealizations* of reality. But as the Princess helps her see, in the world of *animated* porcelain characters such a motionless existence seems a horror, an unreality not in the least ideal. Dorothy must put that particular crayon back in the box. She is learning something.

This scene, which has many parallels in the book, resolves two key questions regarding the appearance-reality distinction kept in tension throughout Baum's *Oz*. First, it helps us address the problem of reconciling the child's appreciation for unrealities and the adult's serving of ideals. We find that, just as the unreality of the porcelain figure in Dorothy's world works in its inanimate context, Kansas, but fails in its animate *Oz*-world, the child's devotion to unrealities becomes a vice in adulthood. It comes to be replaced by ideals. For this reason, social disapproval of excessively "eccentric" interests should not be viewed as wholly misguided, nor should the general transition from loving unrealities in youth to ideals in adulthood. The adult will only become jaded, that is, will come to resent her loss of social license to innocently worship unrealities, if she fails to transmute that experience into a wizened appreciation for ideals.

Baum's *Oz* rings changes on this theme of the contrast between jaded adulthood and childhood innocence through the use of eccentric subcultures such as the porcelain kingdom, and he never suggests that these should be destroyed or even reformed; instead they seem to the outsider to have a right to their own particular customs. Porcelain people have their own ideals.

Imagining Kansas

A second question addressed by the porcelain kingdom, and similar scenes, pertains to the coping function of imagination in times of sudden homelessness, when we suddenly become acquainted with realities wholly unknown before. The leaps of imagination one makes to overcome fears of unknown realities are at least as long as Dorothy's cyclonic transplant into the wonderful world of Oz. When she awakens with Toto and receives thanks for killing the Wicked Witch of the East and freeing the Munchkins from bondage, we're relieved, psychotic episode or no, that it has a favorable outcome for Dorothy. Yet as quickly as relief comes, so too do our feelings of doubt and unsettlement. Dorothy *seems* sane of mind, but Kansas this is not. She and Toto are not only *not* in Kansas anymore: *Kansas is not Kansas anymore*. How to convey this unreality?

That Kansas is not Kansas anymore for Dorothy after her cyclonic emergence is a way of illustrating an existential metamorphosis that all persons undergo at some point in their lives. The adage that "you can't go home again" depends upon how you left and for how long. A vacation is not enough to challenge the reality of home, but a permanent move will always expose the unreality of home.

Dorothy could take a vacation, and probably find upon her return the hues of gray all the grayer. But she would not, for all of that, experience the loss of home the adage laments. One finds upon leaving home for good that its persons and relations never possessed the permanency originally accorded them. Features of the home we thought were permanent come to resemble the animated porcelain figures in Dorothy's Oz. Such features are breakable in any place, but only now, in their animation, are they transformed by our displacement into grotesques.

Imagine seeing your own childhood pet stuffed and displayed as a fancy ashtray in the smoking room of a posh New York men's club. How unreal would *that* seem? Grotesque? Such are all the familiar features of childhood subjected to the cyclones that lift us from home. "Was my childhood even real?" you might be moved to ask. The process of disillusionment with home is an opportunity to understand the homing impulse as such.

The Homing Impulse

The homing impulse impels us to fence out the unknown, to find and create the familiar when surrounded by foreignness. A young couple comforts themselves the first night after an exhausting cross-country move to an unknown state by hanging familiar images of art and photographs on their bare walls. So too the cat who, when removed from a beloved place, mysteriously finds his way back through labyrinthine streets and fields to arrive at the location most familiar to his existence.

This impulse for home explains why Dorothy's heart's desire is to return to Kansas after she is unceremoniously dumped in Oz, yet what she believes home *is* will be forever altered by her encounter with the imaginative land that she finds herself confronting. But she steps into Oz from the stoop of her own house. Dorothy's homing instinct is therefore challenged and optimally strengthened by her reconstructive imagination as she encounters the unrealities of Oz. Home isn't a house. In Baum's book, Aunt Em and Uncle Henry have built a new house, since the old one really did blow away, with Dorothy inside.

Dorothy's famous line as she steps from the tattered house into the visually stimulating and colorful Land of Oz shows that it is color that offers her the chief indication that she's not at home anymore. The multihued landscape of Oz and the washed-out gray of Kansas are familiar to movie viewers and readers alike. Dorothy's Kansas is reminiscent of Aberdeen, South Dakota, where Baum lived for a short period and tried, unsuccessfully, to run a small town newspaper and general store. These years, 1888 to 1891, were marked by severe drought, crop failures, falling crop prices, and, not surprisingly, a fierce cyclone that destroyed much of the city. Oz, on the other hand, is anything but dull and gray. It is happily isolated from the rest of the planet, with an expanding magical technology, and apparently unlimited natural resources. Its luxurious, colorful vegetation and whimsical architecture are vibrant and fit nicely with what every child imagines a place of wonder to be.

Baum describes Kansas as the "great gray prairie . . . not a tree nor a house broke the broad sweep of flat country that reached the edge of the sky in all directions." The sun bakes the plowed earth into a "gray mass, with little cracks running through it." Even the grass resists the fullness of green because the sun has burned the tops of the long blades making them as gray as the other architectural and physical features, including Dorothy's Aunt and Uncle. The house that becomes the murder weapon of a wicked witch had "been painted, but the sun blistered the paint and the rains washed it away, and now the house was as dull and gray as everything else." This dull house lands smack dab in the middle of the vibrant, colorfully rich land of Oz like a dollop of pea soup in a rich vegetable stew: "The cyclone had set the house down very gently—for a cyclone—in the midst of a country of marvelous beauty" (p. 8).

All the Colors of the Rainbow

The Land of Oz is as colorful as Kansas is gray and the contrast is striking to both the viewer of the movie and the reader of Baum's tale. The visual impact of various color combinations, like the cyclonic experience of Dorothy, tempts us to see Kansas as a place where no intelligent person would wish to return. For the Land of Oz is lush and beautiful.

Baum understood that colors occupy a vital part of our lives. They are significant to how we view and *know* the world by way of what we *see* as "real," linking our sensations to what we think and know. We weave a world, a rich tapestry of color that is vital to defining for us our objects, people, animals and landscape. The gray of Kansas is crushed right along with the Wicked Witch of the East, and we are reminded how important color is for our understanding of what is real.

The adult use of imagination on behalf of ideals versus that of the child on behalf of unrealities is also related to how each encounters color. The adult's world is as colorful as a child's, yet the adult will resist the vivid allure of the visual world for the desire to find an ideal that will satisfy her need to know the world. Young children learn their colors as one of the first steps towards identifying themselves in relation to their world, and their imaginative creations are intimately united by color. Even Kansas with its dominant palate of grays has color, though it is drained of all freshness and life.

It Isn't Easy Being Green

Specific colors have unique appearances and the use of green as the dominant color of the only major city in the Land of Oz is indicative of the need on Baum's part to express the differences between Oz and Kansas. Dorothy and her friends are "dazzled by the brilliancy of the wonderful city . . . beautiful houses all built of green marble and studded everywhere with emeralds" (p. 90). They enter through a green gate where the pavement is the same green marble as the houses and even the window panes are of green glass. They are given green tinted glasses to protect their eyes from the dazzling glare of the city and while they are visiting they see the world through the richness of the emerald lens. They are told by the guardian at the gate that if they fail to wear these glasses the "brightness and glory of the Emerald City" will blind them. Even the permanent residents must wear spectacles night and day.

In the film, the city has a cinematic creation in the form of a Horse of a Different Color that changes hue and shade as the companions travel through the green city. This horse flashes blue, red, orange, purple, and yellow, all the colors of the rainbow, radically imposing other colors upon what is supposed to be an Emerald City. This is a departure from Baum's version of the place. An entirely green celluloid city is visually uninspiring, so we can understand why the film-makers went a different direction, but in Baum's book the Emerald City is decidedly green, just as Munchkinland is blue, in shrill contrast to the gray, lifeless land of Dorothy's prairie. In fact, each region of Oz has one distinct color associated with it. The land of the Winkies is yellow and the Quadling country is red. The visual distinction importantly enhances the differences between Kansas and Oz.

Green is not one of the primary colors, but is created out of yellow and blue. The color green has broad and sometimes contradictory meanings in many cultures. In some it is associated with death and sickness, and it is connected with one of the seven deadly sins, envy. In Old English the word green is closely related to the verb *growan*, to grow, thus the connection with the natural world and fertility is established in the history of the language. The most common associations are found in its ties to nature and in this tale it is the ideal contrast to the gray, lifeless land of Dorothy's Kansas.

Dorothy's encounter with the Wizard—the only other human who manages to travel from the gray plains of the central United States to the colorful Land of Oz—tests her ability to distinguish appearance from reality and although she's not in Kansas anymore, Kansas may not actually be that far away. The Emerald City is in the geographic center of the Land of Oz, paralleling Smith county in Dorothy's Kansas. It's often forgotten that the Wizard built the city—there was nothing in the middle of Oz when he arrived. Building a city amused the Wizard and kept the people busy while he settled into his humbug existence. This reinforces the appearance-reality distinction that recurs in Baum's work. The Wizard tells Dorothy the history of the Emerald City:

> "I came down gradually, and I was not hurt a bit. But I found myself in the midst of a strange people, who, seeing me come from the clouds, thought I was a great Wizard. Of course I let them think so, because they were afraid of me, and promised to do anything I wished them to. . . . Then I thought, as the country was so green and beautiful, I would call it the Emerald City, and to make the name fit better I

put green spectacles on all the people, so that everything they saw was green."

"But isn't everything here green?" asked Dorothy.

"No more than in any other city," replied Oz; "but when you wear green spectacles, why of course everything you see looks green to you." (pp. 151–52)

The Emerald City isn't *really* green, it only *appears* to be, just as the Wizard isn't really a wizard. Why does the Wizard do the trick with spectacles? Baum is questioning the accoutrements of science as a means of enhancing our sense of things. The Oz books (published between 1900 and 1919) presciently anticipate many scientific inventions, among them artificial hearts and limbs. We haven't worked out how to do a brain transplant yet, but one wonders. The Wizard symbolizes for Baum the over-reaching enthusiasms of a modern scientific man, a master of technical illusions, but not very adept with deeper realities, like ideals.

A Whiz of a Wiz?

So the Emerald City is governed by a man whose appearance and reality are seriously at odds, and through the use of various inventions he is able to masquerade as the Great and Terrible Wizard when in reality he's only a simple man from Nebraska blown off course in a balloon. The Wizard's demand that the citizens of his Emerald City wear green-tinted glasses is the act of a man well versed in the distinction between the apparent and the real, but not content that his citizens will be happy with reality. They need instruments to see what he wants them to see.

Our so-called Wizard is based on a well-known American type—that of the humbug or charlatan, a person whose very character (or lack thereof) exploits the distinction between appearance and reality. He resembles the American politician, and the traveling nineteenth-century sideshow barker, the archetype of whom in Baum's time was the formidable P.T. Barnum. This becomes explicit in the movie when we meet him as "Professor Marvel." The Emerald City is governed by an incompetent phony without magical powers. In other words, Baum presents us with a trickster whose game is to blur the distinction between appearance and reality in order to advance himself, or save his own skin.

The four companions converge on Emerald City with high hopes. In the 1939 film the Wizard scares all four companions at once in the shape of a giant, grumpy, green smoking head, but in the book the Wizard appears to each of the four friends alone, on four different days, with a different identity. Dorothy is led to the throne room first and encounters a great head "without body to support it or any arms or legs whatever. There was no hair upon the head, but it had eyes and nose and mouth, and was much bigger than the head of the biggest giant" (p. 96). To Dorothy's chagrin she is charged with the task of killing the Wicked Witch of the West in return for a ticket back to Kansas.

The Scarecrow is confronted by "a most lovely lady" (p. 100) dressed all in green and possessing angelic wings. The Tin Woodman hopes to encounter the lovely lady, but instead finds himself face to face with "a terrible beast...nearly as big as an elephant" (p. 102). Finally, the Lion readies himself for a great head, or a lovely lady, or a frightful beast, but discovers that he is to speak with a "ball of fire, so fierce and glowing" that he's forced to avert his eyes to avoid having them burn up in the glare of the great glowing sun (p. 104).

These faces of the great Wizard of Oz are unmasked when the real man behind the parlor tricks is revealed by, of all creatures, the simple dog Toto. Baum devotes two chapters to the uncovering of the antics of the Wizard. The four companions return with the news that they ridded the land of the second Wicked Witch. The Wizard is befuddled by their success. He tells them to come back the next day without granting their request when the Cowardly Lion takes it upon himself to scare the Wizard, and succeeds in scaring Toto enough that he trips over a screen in the corner and "they saw, standing in just the spot the screen had hidden, a little, old man, with a bald head and a wrinkled face" (p. 147). Thus, reality is disrobed by the smallest of creatures. It's hard to get a dog to believe in appearances over realities. Of course, three of the companions discover what Baum's readers knew all along, that they already possess what they desire: the Tin Woodman a heart, the Scarecrow a brain, and the Lion courage.

In the next chapter, "Magic Art of the Great Humbug," the Wizard follows through on his promises by once again exploiting the distinction between appearance and reality. He empties the head of the Scarecrow and he fills it with bran, pins, needles and the remaining straw. The Scarecrow's head is bursting with matter and the Wizard notes that "Hereafter you will be a great man, for I have given you a lot of bran-new brains" (p. 157). The Scarecrow is taken in, and he is proud and pleased by this for his head appears to be filled to capacity with brains, even though the Scarecrow's ability to think has nothing to do with what's in his head. Then for the Tin Woodman, the Wizard installs a "pretty heart, made entirely of silk" (p. 159). The Tin Man believes it. Of course, the ensuing kindness the Woodman exhibits to all living creatures bespeaks a soul with heart that was apparent well before the Wizard was consulted. Finally, he has the Lion drink a potion from a square green bottle and suddenly the King of the Beasts is bursting with knowledge of his courageous nature. There's a sucker born every minute. All along it was his courage that enabled the four companions to escape from wild and savage beasts. Parlor tricks, trinkets and snake oil.

As we all know, Dorothy is the wild card. Seeing that her case is different, that only a real solution will be any solution at all, the Wizard offers a very non-magical solution to her problem, the ill-fated balloon ride. When this fails, Dorothy is forced to go to Glinda, the Good Witch of the South, who counters the Wizard's failure with a magical solution. Glinda informs Dorothy that with three taps of the heel of her slippers they will send her zooming back to the gray prairie of her beloved home.

The impotent, magic-less Wizard is a man deathly afraid of Oz's witches and ignorant of the silver slippers' properties. But when Dorothy rises out of the prairie grass of Kansas, she "found she was in her stocking-feet. For the Silver Shoes had fallen off in her flight through the air, and were lost forever in the desert," as is the Land of Oz from Dorothy's life—until she returns to Oz two books later. (In the film, the ruby slippers are a figment of Dorothy's dream-land, and are also not present when she returns to Kansas.) In the last analysis, the magical world and all of its challenges to Dorothy's sense of reality, dissipates with Dorothy's recognition that her source of imaginative escape was all along at hand, or at foot in this case.

Home Again

So what does Dorothy bring back with her from Oz? In Baum's *Oz*, reality is distinguished from appearance in order to acknowl-edge more fully the overlooked value and meaning of what we previously assumed were mere appearances. Discovery of the true meaning of appearances requires that Dorothy, and all others undergoing similar existential transformations, trade in unrealities for ideals; doing so, they can never return to Kansas, *but they can return to themselves.* Dorothy desires above all else to go home, and in fact, this desire is what allows her to experience the Land of Oz in all of its splendid color. But Oz is where she got her Box of Sixty-Four. Even if Kansas isn't Kansas any more, it's her coloring book. What good is it to have all those crayons and no coloring book?

Why should Dorothy wish to leave this ideal wonderland and go back to her boring life on the gray Kansas prairie? A destitute subsistence in a miserable hut is preferable to the effervescent, multi-hued dreamland of Oz basically because it's home. The truth concealed behind this cliché is that the ultimate desire to engage with the unreal is actually within each individual person, and it is the pathway to serving the ideals we cherish in adulthood. The distinction between appearance and reality that so entices the readers of Baum's books illustrates the existential shift from the outer world to the idea of the imaginative world of the individual person. Not only do children need to find Oz, but adults also need to return to this land of marvelous color, which is simply home, but with an Oz-ian twist.

Baum's tale is ultimately about the role of imagination in radically uncertain times and transitions in life, when the old is swept away and the new is unknown and seems unreal. The child's fascination with unreality points to an ability to imagine, which gives meaning to what would otherwise be a dull existence, where imagination stagnates. A childlike wonder infects those who encounter Dorothy's sojourn to the Land of Oz. The basic way a child's imagination is cultivated is through the art of storytelling, where words can evoke worlds beyond the immediate reality.

Baum understands that the essence of human happiness, the foundation for a vital and healthy life, comes with the fantastical tales that are the provenance of childhood. The wizards, fairies and elves of Grimm, Andersen, Wilde, Tolkien and so many other authors of fantastical stories, as Baum notes in his introduction, have "brought more happiness to childish hearts than all other human creations." Yet, it was Baum's intention to produce a newer kind of story for children, where the creatures of fairy tales are morphed into what he deems "wonder tales" where the moral of

each tale, along with the horror, is eliminated in favor of the pleasure of the imaginative experience. Children are not expected to
learn a deep moral lesson from Baum's work, instead they are supposed to simply enjoy the story and be transported out of Kansas
for the duration of the tale.

Why go back to Kansas? There isn't any other choice. Kansas is
where Dorothy calls home. But we don't return to our own Kansas
unchanged. Optimally we grow by our encounters with foreign
realities. We should not desire to go back to Kansas as it was when
Kansas was *all* there was. The existential understanding that comes
of engagement with foreign realities is possible due to the awe-
some creations that occur in the realm of the imagination.

The adult world is too often shrouded in the grey mist of unser-
viceable ideals. The ideals we inherit from the past become gray
over time. Living for those purposes inherited for others is like
looking at someone else's coloring book, all finished and done.
The colors mean nothing to us because the process of choosing
them and bringing the picture to life was someone else's. Even the
adult must be open to possibilities represented in the fantastical
appearances of Oz.

The ultimate appeal of *The Wonderful Wizard of Oz* is just this
intent, for in a world of radically uncertain times, where world wars
and cold wars and wars on unidentifiable terrorists have under-
mined our sense of what is real and what is not, where global
warming may change Kansas into Mexico and Saskatchewan into
Kansas, Baum's imaginative creation is a salve and a teacher for our
times. Where did you leave your crayons? You may need them
soon enough.[3]

---

[3] The authors extend their gratitude to the editors of this volume, Randall
Auxier and Phil Seng, who offered extensive editorial improvements to this essay.
We thank Randall Auxier for the binding metaphor, our Box of Sixty-Four. Thanks,
Randy.

15

A Sort of Homecoming: Growing Up with Dorothy

PHILLIP S. SENG

The basic Oz story in Baum's first book, *The Wonderful Wizard of Oz*, and in several movie adaptations of it, reiterates the theme of homecoming, a need to return to and affirm one's home. In all versions, the story goes something like this: a young girl of variable age, unhappy at home, finds herself whisked away to a strange and wonderful land where she meets new friends, finds inner strength and wisdom she never realized she possessed, and during her adventures (and even after their happy conclusion) desires desperately to return home.

There's something incongruous about her determination to leave the troubles of home behind and her equally passionate desire to return home, to the place of all her troubles. Dorothy's an ambivalent character who struggles to find something better, something to make her feel at home, so it seems a crucial question to consider is: What is this thing called home? The idea of home seems to change in subtle ways with each new version of the story. It's as if we don't quite understand it ourselves, and we keep rewriting the story to find the answer.

Plato's Cave Allegory: A Rainbow at the End of the Tunnel?

I'm not going to sugar-coat this issue with the simple conclusion that "Home is where the heart is." Whether home and heart are similar depends on your definition of "Home." What seems painfully clear in all the various adaptations of Baum's tale is that Dorothy really searches for something better, something not available to her at home in Kansas, and she winds up finding it while in Oz. But whatever "Home" is, it's not *in* Oz, nor even is it Oz itself; Dorothy finds her home within herself. Dorothy's empowerment is a happy conclusion to a child's tale, but only if the tale ends at that point (more on this later). But the point is that in every version of the tale there's a strong connection made between Home and *self-knowledge.*

The reigning Wizard of self-knowledge in Western history is Socrates, the hero of Plato's dialogues. In Plato's *Republic*—that ever constant touchstone of philosophy even today—Socrates tries to explain, among other things, the process of learning and education, as a process of acquiring self-knowledge. To explain it Socrates uses a visual metaphor that has come to be called the cave allegory. It's a story about the journey a person (or soul or spirit or mind—it depends on which philosophical theory you want to align yourself with) makes when traveling from ignorance to knowledge, and I think it's pretty obvious Dorothy travels this road in Baum's story.

Socrates asks Glaucon and Adeimantus, his main questioners, to imagine what it would be like to have lived one's whole life in bondage in the depths of a cave. You're bound in place, can't even turn your head. You can only look forward, and all you see on the cave wall before you are weird shapes in flickering light and all you hear are garbled sounds. Socrates describes the scene like this:

> The men have been there from childhood, with their neck and legs in fetters, so that they remain in the same place and can only see ahead of them, as their bonds prevent them from turning their heads. Light is provided by a fire burning some way behind and above them. Between the fire and the prisoners, some way behind them and on a higher ground, there is a path across the cave and along this a low wall has been built, like the screen at a puppet show in front of the performers who show their puppets above it. . . . See then also men carrying along that wall, so that they overtop it, all kinds of artifacts, statues of men, reproductions of other animals in stone or wood fashioned in all sorts of ways, and, as is likely, some of the carriers are talking while others are silent. (Plato, *Republic*, Hackett, 1974, lines 514a–515a)

The fire behind casts shadows of the objects and people against the back wall of the cave, and their voices rebound there as well. These shadows and echoes are all the captives know about their world—it's a world removed from actual truth and from any notion of who the captives themselves really are. They don't know they are bound, for they have never known otherwise. What Socrates tries to suggest, in other words, is that when a person's ignorant concerning some bit of knowledge, like when she doesn't know the Pythagorean theorem or where Kansas is on a map, then she's like a captive who can do no better than to believe whatever someone else tells her.

A prisoner's goal, naturally enough, is to get out of the cave and see the world for what it is—kind of like Keanu Reeves's character Neo in *The Matrix*. And that is *you*, your condition, whether you want to admit it or not, Socrates says. When someone finally comes along and frees you of your shackles or you yourself manage to dig up the nerve to do it, you realize that the images on the wall and the sounds are nothing but shadows and echoes, pale imitations of objects and voices bouncing reflected from people and things between you and the fire, and still far removed for the entrance of the cave where a brighter light shines.

In *The Wizard of Oz*, as with *The Matrix*, the journey out of the cave and into the light is fraught with struggles, but I'm not terribly interested in getting mired down in all the stages and battles (Munchinkinland, the Emerald City, two Wicked Witches, The Wizard, and the rest of it). Instead, what I continue to be fascinated by is what Socrates says we have to do once we get outside the cave: *we have to go back in* (line 519d).

You Can't (Quite) Go Home Again

Let's put some more perspective on this example. Perhaps you've left home for an extended period of time, for college or a journey overseas or summer camp, or maybe you've even spent time with other members of your extended family away from home. When you get back home you're different, and your sense of being different makes your home feel different too. It takes time to adjust. Or maybe you realize you'd rather not have come back home at all.

Imagine that you're a prisoner in Socrates's story, and you finally make it outside into the daylight after living in the darkest depths all your life. What would it be like outside? Well, unless it's the dark of night, you will be blinded by the light. This striking image of a person being enlightened is exactly the image Socrates uses to convey the process of education and learning. When one learns and grows, it's like being brought out of the cave.

So, why on earth would anyone ever want to go back home, back to the depths of the cave? Well, the best philosophical answer I can give (and really, don't ask philosophers to ever give a simple answer) is that we already are home, but we also have to return home. Let me try to explain this first in Socrates's terms (not the Greek ones, of course) and then how Dorothy is a Socratic prisoner.

Socrates's story is basically a lesson about the importance of knowing who you are, of gaining self-knowledge. Socrates thought it was a very serious thing to know who you are, to know your limitations, and to have a plan for becoming better. While on trial for his life he even suggested, "The unexamined life is not worth living" (*Apology*, line 38a). But, you might ask, how is learning a way of gaining *self*-knowledge? When I learn about the stars in astronomy classes or rocks in geology exhibits, or even rock stars in the tabloids, I'm not learning about myself. But, in Socrates's way of understanding how everything hangs together in the universe, *all* knowledge is *linked* in some pretty fundamental ways and has a similar origin. We can, by learning something new, make a bit of progress on the steep climb out of the cave.

Of course, some knowledge is better than other knowledge, but to be able to place it all in the proper scheme, to link it together, is to have knowledge of your *self*. For Socrates, the "self" is a rationally-thinking soul, encased in a body (which acts suspiciously like a cave). So, the goal is for a captive to act on the potentiality of the soul in their own body, to find her true home even while being trapped in the cave. In this way she learns that she has her home with her at all times, and also is able to go home at the end of the day.

Home on the Range

Dorothy and Socrates both love their homes. The moral of Socrates's cave allegory is that a person who becomes better (smarter, braver, stronger, whatever) must return to the cave and try to pass on their newfound skills—in effect, those who have learned to know themselves should help others out of the cave too. But remember, being outside the cave is an analogy for gaining wisdom, for learning the truth about things, and for finding out what's right and wrong. For this reason a person's "Home" is found, in Socrates's terms, when she comes to know the truth and give up the shadows and echoes. Home is in the sunlight, where the skies are not cloudy all day, not in the depths of the cave, even though we all begin in the depths of the cave (so it is, in a sense, our home, even where the buffalo roam as shadows and echoes).

Dorothy finds her "Home" while in Oz—the sense of self she gains through her journey makes her a more complete person. Oz isn't really her home, but in Oz she learns from Glinda that she always had it with her already, even when she was back home in godforsaken Kansas. Baum gives Dorothy the key to her shackles in the form of silver shoes (or ruby ones if we're talking about the 1939 movie). They have the power of taking her home. Dorothy didn't know about this power until informed of it by Glinda, but she possessed the shoes almost the entire time she journeyed in Oz. In a sense, then, she never gained anything that she didn't already have with her.

Dorothy wants desperately to go home, to the physical home that shaped her life, but Socrates' prisoner wants nothing to do with the idea of returning to the cave. A person accustomed to the light of truth, who then returns to the darkness of the cave, cannot be considered fortunate, yet Socrates suggests it's a duty that must be performed. Socrates finds home in the ideas of truth and goodness, of being a good person, and to return to the cave after seeing the light is like being the only human in a world of winged monkeys. But Dorothy takes the lessons learned and joyfully goes to her physical home with a fuller appreciation of her family. Socrates's prisoner reluctantly returns home because he fears losing the wisdom he has fought so hard to earn, but tries valiantly to encourage those still in the cave that a better life is possible for them. Both Socrates and Dorothy love home, and each is trying to bring the physical and ideal together, but they act with different emphases, from different concerns.

Kansases

How is Dorothy's home presented to us? Baum's classic first book is the source of all this confusion about home. He sets the story in Kansas, with Aunt Em's and Uncle Henry's home surrounded by "the great gray prairie on every side."[1] The land is a sun-baked

---

[1] *The Annotated Wizard of Oz: Centennial Edition* (Norton, 2000), p. 18.

"gray mass" with both plowed soil and green grass wilting into the "same gray color" under the force of the sun. Even the painted house suffered the weather and depreciated into grayness. Not only did the prairie and buildings become gray, but so did Aunt Em and Uncle Henry, the former from "sun and wind" and the latter from years of working "from morning till night" (pp. 18, 20). And, finally, the day the cyclone swept across the bleak plain "was even grayer than usual." So, Baum's depiction of Dorothy's home—the physical location of it and the people there—isn't very appealing to readers, though the grayness is somewhat alleviated by the Aunt Em's care for Dorothy and Toto's ability to make Dorothy laugh.

There are several movie adaptations of Baum's first Oz book that reinterpret, illuminate or ignore altogether the depiction of Dorothy's home in *The Wonderful Wizard of Oz*. They all show that Dorothy's home is not necessarily a desirable place to be. Instead, I think the conclusion will become clear that home must be understood as an attitude of mind and body, a complex web of relationships a person embodies and acts upon in their life.

In 1910 a short silent movie adaptation of the book was the first treatment of the book for the silver screen.[2] This version of the story doesn't merit much attention—it's a short film that loosely meshes together the storyline from several Oz books. Dorothy's home is a simple farm, and no scenes occur indoors (this fact becomes important later). True to film styles of the early 1900s the camera sits still and angles only change when the shot changes, otherwise life on a Kansas farm simply unfolds before the camera. There is no technique to convey what a "gray" place it is, since the whole movie is in black and white (out of necessity, of course).

A much longer black and white silent movie version came out in 1925, this one simply called *The Wizard of Oz*.[3] This adaptation also meshes together several of Baum's books into a complex story about Dorothy journeying to Oz and becoming the Princess. The director, Larry Semon, frames the movie with the story of a doll-maker reading a story—about Dorothy, the Tin Woodsman, and the Scarecrow—to his young daughter. Thus, Dorothy's journeys to Oz are set in a story about Kansas, and the story about Kansas is read

---

[2] *The Wonderful Wizard of Oz*, directed by Otis Turner from Disc 3 of *The Wizard of Oz: Three-Disc Collector's Edition* (Turner Entertainment, 2005).

[3] Directed by Larry Semon, who also starred in the movie as the Scarecrow, and also on the same three-disc *Collector's Edition*.

to the doll-maker's daughter in his workshop. The Dorothy of Semon's tale is seventeen years old, turning eighteen on the day of the fateful cyclone. Semon develops the subplot of why Dorothy lives with her aunt and uncle, and creates a movie in which Dorothy is the daughter of the King of Oz and, after her travails in Oz, claims the throne that is rightfully hers. In other words, Dorothy does not return to her home *in Kansas*. She stays in Oz and rules the land, or so viewers are left to assume.

The 1925 adaptation is interesting because it gives Dorothy some much needed development that the first book doesn't provide. Filmmakers recognized the limitations of Baum's character when trying to place her on the screen—viewers wouldn't know enough about her and so the character needed development, a back-story as they call it. In Semon's film Dorothy suffers from teenage angst; she is learning about her true parents, she has two young men seeking her affections, and feels generally out of place on the farm. Semon gives to Dorothy an anxiety about her *self* that the character of the novel lacks but which gives the movie—and the movie audience—something to build a meaningful story around, an idea to which we can relate. Who hasn't wondered about the meaning of it all during the teenage years? What kid hasn't thought at some point, "Is this really my family?" In other words, Semon takes the story from Baum's young girl and translates the tale into one of self-development and growth, much as Judy Garland's rendition of Dorothy does some years later.

One more movie version was produced before the classic 1939 movie by Victor Fleming, this one in 1933. Fans will know it's a nine-minute animated movie with little resemblance to Baum's book after the first minute or so.[4] Directed by Ted Eschbaugh and written by Frank Joslyn Baum, the movie actually presents the Kansas scene in black and white and shifts to color animation for the Oz scenes. Within the first minute, Dorothy—who resembles Betty Boop—suffers the cyclone and is transported to colorful Oz, so there's not much made about home or how distasteful it is. Nor does Dorothy return to Kansas, for the movie ends after a big dance number in the Emerald City (perhaps trying to resemble the popular Busby Berkeley productions of the era).

---

[4] *Wizard of Oz*, directed by Ted Eshbaugh, on the same collection. The movie was not released in 1933 due to legal issues with ownership of the title.

Fleming's *The Wizard of Oz* (1939) presents Dorothy as a teenaged girl, polite and desperately wanting to get back to her gray Kansas homestead. Truer to Baum's depiction of Kansas, this version also develops a back-story for Dorothy to suggest why she's distraught about her home life. Aunt Em and Uncle Henry don't have time to listen to her problems with Miss Gulch, the farmhands tell her what to do and point out her insufficiencies for her, without really helping her to save Toto from Miss Gulch's clutches.

The Color of Home

The shift from black and white to color (processed via the Technicolor process which is now all but given up in the US) marks the change between Home and Away in the 1939 film. It's magical to see the change to color for the first time, but it also reminds me of a more recent movie, *Pleasantville*, starring Toby Maguire.[5] In *Pleasantville* Maguire's character, David, is transported into a 1950s sit-com city called Pleasantville, where there are no colors: everything is in black and white. He finds himself stifled with the "cute" morality of the time, and eventually begins spreading color to people and places he touches. Maguire's David took his home with him, and altered Pleasantville into a more recognizable likeness of his own home. In Fleming's *The Wizard of Oz* Kansas never receives any color, but the same lines are drawn: Kansas is stifling, and the colorful land of Oz—even with all of its dangers and oddities—is the place where you go to grow and mature.

It's no accident that the house is taken along with Dorothy in the story; the house encloses her for as long as it can. She is not safe outside, we are meant to believe, and especially so during a cyclone. When Dorothy is inside the house she seems safe, but out of doors she runs away from Miss Gulch, she runs after Toto, runs away from home, runs after Toto some more, and she runs to get inside to avoid the cyclone. Outside, while in Kansas, is very dangerous in Fleming's movie. While in Oz, by contrast, almost everything occurs outside except when the group is held captive or meeting the Wizard.

Outside is also where Dorothy sings her anthem, "Over the Rainbow." Incredibly, audiences don't laugh when she sings this

---

[5] *Pleasantville*, directed by Gary Ross (New Line Cinema: 1998).

song. She's talking about a rainbow, right? And the movie up to this point is in black and white, showing us just shades of gray. What on earth will a rainbow look like in sepia-toned cinematography? How can it be magical? In any case, we know now she's singing a song about getting out of the cave of her discontent, about finding something better for herself. She sings her anthem in the midst of Baum's bleak, gray prairie. About Dorothy and this song Salman Rushdie writes:

> What she expresses here, what she embodies with the purity of an archetype, is the human dream of *leaving*, a dream at least as powerful as its countervailing dream of roots. At the heart of *The Wizard of Oz* is a great tension between these two dreams; but as the music swells and that big, clean voice flies into the anguished longings of the song, can anyone doubt which message is the stronger? In its most potent emotional moment, this is unarguably a film about the joys of going away, of leaving the greyness and entering the colour, of making a new life in the 'place where there isn't any trouble'.[6]

Rushdie identifies and dwells on the irony of Dorothy's preference for Kansas in the film when it stands in such sharp contrast with Oz. A person would have to be crazy to think of Kansas as the "home" that "there's no place like." The whole prairie is like Kansas, and it's all gray. Baum, having lived in South Dakota for a time, knew what the prairie had to offer, and it wouldn't be surprising if that's why he kept on moving around. Rushdie considers the movie a tale for emigrants, for those who desire to leave a place in hopes of something better. In Rushdie's opinion, Dorothy's belief that her "place" in Kansas is special is just ridiculous. Rushdie is partly correct, of course, if we consider Socrates's point of view. Dorothy is trying to leave to find a better place. But she also must return home and infuse her home with her newfound improvements. In other words, she's going to make her home into that better place.

Return to Oz

I could stop there but two other movie versions exist that are important to the idea of home. First, *Return to Oz* (Walter Murch,

---

[6] Salman Rushdie, *The Wizard of Oz* (British Film Institute, 1993), p. 23.

1985) tells the story of Dorothy shortly after she's back in Kansas from her first visit to Oz.[7] Dorothy's family is in dire straits as winter approaches; Uncle Henry is recovering from a broken leg, the house and all the farm buildings have had to be rebuilt following the cyclone, the crops were ruined by the storm, and there's not enough money to cover all the expenses. To make matters worse, Dorothy keeps day-dreaming, and night-dreaming too, about Oz. She's consumed with the reality of the place—even sees images of Princess Ozma in her mirror—and tries in vain to convince her aunt and uncle that her experiences weren't just in her head.

All of the film is in color, so there's no obvious and glorious distinction between Kansas and Oz this time around. Instead, Kansas is almost completely confining to Dorothy in the beginning scenes of the movie—it's full of things she shouldn't or can't do. Dorothy is of no help around the farm, and exacerbates the stressful situation by being preoccupied with her ridiculous fantasies about Oz. Dorothy in this movie (played by a young Fairuza Balk) seems somewhat younger than Garland's Dorothy, but an equal amount of distrust for adults is presented. Aunt Em and Uncle Henry are so up in arms about Dorothy's wild imaginings that Em takes Dorothy to Dr. J.B. Worley for "Electric Healing"—she's to undergo electric shock treatments to cure her of the "excess nerves" causing her vivid imaginings.

Home in this movie is enclosed, mostly dark, and filled with adults who don't trust in the reality of what Dorothy imagines to be real. The doctor's nurse, Nurse Wilson (Jean Marsh, who also acts the role of the evil Mombi) strikes a fearful pose as she watches Dorothy being strapped onto the squeaky-wheeled gurney for her slow, tense journey down the narrow halls to her date with the doctor's "electrical marvel." Dorothy feels claustrophobic in Kansas, as though her imagination is hemmed in and cannot express itself adequately enough, and the closeting she must endure is painful. So when she flees Dr. Worley and Nurse Wilson she runs outside, aided by Ozma, and finds escape in a river (a symbol of her free-flowing thoughts, perhaps). Not surprisingly, the river takes her to Oz.

When Dorothy returns to Kansas, Toto finds her alongside the riverbank from which she made her escape. After a period of recovery she awakens in her bed and gets up to look outside—she

---

[7] *Return to Oz*, directed by Walter Murch (Walt Disney Pictures, 1985).

doesn't yet go outside because she's home now, inside her room—and we see her looking out her window, as *we* look in on her. The house is nearly complete and ready for the cold prairie winter to roll in off the Colorado Rockies. Aunt Em finally suggests she go outside to play, and all seems fine with home in Kansas again. As the credits roll the camera pulls back in a continuous shot of the farm, showing us Dorothy's home. With Princess Ozma visiting her from time to time via a bedroom mirror, Dorothy no longer feels claustrophobic in Kansas.

North of 125th Street

Finally, the last movie to consider for the meaning of "home" in the Oz movies is Sidney Lumet's *The Wiz*.[8] In the movie adaptation of a Broadway musical based on Baum's novel, Diana Ross plays Dorothy, a Harlem school teacher in a large family. Dorothy is young at heart, and we find her in her aunt's and uncle's home helping them prepare Thanksgiving dinner. The family bursts into song before the meal (if I had a dollar for every time that happens to me!) reminding the younger people at the table, "Don't lose the feeling that we have" as a family, as a home. Dorothy spends much of this song in the kitchen—she's not one of the daughters or sons, or in-laws. She's an outsider even while precisely inside the house. She replies in song, "Lose it? Lose it? Don't even know the first thing about what they're feeling. . . . Can I go on not knowing?" From this point forward the movie's trajectory is about Dorothy learning what it means to feel like a part of the family, like she belongs at home (for more reasons than just washing the dishes). Even a Dorothy living in Harlem as an adult can face the problem of not knowing who she is, where she fits in.

Near the end of *The Wiz* Dorothy begins to grasp the full meaning of the lesson she's been trying to learn. "Home? Inside me? I don't understand," she tells Glinda (played by Lena Horne). Glinda tells Dorothy:

> Home is a place we all must find, child. It's not just a place where we eat or sleep. Home is knowing; knowing your mind, knowing your heart, knowing your courage. If we know ourselves, we're always home, anywhere.

---

[8] *The Wiz*, directed by Sidney Lumet (Motown Productions, 1978).

Possession of self-knowledge is what makes a person feel at home, and it is this knowledge Dorothy, in most of the versions of the story, has lacked until the end. She's at home with herself. Dorothy replies to Glinda's song, "If you believe within your heart you'll know" with a stanza of her own:

> "When I think of home I think of a place where there's love over-flowing. I wish I was home. I wish I was back there with all the things I've been knowing [at this point she is shown in a close-up shot against a black background: *she* is *home* as she sings about it, and as she con-tinues galaxies move past her, she travels through space towards home]. And I've learned that we must look inside our hearts to find a world full of love, like yours, like mine, like home."

As she concludes she finds her feet, back in her boots, in the street outside her Aunt and Uncle's home. She rushes to the door and enters, and the movie fades to black. More powerfully and more directly than any of the other versions of Baum's story, *The Wiz* conveys the message that Dorothy finds her home within herself, that *she* is home whether she's in Kansas or Harlem or Oz, or any-where else. All she needs to know is that it's within her wherever she goes. The achievement of this self-knowledge brings her home, to her physical home, because it marks the end of her journey out of the cave. She has learned the required truth, and now can return home.

Must I Repeat Myself?

Returning home is Dorothy's constant goal in Baum's story and in most of its movie adaptations. Now that we can understand that "Home" is more than just a physical location, that it's a realization of sense of self too, we can ask the next question: Can we ever really go home again? I mean, since Dorothy leaves her home in Kansas and travels throughout Oz, she changes as a person. When she gets back to Kansas and her aunt and uncle, can she simply fall back into the same old habits and routines that she followed before the cyclone?

The interesting part of Murch's *Return to Oz* is that it shows Dorothy in her unhappiness in Kansas. Some famous French film-maker noted many years ago that American movies usually end with some happy occasion (a wedding, a celebration, a victory) but French movies were more intriguing in that they took these happy occasions as the starting point and continued on to show how things fall apart after success. *Return to Oz* begins in this novel way, but ultimately proceeds just like the 1939 movie. In any case, at the beginning of the movie Dorothy dwells on Oz, she claims to be able to feel that something is wrong there, and her preoccupation with Oz gets in the way of a happy home life. She seems to prefer Oz *over* Kansas, if you can believe that.

What does Dorothy want now? She wants to return to Oz to see that everything is okay there; she just wants to check in. But by the end of the movie she really wants to return to Kansas again, the same as in all the other versions of the story. So when she's in Kansas, she wants Oz, and when she's in Oz, she wants Kansas. But what is Dorothy really asking for in her desire to return home? We've noted that "home" is a problematic idea, and in the course of her time away from home Dorothy will have certainly undergone some changes. Can she ever really go back to the same home she left?

Her home in Kansas won't remain unchanged while she's in Oz (unless time freezes, and that doesn't happen). The Danish philosopher Søren Kierkegaard provides some concepts to help us sort out what is really going on here. If Dorothy simply desired to get back to her old way of life and the same old farm she left behind, she would be recollecting her memories of Kansas. If, on the other hand, Dorothy wanted to return home for the sake of enjoying life on the farm as a different person, then she would desire the repetition of events on the farm. Recollection and repetition are two of Kierkegaard's concepts, and they are key to parsing out the differences in the many depictions of Dorothy.

Kierkegaard summarizes these two concepts in what may appear to be clear language but naturally is more dense than lead. Here's how he explains the concepts:

> Repetition and recollection are the same movement, except in opposite directions, for what is recollected has been, is repeated backward, whereas genuine repetition is recollected forward. Repetition, therefore, if it is possible, makes a person happy, whereas recollection makes him unhappy—assuming, of course, that he gives himself time to live... (131, 132).[9]

---

[9] Søren Kierkegaard, *Repetition* (Princeton University Press, 1983).

That's pretty clear, right? Let me try to unpack it a little bit and relate it to some of the various Dorothy's we've encountered so far. Recollection is the remembrance of things past, and as such the Greeks, particularly Socrates and Plato, considered recollection a method of gaining knowledge. Knowledge, as a body of facts, most definitely concerns what has happened in the past. For a long time it was understood that the way to learn anything about our future was to learn more about our past—by knowing what *has* happened we will know better how to handle future events. A lot of science seems to work this way: for example, if that levee broke or was not sufficient, when we build a new levee we will have to make some changes. How do we know what changes to make? We look to our past experiences to for the answers.

Kierkegaard believes recollection must begin with a loss, that we feel safe when we recollect because there is nothing else to lose (p. 136). Dorothy's loss is her separation from home, and we find in both Baum's novel and Fleming's movie the reiteration of her desire to return home. She wills the recollection of her home in Kansas. *Return to Oz* is interesting, at the outset, at least, because Dorothy instead dwells on Oz. Kansas is insufficient to the needs of her life, and she desires the repetition of another journey to Oz.

Repetition, on the other hand, looks forward. Repetition is more difficult, and, if you haven't guessed by now, much less frequent in our experiences. Kierkegaard claims that, "it takes courage to will repetition" (p. 132) because there's no safety in willing things to be different. The confusing notion to understand here is how repetition is anything new at all; it sounds like it's just the simple act of repeating something again and again. Recollection, for Kierkegaard, is a yearning for what a person has already experienced (like the glory days of high school), or for some truth that already happened (like the idea of a geocentric universe, when people believed that the heavens revolved around the earth). A desire for recollection is a desire for situations and contexts to stay the same, and thus for *ourselves* to stay the same with them.

Repetition instead looks to the future and all of life as creative and novel. In the face of absolutely new experiences the person who wills repetition proudly strides forth as a unique individual, someone possessing self-knowledge. Instead of willing that situations and experiences return exactly as they were (as with recollection), the will for repetition rests on the condition that the individual, herself, is stable in the face of a world of change. Rather than a repetition of circumstances or laws or environments, one who wills repetition holds firmly to her self-knowledge and lets go of all else. It is, for Kierkegaard, the equivalent of faith. Dorothy in *The Wiz* seems to characterize a person who wills repetition. She sings about finding home within herself, and when she gets home viewers simply know that she won't return to her meek personality.

With Baum's original novel we have very little to go on to indicate how Dorothy receives her homecoming, but she seems to be willing a recollection of her previous life. If we go by the illustrations by W.W. Denslow, Dorothy's a young girl and probably not terribly self-assured in her individuality. Judy Garland's Dorothy, on the other hand, is much older and more capable. But, tied to the spirit of the novel and some of the language, Garland's Dorothy does not seem any more self-assertive or individualized. Only Diana Ross's rendition of Dorothy seems to fully capture the sense of homecoming that is something more than just a mere return to a prior place.

What emerges from this investigation is that in our culture, many of us clearly want repetitions of Oz. We don't settle for recollections of Baum's book, or the 1939 film. We keep pushing the story forward, asking in slightly different ways, "Where's Dorothy *now*, in her journey towards self-knowledge?" Perhaps that's why she keeps getting older in the repetitions. In Baum's book she is a young girl. In Semon's movie she turns eighteen and in the 1939 movie she is in her mid-teens. In *The Wiz* she is twenty-four. We want to track her progress. We face the new version, the repetition, with the question, "Does she know what home is yet? And if so, can she teach us?" In the most recent rendition, having pressed Dorothy as far as she can go, we turn our attention to the Wicked Witch of the West, whom Gregory Maguire also depicts as "homeless," caught between the same two worlds, and as thirty-eight years old. Dorothy becomes uninteresting, but the question of Oz remains the same. Can we find home? The Witch doesn't manage it. We're prepared for another repetition of the Oz question, the question of home.

The significance of understanding this robust view of homecoming is that it lets us believe that Oz really does make a change in Dorothy, and in us. When she returns back to Kansas, or Harlem, she takes from her journey something more than when she first got to Oz. She's found herself, to some extent; she has greater pride and courage and confidence and wisdom gained through struggle.

16

Should Dorothy Have Stayed in Oz?

STEVE BICKHAM

I love *The Wizard of Oz*. The movie captivated me as a child. Then, almost before I could blink, I watched it with my children, and then—another blink—with my grandchildren. One aspect of the work that I have found troubling, though, is why Dorothy was so dead set on leaving Oz and going back to Kansas. Was it a mistake?

Dorothy's Kansas

The Kansas of the movie is bleak. It's the opposite of Oklahoma in the musical where "the wavin' wheat can sure smell sweet, when the wind comes right behind the rain!" The Kansas farm we are shown in the film is plain, with Dorothy's aunt and uncle working hard along with the three hired men—it's not poverty, but a lot closer to that than luxury. Then after Dorothy has decided to run away to save Toto we're shown a few studio shots of the Kansas countryside—a few scraggly blades of grass growing around a dilapidated fence, scrubby trees, withered corn plants, and some tumbleweeds casually blowing past.

The Kansas as presented in L. Frank Baum's book, the source of the movie, is even bleaker. Gray is the color motif Baum gives us for Dorothy's environment. In the paragraph describing her world he uses "gray" four times and "green" once—with a "not" in front of it.[1] And the gray is not limited to the landscape. Aunt Em was once

---

[1] L. Frank Baum, *The Wonderful Wizard of Oz* (New York: Grossett and Dunlap, 2000), p. 2.

a young, pretty wife, Baum writes, but, "The sun and wind . . . had taken the sparkle from her eyes and left them a sober gray; they had taken the red from her cheeks and lips, and they were gray also. She was thin and gaunt, and never smiled now" (p. 2).

As for Uncle Henry, we get one short paragraph to describe him. "Uncle Henry never laughed. He worked hard from morning till night and did not know what joy was. He was gray also, from his long beard to his rough boots, and he looked stern and solemn and rarely spoke." This is the land and the people to which Baum and the script writers have Dorothy, from the very beginning of her adventures to the end, eager and determined to return.

The movie provides more detail about Dorothy's environment. But while her house in the movie is nicer than that in the book and Aunt Em and Uncle Henry in the movie are more appealing people, the Kansas situation in the film is far from inviting. The farm hands are nice to Dorothy, but they have nothing in common with her. There are no other children for her to interact with, and Aunt Em and Uncle Henry are too busy to pay any attention to her.

Then, when Miss Gulch, the earthly wicked witch, arrives with some kind of document from the sheriff, her protectors meekly hand over Dorothy's beloved Toto into Gulch's clawing fingers. And finally, when Auntie Em is furious over how this situation has turned out, her "Christian principles" won't let her even speak, let alone act, hostilely to the villainess. So, of course, Dorothy is driven to run away to save her little pooch, changes her mind and tries to get back home, then is sucked up by the cyclone over the rainbow to Oz.

Baum never lived in Kansas, nor did he apparently ever visit it. He did live in South Dakota for a number of years before he moved to Chicago where he wrote the book. Perhaps he didn't appreciate South Dakota but did not want to alienate his friends there by making it Dorothy's home state.

Oz

What about Oz?

First the color. One of the most memorable scenes in the history of movies, to my mind, is when Dorothy opens the door of her house, after it has landed on the witch, and steps out. The land of Oz is brilliant. There just could not be a greater contrast between the Busby Berkeley choreographed Munchkinland of the movie and Baum's version of Kansas. Munchkinland is full of interesting people singing and dancing their little hearts out—when Dorothy sings in Kansas the most she can do is walk a few paces around the farm equipment, it's in Oz where she can dance. By her fifteenth minute in Munchkinland Dorothy has killed, albeit accidentally, a wicked witch, met and befriended a good witch, freed an entire people from tyranny, accepted their obsequies, obtained magic shoes, and is dancing her way to further adventure—all just to get back to Kansas.

As her journey develops she meets true friends, releases at least one other captive people from oppression (receiving her due adulation from all manner of creatures), risks her life, and does in another evil witch to boot. She accomplishes all of this with beautiful music, costumes, and dancing—and in gorgeous Technicolor. They love her in Oz. Ultimately, the Wizard accidentally flies off alone in his balloon. All she'd have to do to have herself declared queen, wizard, or whatever is just snap her fingers. *So why in the world does she want to leave all this?*

Dorothy's situation in the book and movie bears an unusual relationship to Shakespeare's character, Hamlet. Everyone knows from their English Lit. class that a key element of Shakespeare's play is why Hamlet takes such an extraordinary amount of time to do what it is clear he should do—avenge his father's death by taking action against his uncle. If Hamlet takes entirely too long to make up his mind, Dorothy takes too little. In fact, she never questions in the slightest her desire to leave the fair, green land of Oz, where she is a national or multi-national heroine, for gray Kansas and her isolated, unrewarding situation there.

The point I want to make is that if it is reasonable for us to ask, "Why?" about Hamlet's tardy decision, it must be reasonable to ask the same question about Dorothy's rash one. And not only that, since it is Hamlet's action that critics and students alike ponder, it is reasonable to consider Dorothy's decision in terms of *her*, and not the "alternative cause" of her action. The alternative causes of Hamlet's and Dorothy's actions are Shakespeare and L. Frank Baum. We could speculate as to the reasons or motivations why an author makes his character act as he does, but here we're concerned with the characters' motivations. A good story is an independent, autonomous domain. In a good story there are reasons why characters do things, and, while it's always there as a possibility, we are not at all compelled to shift from the ground of the story to that of the author to figure out why Hamlet and Dorothy do what they do. So our examination of Dorothy's action in terms of her decision seems on solid ground.

Philosophy

But, if it's an interesting problem why Dorothy does what she does, is it a *philosophical* problem? Why would philosophy have anything to say about what Dorothy should have done?

The reason has to do with the similarity or identity between what we feel for Dorothy and what we feel for real people. When we feel affection for someone we don't want to possess them; we want them to have the best. But what's the best that they can have? This question is philosophical—what philosophers call the issue of "the good life." What are the characteristics of the best life? We can ask this of ourselves, since whatever the answer turns out to be, it should transfer to those for whom we have affection (or love) and wish the best. Should we make the pursuit of a key goal the center of our life—say wealth, power, success, fame, excitement? If so, it's because we believe that what we are pursuing is the best.

If there's one thing true about Philosophy it is that there is almost never general agreement among philosophers as to the answers to philosophical questions, so Philosophy is entirely without official or authoritative solutions to its problems. Bertarnd Russell once said that the only thing two philosophers can agree upon is the incompetence of a third. Philosophy's major value is that it makes us consider important questions for ourselves. Philosophy sneaks up on you. In one moment it can seem the most abstract, theoretical, and distant kind of way at looking an issue, and then, pow, it hits you right where you live—What should *I* do? How should *I* act? What's most important in *my* life?

Well, What Is the Best?

When we want the best, ultimately, for ourselves or others, we are asking, "What is the good life?" And the most influential philosopher to address this question almost certainly is Aristotle.

While I think Aristotle is the most influential philosopher to have written on this question, his answer to it is has in no way restricted the diversity of opinion among philosophers. Hedonists are philosophers who, unlike Aristotle, hold that pleasure is the key to the good life. There have been many influential hedonists, but, while they all focus on the notion of pleasure, they also believe that different types of pleasure make for the best life.

Aristippus (who lived in the fifth and fourth centuries B.C.E.), Epicurus, (fourth and third centuries B.C.E.), and Jeremy Bentham, (eighteenth and nineteenth centuries C.E.)—all believe pleasure is the highest of values. But they do not agree at all as to how we should live once we accept pleasure as the key ingredient in life.

Aristippus believes we should simply try to get as much of this pleasure as we can—the college Sophomore position. Epicurus holds that what really follows from the "pleasure principle" is that we should each strive to obtain the most positive *balance* of pleasure over pain in our lives; having only a modicum of pleasure, but only a tiny bit of pain is preferable to having both great pain and great pleasure, because the former gives us this higher balance. Jeremy Bentham, still a hedonist, holds that the pleasure principle has very little at all to do with our *own* pleasure. He argues that since pleasure is the greatest good, it follows that we have a duty to produce as much of it *in the world* as possible, thus not favoring our own pleasure over anyone else's but favoring the pleasure of any group of people over our own individual pleasure.

Plato, Aristotle's teacher, is one of the earliest proponents of the very popular philosophical position of *dualism*. According to this view the intellectual and the physical aspects of life are two completely different and opposed realms of reality. He holds that our physical and intellectual "parts," soul and body, must be separated for us to have the good life. It is by using our intellect and disdaining all physical components of the world, including our own bodies, that we arrive at the best life for a person—which Plato believes, not surprisingly, is the life of a philosopher.

Aristotle, Plato's student, follows his teacher part-way. Aristotle saw the cultivation of the highest of our faculties as crucial to the good life, but he also saw the common-sense benefits and importance of material aspects of life. Aristotle thought it impossible, practically, for someone totally poor or totally alone to be happy, regardless of his or her intellectual attainment. So Aristotle places friendship as an important component of the good life, especially the friendship in which each party wants what is best for the other for his or her own sake. In terms of the contemporary perspective, Aristotle can be seen as advocating the attainment of one's highest potential as the essence of the good life, though—and here is the significant difference from Plato—Aristotle saw the area of our highest potential as determined not by our individual talents but by the nature that we all share as rational beings.

To care for someone, in Aristotle's view, would be to treat him or her as a friend and to wish the best for that individual—especially in the successful exercise of the highest faculties. This concern easily meshes with our concern for Dorothy. If you feel as I do, we wish for her to have the opportunity to develop the qualities (Aristotle would say the virtues) which she exhibits in her Oz story and which are the reason why we have the affection for her that we do. And it looks more unlikely that she will be happy in Kansas than in Oz. So we are understandably perplexed by her desire to return to Kansas.

The Paradox of Fiction

Unfortunately, just like Dorothy's journey through Oz, here we meet yet another unexpected obstacle. Up to now we have used Philosophy to try to get a handle on the slippery issues involved in wishing something for a fictional character—Dorothy. Now we face an objection to our caring for Dorothy arising from Philosophy itself.

This issue arises in aesthetics (the philosophy of art) and is called "the paradox of fiction." In terms of our issue of caring about Dorothy, this paradox is: (1) Of course we care about Dorothy, *and yet it is also true that* (2) to care about a fictional person such as Dorothy is impossible. After all, she doesn't exist. Judy Garland existed, but, of course, not Dorothy.

No paradox can be true, because all paradoxes (at least of this type) are self-contradictory. In a self-contradictory statement, if one element of the contradiction is true the other must be false. So the conjunction of the two statements—in our case both statements being true—must always be false, because by definition a conjunction must be false if either component is false (or if both are). Here, put in terms of our issue, is a bit more detailed presentation of this paradox.

We care about and have emotional reactions to characters in fiction. We wish Sydney Carton did not have to die in *A Tale of Two Cities*, but, under his circumstances, we are glad he made the decision he did. On the other hand, such common reactions seem impossible. To say that we wish Dorothy had decided differently about her location after her adventure simply makes no sense. As a fictional character Dorothy is not a real person. Since she is not real, she could not have made any real decision, and thus did not do so. Moreover, since she never made a decision, we cannot wish she had made one different than she did. And, just as it is impossible for us really to wish that a non-existent person had done something she did not do—remain in Oz—it makes no sense for us to think we are caring about her. One cannot "wish the best" for an "individual" who never did nor never could exist.

The two possible ways to defeat this paradox would be either to explain how it *is* possible to care for Dorothy or to establish that we *do not really care* about her, even though we *think* that is what we are doing. If either of the two previous could be proven, the paradox would fall to pieces because then its two components (one of which would be a new one mentioned in the previous sentence) would not consist of a contradiction when they are conjoined.[2] Each of the two philosophers we are going to examine briefly chooses one of these two strategies.

Currie-ing Favor

Our little effort to see if caring for Dorothy makes sense, and whether she made the right decision, is a bit like Dorothy's own adventure in Oz. When Dorothy and company arrived at the city of Oz the first time, they thought their quest was over, only to have the Wizard tell them that before he'd help them they'd have to bring him the broomstick of the Wicked Witch of the West. And that proved to be much more difficult than just getting from Munchkinland to the Emerald City in the first place.

Well, onward comrades! First up is an argument presented by the English philosopher Gregory Currie. Currie proposes to show how it is possible to care for a fictional character, in our case Dorothy, even though we know the fictional character doesn't exist. The reason, Currie holds, that people think it's impossible to care for a fictional person is because doing this seems to commit us to the existence of someone whom we know does not exist, and that is impossible. Currie utilizes the cognitive psycholgical idea of

---

[2] The last three paragraphs are about the branch of Philosophy known as Logic. It's always a good idea to read anything in logic over at least a couple of times. Sorry.

"simulation" to show how we can care for Dorothy without also committing ourselves to her actual existence. Simulation theory, according to Currie, holds that sympathizing with someone involves having the same emotions as the other person, *but without the same connection to action that the other person has.* For example, I do not act exactly like the person with whom I am sympathizing as she grieves for her dead husband, even though I have her emotions. I don't throw myself onto the coffin or develop clinical depression.

Currie proposes the following: Caring for a fictional character, say Dorothy, involves our simulating a hypothetical reader who is reading what is proposed to him as a *factual* account of a girl who is blown over the rainbow by a tornado, lands in Munchkinland, meets a talking scarecrow, and so forth. That *hypothetical* reader has what Currie calls states of caring for Dorothy because he sympathizes with her. He also, of course, believes she exists, so he might possibly try to determine where in Kansas Dorothy lived so he could visit her. When we, in turn, sympathize with the fictional reader, play his role, as it were, we come to share his states of caring (that is, just his emotions) but without sharing his belief that Dorothy is real and could be visited by us. We get the emotion of caring, but without the action relating impulses. Thus, the hypothetical reader is caught in the paradox, but we are not.[3]

Currie's position is very convoluted, even if it should turn out to be correct. Currie has to involve a *hypothetical* person—the hypothetical reader—as an intermediary between the real reader (you) and the fictional Dorothy to explain how you can care about her. I'm not saying this is wrong, and it certainly is ingenious, but creating a non-existent reader to explain how we can care for a fictional character just doesn't *look* right; it makes us feel that there's just got to be a simpler way out.

A Walt-on the Wild Side

By contrast, here is the position of a philosopher who wants to refute the paradox by attacking the first part of it—by establishing, in other words, that we *do not indeed care about fictional characters,* including Dorothy, though we may think we do. If we don't

---

[3] Gregory Currie, "The Paradox of Caring," in Mette Hjort and Sue Laver, eds., *Emotion and the Arts* (Oxford University Press), p. 69.

really care for fictional characters there's no paradox, because the statement that we don't care for them is perfectly consistent with the second part of the (now defused) paradox that it is impossible for us to care about them.[4]

This solution comes from Kendall Walton, perhaps the best known philosopher to write on this issue. Walton states, "The very fact that people make up stories and tell them to one another, the fact that they are interested at all in what they know to be mere fiction, is astonishing and needs to be explained."[5] And, "We frequently become 'emotionally involved' when we read novels or watch plays or films. But to construe this involvement as consisting of our having psychological attitudes toward fictional entities is to tolerate mystery and court confusion."

So Currie gives us an ingenious, though convoluted, explanation of what we are doing when we care what happens to Dorothy. Walton thinks it's amazing and unlikely that there are stories in the first place and then holds that we are misleading ourselves when we think we do care about her.

How Stories Work

I don't want to wrestle the Witch of the West for her broomstick so much as just sneak in and steal it. I don't want to solve or resolve the paradox; I want to *dissolve* it, sort of like Dorothy dissolves the witch. As a matter of fact this tactic has become a recognized strategy in philosophy made famous by philosophers as noted and different as William James and Ludwig Wittgenstein. The idea is to show that what seems like a puzzle or a problem in philosophy really just rests on a misunderstanding. Once the misunderstanding is removed, the problem just vanishes.

Well, maybe it's a dual misunderstanding. The first is to think of fiction, as do both Walton and Currie (and everybody else I know of in this dispute), *from the perspective of logic rather than that of literature.* And the second is not to see that the base form from which literature (or fiction) needs to be understood is not novels, poetry, drama, or film, *but audible story-telling.* I think that the entirety of this paradox stems from Walton's idea, which Currie accepts, that the very existence of stories is "astonishing" because

---

[4] More logic. See note #2.
[5] Kendall Walton, *Mimesis as Make-Believe* (Harvard University Press), p. 5.

they move us to act in an irrational (that is, illogical) fashion. And the concern with logic rather than our bodily, sensible, emotional responses reveals how current philosophers are still caught up with Plato's ideas.

In my view we are not involved in a logical contradiction when we care for a character such as Dorothy, because by entering into the story, or entertaining it, *we have removed ourselves temporarily* from the world in which logic reigns. The key to accepting this idea is to understand in some depth what attitude we take, what role we play, when we listen to a story (though this will also apply by extension to interacting with the other forms of fictional narrative).

It is essential when listening to a story to put yourself into the right frame of mind, a receptor or participant mind-frame. This fact was as true for the ancient Greeks listening to a rhapsode recite the *Iliad* in the local prince's court as when a child listens to a bedtime story today.

One of the absolutely central aspects of story telling and story listening is that they are "special." The child at bedtime knows mother is not telling her to do something, nor is she explaining anything. The child soon learns that strange things can happen in a story; a young girl can meet a talking scarecrow or have her flying house land on a Wicked Witch. Interesting, exciting, and sometimes dangerous things occur that the child has never imagined, let alone experienced. Sometimes a very young child is not quite sure about the relationship between the story and reality. "Mommy, could the Wicked Witch come here?" "No, darling, this is just a story." By around age five, so my wife the reading specialist tells me, the story-reality distinction has been cleared up for almost all children.

There are also true stories, as well as stories that might be true and might not be. (The comedian tells us, "Let me tell you a true story . . ." There's about a 96.2 percent chance, of course, that it's not.) But whatever type the story is, it has to be captivating so that the listener "enters in." Our regular life mode—including logic—must be exchanged for the time being for that of story life, in which anything can happen. Otherwise the story simply fails.

Nor are stories simply light entertainment. Often the most meaningful and important cultural possessions of a people are their stories. What made all the Greeks think of themselves as one people despite the fact that they were always at war among themselves? More than anything else, it was the the Homeric epics. The sacred scriptures of the Hindu and Jewish religions, and quite likely some of the Christian Gospels, began as oral stories. What we think of as Homer, the Bhagavad Gita and Upanisads, and the Torah are all older than writing itself, so we are certain that they began as verbal accounts. All of these texts were seen by their peoples as defining documents for establishing their view of the world and themselves, their cultural heritage, as it were. These sacred stories exemplified the beliefs, including identification with the characters, that one simply *had*, as a Jew, a Hindu, a Greek, or a Christian. To be a Jew, for instance, meant to be not just a member of a certain population but to see oneself in a certain context—the context of the covenant with Abraham and how this worked out with Moses, David, and all of the rest of the characters with whom all of us are familiar. And the same relationship exists between the people of the Hindu religion and the Bhagavad Gita and the Upanishads. And if the degree of total cultural identification was a bit less for the Greeks and still a bit less for the Christians, for these groups, too, the stories were central and held to be true. And yet they were stories, with the impact that only stories can have.

What these people and their stories did not have was precisely what Currie and Walton are insisting on—that there be a *logical* difference in kind between the emotional attachment to "real people" and to "fictional characters." Did all Jews believe that the whale actually swallowed Jonah, that Aaron's rod really became a snake, that Lot's wife became a pillar of salt, or that a snake truly spoke to Eve? Probably many did. Almost certainly many did not. The point is that the truth of a story lies in its structure, not in whether something "actually happened in exactly that way," which we can never know, anyhow, in the case of many stories. The truth of the Jonah story is that if God calls you to be a prophet and gives you a mission, you'd darned well better do it, even if it goes against the grain. The Hebrew words we transliterate as "Adam" and "Eve" mean in Hebrew "the ground, or earth" and "mother of all." Jesus didn't invent the parable form of teaching in his culture; it is perfectly clear that this method abounds in the Hebrew and Sanskrit scriptures.

Let's look at Job for just a second. Was there really a Job? Probably not, but the question is completely moot. People who are wondering or worried about whether there ever was a Job are just missing the point. It's about separating good and bad fortune from faith. Does the very likely non-existence of Job as he is described in the Old Testament book named for him mean that it makes no sense for us to debate whether he did the right thing in his response to his fall from good fortune? Does it mean we cannot really have any emotional connection with him? Take away any emotional connection with the hearer (or reader) and the story loses all its force.

And the crucial idea for our project is that we and the readers of *The Book of Job* knew all this from the start, just as we and all the other readers or viewers of *Hamlet* and *The Wizard of Oz* knew it, also. We knew just exactly what we were doing—relating to a character in a story. Despite Kendall's and Currie's ideas, there is simply no great mystery to explain. As human beings few things are more natural or straight-forward than listening to and reacting to a story. What is a little *less* natural is treating this emotional activity as a paradox.

So it does make sense for us to care for Dorothy, for us to wish for her the best, and for us to consider whether she made the right decision in returning to Oz.

Dorothy's Decision

Now that we know that we can really care for Dorothy, we need to look back at her decision, or perhaps it is her compulsion to return to her Kansas home, and to the issue if she was better off there than over the rainbow.

The movie version of *The Wizard of Oz* goes beyond the book in providing an explanation of Dorothy's final situation that would eliminate any decision on her part. As Dorothy is lying with a cold compress on her forehead, in her own sepia-toned Kansas room, after beaming herself down from Oz at the end of the movie, Auntie Em says, "There, there, lie quiet now. You've just had a bad dream." If Dorothy's adventure was just a bad dream, then, of course Dorothy is better out of it. This interpretation is strengthened by emphasizing the resemblance of the three farm hands, also not in the book, with the Scarecrow, Tin Woodman, and Lion of the adventure, thus lending credence to the Tin Woodman, Scarecrow, and Lion as dream creatures.

But is the movie right?

Dorothy's Oz experience does not have the qualities or characteristics of a dream. Dreams are disjointed and fuzzy. Dorothy's adventure is anything but. The inhabitants of Oz—Munchkins, witches, flying monkeys, talking scarecrows, and the rest—are fantastic to Dorothy, but they all play their parts with consistency and believability. We often react with great emotion in our dreams, regardless of whether this is our normal mode of action. Some people suffering from nightmares are routinely terrified during these. But Dorothy acts always with reasonableness, courage, and sympathy. She is in no way overcome or overawed by these unusual goings on.

Aristotle wrote a short account of dreams, and whatever Aristotle wrote, despite its being over two thousand years old, is worth a look. Aristotle defines a dream as a presentation, or an imagining that occurs in sleep (*De Somniis*, line 462a). Part of his point is that a dream is something that happens *to* us, not something we voluntarily do. But Dorothy's experience in Oz is something that she *lives*, not something she experiences passively. Dorothy's experience was an adventure. She is not a poor, passive waif. She charts her own course, does what she decides is best—even at great danger to herself—and succeeds brilliantly.

My guess is that no one has ever experienced a dream with such continuity, detail, plot development, dialogue, music and choreography as Dorothy's adventure, so Auntie Em just seems to be wrong here when she says it was a dream. Perhaps that is why Dorothy immediately questions Auntie Em's verdict: "No. But it wasn't a dream—it was a place." It seems to me that the script writers saw the inadequacy of Dorothy's just returning to Kansas no matter what, and tried to fix it with a bit of ambiguity. But it's a slap-dash job. Her adventure does not have anything like the wild, discontinuous structure of a dream.

In the movie Dorothy wants to go home. She says, "There's no place like home." But does this establish home as indeed where she should be? What I said earlier about whether Dorothy would have the better chance in Kansas or Oz is relevant here and a good case can be made, as we have seen, for Oz being the best place for her. However, there are a couple of relevant, problematic factors that emerge here. The first is that *the emphasis on home as Dorothy's goal, so strong in the movie, just is not present in Baum's book*. In the book Dorothy is glad to be home, but she states that now that her friends have all gotten what they most desired, she wishes to go back to Kansas.[6] The implication is not that there's no place like home, but rather like the Lone Ranger always said to

---

[6] *The Wonderful Wizard of Oz*, p. 204.

Tonto—"Our job here is done." The only other statement that Dorothy makes to Glinda the good witch at the end of the book resonates somewhat bizarrely, "My greatest wish *now* is to get back to Kansas, for Aunt Em will surely think something dreadful has happened to me, and that will make her put on mourning. And unless the crops are better this year than they were last, I am sure Uncle Henry cannot afford it" (p. 201).

There's also an important, unresolved attribute of Dorothy that makes the "no place like home" argument hard to evaluate fairly. *We don't know Dorothy's age.* Dorothy is called a "little girl" several times in the book. The first few illustrations make her look about four or five years old, but it is hard, for me anyway, to imagine anyone that young acting as maturely as she does in the book or the movie. And there is no consistency to her age in the illustrations. In general, she seems to be depicted as older later in the book (especially on pages 92, 96, 99, and 136), but this is not clear cut. To complicate matters further, the cover art on my edition portrays her as clearly eleven or twelve years of age, but the cover art is copyrighted 1994, while the other illustrations are much older. If Dorothy is a five-year-old as she is depicted in a good many of the illustrations, then it makes sense to say that she should go home where people can take care of her. However, in both the book and the movie she has been taking care of herself quite well, thank you, as well as leading three other adventurers on a perilous quest involving the risk of their very lives.

I regard Dorothy as twelve or thirteen years of age. This is based partly on her actions, but mostly on the picture we all have of her as played in 1939 by Judy Garland. Garland was seventeen as she played the part, but the wardrobe and make-up people did their best to take off as many years from her as they could. There is no indisputable answer as to Dorothy's age, and my interpretation of her character has been influenced throughout this chapter by my mental vision of her. I can only suggest that you close your eyes, think of Dorothy, and see what you see. Certainly if Dorothy is thirteen, the necessity of the return to Kansas is mitigated. Her future there is cloudy at best—dismal at worst. But there's plenty of room for dispute for those who take my "shut your eyes" test and see a dependent five year old little girl.

Finally there is one last possible perspective on the story of Dorothy in Oz that would either eliminate Dorothy's decision or else determine that she choose Kansas as her living environment.

This interpretation, never overtly stated but implied, especially in the movie, is that if Dorothy's adventure was not a dream it was at least a fantasy. And one should always choose reality over illusion and fantasy. Well, I agree with the first part of this interpretation. I think what Dorothy lived through is best described as a fantasy, a fantasy adventure.

But it's not at all clear that fantasy Oz, as Dorothy, the Scarecrow, and the rest experienced it, is any less real than the unpleasant fantasy Kansas in which Aunt Em and Uncle Henry find themselves. I've been to Kansas; it's not as bad as Baum or Fleming depict it. So the choice is really between a fantasy Oz and a fantasy Kansas. This is fiction, after all. It's not as though the Kansas of the Wizard of Oz is *really* Kansas. Nor is it always right, no matter what the circumstances, to choose reality over fantasy—specifically when the fantasy is wonderful and the reality quite bleak, as it seems to be in Dorothy's situation. The basic decision to be made is not between fantasy and reality but rather where Dorothy belongs *in the story*, according to our sympathies. Hmmm. Maybe we're ready for . . .

A Happy Ending

Have we arrived at any conclusions? I think so. Our reservation about Dorothy's determination to return to the Kansas of the movie now seems justified by our investigations of the good life as being one involving one's highest capacities. Likewise our examination of whether it's reasonable for us to have positive feelings for Dorothy has shown that this is at least philosophically respectable by our treatment of the "paradox of fiction."

Some time ago I mentioned that when we're thinking about a work of fiction, we can put our question in terms of a character, such as "Why does Hamlet hesitate?" or the same question in terms of the author, "Why does Shakespeare make Hamlet hesitate?" In our discussion of Dorothy we've been considering her motives, or mind set. I want to change our focus now to L. Frank Baum and the writers of the 1939 Oz musical, Noel Langley, Florence Ryerson, and Edgar Allan Woolf. We can see now that both the script and novel writers did not succeed in one of their objectives—giving their work a happy ending. Baum thought of himself as writing a modern fairy tale, one without all the gore and violence of the Grimm stories which were the only fairy tale versions available to the children of his day.[7] And fairy tales always have happy endings.

The standard fairy tale ending is, of course, "And they lived happily ever after." Well, this is fine for getting a five year old off to sleep at the end of a story, but when you think about it a little, it's easy to see that this simply can't happen. Life just isn't like this. The Stephen Sondheim musical, "Into the Woods" treats of this phenomenon. The play deals with several fairy tales at once, including Cinderella, Jack and the Beanstalk, and Rapunzel. The first act dramatizes these stories in parallel to their traditional happy ending. But the second half is what happened afterward. Jack and his mother are quarreling, and the two married princes are bored and looking around for new damsels to conquer.

There's also a darker and more serious side to this business of ending. Martin Heidegger (1889–1977), a German philosopher, made the famous statement that for us humans, our *being* is *being unto death*. We're the only beings, according to Heidegger, who live life fully conscious of the inevitability of our own deaths. I think he was right. How could an animal, even a chimpanzee, understand not only that it might die, but that it *must?*

Since it's a practical impossibility that we live our whole lives happily and an absolute impossibility that we live forever, living happily ever after just isn't going to happen. It makes no sense, even for a character. So we ought to have some sympathy for Baum, Langley, and the other writers who were just trying to tell us that everything for Dorothy was going to be all right. That's a fine thing to tell children, and *The Wonderful Wizard of Oz* was intended as a book for children. But the movie is not just for children. It's for all of us.

Is a happy ending possible for Dorothy in our story? The appeal of Oz as Dorothy's home over fictional Kansas is that it is easier for us to imagine her living in Oz, not necessarily happily ever after, but living a good life, a life of accomplishment and satisfaction. Well, let's make the question harder. Is it possible to have a happy ending for Dorothy *in Kansas?*

I could formulate such an ending. (I don't know how much you would like it.) But in fact I'm not going to do so. Maybe you can, instead. This might not be so hard, but don't be too sure. No fair having Dorothy become a doctor, say, and meet a handsome young

---

[7] See *The Wonderful Wizard of Oz*, Introduction.

man in town who went into politics and became a U.S. Senator from Kansas, while she establishes a string of hospitals in small Kansas towns—too easy. A good ending would have to really *fit* the Oz story and Dorothy's character. This would take some thought, all right, but it might be fun, and a philosophical kind of fun, too.

So, this is your mission—if you decide to accept it. Write a two page happy ending of the *Wizard of Oz* story with Dorothy returning to Kansas. You've thought about *The Wizard of Oz*. You got hold of this book. You even read my essay clear to the end. You're qualified, kid. You can do it.

17

There's No Place Like Home: Dorothy Gale's Relations

AARON FORTUNE

"I have a feeling we're not in Kansas anymore . . ." Wait, why is that a bad thing?

Like most Americans my age, I grew up watching *The Wizard of Oz*, but before revisiting it to write this chapter, I had not seen it in over a decade. Seeing a familiar movie after such a long lay-off is a bit like seeing it for the first time—you see things you never saw before, things you perhaps were not equipped to see the first time, especially if the first time was when you were very young. In this case, I saw that *The Wizard of Oz* is a very strange children's story, not at all like most of what is put out today.

First, there's Dorothy, who lives in Kansas. Not the kingdom of Far, Far Away, not an idyllic cottage in an imaginary wood, just Kansas. Now, there's nothing wrong with Kansas, as these things go. I'm sure a lot of really decent people hail from Kansas, and if you need a whole bunch of wheat, there's no place better (except Montana and the Dakotas, of course). But as the launching pad for a fairy tale, Kansas has about as much going for it as . . . as . . . well, I can't think of a more unlikely place to start a fairy tale, to be honest.

Dorothy lives with her Aunt Em and Uncle Henry. Is this an after-school special about living in a broken home? No, it's a fairy tale, and the absence of Dorothy's parents (in the movie, anyway) is never even touched on, much less explained. In 2008, that's a little odd. In 1939, I imagine, that would have been downright bizarre. While Dorothy's love and respect for her aunt and uncle are solid from the beginning, it looked to me, upon further review, as if some of that love and respect is a tad undeserved. The only action we see early on to establish Aunt Em and Uncle Henry's characters is their giving in, after some halfhearted opposition, to Miss Gulch's demand to exterminate Toto because "we can't go against the law." If some mean old bit—I mean—witch came to my door brandishing an order from local law enforcement and wanting to kill my daughter's obviously-not-harmful terrier, you can bet I'd put up more of a fight than Henry and Em do.

But Em and Henry do roll over, and Toto is taken away, though he manages to get back. And then Dorothy has to run away because she wants to protect her dog, because her aunt and uncle still won't, and that's how she gets caught out in the storm to begin with. And the tornado takes her to Oz. That's got to be a good thing, right? I mean, yeah, Oz has a problem with witches, but not all witches, we find out, are bad, plus there are Munchkins, talking scarecrows, and a wise, beneficent wizard who seems to be in position to right what few wrongs there are. Oz, to put it mildly, has a few things going for it that Kansas does not—at least one of them being the lack of law enforcement officials who are apparently employed by old spinsters who own half the county.

Home Is Where the Home Is, Even When Home Is Kansas

So the plot of this story is going to revolve around getting Henry and Em to Oz, isn't it? Or recruiting an army of winged monkeys to come back to Kansas and save Toto's life by dropping Miss Gulch in a lake? Or if the tale is a morality tale, Dorothy should probably learn something like "Home is where the heart is," something that will make it okay to abandon Uncle Henry and Aunt Em for her new friends, friends who have surely treated her more like family than her blood relations ever did. One of those ways, or some combination thereof, should be the way the story should go, right? Because there's no way, under the circumstances, that Dorothy would want to go back to Kansas.

Wrong. Not only does Dorothy go back home, but going back is all she talks about for the whole movie. Her longing to get home drives the plot. The story's resolution is her realization that "There's no place like home." And home is Kansas. Home is Uncle Henry and Aunt Em, and not much else. Home hasn't changed—it still offers no real answers, and it's still grey. Toto's life is still at risk at the end of the movie, best I can tell, at home. The Wicked Witch of the West is gone, but Miss Gulch isn't. *Maybe* the cyclone got her, but we never find out.

So when I say this story wouldn't make it as a children's movie today, I mean that the ending, while positive, isn't formulaically happy. Dorothy gives up Oz for Kansas, and nothing about her experiences in Oz concretely improves her situation back home. What changes is Dorothy's character, her attitude toward her surroundings. The moral of, "There's no place like home," implies a stoic acceptance of home for *everything* it is, both good and bad.

This message isn't one we hear very often these days, and the reasons we don't are deeply philosophical. They have to do with what we think it means to be a person. Everyone has a concept of what it means to be a person, and our notions of personal identity are intimately linked to our notions of home. The notions of person and home exemplified in Dorothy's character are not notions that we see much in popular culture anymore—but they are notions that still resonate with us today.

On the "Wonderful" Wizard of Oz; Or, Everything I Needed to Know about People I Learned at Chuck E. Cheese

To understand why this story is so unusual yet so popular and philosophically interesting, we need to understand the difference between Dorothy and the Wizard. Both Dorothy and the Wizard came to Oz from our world, and both arrive in very public ways that led the natives of Oz (Ozzians? Ozymandians? Ozzites?) to ascribe them both important places in society.

While Dorothy makes friends in Oz, she's honest about who she is and what she wants—she's no witch, and she wants to get back home. The Wizard, on the other hand, milks the gullibility of Oz for all it is worth, setting up his little humbug shop in the Emerald City and holding the naïve inhabitants of the City in his thrall. Clearly, these two characters exemplify two very different ideas of home, since the Wizard seems to think of home as wherever he can most effectively run his dog and pony show. With different notions of home come different notions of what makes a person, and these different notions of personhood are the philosophical meat of this story.

Ask a thousand people what it means to be a person, and you're likely to get a thousand different answers. To understand the difference between the Wizard and Dorothy, we can reduce those thousands of possible positions to two, based on their answer to a single question: do persons require direct, intimate relations to other persons to be what they are? To put the question another way, could a person *remain* a "person" on a deserted island?

People who think that people can be people all by themselves are called *atomists*. The atomist picture of people in the world is like the ball pit at Chuck E. Cheese. The thing about the ball pit is that there are just so many damn *balls* in it. It's the aggregate of all those balls that makes the ball pit what it is—fun to roll around in. But do the balls really affect one another? Not really. Take a ball out of the ball pit, and you've still pretty much got a plastic ball. Take it to the other Chuck E. Cheese across town, chuck it in that pit, and it sits there being what it has always been—a ball in a ball pit. The balls in the ball pit are almost identical to each other, which is why this idea of atomism works. They're different colors, but they're all made of the same stuff, are roughly the same shape, and serve an identical function.

For the atomist, people are the balls. Different atomists will have different answers for what all the balls are made of, but each atomist is likely to list one essential philosophical "stuff" (rights, appetite, and so on) out of which people are made, or one essential function that makes them what they are. And atomism tends not to think of people as essentially connected to a physical place, just like the balls that can be moved from one pit to another while remaining essentially the same things. The balls may bounce into one another, may even damage one another under certain circumstances, but they don't *need* one another to be what they are.

The Wizard is like a ball, and he sees the world as so many ball pits. That balloon of his lifted him out of one pit (Omaha, apparently) and dropped him in another (Oz), but that doesn't matter. He can go on doing what he does, floating on his own hot air, if you will. To an atomist, folks in Oz are not that much different from folks in Kansas. They're still gullible, still willing to be fooled and entertained by trickery, sleight of hand, and good old humbuggery. There's a sucker born every minute. The difference in location is just a difference in scenery because people everywhere are the same, and the Wizard is philosophically and psychologically self-sufficient.

Pineapple in the Ball Pit

If atomists see the world as a ball pit, relationalists see the world as a pizza, or like a whole bunch of pizzas. Pizza is yummy, but it's not just a homogenous aggregate of a single ingredient, like a ball pit. There are fundamental, essential differences among pizza ingredients. Pepperoni is different from mozzarella cheese, which is different from Italian sausage, which is different from mushrooms, and so on. But the unity in diversity that comes from *cooking* those ingredients together makes a pizza what it is. A pepperoni pizza doesn't taste like a stack of uncooked pepperoni or like a bowl of pizza sauce. It tastes like those things cooked in the right proportion with crust, cheese, and so on. You've had pizza.

When it comes to pizza, location matters. Cook a stray mushroom into an otherwise strictly pepperoni pizza, and you'll know. Try to serve a Chuck E. Cheese pizza at a Pizza Hut, and someone will notice and sue for damages. Order a Canadian bacon and get served a sausage and mushroom, and you're probably sending it back. *Or* take a slice of bell pepper out of the pizza line, and put it on a sandwich. Rescue the mushroom from the oven and put it on a salad bar. You've got a different ingredient, a different flavor entirely. Maybe better, maybe worse, but unquestionably *different.* And the different combinations of flavors make for different gustatory experiences, so that a Chuck E. Cheese pizza is fundamentally different from a Papa John's pizza, and double onion with bacon is essentially different from hamburger with extra cheese.[1] A person might like onions, and that same person might like pineapple, but from those preferences it does not follow that onions on a pineapple pizza would be doubly tasty. Some ingredients just don't belong on some pizzas. The British put corn on their pizzas and call it "American style." I don't think you could even convince someone from Kansas to put corn on a pizza. It just doesn't belong. And this is one case where Kansans are right and the British are emphatically wrong.

Dorothy is like a sweet little piece of pineapple. I like pineapple, but not on pizza. And even the people I know who like

---

[1] Usually the crust is on the bottom, but sometimes (like in Chicago) there are two crusts, and on very portable occasions the crust is folded over and baked shut (as in a calzone—is that still a pizza?).

pineapple on pizza would admit that pineapple doesn't belong on just *any* kind of pizza. There are only a few other toppings in the pizza universe that really go with pineapple. So Dorothy is a chunk of pineapple that gets lifted off of the Hawaiian pizza on which it belongs and plopped down on an extra large meat lovers' pie.[2] She's about to get cooked in with a whole mess of pepperoni, Italian sausage, ham, and bacon, and she knows she doesn't belong there.[3] So she spends the whole story trying to get back to her own little slice of existence, the place she belongs. To say "there's no place like home" is to say that while I am different from the people who constitute my community, I make them who they are and they make me who I am, so to leave my community, to leave my home, is to put me fundamentally out of place and destroy an essential part of who I am. A pineapple chunk on a Hawaiian pizza might be a welcome addition to the whole dish, if you like that sort of thing. That same chunk of pineapple lurking under a pepperoni slice is something you're likely going to spit out.

In *The Wizard of Oz*, we've got the relationalist view of personhood and home driving the plot, looking to atomism (in the person of the Wizard) for help, and *and atomism has no answers*. The Wizard can only send them on an idle quest to get them out of his ball pit. Think of the mess—pineapple in a ball pit. In the movie, atomism reduces heart to a testimonial, brains to a diploma, and courage to a medal. Atomism objectifies, and runs for the hills. But how are you going to get Dorothy home? The relation to home is essentially and irreducibly connected to the kind of person that drives Dorothy's character. There is no object to reduce it to, no way to cook who she is into something that belongs in the ball pit. Throwing pineapple in the ball pit does not make it a ball.

The Wizard of Oz is a morality play that juxtaposes relationalism and atomism as methods of creating persons, and in the movie, anyway, relationalism wins. If you want to make yourself a functioning person, the movie says that "There's no place like home" just works better than "Go where the money is." Now, just because

---

[2] Yes, I just indirectly compared Kansas to a Hawaiian pizza, and Kansas is about as different from Hawaii as possible. Perhaps we could say that Kansas, like Canadian bacon and pineapple (otherwise known as Hawaiian) pizza, is not for everyone. Personally, I am ambivalent toward Kansas, but I loathe Hawaiian pizza. Or perhaps this is just where the metaphor breaks down.

[3] Okay, so now she's a self-conscious pineapple. Whatever, just go with it.

a movie says something doesn't make it so. But this particular movie has been central to American popular culture for at least the last half-century. So the fact that this movie has this message may tell us something about ourselves, even if it doesn't tell us for sure what is true.

Seeing Our Reflection in the Crystal Ball:
What *The Wizard of Oz* Tells Us about Ourselves

The Wizard of Oz was Warner Brothers' answer to Disney's *Snow White*, released the previous year, but during its initial theatrical run *Wizard* did not approach *Snow White*'s success.[4] While the movie was critically acclaimed, it lost the Oscar for Best Picture in 1939 to *Gone with the Wind*. It would probably overstate the case to call the movie a flop, but it's generally agreed that *Wizard* underperformed relative to expectations in its initial release and that it did not really catch on until it began its regular appearances on network television, starting in 1956. Since the 1950s, *Wizard* has been at least as influential in American culture as *Gone With the Wind*, and both of these are ahead of *Snow White* in that regard, though the latter is hardly forgotten. Given what we know about this movie, why did it catch on years after its release? What kind of people are we, so that this kind of movie stuck with us through several generations?

Saying that a philosophical idea or system "caused" something in popular culture is tricky because there are so many factors that fall outside the scope of philosophical analysis. Why did *Wizard* not catch on in 1939? Maybe it was just marketed improperly. Why did it catch on in 1956 and following? Maybe its popularity increased as color televisions were becoming more widely distributed through the 1960s, and *Wizard* was one of the first feature films to use Technicolor. There are so many factors that go into a cultural phenomenon of this scale that it would be presumptuous to say that some philosophical notion "caused" it. Nonetheless, it would be just as presumptuous to suggest that a movie's ideas have no impact on its place in popular culture. So I would close with a

---

[4] All my specifics about the critical and popular reception of *The Wizard of Oz* are drawn from the special features of the two-disc special edition of the movie itself (Turner Entertainment, 2005).

few words about why I believe *Wizard* plays the central role it does today.

You Can Go Home Again

Two major functions of fairy tales are escape and moral instruction. These stories remove us from the humdrum of everyday existence and, in so doing, show us what the world could be, what it should be. Fairy tales work when the audience identifies with and buys into the moral vision the tale puts forward, when the audience wants to make the fairy tale come true, morally speaking. These tales succeed at moral instruction when the vision they espouse is close enough to the audience for the audience to see what should be, but far enough from the audience's everyday existence that we see that something needs to change.

The morality of *The Wizard of Oz* centers on a relationalist view of home and family that I would suggest was commonplace in 1939. Audiences didn't need a morality play in 1939 to tell them there's no place like home; relationalism was foundational to this country's political, social, and moral existence for its first 150 years. By 1956, that was starting to change, as a whole slew of philosophical, sociological, and political factors that philosophers like to lump together and call "modernity" had filtered into the American consciousness in a way that they had not seventeen years earlier. By 1956, huge migrations of our population were underway, we were becoming a rootless society, people were starting to feel alone in a crowd, and as much as we like to dress it up with prettier, more positive-sounding words (rugged individualism, self-sufficiency, self-expression, and so forth), that isolation has grown increasingly pronounced over subsequent generations. Next time you're at the food court, take a look around. See and count how many people are wearing ear-buds or headphones.

Today, we all want to be the Wizard. We're all too likely to go where the money is. We're becoming a nation of snake oil peddlers, rolling all over the map, trying to set up shop. Today, *Oz* works as a morality tale because the morality it espouses is no longer pervasive—but also because its moral vision is close enough to our history for us still to feel its pull. Today, the nostalgia we feel for this story is existential: it calls us to a way of being that we have lost, but not that long ago.

Deep down, we know that Dorothy is right, that there is no place like home, because that's the country we grew up in—that's what's in our blood. But today we need to hear it a little more often, because the voices of those who would tell you otherwise are getting awfully, awfully loud.

VI

Something Wicked
This Way Comes

18

Wicked Feminism

PAM R. SAILORS

I've lost all respect for Dorothy. First, she simpered her way through *The Wonderful Wizard of Oz*, letting the Scarecrow, Tin Man, and Lion maneuver her through every obstacle L. Frank Baum could dream up. Not only did they do all the heavy lifting, they also chivalrously tried to give her credit for their gains, simply because she invited them to come with her to see the Wizard. And, being the crowd-pleaser she was, she took the credit and proclaimed herself happy just because they were happy:

> "I am glad I was of use to these good friends. But now that each of them has had what he most desired, and each is happy in having a kingdom to rule besides, I think I should like to go back to Kansas."[1]

Perfect example of the stereotypical female: let the men do the work, coyly accept their compliments, base your own happiness on the happiness of others, and then return to the domestic front where you can, once again, be invisible.

The cinematic version of Dorothy in Victor Fleming's *The Wizard of Oz* was a slight improvement. In fact, if you squint your eyes just right, you can almost see Dorothy's backbone. She does try to stand up to Miss Gulch to save Toto, but he ends up in Miss Gulch's basket nonetheless. She thinks about running away from home, but when Professor Marvel tells her that Aunt Em will be sad without her, she gets weepy and runs right back. Just like the Dorothy of the book, all she wants is to get back home; she's not

---

[1] L. Frank Baum, *The Wonderful Wizard of Oz* (Modern Library, 2003), p. 182.

interested in acting to improve the conditions for anybody she meets along the way. And she's protected by the Scarecrow, Tin Man, and Lion; it's actually they who solve the problems encountered on the Yellow Brick Road.

This Dorothy accomplishes two things at least partially on her own: killing the Wicked Witches. But she refuses to accept responsibility for either act. When the Wicked Witch of the West asks Dorothy if it was she who killed her sister, Dorothy denies it. "No. No, it was an accident. I didn't mean to kill anybody." Later, when Dorothy kills the Wicked Witch of the West, she again refuses to accept responsibility for the act. "I didn't mean to kill her. Really, I didn't. It's just that [the Scarecrow] was on fire." Only after the Winkies tell her the Witch's death is a good thing does she "own" her act. By the time she gets back to make her report to the Wizard, there's no mention of an accident, instead: "We melted her." Of course, she lets the Wizard himself bully her until he's revealed as a fraud. And, even then, she can't bring herself to condemn him for his deception; she accuses him of being a very bad man, but softens after he gives everyone else what they want.

Wicked **Women**

In *Wicked*, Gregory Maguire offers a third version of Dorothy, one who panics and runs away from an impending storm in her first appearance—not an auspicious initial impression. Indeed, no one seems to take Dorothy to be a threat; most are charmed by her. Glinda refers to her as a "harmless" and "timid" child, and says "no one should take her seriously" (p. 346).[2] Boq the Munchkin expands on this description, saying: "Dorothy is a child, but she has a heaviness of bearing like an adult, and a gravity you don't often find in the young" and admits to being charmed by her (p. 360). For all her harmless charm and gravity, however, she's no better than her previous incarnations at taking responsibility for her actions. When accused of killing Nessarose, the Wicked Witch of the East, Dorothy points out that she doesn't actually own the house that crushed her: "the Mechanics and Farmers First State Bank of Wichita holds the mortgage so they're the responsible par-

---

[2] *Wicked: The Life and Times of the Wicked Witch of the West* (HarperCollins, 1995), p. 346.

ties" (p. 396). We aren't treated to the scene between Dorothy and the Wizard after she's killed Elphaba, the Wicked Witch of the West, even in the sequel to *Wicked*, where Maguire might have recounted it, but I expect she tried to lay the responsibility for that one on someone else as well . . . unless she received praise from others for the death.

This Dorothy also shares with the previous ones the craving to please others. She can't even get through a meal with a cordial Elphaba without dissolving into tears, not for herself but because she's worried that Uncle Henry and Aunt Em will be upset by her absence (p. 397). In fact, it turns out that her motivation for coming to see the Witch is to continue her quest to be liked by everyone, asking for forgiveness for the death of the Witch's sister.

We're given few details about Dorothy's trip down the Yellow Brick Road, but we do see that it's the Tin Man, Lion, and Scarecrow who save her by defusing the weapons launched as she approaches the Witch's castle. It comes as no surprise, then, that when Toto is grabbed by the Witch's monkey, Dorothy expects someone else to intervene, calling out, "save him, someone!" (p. 398). Maybe this is wise, since her later attempt to save the Witch from a burning skirt by dousing her with water ends, as we all know, in miserable failure (p. 402). Or maybe it's a success, since Dorothy's main role in *Wicked* is to bring the story of the Witch to an end; there are only a few more sentences about Dorothy after she kills the Witch, and precious little in the sequel.

Wicked is very much the Witch's story, as Elphaba demolishes all the many feminine stereotypes that Dorothy reinforces. Unlike Dorothy, Elphaba leaves her home behind to fight the injustices she has encountered. And unlike Dorothy, Elphaba has no clear or consistent protector. And completely unlike Dorothy, Elphaba is the perfect embodiment of a "feminist hero." That name might apply in various ways to various figures in our world or Oz, depending on what sort of feminism one favors. Like the inhabitants of Oz, philosophical feminists are not all the same.

Many philosophers can be characterized as "feminist," some as different as Gillikinese and Quadlings. "Liberal feminists" believe that it's social practices that hold women back, so those practices—especially ones that hinder women's access to career and educational opportunities—must be reformed. So liberal feminists act to change the system from within. "Radical feminists" believe the system is beyond repair. Rather than change from within, they argue for complete overturn of the social, political, and cultural institutions that have functioned to block women. Instead of working for women to be allowed to participate more fully in hierarchical institutions where power and competition are virtues, radical feminists want institutions with different values.

"Marxist feminists" locate the source of women's oppression in the creation of private property, and the class system that comes along with the idea of ownership. It is capitalism, not patriarchy, that must be overcome to eliminate the oppression of women. The goal for Marxist feminists is to move to a socialist system where everyone contributes according to ability and is provided for according to need.

"Postmodern feminism" goes in a different direction, claiming that no theory has a claim to Truth with a capital "T," and any theory that tries to claim it ignores the essential condition of human "differentness." There's no consistent and unchanging big-T truth, no essential male or female nature, and no unified "self." Instead there are local and malleable truths, a fluid continuum between male and female. and fragmented selves. To think otherwise is to worship logic and reason, that is, to think like a man. The antidote is to acknowledge the vital place of emotion and playfully embrace inconsistency. If there's no essential and unchanging nature, no one true fact of the matter, then there's nothing necessary about the way things are and no impediment to changing them for the better.

There are examples of each of these types of feminism within *Wicked.* And there are more types of feminism than I have laid out here. My own view and the claims I make in what follows are formed from bits and pieces of all of them. Likely, there are feminists of every type who would object to my characterizations, but that's to be expected. Not every Munchkin agrees with every other Munchkin; why should feminists be different?

The Mystery of Elphaba's Gender

Maguire's main character begins her life not as the Wicked Witch of the West, but as a baby, named Elphaba, born in mystery. She's delivered by midwives and left hidden with her mother, Melena, inside the Clock of the Time Dragon, a strange puppet show that seems to foretell the future. From the beginning her gender is in doubt, with the midwives in disagreement. The fishwife says it's "another willful boy," and proposes killing it. The crone says there's no need to be nasty because it's a girl. The maiden suggests they recheck because the child has the usual male equipment (charmingly referred to as "the weather vane"). Although they have the naked baby in front of their eyes, they can't agree on whether it's a boy or a girl. Finally, after several rubbings, the sex is revealed as female, and the uncertainty attributed to "some bit of organic effluvia" having been "caught and quickly dried in the cloven place" (p. 20). Simple confusion, simply explained, except that there are other hints that raise questions about Elphaba's gender.

Although Elphaba and Fiyero are lovers, she never allows his hands to touch her below the waist (p. 192); when her blanket slips off as she is sleeping, Fiyero notices "an odd shadow near the groin" and wonders if it might be a scar, but Elphaba wakes and covers herself before he can look more closely (p. 197). Much later, after Elphaba has taken on the name of the Wicked Witch of the West, The Tin Woodman spreads the rumor that "She was castrated at birth. . . . She was born hermaphroditic, or maybe entirely male" (p. 1).

Perhaps Elphaba is neither fully male nor fully female, but somewhere in between. Feminist philosopher Marilyn Frye, in writing about how important it is to us that we be able to identify people as male or female, explains that some babies cannot easily be assigned to one sex or another. We find this to be a problem, she suggests, because the easiest way to oppress a group of people is to make sure that the group can be easily identified. If men are to be the oppressors, then there must be clear and immediately obvious differences between men and women.[3] Elphaba is a strong character who always appears in control of her situation, almost never controlled by others. Maybe this is because she cannot be oppressed if she is not clearly and obviously a woman. Her in-between place and her innate cleverness create enough uncertainty for her to break the rules.

---

[3] Marilyn Frye, *The Politics of Reality: Essays in Feminist Theory* (Crossing Press, 1983). Regarding indeterminate gender, Frye claims: "There are people who fit on a biological spectrum between two not-so-sharply defined poles. In about five percent of live births, possibly more, the babies are in some degree and way not perfect exemplars of male and female. There are individuals with chromosome patterns other than XX or XY and individuals whose external genitalia at birth exhibit some degree of ambiguity" (p. 25).

Types You Can Play in Stereo

It's not like Maguire's Oz is so enlightened that there aren't obstacles based on one's gender; the usual stereotypes that go along with a culture where women are in an oppressed position are all there. For example, giving birth to a boy is cause for celebration; having a girl is generally cause for disappointment.

Elphaba's parents both have trouble dealing with the reality that their child is not a boy. Her mother was so sure she would have a son that she has to work to change her thinking about the child: "It was a she. It was a her. Melena practiced conversions in her thinking when she was alone. The twitching, unhappy bundle was not male; it was not neutered; it was a female" (p. 22). Elphaba's father, Frex, is so upset by the child that he suggests being female is a defect. He tells Nanny: "It's worse than we thought. . . . The baby— you had better be prepared, Nanny, so you don't scream—the baby is damaged." Nanny steels herself for the news and asks to be told everything. To which Frex replies, "It's a girl" (pp. 22–23).[4]

Seeing this situation as "damage" may have several related explanations, all reaching into stereotypes. First, Melena and Frex were probably disappointed that their child was not a boy because they bought into the stereotype that men are smarter than women. Elphaba recognizes that men only present themselves as smart and logical out of their insecurity. "Elphie had come to think, back in Shiz, that as women wore cologne, men wore proofs: to secure their own sense of themselves, and thus to be attractive" (p. 231).

Second, maybe Elphaba's parents worried that their daughter wouldn't be able to defend herself against some man, because they believed the stereotype that men are more aggressive than women. Sarima gives a great illustration of this stereotype when she explains to Elphaba the difference between hot and cold anger. She says children have both kinds of anger, but grow to have only one according to whether they are boys or girls. "Boys need hot anger to survive. They need the inclination to fight, the drive to sink the knife into the flesh, the energy and initiative of fury. It's a requirement of hunting, of defense, of pride. Maybe of sex, too." Girls, however:

---

[4] As strong as Elphaba turns out to be, her parents' unhappiness at her birth never stops causing her sadness. She tells Nanny she would've been a boy if she'd had a choice. "Not to be simplistic, but it always made me feel horrible, to know how I'd disappointed her so early on" (p. 299).

need cold anger. They need the cold simmer, the ceaseless grudge, the talent to avoid forgiveness, the sidestepping of compromise. They need to know when they say something that they will never back down, ever, ever. It's the compensation for a more limited scope in the world. Cross a man and you struggle, one of you wins, you adjust and go on—or you lie there dead. Cross a woman and the universe is changed, once again, for cold anger requires an eternal vigilance in all matters of slight and offense. (pp. 285–86)

The characteristics assigned to men and women here map right onto the stereotypical characteristics we require of men and women. Men are hot-headed fighters and women are cold grudge-holders who will never forgive or forget.

But Elphaba refuses to accept the distinction between hot and cold anger, realizing that having both is the strongest way to be, which sets her aside as stronger than both. She watches the sun melting snow that will become icicles and sees "warm and cold anger working together to make a fury, a fury worthy enough to use as a weapon against the old things that still needed fighting" (p. 286). It's the hot male anger that Elphaba has always felt like she had, but she comes to see in this moment that she will also need the cold female anger. In order to succeed in making things right, she'll need to go beyond the gender stereotypes and become a different kind of being.

Making things right usually requires power, which means over-coming a third stereotype—that men are more powerful than women and make better leaders. Even before Elphaba learns the difference between hot and cold anger, she talks as if she believes this idea, at least to a degree. In discussing wickedness with her lover, Fiyero, she claims that men and women are wicked in different ways. She says men's wickedness "is that their power breeds stupidity and blindness. . . . Women are weaker, but their weakness is full of cunning and an equally rigid moral certainty. Since their arena is smaller, their capacity for real damage is less alarming. Though being more intimate they are the more treacherous" (p. 197).

Elphaba must have been listening too well to her school's Headmistress, Madame Morrible, who said years earlier that "a man is always good for the public face of power," but when the man (in this case, the Wizard) finds that his tricks aren't working, he needs help from those who are more intimate and treacherous. He "needs

some agents. He requires a few generals. In the long run. Some
people with managing skills. Some people with gumption. In a
word, women" (p. 158).[5] In the end, however, we see that, alone,
neither the public appearance of power nor the intimate treachery,
gumption, and managing skills is enough. To make things right,
Elphaba will have to have the ability for all these.

What's a Woman to Do (Philosophically)?

Why do we believe that men are smarter or more aggressive or better leaders in positions of power? Because society has assigned
these characteristics to them and expects them to conform. Early
feminist philosopher Simone de Beauvoir famously claimed that
"One is not born, but becomes a woman."[6] Even earlier, John Stuart
Mill, put it this way: "What is now called the nature of women is
an eminently artificial thing—the result of forced repression in
some directions, unnatural stimulation in others."[7]

The point that both Mill and de Beauvoir were making is that
we become who and how we're expected to be. We don't just
choose how to dress, or act, or speak. Instead we are instructed, in
subtle ways, what to do.

Women are expected to exhibit certain characteristics and public opinion is used to make that happen. Be different from how you
"should" and you'll feel the full measure of social disapproval.
Unfortunately for women, the expected ways of being almost all
contribute to their oppression by men. If women can't vote, as was
the case when Mill wrote, they can't get into positions of power
and men are able to make laws that discriminate against them. If
women are expected to wear skirts and heels and be passive, and
men are expected to be aggressive, women are easy prey for
rapists.

But Elphaba is on a mission and she lives her life without regard
for what is expected or how she "should" be. From the moment of
her birth, when it wasn't clear whether she was male or female, she

---

[5] Although he's commenting on the film version of the story, Salman Rushdie
makes a similar claim. He says: "The power of men, it is suggested, is illusory; the
power of women is real." Salman Rushdie, *The Wizard of Oz* (British Film Institute,
1992), p. 42.

[6] Simone de Beauvoir, *The Second Sex* (Vintage, 1973), p. 301.

[7] John Stuart Mill, *The Subjection of Women* (Orchard Park: Broadview), p. 29.

seems to have had little concern for acting like a woman. Fiyero thought that Elphaba "wasn't just a different (not to say novel) provincial type—she seemed an advance on the gender, she seemed a different *species* sometimes" (p. 207). Is it possible that Elphaba isn't just somewhere between male and female, or some combination of male and female, but a bridge between human and animal?

Elphaba's Connection with Animals

Some philosophers who are concerned with the treatment of women have pointed out the connection between attitudes toward women and animals. Feminists have highlighted the ways that women have been seen as closer to animals than to men because neither woman nor animal has been thought to possess the ability to think fully rationally. Men are associated with the soul and thinking, while women are associated with the body and nature, including animals. This reasoning goes a step further, though, because unless you are able to think rationally, you don't matter morally, so people who are thinkers (men) can treat those who aren't thinkers (women and animals) however they please.

Since women and animals have both been oppressed, based on the same assumptions, the mistreatment of one is connected to the other—changing the assumptions is necessary for eliminating the mistreatment of either. Women and animals have both been mistreated, but not on the same level. Women are placed between men and animals in the scale of importance, "so that women, and especially women of color, were traditionally viewed in Western culture as neither man nor beast."[8]

Elphaba certainly is a woman of color, even if the color is not what was intended in the quote. And she definitely seems to be neither man nor beast; connections between Elphaba and animals are made throughout *Wicked.* She is born in the clock of the Time Dragon. She is described as "crablike," "a dragon child," "a frightened spring turtle" (pp. 1, 44, 50). Her father, Frex, calls her "little frog," "little snake," and "lizard girl" (p. 61). Her mother, Melena, is struck by the idea that Elphaba "is more grasshopper than girl, with those angular little thighs, those arching eyebrows, those poking

---

[8] Carol J. Adams, *Neither Man nor Beast: Feminism and the Defense of Animals* (Continuum, 1994), p. 11.

fingers," and thinks she looks "like a sphinx, like a stone beast," like "a naked green kitten after an invisible butterfly" (pp. 33, 46). Elphaba will not allow Nanny to bathe her in lake water; at the attempt, "she twisted like a cat in panic" (p. 30). Her roommate, Glinda, sees a resemblance to "a pointer on alert. Her chin was out, her nose high and nostrils flared, her dark eyes squinting and widening" (p. 172). Ice skating with Fiyero's widow, Sarima, "Elphaba looked like one of her crows: knees out, elbows flailing, rags flapping, gloved hands raking for balance" (p. 271).

When she is finally found after going missing as a child, Elphaba turns up in quite a scene. "Behind her was a low growl. There was a beast, a felltop tiger, or some strange hybrid of tiger and dragon, with glowing orangey eyes. Elphaba was sitting in its folded forearms as if on a throne" (p. 62). Her obvious connection with animals goes beyond mere sympathy; Elphaba may even bridge the gap between Animals, who have souls and the ability to use human language, and animals, who do not. We're told: "Elphaba looked like something between an animal and an Animal, like something more than life but not quite Life" (pp. 77–78), or, as already said, "neither man nor beast." Late in her life, Elphaba encounters a dwarf who tells her she is

> ". . . neither this nor that—or shall I say *both* this and that? Both of Oz and of the other world. . . . You are a half-breed, you are a new breed, you are a grafted limb, you are a dangerous anomaly. Always you were drawn to the composite creatures, the broken and reassembled, for that is what you are. Can you be so dull that you have not figured this out?" (p. 374).

Witch Liberation?

Peter Singer is a philosopher who is famously concerned about the treatment of animals. Singer claims that all liberation movements follow a common logic; they all claim that there are more similarities than differences between the group holding rights and the one seeking to share those rights. He also recognizes that the connection between rights for women and for animals is not new, recalling that early feminist Mary Wollstonecraft's 1792 *Vindication of the Rights of Women* was parodied in Cambridge philosopher Thomas Taylor's *A Vindication of the Rights of Brutes*. Taylor's publication:

tried to refute Mary Wollstonecraft's arguments by showing that they could be carried one stage further. If the argument for equality was sound when applied to women, why should it not be applied to dogs, cats, and horses? The reasoning seemed to hold for these 'brutes' too; yet to hold that brutes had rights was manifestly absurd; therefore the reasoning by which this conclusion had been reached must be unsound, and if unsound when applied to brutes, it must also be unsound when applied to women, since the very same arguments had been used in each case.[9]

Singer turns the argument on its head, claiming that since we now know that women have rights, and we now know that animals are similar to women in all the ways that matter, we must grant rights to animals. Elphaba, however, takes the argument back the other way.

Elphaba, the Political Animal

In Oz, women occupy a position between Animals and animals. Elphaba's biology professor, Doctor Dillamond, himself an Animal, devotes his research to proving that there are no relevant differences between humans and Animals. This is because he is alarmed about the ways that the Wizard's government was slowly but surely taking away the rights of Animals. Elphaba serves as the Doctor's research assistant and becomes passionately committed to his project and the welfare of Animals. In words that recall Wollstonecraft and Singer, she sketches for her friend, Boq, the main logic underlying the research, saying:

> ". . . the real interest of it to me is the political slant. If he can isolate some bit of the biological architecture to prove that there isn't *any difference*, deep down in the invisible pockets of human and Animal flesh—that there's no difference between us—or even among us, if you take in animal flesh too—well, you see the implications." (p. 110)

When Boq claims not to be able to see the implications, she's more explicit, explaining that the current legal restrictions on the freedom of Animals cannot be maintained unless Animals are different from humans in some relevant way. But Elphaba's goal isn't only

---

[9] Peter Singer, *Animal Liberation* (Avon, 1990), p. 1.

that Animals be granted the same rights as humans. She has a more feminist goal in mind. "And when the good Doctor is finished ferreting out the difference between Animals and people, I will propose that he apply the same arguments to the differences between the sexes" (p. 111). Even though Elphaba's argument begins with a slightly different concern (with Animal rights coming before women's rights), Wollstonecraft would approve of the logic and the goal.

Thinking Globally, Acting Locally

And Elphaba has the courage and strength of conviction to go beyond mere academic arguments. She confronts Madame Morrible about a poetry reading where Animals are ridiculed and cast as second class citizens and refuses to back down when the headmistress blatantly accuses Elphaba of ignorance (p. 90). She challenges her professor, Doctor Nikidik, when he tries to use a lion cub to prove that animals do not feel pain, eventually assisting in the escape of the cub from the classroom (pp. 145–46). She comes up with a ploy to convince the Wizard himself to see her, and then chastises him for his government's policies regarding Animals, going so far as to call those policies immoral. In her speech to the Wizard, Elphaba is "at once hard and soft, proud and pleading," exhibiting again both male and female characteristics (p. 175).

Her overall political framework also exhibits both male and female traits. On the male side, she can be focused on concerns of justice, of playing by the rules, of getting what one deserves. She proudly tells an old schoolmate, Avaric, that she has killed Madame Morrible. When he asks why, she has a simple response: "Because she deserved it." And she grins with happiness when Avaric calls her "The Avenging Angel of Justice" (p. 368). In the end, it's this obsession with getting what she deserves that gets her killed, as she does everything in her power to obtain the infamous shoes that she is convinced should be hers.

Despite this sign of male aggressiveness, Elphaba's political ideas show traits more often associated with females. When Glinda asks for more information about her childhood, Elphaba talks about what her family witnessed in Quadling country, moving quickly from the local acts of the Wizard's men to the more wide-ranging effects of his policies, all the way around to the erosion of Animal rights and claims of "a systematic marginalizing of populations." When Glinda objects that Elphaba was supposed to be talking about her childhood, Elphaba responds: "Well, that's it, that's all part of it. You can't divorce your particulars from politics" (p. 135).

This might sound familiar, since it's almost a direct quote of one of the most famous claims of early feminism—"personal problems are political problems. There are no personal solutions at this time. There is only collective action for a collective solution." The personal *is* political.[10] Feminists have never accepted the idea that one's private life has no connection to politics, in large part because political views and policies about the place of women have had such an impact on women's personal lives. Decisions about reproduction, for example, are intimately personal and also stand behind some of the most explosive political laws and policies.

Elphaba's Fractured Self

I've suggested that Elphaba may be between or a combination of male and female, that she may be between or a combination of Animal and human, and that her political self is between or a combination of male and female views. I'll finish with one more suggestion—that Elphaba's nature is so uncertain because her soul is between or a combination of identities. This idea—that there is no stable core self—is found in much of feminist theory and Elphaba embraces the idea repeatedly throughout her life, adamantly claiming that she has no soul/self/identity. Others suggest that the more accurate claim is that Elphaba's soul is a combination of fractured aspects.

When Elphaba is a little girl, Frex gives her a little wooden sparrow he has whittled for her. Within minutes she snaps the wings off the bird, leading the mysterious Turtle Heart, a man with the ability to see things that others cannot, to remark that Elphaba "is herself pleased at the half things," and that she likes "to play with the broken pieces better" (p. 39). Remember also that the dwarf, another mysterious being with an ability to see beyond the obvious, told Elphaba, "Always you were drawn to the composite creatures, the broken and reassembled, for that is what you are" (p. 374).

---

[10] Carol Hanisch, "The Personal is Political," in *Notes from the Second Year: Women's Liberation,* edited by Shulamith Firestone and Anne Koedt (New York: Radical Feminism, 1970).

The best example of the multiple aspects of Elphaba's self is that
she has two quite different identities. Somewhere along the line,
Elphaba the unusual child with the even more unusual color,
becomes The Wicked Witch of the West, considered by many to be
the very embodiment of evil. And Elphaba embraces the new identity in public while holding on to the old in private. When she asks
an Animal for her name, the Animal tells her she no longer uses
her name in public because "It's not afforded me any individual
rights to have an individual name. I reserve it for my private use."
Elphaba says she understands: "I feel the same. I'm just the Witch
now" (p. 315). She more gleefully embraces the public identity in
conversation with Boq, saying:

> "People always did like to talk, didn't they? That's why I call myself a
> witch now: the Wicked Witch of the West, if you want the full glory of
> it. As long as people are going to call you a lunatic anyway, why not
> get the benefit of it? It liberates you from convention." (p. 357)

Elphaba accepts the multiple pieces of her self because she recognizes that forcing oneself into a single identity is deforming. She's
not alone, since "a number of feminists argue that conceptualizing
the self as a seamless whole has invidious social consequences. To
realize this idea, it is necessary to repress inner diversity and conflict and to police the boundaries of the purified self."[11] Put very
simply, it's better to accept the pieces of your self than spend your
whole life trying to be someone you're not because that will condemn you to denying parts of yourself.

Mirror, Mirror

Elphaba knows that her self has multiple, sometimes contradictory,
aspects; she also knows that there's no unchanging *thing* holding
those aspects together. Told that "playing the Lady Rebel" is unbecoming, she agrees. "A perfect word for my new life. Unbecoming.
I who have always been unbecoming am becoming un" (p. 188).
Told that the interior of a person doesn't change, she responds, "I
have no interior" (p. 239). "I'm not a harem, I'm not a woman, I'm

---

[11] Diana Meyers, "Feminist Perspectives on the Self," *The Stanford
Encyclopedia of Philosophy* (Spring 2007 Edition) URL = <http://plato.stanford.edu/
archives/spr2007/entries/feminism-self/>.

not a person, no," she says (p. 191). And "I have no *self.* I never did, in fact" (p. 198). When she looks in the mirror, she can find no answer to who she is, nothing apart from all the various aspects of her. "I just think it's our own lives that are hidden from us. The mystery—who is that person in the mirror—that's shocking and unfathomable enough for me" (p. 267).

Yet, finally, near the very end of her life, Elphaba sees something in the mirror that isn't just shocking and unfathomable, but instead is revealing. She sees Dorothy and realizes their similarities. "Who do we ever see but ourselves, and *that's* the curse—Dorothy reminds me of myself" (p. 381). Looking into the mirror, seeing scenes from her childhood reflected, the Witch sees again her younger different self.

> I see myself there: the girl witness, wide-eyed as Dorothy. Staring at a world too horrible to comprehend, believing—by dint of ignorance and innocence—that beneath this unbreakable contract of guilt and blame there is always an older contract that may bind and release in a more salutary way. A more ancient precedent of ransom, that we may not always be tormented by our shame. Neither Dorothy nor young Elphaba can speak of this, but the belief of it is in both our faces. (p. 383)

This revelation drives the Witch to drug herself, "hoping for miracles, seeking some version of the fabulous alibi Dorothy was unwinding" (p. 383). This revelation also drives me to reconsider some of my earlier harsh comments about Dorothy and her apparent inability to accept the blame for her actions. I guess I'll have to take a lesson from Elphaba, the Wicked Witch of the West, that there's always more to any story if we see it from a different perspective. Dorothy might be a feminist after all—we just need more information to know for sure.[12]

---

[12] For that information, see the forty books after *The Wonderful Wizard of Oz* in the series created by L. Frank Baum, and the next book, *Son of a Witch*, in the more recent Oz series by Gregory Maguire.

19

"I'm Not That Girl"

RICHARD GREENE

> Wicked thoughts and worthless efforts gradually set their mark on the face . . .
>
> —Arthur Schopenhauer

In his novel *Wicked: The Life and Times of the Wicked Witch of the West* (1995) Gregory Maguire offers a somewhat "revisionist" account of the events detailed in L. Frank Baum's classic work *The Wonderful Wizard of Oz* (1900).

As with *The Wonderful Wizard of Oz*, *Wicked* is beautifully written, is ripe with social commentary, and raises pertinent questions about human nature and the various bases for making certain value judgments. A central theme of *Wicked* is the nature of evil, raising the question what makes a person wicked. The Wicked Witch of the West, Elphaba, as she is called, makes a perfect test subject, as we attempt to get clearer on the nature of evil. Elphaba certainly performs actions that lead to bad consequences—among other things she causes bodily harm and death, commits crimes, and plots a political assassination. Moreover, she practices witchcraft and routinely casts spells taken from a book of black magic—*The Grimmerie*. Alternatively, she is a dutiful sister and daughter, a loyal friend, devotes her life to rectifying injustices towards Animals (which are sentient animals, such as the Cowardly Lion) brought about by a corrupt government, and has generally good intentions, despite the bad results her actions occasionally bring.

Is Elphaba wicked or evil? To sort out this issue we'll need to address a number of questions: What is the nature of evil? Is evil

something that exists in persons? Is evil something that exists apart
from persons (that is, is it something that is just a free-wheeling part
of the universe)? Is having an evil reputation sufficient for something's being evil? Is "evil" a term that more appropriately applies
to actions, and not to persons?

"Wicked" and "Evil"

To this point we have been using the terms "wicked" and "evil"
interchangeably. Strictly speaking, it's not clear that they mean the
same thing. In fact, there's reason to think that they don't. Here's
why. "Wicked" is a term that applies only to things or actions. It is
strongly suggested by Maguire that Madame Morrible (aka
"Morrible the Horrible") and the Wizard are wicked. They do bad
things, they have bad intentions, and they don't seem to be concerned with things such as justice, rights, fairness, or the welfare of
others. They use people to further their own ends. It's also appropriate to call them evil.

On the other hand, one might at least wonder whether evil
really exists, without necessarily being used to describe some particular thing. Sometimes people say things like "the universe is an
evil place" or "evil lurks." For our purposes, this distinction does
not really matter. If Elphaba turns out to be wicked, she will also
turn out to be evil and *vice versa*. So we'll continue to use the terms
"evil" and "wicked" interchangeably.

So what do we mean by "evil?" Philosophers, while discussing
things such as "the problem of evil" (how there can possibly be evil
if there is an all-loving God) make a distinction between physical
or natural evil, on the one hand, and moral evil on the other.
Examples of physical or natural evil would include Elphaba's experiencing great pain upon even the slightest contact with water,
Nessarose's being born without arms, and Dorothy's house being
destroyed by a tornado. Physical or natural evils are things that are
bad purely in virtue of the way the universe is, meaning that their
badness stems from purely physical facts and accidental occurrences. Moral evils, by contrast, require something like bad intentions or bad character traits or bad outcomes (when resulting from
choices we make). Examples of moral evils would include
Elphaba's feeling self-conscious or being upset about her green
skin (provided the bad feelings resulted from others teasing her
about it), Glinda's snobbery, Liir's nearly dying at the bottom of a

well (Liir was coerced by another child, Manek, who was just plain mean-spirited!), and Madame Morrible's having Doctor Dillamond (a Goat and university professor) killed in order to silence his research on the equality of humans, Animals, and animals.

If it turns out that Elphaba is wicked, then it will be due to her being morally evil. It will either be a feature of her character that is evil or, perhaps, something about her nature is evil, or, possibly, she is evil as a result of her performing morally evil acts. We'll explore each of these possibilities in due time. For now, the important thing to note is that Elphaba's being wicked can't solely be due to physical or natural evil.

I Don't Give a Damn about My Bad Reputation

In *Jane Eyre* (1847) Charlotte Bronte writes, "If all the world hated you, and believed you wicked, while your own conscience approved you, and absolved you from guilt, you would not be without friends." This passage indirectly suggests that having a reputation for being wicked is not sufficient for actually being wicked. (The tacit premise in my argument is something like: if you can live with yourself, then you must not be wicked.) The possibility that having a reputation for being wicked is what makes one wicked is one that is explored throughout *Wicked*.

Elphaba largely gains a reputation for being wicked because she spends much of her adult life in hiding and when she appears in public she's disguised as a witch (mostly for safety's sake, as she lives in a tribal wilderness, among warring factions). It's only after her reputation is secured that she actually becomes a witch (it is towards the end of the novel that she begins working with *The Grimmerie*). Most of the spells she casts are actually aimed at good. She engages in experiments, for example, designed to give sentience to animals.

Part of Elphaba's reputation for being evil is due to her sister's actually being evil. Nessarose, upon inheriting a position of political power, becomes something of a tyrant. She rules Munchkinland with an iron fist, with an eye toward promoting her own religious (called "Unionist") values, and is not beyond profiting from the misfortune of her subjects (though her doing so always seems to have a "moral" pretense). For example, the Tin Woodman, previously a human and a Munchkinlander, becomes tin as a result of a spell that Nessarose casts in exchange for a Cow and a Sheep

(Nessarose justified this act by stating, "The righteous person can work miracles in the honor of the Unnamed God."). Citizens of Oz assume that Elphaba also is evil. Finally, her reputation for being wicked, to some extent, is a product of her general demeanor— Elphaba, throughout her life, was disagreeable, standoffish, cantankerous, and just plain nasty with people. Presumably, these traits had to do with her physical appearance, specifically, her being green. Perhaps this type of behavior was a sort of defense mechanism. Even if Elphaba turns out to be wicked, there doesn't appear to be a strong correlation between her wickedness and her reputation for it.

Naughty by Nature

The Bronte quotation given above is suggestive of something Plato raised in *The Republic*. Glaucon is challenging Socrates to show that to be good or just has intrinsic value, that is, he wants Socrates to show that being just or good is its own reward. Glaucon, on the other hand, holds that being just or good has only instrumental value—being good or just is valuable only for the consequences it brings. To make his case, Glaucon asks Socrates to compare the life of a perfectly just person, who has a reputation for being perfectly evil, with a perfectly unjust person, who has a reputation for being perfectly good. Glaucon contends that the perfectly unjust person is better off, since he gets all the good consequences of being just (because of his reputation for being perfectly good). Socrates, of course, holds that the perfectly just person is the one who is better off (even though his reputation prevents him from getting the good consequences).

On both Glaucon's view and the view of Socrates there is a disconnect between one's reputation and whether one is actually good or wicked. This distinction suggests that being wicked must be due either to features of one's nature or is so in virtue of the actions one performs. We will consider each of these possibilities in turn.

Certainly one way a person could be evil is by having an evil nature. This would involve having some metaphysical property that makes it the case that one is evil. Vampires, for example, have an evil nature, in virtue of having the metaphysical property of being cursed. They couldn't be good no matter what they do. Is Elphaba evil in the way that vampires are evil?

Elphaba eventually becomes a witch. Perhaps witches are evil in the way the vampires are evil. This comparison may be so in some worlds, but in the worlds of Oz created by Baum and Maguire, it appears not to be the case. The obvious counterexample in both worlds is Glinda—the good witch. In Maguire's Oz, Glinda does not start out good by nature. Prior to her becoming friends with Elphaba (Glinda was called "Galinda" then), Galinda was shallow, superficial, deceitful, and manipulative, but eventually she grew to be good, by and large devoting her life to charity work. Of course in Baum's Oz Glinda is always good (or so the reader is led to suppose), although in the book, she is the Good Witch of the South, and the Witch of the North is a different character. Maguire also introduces a second good witch—Nor. Nor is a child, who upon going through puberty, begins to realize that she has certain powers (she has considerably less trouble, for example, getting Elphaba's broom to fly than Elphaba herself has). There is no evidence in the text to suggest that Nor is anything but good, although bad things befall her, both in that book and the sequel, *Son of a Witch*. Thus, the possibility remains that Elphaba, in virtue of practicing the black magic of *The Grimmerie* is evil, but it is not plausible to suppose that she is evil purely in virtue of being a witch.

Perhaps Elphaba was just born evil. This possibility is actually raised a number of times in the text. The circumstances of Elphaba's birth were odd, to say the least. She was born in the bowels of The Clock of the Time Dragon—a blasphemous, pagan future-telling tiktok (mechanical) contraption—as it prophesized the birth of a "little dragon." The midwives who helped with her birth thought that killing her would have been "the kindest course of action." One midwife declared, "I think it's rotten." She was born emerald green with baby teeth that resembled those of a mature shark. Her first act wasn't crying; rather, she bit off the finger of one of the midwives. Her father, Frexspar, a Unionist minister, around the time of her birth considered her to be "a terror," "a beast," "damaged," "the devil," "cursed," and "born to plague" him.

Elphaba, in response to these claims, asked him, "why was I cursed to be different? . . . You are a holy man, you must know." On occasion Frex was driven to musing on "the nature of evil," attributing Elphaba's existence to "a vacuum set up by the inexplicable absence of the Unnamed God, and into which spiritual poison must rush." At one point he held an exorcism. Elphaba's nanny referred to her as "a demon," "a horrid little thing," and wondered whether she was "devil's spawn." Her own mother considered her to be "a monster."

That Elphaba was considered to be a form of evil, even by those closest to her and charged with loving her, does not make it true that she was, in fact, evil. Just as having a reputation for being evil doesn't make one evil, being perceived as evil doesn't make one evil, either.

But what of the prophecy of the Clock of the Time Dragon? Like all portents and premonitions, it's a bit lacking in detail. The Clock of the Time Dragon correctly predicted that Elphaba and her sister, Nessarose, would play important roles in the distant future of Oz, but fell well short of establishing that either was evil by nature.

Elphaba's first act—biting of the finger of a midwife—certainly looks to be an evil act, but is it evidence of Elphaba's being evil in the way a vampire is evil? At least one alternate explanation presents itself. Elphaba was merely doing what all infants do; she was suckling. She just happened to have really sharp teeth, such that she couldn't suck on a finger with out severing it. Thus, the textual evidence for Elphaba's being wicked by nature just isn't there.

One final proposal along these lines is that Elphaba just has some odd metaphysical property that causes badness to result whenever she is present or involved in something. The badness could then be attributed to Elphaba in some respect, but this wouldn't be sufficient for Elphaba's being evil, as this would be an instance of natural evil (despite the supernatural overtones). Notice the contrast in this scenario with the kind of curse that vampires operate under. Their curse forces them always to choose badness. They actually desire badness and seek it out. Under this proposal Elphaba makes no such choices and has no such desires—the universe is just constituted such that as a law things Elphaba affects go badly.

As Nasty as I Wanna Be

Thus far we've considered whether the Wicked Witch of the West is wicked in virtue of either her reputation for being wicked or some property of her essential nature. In each case, we've not found sufficient reason for considering her to be evil or wicked.

Perhaps we've been looking at things backwards. It may well be the case that evil or wickedness is not a property that attaches to people because of how they are (or how they are perceived); rather, one is evil in virtue of the things one does. In other words, it's not the case that being evil leads to evil actions; instead, performing evil actions is what makes it the case that one is evil. This conclusion sounds right. When we declare people such as serial killers or fascist dictators to be evil, we are not typically asserting that they have metaphysical properties that most people lack. We think they are evil because of the things they do. So provided that someone does enough bad things, or has certain propensities to do bad things (or possibly does some single thing that is so horrendous, like blowing up the planet) such a person appropriately can be called "wicked" or "evil."

David Hume, in arguing for a kind of moral subjectivism, points out that morality is not something that is in the world (*A Treatise of Human Nature*, Book III, Part I, Section I). It's not the case, on Hume's view, that we observe morality and form moral judgments on the basis of our observations. Rather, we observe facts and then form moral judgments on the basis of those facts. Following Hume, we might also hold that wickedness or evil is not something actually found in actions, but rather in our assessment of the actions. Our proposal then is that being wicked or evil is a matter of routinely or sufficiently often performing actions that we feel are evil. Such an approach dovetails nicely with our intuitions about persons we want to consider evil (for example, the aforementioned serial killers and fascist dictators) whose actions we didn't actually witness in person.

So is Elphaba evil in virtue of the actions she performs? It depends on whether she performs bad actions often enough or whether certain of her actions are severe enough. To sort out this situation we need to get clear on what we mean by "actions." The essential or defining characteristic of an action, at least as far as determining whether an action is bad or not, could be either the intention of the act or the outcome of the act.

There is a connection here between wickedness and evil, on the one hand, and normative ethical theories, on the other. Some moral theories that hold that the moral worth of an action is found in the intentions upon which it's based, will also hold that wicked people are people with bad intentions. Conversely, other moral theories that hold that the moral worth of an action is found in the outcome of an action, will hold that wicked people are those who bring about bad consequences.

Let's look at a few episodes from Elphaba's life to see if on either account a clear verdict of her wickedness emerges. As we saw, as a newborn, Elphaba bit off the finger of a midwife. Here we have a bad result, but it's not obvious that she acted with a bad intention. In fact, the greater likelihood is that she was acting instinctively, and without any particular intention, given her age (a few minutes old).

While at college Elphaba disrupted classroom science experiments. One consequence was that a small Lion cub she helped remove from the classroom grew up to be the Cowardly Lion. Again, the outcome was bad, but her intentions were good. She was trying to prevent an eventual loss of sentience in Animals, and to speak up for the rights of this particular Animal.

Eventually Elphaba devoted her life to becoming an Animal rights activist. Her early attempts to promote Animal rights by working within the system were met with resistance. Later she ended up working as a sort of Animal rights terrorist. She plotted and intended to assassinate Madame Morrible (an agent of the Wizard's in his attempt to oppress and eventually eliminate Animals). Her plan failed as a group of school children interfered with her target, causing Elphaba to abort her plan. Further fallout from her activism was the death of her lover, Fiyero, although the badness of his death may more appropriately be attributed to agents of the Wizard. Still, Elphaba's activities put him at risk, as she well knew. Here, with the assassination plot, we have the opposite case: bad intentions without bad consequences (for the target). A second attempt on Madame Morrible's life yielded similar results. Years later Elphaba went to kill an aging Madame Morrible. This time, fate intervened. When Elphaba was ready to kill her Madame Morrible had already died of natural causes. So again we have bad intentions without bad consequences.

Fiyero, while carrying on with Elphaba, was married to an arranged bride named Sarima. Elphaba blamed herself for Fiyero's death so she traveled a great distance to Sarima's home, Kiamo Ko, to make amends. As Elphaba was under the watchful eyes of Madame Morrible and the Wizard (as a result of her activism), she brought unwanted military attention to the home of Sarima, which ultimately resulted in the political executions of Sarima, her son, and her sisters. Once again, Elphaba's good intentions yielded an unwanted and undesirable result.

Let's look at two other incidents. While traveling to Kiamo Ko, Elphaba became angered at their caravan's chef. Her anger resulted in a swarm of bees (pets of Elphaba) killing the chef. When Sarima's younger son Manek had coerced Liir (Elphaba's son) into a fishwell, where he was nearly drowned, Elphaba's anger caused an icicle to fall, impaling Manek and ultimately killing him. Presumably Elphaba had no evil intentions in these cases. The deaths are attributable to her only insofar as they resulted from magical abilities that she was not yet even aware she had. She entertains some bad intentions along the way, but these intentions are transient and ineffectual, and offset by intentions and remorse that are contrary—harboring malicious intentions is not a mark of her character.

So with the exception of the two attempts on Madame Morrible's life it seems that the case for Elphaba's wickedness lies mainly in the bad results that her actions brought about. She typically had good intentions. Moreover, there's an argument to be made that her intentions with respect to Madame Morrible weren't all that bad. Madame Morrible did horrible things and needed to be stopped. Elphaba's intentions can be characterized as an attempt to stop injustice. When framed this way they actually seem like good intentions. It, thus, seems implausible to attribute wickedness to Elphaba on the basis of her intentions.

So do Elphaba's actions that so often bring bad consequences serve to make her wicked? Elphaba seemed to think so. From her perspective her life was a failure: very few things turned out as she intended (in most cases she made things worse), and the results of her actions were tragic. She felt as though she deserved to die and intended to do so once she made her amends to Sarima. This plan, of course, also ended in failure. She certainly brought about a number of horrific and devastating outcomes. Whether Elphaba can be construed as wicked on the basis of her bringing about bad consequences, I suppose, depends on the plausibility of consequence-based moral theories. We can conclude that if Elphaba is wicked, it is in virtue of the effect she had on the world, as we've ruled out all the other possibilities.

As for my opinion on Elphaba's wickedness, well . . . I could tell you what I think but to not say anything seems more wicked.

20

Wicked? It's Not Easy Being Green

KEVIN DURAND

"Are you a good witch or a bad witch?"

—Glinda, the Good Witch

A scarecrow and a tin man walk into a bar to meet a lion who was awaiting their arrival. In the smoky semi-darkness, the scarecrow sees a fight break out. A card-carrying member of the Lollipop Guild rocks a Lullaby Leaguer to sleep with a sucker punch. The scarecrow is appalled at such uncivilized behavior. He turns to his metallic companion and says, "That was a very bad thing that Munchkin did. Somebody oughta teach him a lesson." The tin man nods in agreement. Rather than agree, the third of their group, a regal, yet cowardly lion who had been sitting at the bar prior to the fight and had seen its development says, "Well, perhaps, but the Lullaby Leaguer had tried to poison the Lollipopper's drink with one of those poppies. He popped him in self-defense."

Our natural reactions to the example (or our intuitions about what the reactions of the characters at the various points in the story would be) are probably a bit mixed. At first, along with the scarecrow, we might disapprove of a seemingly unprovoked attack. Then, with new information, likely our view shifts—the attack wasn't unprovoked; the punch was self-defense; the Lullaby Leaguer isn't a bullying swine, but rather is the praiseworthy party.

David Hume (1711–1776), perhaps the greatest English speaking philosopher, thought that all of our moral thinking starts with experiences such as these. We see something happen and that causes a feeling—I like that, or I don't like that. And that feeling, over time and through many repeated experiences of similar sorts, gets refined even further until we consistently (more or less) begin to praise those we feel to be good and to blame those we feel to be bad.

Of course, this sort of rough-and-ready moral feeling and thinking is rather imprecise. Sometimes we might get it wrong. Sometimes we might see a friend do something and cut him far more slack because he's our friend than we would if we saw someone we didn't like at all do the same thing. When our feelings are so much a part of praise and blame, these are the risks we run. At the same time, we can hardly separate how we feel from what we think, especially about such important matters as good and evil.

Then there are those times that we get more information and, as a result, our feelings change, and we see the situation in a new light. Such is the case with Gregory Maguire's *Wicked*. Maguire radically reimagines *The Wizard of Oz*, both the movie version and L. Frank Baum's multi-volume world. Experiencing Maguire's retelling of the story, and the musical made from it, the reader becomes like that Scarecrow in the bar I mentioned above. With more information and a new perspective, perhaps the initial intuitions about who is good, who is evil, and who is to blame, and why they are so perceived, become somewhat less clear, somewhat more muddied.

Hume and the Moral Sentiments

What if the Wicked Witch of the West weren't all that wicked? What happens if Dorothy is a misguided young woman, ill-used by a tyrannical and power hungry "man behind the curtain"? Is Dorothy's triumph over the Wicked Witch of the West a victory of good over evil, or is it the reverse? Or, is it worse? Is Dorothy a victim of the inertia of power—the pawn, checkmating the rebellious, if flawed, queen and voice of the politically oppressed? Might we instead suppose the Wizard is the Oz equivalent of Grand Moff Tarkin of *Star Wars*, tightening his grip while more and more systems slip through his fingers?

The time-honored movie stands before us as a series of first-impressions, a maker of intuitions and a shaper of feelings. Miss Gulch gives us our first impression of the character of the Wicked Witch of the West; the farmhands prefigure their Oz counterparts; and the traveling snake-oil salesman is our first glimpse of the Wizard. Our moral sentiments begin to form, and they take shape in the Gale's living room as Auntie Em addresses Almira Gulch with the powerful, "Almira Gulch, just because you own half the county doesn't mean that you have the power to run the rest of us. For twenty-three years I've been dying to tell you what I thought of you! And now . . . well, being a Christian woman, I can't say it!" Walking in on such an exchange would likely set our initial moral sentiments quite well—very much in favor of Em and Uncle Henry; very much out of favor toward Gulch.

The fairly standard interpretation of the *Wizard of Oz* plays on that feeling. And, it's quite difficult to see the Witch as anything but Wicked. She does, after all, try to eliminate Dorothy's companions, to poison them all in a field of poppies, to kill Dorothy with a cursed hour glass, and to ignite the Scarecrow. But, what of Oz? Perhaps, like the first impression of the fight in the bar, our moral intuitions are clouded with apparently obvious malevolence that hides a greater sense of the sinister. Is the Witch the only villain in Oz?

Here, Hume comes to our aid again. It's often quite easy to feel approval for our friends and disapproval of our enemies simply because they are our friends and enemies. Hume suggests, however, that to be truly morally consistent, if we see our enemies doing something and we approve of our friends when they do it, then we should approve of our enemies doing it. So, if our best friend acts courageously, and we see an enemy doing the same thing, then we should, however grudgingly, acknowledge that perhaps our enemy is brave, too. For example, Achilles and Hector squared off against each other outside the gates of Troy, but both had great respect for the courage of the other. In the same way, if we see our friends doing something that we would find blameworthy in our enemy, again we ought to react in similar ways, giving our disapproval to both.

So, what of Oz? To paraphrase Glinda's question, "Is he a good wizard or a bad one?" Clearly, in Maguire's hands, the Wizard becomes a malevolent despot. In truth, there is more reason than simply Maguire's *Wicked* to fuel this question of the Wizard's character. I well remember my own first encounter with *The Wizard of Oz*, and more particularly, with the Wizard. Growing up in "Twister Alley" (those parts of Kansas, Oklahoma, and Arkansas that see dozens of them a year) was an intriguing experience; one where tornados are far more than sepia-toned special effects chewing up prefab Hollywood movie sets. Yet, it wasn't the tornado that caused the occasional nightmare, in my case. It was the "Great and

Powerful" Wizard of Oz. His green, disembodied head, floating in front of what seemed a creaky, old pipe organ with smoke and flashes of light and fire and thunder caused more than one night-time shudder. It never struck me as odd in the least that the Cowardly Lion should go barreling down the corridor and leap through the emerald green cathedral windows to escape the presence of such a horror. The Wizard was a terror.

As I got a bit older, and less susceptible to disembodied head nightmares, it still seemed to nag at me that the Wizard certainly seemed more than a bit unreasonable. After all, he sends a poor and rather simple young girl, armed only with her little dog, and escorted by three out-of-place and unprofessional guards, to kill a Witch so powerful that he himself evidently cannot do the deed. This ragtag band is supposed to march right into the Witch's stronghold, past soldiers and flying monkeys, kill her, escape with their lives, and return her broomstick to Oz. It can't be supposed that the Wizard doesn't know what he's asking—the Scarecrow's quite clear that to bring back her broomstick will mean that they'll have to kill her. But, the Wizard ignores their offerings and merely sends them on their mission.

Perhaps the Wizard and the Witch share more than an emerald hue. At worst, our revised intuitions might suggest that the green Wizard and the green Witch are both scheming; both are prepared to kill and both plot assassination in order to cement their power and authority. Dorothy and her band are caught in the middle. Our moral sentiments likely experience a bit of flux, shifting from "Wizard, good; Witch, bad" to something a bit more muddled.

Roots of Evil

The events of the movie begin well past the three-quarter point of the book, *Wicked*, picking up at that late stage with the architectural mishap suffered by Nessarose (the Wicked Witch of the East and sister of Elphaba, Wicked Witch of the West). Like those wandering into the bar at the moment of the fateful Lollipop punch, Maguire suggests that the movie audience has come onto the scene, with Dorothy and her house, well into the telling of a very complicated story; a story incomplete on a mere viewing. Indeed, readers of L. Frank Baum's several Oz books generally find the 1939 film rendition to be a wonderfully cinematic visual companion to the far richer and more complex fantasy reality he created there. So, too, viewers of the Tony Award-winning musical, *Wicked*, generally are pleased to find that they can lose themselves in the rich and full world of Maguire's book; a world only hinted at in the musical. Thus, the two books and their musical counterparts all tell stories of the same world, with differing levels of depth.

If moral sentiments and certainties are a bit unsettled by closer attention to the movie, they are in for a tornadic shaking in *Wicked*. The book opens with the vaguely ominous chapter, "The Root of Evil." Elphaba (whose name is constructed from Baum's initials—L, F, and B) is the emerald green daughter of Melena and her clergy husband Frex. Frex represents the sort of clergyman, vaguely Calvinist but sort of old school Unitarian, who is so convinced of his call from "the Unnamed God" that he leaves his pregnant wife on the eve of her deliverance to travel several towns over to stamp out a Clockwork evil. To say that his reception by the (un)faithful is less than jubilant is rather an understatement. A Tiktok machine called the "Time Dragon" skewers the religiosity of Frex and the priestly class. Rampant and wanton pleasure is to be preferred to the self-denial and self-importance of Frex and his ilk.

Reflecting on her father's ministry and its ineffectiveness at convincing her of the existence of any life beyond this one, Elphaba recalled that her father "used to orchestrate proofs about evil as a way of persuading his flock to convert. But, surely evil was beyond proof." That Frex was made a cuckold during one of his many missionary trips is lost on him, though the Tiktok Clockwork Dragon that he has come to thwart rather explicitly tells the tale. As the night of Elphaba's birth comes to an end, so enraptured are the people by the irreverent machine that they make to do Frex in. As the chapter ends, the reader is left wondering what the root of evil is—is it Frex's sentimental and empty mysticism, is it Elphaba (the little green girl born out of the marital bond), is it the mysterious father of the little green girl, or is it found somewhere else?

Frex justifies his absenteeism with a telling line that suggests maybe the roots of evil are contained in the varied perceptions of those caught in the cross-currents of events. Says Frex, "History crawls along on the peg legs of small individual lives, and at the same time larger eternal forces converge. You can't attend to both arenas at once" (p. 9). He sees himself as a major player in the war of eternal forces, on the side of good as the battle against evil is joined in an epic, Zoroastrian struggle. While his moralizing fails rather terribly, one can see in Frex the intentions of the collaborationist clergy—encouraging the people to still their restless and rebellious political inclinations in favor of a brighter and more gifted future in the afterlife. The ministry of "good" for which Frex lives, calls to mind the Marxist critique of such "reward in the afterlife for patient endurance of suffering now" kinds of religion. For Marx, such religions are the "opium of the masses." Indeed, Frex's encouragement of self-denial, and of peaceful acquiescence to the temporal powers in favor of the eternal ones, is so strident that one cannot help sensing the very Marxist reactions of the crowd; a crowd that, finally overtired of seeming moral platitudes, revolts against Frex and his religion.

Wicked suggests a healthy skepticism of moral absolutes. Frex is a mostly well-meaning, if bumbling, man of the cloth. In many ways, he's a self-important clergyman trying to propagate and prop up a feeble sort of mysticism that is steadily waning in relevance. It's in decay because it has become disconnected with the real lives of the Munchkinlanders, a shell of faith with tired rituals that no longer seem to convey meaning to its adherents, and little power to attract new followers.

If Frex is convinced of his own holiness, however, his youngest daughter, Nessarose, is convinced of the power to be found in religion itself and its trappings. Whether or not she is a true believer is unclear. What is exceptionally clear, however, is that she rejects the style of exhortation employed by her father in favor of arguing from positions of power. She ascends to the throne of the Eminent Thropp (the fabled ruling position of Munchkinland) and increases its reach and influence through cunning use of religion. Her brand of fundamentalism establishes orderliness in her kingdom and an uneasy détente with the empire of the Wizard. The celebration of the Munchkinlanders at her demise, in book and movie, suggests that the rigid absolutism of father and daughter (bumbling, on the one hand, sinister and controlling, on the other) fails to square with the moral sentiments of their subjects—the Munchkins prefer a little less structure, unless the structure in question is a four-square descending from Kansas.

Whatever Nessarose's faults, she kept the land of the Munchkins independent of the growing power of Oz. After her death, however, the Wizard sought to thrust himself into the power vacuum and reclaim Munchkinland for his own regal and imperial rule. His intentions are made abundantly clear to Elphaba at the memorial for her sister. Rather than offer much in the way of unfelt sympathies, he simply asks if she, as the rightful heir to the position of eminence, intends to try to consolidate Munchkinland under her own aegis. He warns against trying, pointing out that the shoes of power Elphaba needs are currently out of Munchkinland and on their way to Oz (and, to him). "Reunification is under way," said the Wizard, "even as we speak. I understand that Lady Glinda, bless her well-meaning foolishness, has sensibly evacuated both the unfortunate girl [Dorothy] and the totemic shoes from the district, which should make annexation less troublesome." Notice, "reunification," with its more positive connotations becomes, in less than a full sentence, "annexation," expressing much more accurately the Wizard's sentiments. His is an exercise in power and control; empire-building, not consensus-making or home rule.

While Nessarose rejects the priestly approach of her father in favor of using religion as a power all its own, the Wizard rejects religiosity altogether, especially the religions of the various segments of the Land of Oz he intends to rule. As he and Elphaba spar verbally after Nessarose's memorial, she charges him with not only murderous intentions, but with murder itself. This charge actually seems to amuse the Wizard. He says, "*Murder* is a word used by the sanctimonious. It is an expedient expression with which they condemn any courageous action beyond their ken. What I did, what I do, cannot be murder. For, coming from another world, I cannot be held accountable to the silly conventions of a naive civilization. I am beyond that lisping childish recital of wrongs and rights" (p. 352).

The Wizard isn't a not a wizard because of the wonderful things he does. No, he's a wizard because of the power he wields and the complete rejection of conscience that his exercise of power embodies. Hume argued that from individual senses of praising and blaming, from approval and disapproval, a common moral sense arises within a community. On balance, the members of a community come, over time, generally to assign praise and blame in roughly the same ways for roughly the same reasons. This "common sense" morality is then inculcated in the next generation, and eventually, a rather comprehensive system of moral rules and intuitions takes hold.

The Wizard, as an outsider to Oz, recognizes neither the moral rules present in the societies he seeks to annex nor that they have any hold on him. In this way, the Wizard is a rogue power, and, in the view of Maguire and *Wicked*, quite possibly the root of the present evils experienced by the people of Oz. In short, the Wizard is an alien tyrant, beyond good and evil himself, and the effect of his rule must be adjudged evil by the conventions, rules, and intuitions, that is, the "common sense" of Oz. The suggestion is that the root of evil is beyond good and evil.

The Habit of Vengeance

Despite this case for the root of evil, Elphaba is conventionally thought to embody something like evil herself, by many of the inhabitants of Oz. One feature that is consistent between book and film is the assumed "wickedness" of the Wicked Witch of the West, a wickedness assumed by characters from the lowliest Munchkinlander to the Great and Powerful Oz (including our intrepid travelers—Dorothy and her companions). Elphaba is separated even from a spectacularly diverse fantasy world by the green hue of her skin and her "reputation for malice." She's the only green person in Oz, and difference breeds suspicion. Indeed, that greenness seems to be a visual cue that she is not only different, but dangerous. Maguire makes it clear that she isn't a "witch" until she is instructed by an enchanted being, a princess of the Scrow tribe, to disguise herself as a witch. In college, Elphaba was a biology major, specializing in animal husbandry, a naturalist and not a sorceress at all. While she's not an adherent of the religious views of her father and sister, neither does she disregard the traditions and cultures of her people. Yet, she suspects her own character of tending toward something blameworthy, and she doubts she has a soul.

In conversing with a childhood friend after the death of Nessarose, Elphaba, now referred to as "The Witch," is world weary. The tale says, "The Witch sighed, 'You may be right. You know, I'm getting used to stiff muscles in the morning. Sometimes I think that vengeance is habit forming too. A stiffness of the attitude. I keep hoping that the Wizard will be toppled in my lifetime, and this aim seems to be at odds with happiness. I suppose I can't take on avenging the death of a sister I didn't get on all that well with anyway'" (p. 343).

Vengeance, then, is a habit, one developed through a series of vengeful actions borne of a series of vengeful attitudes. Elphaba, from birth, has had a variety of injustices come her way for a variety of reasons; most obviously her green color, but also her

Munchkinland heritage and her family's strained socioeconomic condition. Her approach to these injustices has been to fight back, to wreak vengeance directly where possible and to fight guerilla campaigns against the Wizard where necessary. She bides her time. She conspires, she plots, she broods Having attained a certain level of power, she attempts to murder the college headmistress who had been so very cruel to her as a girl—but she's too late. The woman dies of natural causes only minutes before Elphaba arrives to kill her.

Elphaba also waits for Dorothy, whom she recognizes as the accidental occupant of the falling house and whom she knows is innocent of stealing her sister's shoes. Dorothy and her friends are on their way to kill Elphaba, and yet the Witch seems tired rather than vengeful. The fiery intent is gone; vengeance has become a habit, not a passion. World-weary, she recognizes her attitudes have stiffened, but the careful reader knows that those stiffening attitudes have been the product of thirty-eight years of fighting, if not always the good fight, then at least the fight that was before her. In other words, Elphaba's native intuitions of good and evil, of praise and blame, have, through repeated use, become habits of actions. Her own moral compass has been fixed. Even though others, from Glinda to her old friend, Boq, try to give her more information that should dissuade her own vengeance-ridden intuitions toward Dorothy, her perceptions of the situation remain unchanged.

Thus, Maguire's telling of the Witch's story is itself like the Scarecrow and Tin Man walking into a bar. We get a bit more information and with it greater insight into the Witch. Further, perhaps it helps us see the original movie more clearly, gaining more insight into, well, everything green, like the Witch and the Wizard, and the wicked Emerald City itself. Green they may be, but we don't envy them, and they don't envy one another. Our own internal mechanisms of approval and disapproval are refined by Maguire's imaginative exposition. Let's refine them a bit further, moving from the roots of evil to a touch of revolution before returning to some final reflections on evil and our perceptions of it.

Revolution: Marx in Munchkinland

While religion may be the opium of the masses, administered to the Munchkinlanders by Frex to encourage them to stay in their place and by Nessarose to force them to do so, the true center of Marxism is power, not religion, and the Wizard is the one wielding the power. The Wizard has established his unquestioned rule in the center of Oz, has stationed an army of "observation" just outside the Witch of the West's domain, has Quadling Country in the south under his colonial authority, and has subverted the institutions of education into bastions of "right-thinking." He has played on the superstitions and prejudices of the different groups to introduce a rigid caste system in which talking Animals, those with a spirit, are reduced to nothing more than their dumb animal counterparts.

And, the Wizard wants to annex Munchkinland. The ruby slippers are one avenue to that annexation which will allow him to extend his power into the relatively independent county that had been ruled by Elphaba's sister, the Wicked Witch of the East (or, with her proper title, the Eminent Thropp). Under Nessarose's authoritarian and religiously fundamentalist rule, Munchkinland was independent of the despotic and authoritarian rule of the Wizard. The fall of the house of Gale from the sky freed the Munchkinlanders of one tyrant, perhaps only to subject them to bloody civil war and subjection to another. Glinda, the "good" witch, dispatches Dorothy to the Emerald City to remove her and the symbolically powerful slippers from Munchkinland. Dorothy readily heads to see the Wizard in hopes that he can send her home, but she's blissfully unaware that the slippers upon her feet have great power—magically, to be sure, but politically as symbols of authority and power (and because the Munchkinlanders are superstitious about the shoes).

Arriving in the Emerald City, Dorothy discovers a Wizard in a bargaining mood. Here the separate tales become murky. In the movie, Dorothy must rely on the doorkeeper's pity—after all, he had an Auntie Em once, too. The audience with the Wizard is a terrifying one in which he directs the travelers to kill the witch without actually saying it in so many words. *Wicked* does not record any of this, but rather has a spy for the Witch report to her that the Wizard has explicitly directed Dorothy to dispose of her. In Maguire's tale, the spy tells the Witch, "The Wizard told Dorothy he would grant them their wishes—when they had—when they had . . . Dorothy and her friends have to come here and kill you." Baum's record of the encounter between Dorothy and the Wizard actually squares more closely with *Wicked*. He records the following dialogue:

"Well," said the Head, "I will give you my answer. You have no right to expect me to send you back to Kansas unless you do something for me in return. In this country everyone must pay for everything he gets. If you wish me to use my magic power to send you home again you must do something for me first. Help me and I will help you."

"What must I do?" asked the girl.

"Kill the wicked Witch of the West," answered Oz.

In both cases, fresh light shines on the fateful encounter between Dorothy and the Wicked Witch of the West. Elphaba is troubled, bedeviled by ill-fortune, petulant, impetuous, and unrepentant, but she is not the demonic, evil Wicked Witch of Imperial propaganda. As Maguire writes in the prologue of *Wicked*, "The punishing political climate of Oz had beat her down, dried her up, tossed her away—like a seedling she had drifted, apparently too desiccated ever to take root. But surely the curse was on the land of Oz, not on her. Though Oz had given her a twisted life, hadn't it also made her capable?" (p. 4). Thus, it is a world-weary Witch who prepares for Dorothy, sent on a mission to kill her. An army of observation on her doorstep, an innocent assassin on the way to destroy her, and a life of constant battle providing her with a nearly *Soprano*-like practicality, Elphaba awaits her killer and prepares.

The Good, the Bad, and the Wicked

And she fails—fails to survive, that is. That fateful moment atop the tower in the Witch's castle is another of the murky spots in the tales. You know how different people who have seen exactly the same accident or episode will describe it in contradictory ways. It's hard to get at the final truth of the matter. In the 1939 movie, the witch is caught by Dorothy's fire brigade act because the Scarecrow was aflame, but in *Wicked*, the Scarecrow is nowhere around, and Elphaba, herself, was on fire, accidentally by her own hand, and Dorothy was actually trying to save her life. Either way, the Witch melts and her evil, her "beautiful wickedness," melts alongside her. Yet, is she evil? Is the Wicked Witch of the West wicked?

While apparently a self-evident truth in *The Wizard of Oz*, it's not nearly that quick a judgment in *Wicked*, despite the title of the work. Indeed, there is much debate in the book itself about what evil really is. For example, at just past the halfway point of Maguire's tale, the concept comes in for serious reflection. Evil is represented as some sort of objective thing, a thing with physical, tangible existence. Maguire reflects, again with a Marxist undertone, "To the grim poor there need be no *pour quoi* tale about where evil arises; it just arises; it always is. One never learns how the witch became wicked, or whether that was the right choice for her - is it ever the right choice? Does the devil ever struggle to be good again, or if so is he not a devil? It is at the very least a question of definitions" (p. 231).

It's easy to imagine the speaker having a view similar to something like the following—"The Devil made me do it. The Witch is evil and it doesn't matter how she got that way. All that worrying about how evil is perceived and how much of evil is a matter of perception is just so much claptrap. She's evil. End of story."

While this defense is a bit more forceful, perhaps, than the speaker intends, there is a finality of statement here. This is the sort of attitude one might find in the bar. When asking why the Lollipop Guilder popped the Lullaby Leaguer, the response along these lines would be, "He's just a bad guy. That's what bad guys do." The circumstances of the action would have no real bearing on the analysis of it. Yet, there's that bit of poignant attenuation of the view—"was [it] the right choice for her?" This question entertains at least the possibility that the Witch made choices that made the best, or the worst, of bad situations; the cumulative total of those choices and situations rendering her "wicked" in the eyes of others. Says the Witch, "People always did like to talk, didn't they? That's why I call myself a witch now: the Wicked Witch of the West, if you want the full glory of it. As long as people are going to call you a lunatic anyway, why not get the benefit of it? It liberates you from convention." What's important about this explanation is that the Witch doesn't see *herself* as wicked; rather she's simply taken the view, "people will think what people will think; why trouble myself with that?"

That the Witch adopts something like this view is clear when we read from perhaps the most obvious treatment of evil that Maguire puts in a conversation between several characters at a disturbing dinner party at which the "Wicked Witch" is the guest of honor, late in the book.

Avaric said, "Evil is an early or primitive stage of moral development. All children are fiends by nature."

". . . I think it's a presence, not an absence," said an artist. "Evil's an incarnated character, an incubus or a succubus. It's an other. It's not *us*."

"Evil isn't a thing, it's not a person, it's an attribute like beauty..."

"It's a power, like wind . . ."

"It's an infection . . ."

"It's metaphysical, essentially: the corruptibility of creation—

"Blame it on the Unnamed God, then."

"No, you're all wrong, our childhood religion had it right: Evil is moral at its heart - the selection of vice over virtue; you can pretend not to know, you can rationalize, but you know it in your conscience."

"Evil is an act, not an appetite."

"The real thing about evil," said the Witch at the doorway, "isn't any of what you said. You figure out on one side of it—the human side, say—and the eternal side goes into the shadow. Or vice versa. It's like the old saw: What does a dragon in its shell look like? Well no one can ever tell, for as soon as you break the shell to see, the dragon is no longer *in* its shell. The real disaster of this inquiry is that it is the nature of evil to be *secret*."

Nothing in *Wicked* so clearly summarizes the view of Oz and the tumultuous personal and political relationships that have conspired to put the Witch into the position she holds. Her childhood religion, given life by Frex and Nessarose; her years in college at Shiz (the Oxford of Oz), where her scholarship status and her green hue set her apart for ridicule and suspicion; her failed love life, in which her beloved dies suddenly and tragically; her Munchkinlander heritage in a society in which Munchkins were thought backwards bumpkins. All these have been facts of her life, but these are not the things we need in order to understand as the root of evil. It's the choices she has made that have shaped who and where she is.

Elphaba rejects blaming evil on physical entities or metaphysical forces—hers is not an approach that blames some devil or the Unnamed God. Evil is something like an action and, her action is the quite practical one of continuing her ongoing opposition to the Wizard, futile though she senses it to be. But, even more, the name "evil" is assigned to shadow; it is assigned to a set of perceptions, perceptions that may be as fluid and difficult to fully grasp as discerning the nature of the dragon in its shell. If one could perceive the dragon in its shell, that perception would alter, perhaps, our view of the dragon outside its shell. This is beyond us, however. So, in a sense, Elphaba is the dragon, never perceived as she is. She is inextricable from her greenness, her Munchkin heritage, and her place. So, rather than present the conundrum to all, she rather embraces the view others have of her, perhaps for no other reason than that it does tend to make some things easier and to render the people she encounters more pliable to her will.

For the Witch, there isn't really any truth to the notion that she's evil. Instead, "Wicked" is simply a name attached to her and, because it has been, she has embraced it for herself. It's almost a condescending recognition of what others say.

She is a practical woman who seems to embody the view that evil and good are simply names attached to things we perceive and then either disapprove or approve, respectively. However, there's an ironic twist to this naming business. To her claim of wickedness, her old friend Boq replies, "People who claim to be evil are usually no worse than the rest of us." Sighing, he adds, "It's people who claim that they're good, or anyway better than the rest of us, that you have to be wary of" (p. 357). The attention of the careful reader, here, falls on the man behind the curtain. As the Wizard is discovered to be something of a fraud by Dorothy and her friends in *The Wizard of Oz*, Dorothy says, "You are a very bad man." He's appalled that someone would say that of him and responds quickly, "No, no. I've a very *good* man. I'm just a very bad wizard."

Ineptitude or Wickedness?

The words "good" and "bad" get tossed around a lot here and each seems to be carrying a different load. Indeed, the movie's Wizard and the book's Witch suffer similar shortcomings. Neither is very good at the magical office to which each pretends. The Witch is has difficulty understanding the "Grimmerie," a book of spells which originated outside of Oz. Any self-respecting witch ought to make short work of such a tome, but she works at great pains to decipher it and to perform the magic it contains. For the most part, she has to stay with biology, so from "magic," she is reduced to genetically breeding and altering snow monkeys surgically, so they can fly; she cannot simply magic the wings onto them. Similarly, the Wizard fails to be able to magic Dorothy back to Kansas or to perform much beyond fairly literal smoke and mirrors. Neither Witch nor Wizard is particularly talented. If the Wizard is a bad wizard, in the sense that the movie gives us, then the Witch is a bad witch, but not a wicked one.

We should examine that conclusion a bit further because it seems that Maguire has offered us a very important distinction. To be a "good" witch, Elphaba (or Glinda) must be both good persons and talented witches. So, Elphaba, an only moderately competent witch, would not be considered a "good" witch. Even if she were a good person, she would fail to be a good witch. At best, she could be a good person. However, since she is not a talented witch and perceived by others to be evil, she gets the moniker "Wicked Witch."

We can see Glinda in a similar light. She may be less talented than Elphaba, although Maguire doesn't make it entirely clear, but in any case she isn't exactly at the head of her class in Sorcery, a desultory student, so she could be at best a good person. However, because she's perceived to be of wholesome character by others, a perception that readers of *Wicked* would surely question, she is labeled inaccurately the "good" witch. Her motives for the sorcery she does practice have more to do with furthering her wealthy husband's business ventures than anything else, and she is vain and given to shallowness. It doesn't look like anyone here is unequivocally "good" at anything.

The Wizard, on the other hand, could be a "good" wizard only if he were both a good person and a talented wizard; he would be a "bad" wizard in two cases—if he were a bad person and a talented wizard, or if he were a bad person and a poor wizard. As it happens, he's worse than both Elphaba and Glinda, on all counts. He is neither a competent Wizard nor a very good man. So, when the Wizard tells Dorothy that he is a good person but a bad wizard, he is saying that his talent for wizardry isn't up to scratch. However, if one were to take the movie Wizard's line here and move it into the book, one would hear the "I'm a very bad wizard" very differently—bad, here, becomes "evil." This would, of course, tell against the statement "I'm a very good man," but would also make it consistent with Boq's statement to the Witch, namely that is it only those who claim to be good who warrant wariness on our part.

Throughout the morality play that is *Wicked*, the question of whether or not Elphaba is truly an evil person has been up for grabs and, as one episode folds into another, always providing us with more and more insight into her motivations, her development, and her character, it seems we come to but one conclusion. Elphaba isn't a Good Witch because she is, at best, competent at witchcraft, and only perhaps a bad person. At the very least, she is no worse than the Wizard. After all, she is willing to defend herself and her people; she does not dispatch a rather dim innocent to do her dirty work, and she has an on-going devotion to justice, as she understands it. Even after she knew of Dorothy's mission to kill her, she resisted the Wizard more than the companions. Dorothy, after all, had been the passenger, not the driver, of the house that killed Elphaba's sister and she was a reasonably innocent pawn in the match played by the Wizard and the Witch.

Indeed, Maguire says, "The Witch began to think about how she might disarm the girl. It was hard to tell what her weapons were, except for that sort of inane good sense and emotional honesty." These are not the actions of a power-mad despot like the Wizard. They are the actions of a world-weary woman whose fondest dreams of seeing her people free and the imperial Wizard over-thrown seem further away and perhaps beyond the span of her life.

Elphaba, the little green girl grows up to be the "Wicked" Witch of the West, but much like the Scarecrow and Tin Man in the bar, after we have heard more of the story, it seems very difficult to call her "evil." Thus, it turns out that Kermit was right. It's not easy being green.

21

In the Merry Old Matriarchy of Oz

RANDALL E. AUXIER

> "The Wonderful Wizard was never so wonderful as Queen Ozma," the people said to one another, in whispers; "for he claimed to do many things he could not do; whereas our new Queen does many things no one would ever expect her to accomplish."
>
> —L. Frank Baum, *The Marvelous Land of Oz* (1904)

It doesn't take a genius to notice that something unusual is going on with women in L. Frank Baum's little land of Oz. There is, to say the least, an estrogen build-up. In the first book the situation is not as obvious as it becomes in the later installments of the Oz series, but the stage is set from the get-go. It's not just that Dorothy is a little girl (not a little boy), or that the four powers of Oz who oversee the four directions of the compass are "witches"—two good, two wicked—or that all the witches seem to have odd relations to the reigning patriarch of Oz, that usurper of a Wizard from Omaha. Things are way more complicated than *that*.

By the end of Baum's second book we've learned how the Wizard stole the throne and how the rightful princess who was destined to rule came to be hidden away by an old witch named Mombi. The princess, under an enchantment, was made to believe she was a *boy*, named "Tip." Meanwhile, in the Wizard's absence, an army of disgruntled women armed with knitting needles, led by one angry woman named General Jinjur, has taken control of the Emerald City in a bloodless *coup d'état*. They're making the men cook and clean house while the army eats bon-bons. The climactic scene in the second book involves a gender-bender in which the boy named Tip resumes his or her identity as Ozma Tippetarius, the Queen of the Emerald City, and having transformed from a pretty boy into an even prettier girl, Tip says: "'I hope none of you will care less for me than you did before. I'm just the same Tip, you know; only, only'—'Only you're different!' said the Pumpkinhead." Never you mind who the Pumpkinhead is. The point is that Baum started something that was too interesting to stop. The "woman thing" continues for another thirteen books.

Gregory Maguire decided to explore this feminine dimension of the Oz myth with great thoroughness in *Wicked: The Life and Times of the Wicked Witch of the West*. Here he fills in the details of this woman-thing and presents a picture of a world in which the transition from a "matriarchal" to a "patriarchal" social order is happening. In *our* world the transition from matriarchy to patriarchy happened so long ago that it's difficult for many people to believe these days that there ever was a pre-eminence of matriarchal societies. But the evidence for this earlier form of social life has been piling up for quite a while now, about 150 years, and it is becoming more plausible every year to entertain the idea that it really happened: over the course of about two thousand years, patriarchal forms of social life replaced an older, long-standing matriarchal order.

It's difficult to determine how much Baum may have known about the matriarchy theories that were being suggested in his day, and whether he set about consciously to explore them in his Oz books. People have speculated on his views about women for a long time, but the messages in his books are somewhat ambiguous. He certainly doesn't make *all* males into bad guys (although most of them are either hollow, silly, or downright bad), and he doesn't exalt *all* females. For every Ozma or Dorothy, you find a Mombi or Jinjur, and Baum's women are just as problematic as any man could hope to be. Maguire, on the other hand, is clearer in his judgment. Men are pigs, pretty much, or they may rise to bumbling oafs in their best moments. All the interesting characters, both good and bad (and those who are both), are female.

What *is* all this? Well, I don't know who else besides a philosopher might try to explain it. I will tell you some stories of matriarchy and let you decide for yourself what'is going on here, but you shouldn't quite think of this as "feminist philosophy." Some of the ideas from matriarchy theory *have* made their way into feminism, but the whole idea of matriarchy is, to say the least, far from creditable in the view of most feminists. And the irony is not lost on me that I'm not exactly a woman. I expect to be shunned, chided, and ridiculed for even discussing this stuff. But hey, the Oz tales are just full of this stuff, and *someone* ought to talk about it.

Most of what we have learned about matriarchy comes from areas beyond philosophy, primarily from the fields of anthropology, archaeology, classics, psychology, and history. When we combine all that's said by these other disciplines, both their evidence and their theories, we have the raw materials for a "philosophy," but it would not be accurate to say that such a philosophy has been worked out or advocated by anyone (or at least by anyone who has the respect of our exalted professoriate). But I have noticed, and this is curious, that *men* seem to like these theories and stories as well as (or better than) women do. Hence, you may have noticed that Baum was a man, Maguire is a man, and so was the most important early pioneer of matriarchy theory. I will get back to Oz, but I have to take a detour through the theory of matriarchy for a while. I know you won't be bored.

Crazy Johann (and Why Haven't I Ever heard of this Guy?)

There was a Swiss professor of classics and jurisprudence named Johann Jakob Bachofen (1815–1887) who kept poking around in ancient graveyards, old law books, and classical writings in dead languages, until he arrived at a startling conclusion about human pre-history. He suspected the world was not ready for his conclusion, so he apologized profusely before offering it, almost begging people to believe he hadn't lost his mind. What was so crazy? Bachofen had come to believe (on the basis of some pretty extensive evidence) that human culture originated in *motherhood*, and that human cultural evolution was primarily influenced by womanly virtues (and vices) for a very, very long time before it ever came to look like it does now. Most people in Bachofen's day were used to assuming that God is male, Adam was a man, Eve was a rib (and maybe not Adam's *best* rib at that), and that women brought sin, death, and evil into the world. Arguing for the idea that women pretty much created human culture and then ran it for about twenty thousand years, long before men had very much to say or do, was not exactly the best way to get tenure at the university. But Crazy Johann already *had* tenure (or the Swiss equivalent of it), so he wrote the books anyway and waited for the storm.

The storm never really came. The idea that women created human culture, and that men gradually stole it away, was so *far out* as to be threatening to almost no one. It was regarded as a kooky and quaint idea that belonged in the same category as life on other planets, flying to the moon, and stuff like that. People mainly ignored Bachofen, and they didn't take his evidence seriously. That may have been good, because what happened instead of a storm was a slow, anonymous advance of his ideas in the direction of basic respectability, mainly through back channels. Let me tell you the story, in brief. You'll see why this is worth hearing when we get back to Oz.

Freddie and the Gods

The most interesting back channel for the matriarchy idea was also one of the most infamous. Bachofen was on the faculty at the University of Basel when a young upstart named Friedrich Nietzsche (1844–1900) showed up there in 1869. Bachofen had published his crazy theory in 1861, eight years earlier. Nietzsche picked up a lot of stuff from Bachofen, and hung around his house, and ate his food, until the *real* bombshell was ready to drop, which was a book by Nietzsche called *The Birth of Tragedy out of the Spirit of Music* in 1872. *Then* there came a storm.

In effect, Nietzsche had quietly pilfered and adapted Bachofen's way of distinguishing the "Dionysian" and "Apollonian" modes of existence (more about that later), which were the two late forms of matriarchy that cleared the path for *patriarchy* in Bachofen's theory. Nietzsche put these categories to his own uses in *The Birth of Tragedy*. He wasn't very much interested in all the stuff about women, but he loved the play and tension among the kinds of male energies Bachofen described. In Bachofen's story, this tension of Dionysian and Apollonian life was a *part* of the story about how matriarchy declined and patriarchy ascended to dominance. But in Nietzsche's telling, it's pretty much all about the men. I think Nietzsche had too much womanly energy focused on him while growing up, and he didn't need to encourage more of the same when he finally broke free of all those women who (sort of) raised him. Because Nietzsche got so much attention with his proto-mythical philosophizing, a *few* people, here and there, started digging around among his sources. Some found Bachofen and started thinking about their mothers. Most didn't.

Freddie and the Malcontents

Around 1884, Friedrich Engels (of *Communist Manifesto* fame) picked up Bachofen's ideas and used them in a scandalous (and thus widely read) treatise on the origins of the family. He said that women had eventually *become* slaves to men due to competition among men for a scarcity of women. This competition had destroyed the original (and healthier) family structures, structures which were . . . you guessed it, matriarchal (or in his terms, "communistic"). As Engels put it:

> The communistic household implies the supremacy of women in the house, just as the exclusive recognition of a natural mother, because of the impossibility of determining the natural father with certainty, signifies high esteem for women, that is, for the mothers. That woman was a slave of man at the commencement of society is one of the most absurd notions that have come down to us. . . . Woman occupied not only a free but also a highly respected position among all savages and all barbarians of the lower and middle stages and partly even of the upper stage.[1]

Engels then goes on to quote some long passages from anthropological studies of the Seneca and Iroquois Indians that describe matriarchal societies. I'm sure it's cold comfort to women to be informed by a man that their sex was in charge of savages, barbarians, and even a few civilized people. Engels's point was that the situation was at its very worst under capitalism, where what he calls "bourgeois marriage" was really the complete subjugation and enslavement of women, who had become property and then even *less* than property. Some people believed Engels about all this, mainly men. So another part of Bachofen's theory, adapted and altered, found its way into wider discussion, but Bachofen was no Marxist and no one cared where Engels got these ideas.

---

[1] Robert C. Tucker, ed., *The Marx-Engels Reader*, second edition (Norton, 1978), p. 735.

With Friends Like These . . .

Of course, Nietzsche and Engels were radicals, fringe characters in their own time, so it's not like their fascination with Bachofen's ideas was doing him any great service in the eyes of the dull middle class or the conservative academies. On the other hand, Bachofen wasn't being damaged either, since no one really noticed where Nietzsche and Engels were getting those ideas. As time passed, the radicals were taken more seriously, but the "respectable" scholars and journalists still did not trace the path all the way back to Bachofen. Yet the basic ideas of matriarchy kept creeping into the culture.

Then, a radical but formidable Cambridge historian named Jane Ellen Harrison (1850–1928) developed Bachofen's ideas more directly, on their own terms, and filled them out (and corrected them) with impressive new research. She wrote big books and was a hugely popular lecturer, although the fact that mainly women attended her talks served to marginalize her. More importantly, Professor Harrison took a young writer named Virginia Woolf under her matronly wing and some of the matriarchy ideas found their way into a popular succession of new novels. Woolf was taken seriously early on, and her prominence brought some attention to Harrison's (wonderful) histories of matriarchy, but the public still didn't catch on, and even fewer followed the trail back to crazy Bachofen.

Carl Gustav Jung (1875–1961) also took up the ideas and developed them for his own ends, notably in a treatise called *Aion: Researches into the Phenomenology of the Self.* Jung had grown up mainly in Basel, and he studied medicine at the university there. Apparently he had always known about Bachofen and his ideas, from childhood, but Jung's followers, just like those who study Woolf and Nietzsche and Marx-Engels, tend to take their own heroes as a *starting points*—these disciples are so enamored of the genius of a Nietzsche or Woolf or Jung that they act as if these people *made up* all the important ideas (about women and everything else) that appear in their writings. And I have to agree with them about the genius part. The fact that Woolf or Nietzsche or Jung said something *is* reason enough to think about it for a while. But (and here I will make a confession), speaking as someone who has read more thoroughly than most in the field of matriarchy, I think it's a shame that more people don't read the serious evidence for matriarchy in Bachofen and Harrison. But Bachofen and Harrison are *difficult* and ponderous to read; they are not great writers like Nietzsche and Woolf and Jung.

The Public Catches On, Sort Of

The basic ideas about matriarchy seemed to surface into more general awareness when Joseph Campbell (1904–1987) suggested they were important. People became widely aware of Campbell as a result of the efforts of the journalist Bill Moyers, who seems to have taken an interest in matriarchy and myth, for whatever reasons he may keep in his bosom. Moyers also brought the poet and essayist Robert Bly to the attention of a wider public, and Bly was developing a "men's movement" in light of the *truths* of matriarchy, training sensitive wounded men to get in touch with their ancient spears, or some such. As a result of the attention gained from the publicity of Campbell and Bly, some of Bachofen's works (translated into English in 1967 and introduced by Campbell, but ignored until Campbell got so famous) became more widely known, and a few brave souls began to investigate the evidence and ideas associated with matriarchy.

Then two things happened, one good, one very bad. The good thing is that an able and astute archaeologist from UCLA named Marija Gimbutas (1921–1994) went out to dig up the layers of matriarchal civilization. Her many discoveries, scholarly essays, and subsequent popular books supplemented and enriched our human understanding of what must now be admitted as well-documented fact: women effectively founded human culture and led human society for many thousands of years. Their social order was gradually replaced by a different social order dominated by men. Anyone who now doubts this is in denial about the evidence, thanks in great part to the tireless work of Gimbutas. Her evidence is far more nuanced and detailed than anything we can find in Bachofen or Harrison, so if you are interested in the evidence for matriarchy among humans, you would do well to pick up some of Gimbutas's popular books, and then perhaps proceed to her scholarly writings. But Gimbutas was no theorist, so you might want to get a couple of Harrison books to help you sort it out. It isn't light reading, I'm afraid, but it's worth the effort.

The very bad thing that happened was that a pseudo-scholarly, highly ideological, and ill-informed book called *The Chalice and the Blade*, by Riane Eisler, was published in 1987 and became a best-seller—half a million copies sold, it says on the cover of my copy of this sorry-excuse-for-a-book. Eisler succeeded in taking the hard work of 150 years and turning it into popular swill for the semi-educated and selfish bourgeois masses to consume, all with a glaze of absolute certainty and cocky self righteousness. Eisler has ensured that the ideas associated with matriarchy theory will not be taken seriously for another generation at least. She turns very serious ideas into a program for blaming men for every ill and a ridiculous call to restore the feminine wisdom, as though that were any kind of real option for our present world. Few women have ever done more to set women back, in my not so humble opinion.

Boys and their Myths

As you can see, the matriarchy ideas were out there during L. Frank Baum's lifetime. I have no idea how much of this stuff may have been known to him, but it looks to me like he probably knew the sorts of stories one finds in Engels's version of the matriarchy. Baum's contrast of the bourgeois revolt of the knitting needles and the more permanent wisdom of the line of the Ozmas seems to indicate a kind of rejection of "liberal feminism among the capitalists" and an endorsement of something more akin to socialism. Baum's connections to socialism and its sort of feminism have been speculated on for many decades. But I will leave Baum aside now and concentrate on Maguire's Oz, which is ever so much more interesting.

I would surmise that Maguire's ideas about matriarchy come mainly from the Joseph Campbell strain, and that there is some Jung and Nietzsche mixed in, but quite possibly he actually read Bachofen and Harrison. I'll tell you why I think so later. There is some stuff in Maguire's depiction of Oz that can't be found in sources other than Bachofen and Harrison. It seems that Maguire may know Eisler's awful book also, but fortunately it didn't seem to damage his understanding. Maguire's presentation preserves much nuance and ambiguity that Eisler reduced to simple ideology. But there's one other thing to consider before we get to specifics about Maguire's matriarchy, and that is myth.

Philosophy has always had an uncomfortable relationship with myth. In a sense, the dawn of recorded history was marked by a struggle by humanity to extricate ourselves from mythic consciousness and to embrace *reason* as our future guide. Philosophy led the way, which is why the works of Plato can be cast as a contest between poetry and philosophy –where "poetry" is understood as the term for the traditional mythic wisdom, with its rituals and social order. In every facet of human life, Plato and the Greek philosophers questioned Homer, questioned myth, and questioned traditional dogmas that had been handed down in the form of myths. They did not *intend* to be displacing the traditional authority of women, however.

Quite clearly, Socrates, who was an initiate of the Eleusinian Mysteries (a late form of the matriarchal cult of Demeter, the corn goddess), sought the authorization of the matriarchy for his life's work. The Oracle at Delphi, another of the traditional matriarchal powers (a pretty scary gal who delivered her wisdom while squatting over a big crevice in the earth), had set Socrates on his quest for self-knowledge. The enigmatic left-handed compliment she paid him can be read as saying that he was the wisest *man* in Athens, because he knew the full extent of his ignorance. The Delphic Oracle, while still a priestess, was at that time devoted to the god Apollo, which means it was already fully developed in the direction of *patriarchy* (Harrison's history in the book *Themis* explains the whole development), and that it was an Apollonian Oracle that set Socrates on the path of reason.

Socrates also understood himself as a "midwife" of ideas, helping others give birth to their thoughts, and in one of the most important discourses he ever gave, at the famous "Symposium," he reports the wisdom he learned at the feet of Diotima of Mantinea, the woman who taught him philosophy. Plato himself was also devoted, in his way, to the wisdom of women, having called the poetess Sappho the "Tenth Muse," in admiration of her unmatched poetic skill and wisdom. The point is that even while the early philosophers were struggling against myth, and trying to give authority to reason, they did not foresee the effect this effort would have on women. But the traditional authority of women was in fact intimately tied to the authority of myth, as it turned out. When myth and its traditions were pulled down and replaced by reason, the authority and wisdom of women went down with it.

From its beginnings, then, philosophy has tried to distance itself from myth, claiming that reason is an *alternative* to myth, completely superior to myth, and doing everything possible to obscure or deny whatever debts to mythic consciousness philosophy may have. A few philosophers along the way have argued that this sharp distinction between reason and myth is a bad idea— Giambattista Vico (1668–1744), J.G. Herder (1744–1803), F.W.J. Schelling (1775–1854), Ernst Cassirer (1874–1945), and Susanne Langer (1895–1985) are a few of them, and all of these philosophers of myth are well worth reading. But philosophy was too heavily invested in defining reason as contrary to myth. Still, Bachofen, Nietzsche, Harrison, Jung, and others, were willing to delve into myth and ritual, and all their mercurial forms, and that is where they learned about matriarchy.

The ideas associated with matriarchy never really received the type of conceptual clarification that we now associate with truth, science, and reason—or philosophy. Most of the philosophers who sought to interpret the philosophical meaning of myth paid little attention to matriarchy. So the "principles" of matriarchy, if one could call them that, remained embedded in stories, sayings, and the oral tradition. At the same time that the boys were whittling away at the authority of myth, they were developing a phobia about women and oracles and earthy rituals, things women had always presided over. During the course of a few centuries of "reason," the boys who had given their souls to reason started calling the women who hadn't done so "witches." The only difference between the veneration of the Oracle at Delphi and the burning of the same woman as a "witch" is about five hundred years of "reason," and a nervous and fearful patriarchy that didn't *want* to know where it came from. The boys became downright superstitious about the power of reason, and refused to admit that its power was also embedded in myth.

Feminist philosophers of the last forty years have rightly identified this narrow and stilted devotion to reason among the boys as a "logic of domination." The exclusion of all emotion and all wider experience from "respectable philosophy" has had the effect of perpetuating male supremacy in the academies and the profession of philosophy, making it a boy's club that runs on "boy logic." It's not that women can't do boy logic. Of course they can. But why should they? It isn't very important, a barren womb, one might say (but one should not). This is all true. It isn't so much a plot by the boys to keep the girls out, but rather it's a bad habit that the boys exploit to their advantage. Yet, women philosophers have not been eager to take up the mantle of the matriarchs and explore the direction it might lead, if the old myths were to receive a more contemporary voice. They seem concerned to maintain their own intellectual credibility, and so this matriarchy stuff remains on the fringes. So that task of further articulation has also fallen largely to men, such as Bachofen and Jung and Campbell, and now Gregory Maguire. And it's not like the boys in the academy are listening to these men either.

The Matriarchal Myths of Oz

At long last we arrive in the Matriarchy of Oz. You now know the *story* of the ideas associated with matriarchy, since I've been prattling on about it for several pages. So what about these ideas themselves? In Maguire's mythology of Oz, there are two dominant, recurring mythical motifs: the cult of Lurline and the Kumbric Witch. What the heck is this?

One thing that happens over the course of thousands of years, as Maguire understands, is that ideas and stories that once belonged together eventually come to be separated and they stultify. They become mysterious "dead ends." No one in Elphaba's Oz knows quite what to make of the folk religion of the Fairy Queen Lurline, or of the ominous legends of the Kumbric Witch. These stories have been passed down for so long that their origins are now shrouded in the mists of time. But they actually represent different stages in the development of the same culture.

I greatly admire Maguire's handling of this matter because it reminds me of the way J.R.R. Tolkien dealt with similar issues in his epic works. Tolkien had, as we all know, worked out the full history of Middle Earth (although he was not sensitive to the matriarchy ideas), and he had determined exactly the spot in its history to situate Frodo's story. He knew how much (and how little) the hobbits and elves and humans in Frodo's day would understand their own history, and he carefully filtered their understanding on the basis of how myths and legends really do develop over many millennia. Maguire has done that too, and very adeptly.

I don't know whether Maguire has a work like Tolkien's *The Silmarillion* piled up in his writing studio, and I doubt that he does, but there is no real need to work out the history of Oz in that kind of detail. Maguire has the lattice of Baum's fifteen books, and he locates his own two books carefully between Baum's first and second books.

Maguire's *Wicked* transpires in the immediate pre-history of Baum's first book, and closes with the death of the Wicked Witch of the West, well before Baum's first book ends. Maguire's second book, *Son of a Witch*, takes up and finishes the events of Baum's first book and then extends a little ways into Baum's second book, *The Marvelous Land of Oz*. Maguire's second tale ends before the revolt of the knitting needles occurs, but Elphaba's son Liir, the protagonist of *Son of a Wicth* (and he is a protagonist, not a hero –heroes are for the patriarchy), briefly meets Mombi and Tip on the road, the latter being destined for a magical sex-change operation and restoration to the throne in the not-too-distant future. Maguire has his history in place, with his Campbell-esque understanding of where his characters reside in their own history, and he builds from there—and does so very well.

The Kumbric Witch

The tales of the Kumbric Witch in Maguire's Oz would be much older than the cult of Lurline. The Kumbric Witch derives from what Bachofen calls the "Tellurian" period of human cultural development, which is the earliest and darkest time. The elemental principle is "earth" (as opposed to water, air, and eventually fire, since fire was the Apollonian principle of late matriarchy, opening the way to pure patriarchy). For Bachofen, the social system at all stages of culture is exemplified by the changes in marriage and mating rituals, and at this early stage of culture, the Kumbric period in Maguire's terms, marriage is by "natural" association. Here women take the men they choose, ritualistically and under the direction of the crones, but the men are essentially just visitors to the clans of the women. Women have here banded together during this epoch for mutual support and protection, and men are kept in abeyance by being unable to control the raising of children. The male children are eventually taken away from the clan by the men in an important coming-of-age ritual. If this banding together of women had never occurred, we would still have no culture, Bachofen believed.

The rituals associated with this stage are earthy, to say the least, dominated by the images of swamps and snakes, reptiles and mud. These symbols of Tellurian matriarchy persist in our own world, of course, but the reptiles and swamps, especially the serpent, are increasingly hated and discredited as the patriarchy becomes more powerful. That puts a new twist on the Adam and Eve story, doesn't it? That story is the work of the patriarchs, you can rest assured. But it's impossible to conceal entirely the traces of the earlier time when the snake meant positive things to human beings, like health, life, power, wisdom, and well-being. Check out the logo of the American Medical Association, and consult the description of the Rod of Aaron in the Book of Exodus (see 7:8–13), and while you're at it, you might look up Miriam, Moses's sister, and ask yourself what's going on with her.

The Kumbric Witch in Maguire's tale is held in ominous fear, but also awe and respect. Her power is mysterious and extensive, unknown and unfathomable. The stories about her retreat into her cave, told by mothers to their daughters (and with which Maguire closes his book), symbolize the decline of matriarchy, and augur its possible resurgence. When a little girl asks her mother whether the witch ever comes out of her cave, the traditional answer is "not yet." There is both fear and anticipation of the return of the Kumbric Witch. This witch is described by Maguire in an ancient image discovered by his character Boq, a Munchkin man who reminds me of Bachofen, and yes, I suspect that "Boq" *is* Bachofen. I am pretty sure Maguire is playing with us about this, waiting for someone to notice who "Boq" is. Well Greg, I'm onto your game (I think). Boq finds a portrait in the library at Shiz, the Oxford of Oz. Here is how Maguire describes it:

> The Witch stood on an isthmus connecting two rocky lands, and on either side of her stretched patches of cerulean blue sea, with white-lipped waves of astonishing vigor and particularity. The Witch held in her hands a beast of unrecognizable species, though it was clearly drowned, or nearly drowned. She cradled it in an arm that . . . lovingly encircled the beast's wet spiky-furred back. With her other hand she was freeing a breast from her robe, offering suck to the creature. . . . She was nearly motherly, with miserable child. Her look was inward, or sad, or something. But her feet didn't match her expression, for they were planted on the narrow strand with prehensile grip, apparent even through the silver-colored shoes, whose coin-of-the-realm brilliance had first caught Boq's eye. (pp. 124–25)

There's more to this, but you get the picture. This is an image of the transition from the earth principle to the water principle in the development of matriarchal culture. The silver slippers symbolize for Maguire all the feminine powers, both good and evil. It becomes easier to understand why Elphaba wants those shoes. She can't get this image out of her mind, once she sees it. Poor Boq. What can he ever do with such a discovery, except give it to Elphaba and hope that she can do some good with it?

The Yackle Moon

The second stage of cultural development is a "lunar" stage, according to Bachofen, dominated by the water principle. Water is purified and rarified earth, and its association with the moon comes from the relationship of moon and tide. In some regions, this move from Tellurian to Lunar matriarchy was a painful and disorderly transition. Men banded together to enslave women. When that happens, all hell breaks loose, and women become militant in resisting the tyranny of the physically stronger men. It is in this period that some women become Amazonians, warriors. They ultimately lose the battle and are increasingly subjugated.

Such an ugly battle (men butchering women) is depicted on the famous shield of Athena Parthenos (you can see her on display in Nashville, Tennessee, at the full-scale replica of the Parthenon, and she's very big). This "parthenos" is the final form of Athena, and yes, "parthenos" means "virgin," and yes, Athena is the enforcer of chastity, and yes, she is the model in many ways for the subsequent cult of the Virgin Mary, all according to Bachofen. You can see how enforced chastity and monogamous civil marriage removes the obstacle to patriarchy that arose from the problem of not knowing who the father of a child was. Of course, now we have DNA tests. That invention should pretty much dissolve the issue forever (or until the Apocalypse).

When the women are thus defeated, they may go "underground," so to speak, re-establishing their sisterhoods in the forests and deep hills, and keeping their traditions on the edges of the civilization. The witches at the opening of Shakespeare's Macbeth are such sisters, and so is Maguire's character Mother Yackle. She just keeps popping up throughout both books, and seems immortal. The best description of her, in mythic terms, comes when Elphaba finds an image in the Grimmerie, a magic book from another world:

> What was more interesting, in [Elphaba's] reading, was a small drawing she saw next to a section marked Evil Particulars. The drawing . . . was a clever sketch of a broad-faced woman-fiend. Written in an angu-

lar bronchiating script with elegant tapering seriphs, all around the illustration, were the words YAKAL SNARLING. Elphaba looked again. She saw a creature part woman, part grassland jakal, its jaws open, its hand-paw lifted to rip the heart out of a spiderweb. And the creature reminded her of old Mother Yackle from the mauntery. (p. 293)

Mother Yackle is essentially a witch-midwife whose purpose in life seems to be the creation and perpetuation of Elphaba's family line. After Elphaba dies, Yackle continues her function by making sure that Elphaba's son Liir, even though he is gay, lives long enough to conceive a daughter. Unkown to Elphaba, Mother Yackle also oversees a degraded version of the Dionysian orgy rites in a seedy establishment called, cleverly, the Philosophy Club.

In Bachofen's theory, the Dionysian wine and fertility cult arises in counterbalance to the cult of Apollo, as it strives through the air (Olympus) principle, and toward the solar principle, that is, a sun cult. The dispossessed earth-women and the displaced moon-women (those who don't become witches) form a sort of alliance in which *earth* and *water* (put those elements together rightly and you get wine, Dionysus's favorite libation) becomes the basis for the continuation of their social forms, although greatly altered by the influence of a dawning patriarchy. The ritual comes to be largely degraded over the course of centuries until it looks something like the shenanigans described by Maguire at the Philosophy Club (see pp. 164–69, pretty racy stuff). So the character of Mother Yackle is the key to understanding how Maguire deals with the decline of matriarchy into a perverse cult.

Not all lunar matriarchies became perverse, however, as Maguire shows in the folkways of the Scrow tribe, who venerate an elephant princess named Nastoya. She plays a crucial role in showing Elphaba the constructive side of the sisterhood, how content and constructive the men can be, and how a nomadic but highly cultured life can be maintained in the matriarchal social forms. Of course, Maguire knows (as do many people) that elephant social order is matriarchal, so it's not like he is trying to make a secret of what he does with Princess Nastoya. She is the counter-balance to Yackle, and the elephant princess continues to play an important role in Maguire's story throughout his second book. With her death at the end of *Son of a Witch*, which is a long time coming, the Scrow also become patriarchal, but they do so peacefully and reverently, and with a memory of what they had been. It's difficult to miss the parallels here to certain Native American and African tribes.

A Pair of Spirits

The flipside of the decline of earth and water matriarchy (associated with Aphrodite and Artemis in the Greek civilization) is the rise and ascent of the Olympian and solar matriarchy. Obviously, air is rarified water, and fire is rarified air. Keep squeezing the earth, and eventually you will discover fire. The way that Bachofen tells the story is one of cultures gradually shedding what *weighs down* the human spirit, from earth to water to air to fire, a purification and rarifying process, until only spirit remains and the body has been left behind, in the primal mud.[2]

As culture "rises" to these new heights, we see the emergence of the two gods who will eventually dominate the last stage of matriarchy, Apollo and Athena. They're both pretty ruthless when they want to be, but they were deeply venerated during the most prosperous and creative phase of ancient life. Marija Gimbutas did much to demonstrate that the civilization of the late Minoan and Mycenaean periods (about 2000–1100 B.C.E.) had a social organization along these lines of high matriarchy.

When Socrates and his buddies came along some 600 years later, they were brought up in the (by then) declining days of this matriarchal civilization of Apollo and Athena. With the development of phonetic writing, pure patriarchy was beginning to prevail. One doesn't *need* oracles when one has holy books. The oracles persisted for a long time, of course. There were still prophets and prophetesses, seers and enchanters, but their role was less important and more suspect. It was during this period (give or take four hundred years) that nearly all of our most traditional sacred writings took their solid forms, such as the Hebrew Bible, the epics of Homer, the Vedas, and so on, moving from a primarily oral tradition to a written one. These writings congealed and finally coagulated, and with this new stability, the canons of reason began to replace folk wisdom. That was the final blow to the matriarchy. The logic of imagination was replaced by the logic of language and

---

[2] For a bit of wisdom on all this earth, water, air and fire stuff, see Jane Ellen Harrison, *Themis: A Study in the Social Origins of Greek Religion*, second edition (London: Merlin Press, 1989 [1927]), pp. 390–94.

grammar, and myth yielded to the onslaught of reason.

Here Maguire ventures an intriguing hypothesis. What would history look like if there had been no Axial Age religions? The "Axial Age" is a phrase that historians of religion use to describe the transformation in history that occurred as a result of the "paradigmatic individuals," that is, primarily Confucius, Lao-tze, Socrates, Buddha, and Jesus. One does well to include Rabbi Hillel on this list, in my view. Each of these figures introduced tremendous reforms into the traditional religions, reforms that had the principles of a more compassionate patriarchy embedded within. The paradigmatic individuals all moved their traditions from visible to invisible principles, beyond the solar patriarchy to an *unseen* order.

But Maguire's Oz has *no* Axial Age and *no* paradigmatic individuals. His suggestion is that even without these individuals, *monotheism* would *still* arise and develop, and history would still move beyond sun cults into ethical religions of an invisible god. Maguire calls this deity the "Unnamed God," in his Oz religion of "Unionism." No one in Oz assumes that the Unnamed God is male, which I take to be another result of the removal of the Axial Age and the paradigmatic individuals (all of whom are men, if you hadn't noticed). Maguire's Unionism looks sort of like Unitarianism, except far more pious, and it does try to fight or discredit the folk religions. But without any paradigmatic individuals and without the threat of hellfire and damnation, the Unionist Church in Oz is largely ineffectual. They simply have no good stories, and they still have the same theological problems that go with any religion based on an invisible god or cosmic order. The value of Maguire's idea of removing the Axial Age and the paradigmatic individuals is that it clears the way for another two thousand years of decline in the matriarchy, without any serious effort of the part of a church to stamp it out. And that Oz is the one Elphaba inhabits.

As Slow as Lurlinemas

At the moment in the history of Oz depicted by Maguire, the stories of Lurline the Fairy Princess still dominate the superstitions of the ignorant peasant class, well represented in the delightful character of Nanny. Nanny is a crone who raises three generations of Munchkin Thropps, Elphaba's mother Melena, then Elphaba, and then her illegitimate son Liir. Nanny is simply filled with folk sayings and oral traditions, such as this little poem:

Boys study, girls know
That's the way the lessons go
Boys learn, girls forget
That's the way of lessons yet[3]

It's actually a warning about the emerging patriarchy and a resigned notification to the girls that they will forget who they are—indeed, they almost *have* forgotten when Elphaba comes on the scene. Nanny does not know or understand the full significance of the sayings and traditions she keeps, and is not very concerned to help Elphaba's generation continue those folkways. But everyone still celebrates around the time of the winter solstice a festival called Lurlinemas. It has been commercialized to some extent, and no one takes its religious meaning seriously (in fact, no one even seems sure what the meaning was supposed to be). But for children the holiday is slow in coming, about as slow as the decay of matriarchy. Lurline is, as far as I can make out, what is left of something like Aphrodite when such a long epoch of forgetfulness has passed.

The Hymn of the Kouretes

Maguire's Oz contains much that may remind us of a matriarchy long dead, but I find this passage especially informative. Elphaba has arrived for university study in Shiz, where she attends a woman's college called Crage Hall, and Maguire describes a curious event she sees:

> On one noble occasion, which no Crage Hall girl present ever forgot, the senior boys from Three Queens College across the canal, for a lark and a dare, had tanked themselves up with beer in the middle of the afternoon, had hired a White Bear violinist, and had gone down to dance together under the willow trees, wearing nothing but their clinging cotton drawers and their school scarves. It was deliciously pagan, as they had set an old chipped statue of Lurline the Fairy Queen on a three-legged stool, and she seemed to smile at their loose-limbed gaiety. The girls and Amas pretended shock, but poorly; they lingered, watching, until horrified proctors from Three Queens came rushing out to round the revelers up. Near nudity was one thing, but public Lurlinism—even as a joke—bordered on being intolerably retrograde, even royalist. And that *did* not do in the Wizard's reign. (p. 76)

---

[3] Gregory Maguire, *Wicked: The Life and Times of the Wicked Witch of the West* (HarperCollins, 1995), p. 53.

There's so much going on in this passage that I can't begin to untangle it for you. But suffice to say, that ritual was no joke. That's basically the same ritual Jane Ellen Harrison spent over five hundred pages untangling in her book *Themis* (second edition, 1927), her masterwork. A mysterious fragment called the "Hymn of the Kouretes" had been discovered, and for Harrison it was the Rosetta Stone of the history of matriarchy. Based on Maguire's description above, not only do I suspect he has studied this book of Harrison's, but he also projected the ritual two thousand extra years into the future and described it as it would have been, given the lapse of time and memory. I could be wrong, but I don't think so. Maguire understands exactly how to dress the boys and how to describe their "gaiety." Yes, that is "Gaia," the earth goddess, right there in his word-choice, as he well knows. And there is more, but you'll have to get Harrison's book and decide for yourself. Having decided for myself that Maguire is consciously tracing matriarchy, unimpeded by the church, for another two thousand years, something else dawned on me . . . something about Elphaba, the Wicked Witch of the West.

Who's Afraid of Virginia Woolf?

There are wolves alluded to throughout *Wicked*, but their meaning and themes are never quite developed. They are feared by everyone in Elphaba's childhood (except her), and they seem to stalk her and her Nanny throughout the book, until Elphaba befriends one half-wolf she names Killyjoy. I think Maguire actually means for us, for someone, to detect Elphaba's true mythic identity in this symbol and many others, if we will just use our imaginations. Elphaba is Virginia Woolf. The more I considered it, the more sense it made to me—Elphaba's psychology, her vexations, her temperament, her feelings of not belonging in the world, her politics, her ambivalence about men, her dreams about the waves, all of it reminds me of Virginia Woolf.

So I did what any conscientious researcher would do: I Googled "Gregory Maguire" and "Virginia Woolf." It turns out I'm not the first person to notice this connection. A number of commentators and bloggers have noticed how Elphaba's group of college friends, whom Maguire terms "The Charmed Circle," seems to be modeled on the Bloomsbury Group, the bohemian circle of writers, artists and aesthetes to which Virginia Woolf belonged. I hadn't noticed that, but yes, obviously. And then, a few hits in on my Google, there's an interview with Gregory Maguire in the Kansas City *Star* in which he explicitly says he modeled the character of Elphaba partly on Virginia Woolf.

Thus, the reason Elphaba dreams of and fears water has to do with both the difficult transition from earth principles to water and lunar principles, but also with the incomprehensible nature of woman in a patriarchy. That's why Elphaba hates the Wizard. And like Virginia Woolf, Elphaba simply cannot work it all out—she's too much a product of the modern world, she can't remember. The reason Maguire offers for Elphaba's aversion to water, then, in mythical and imaginative ways, is that Virginia Woolf drowns herself, and baptizes herself in death. Maguire describes Elphaha's "baptism" in similar terms, as she toys with the idea of suicide.

Yet, Maguire has Elphaba perish in both fire and water, indicating that the Witch is perhaps even a greater sufferer under the weight of patriarchy than was Virginia Woolf, who only "returns" to the water in her suicide. The writer found a feminine guardian in Harrison, whereas Elphaba's world had fallen further into forgetfulness. She found only the horrible Madam Morrible, the Headmistress of Crage Hall, whom Elphaba wants only to kill, and who serves the Nietzschean overlord, the Wizard of Oz. Unless Maguire knows something I don't know about the relationship between Virginia Woolf and Jane Ellen Harrison, I'm assuming that Madam Morrible is *not* modeled on Miss Harrison (who even moved in with the Bloomsbury Group when she retired in 1922, so I'm assuming she was on very good terms with Virginia Woolf). But when I said in another essay in this volume that I didn't "know" why water melts the witch, that wasn't quite the truth. I was doing boy-logic there, and boy-logic doesn't lead to an answer to the vexed and mythical question of water and witches. It isn't logical knowledge, it's imaginative knowledge. Elphaba fears water because she *is* Virginia Woolf, and Virginia Woolf drowned herself. So there.

I have overstayed my welcome among women, if indeed I was ever welcome at all. Having brought to the table this portrait of the Matriarchy in Maguire's Oz, I will now do as Bachofen and Boq did, which is give the portrait to all you Elphabas out there and hope it is of some value to you. I shall retire quietly to my home now, and, like Bachofen and Boq, seek to live a quiet life until I am very old. If anyone asks whether I have come out of my cave, you may tell them "not yet."

Doctors of Thinkology

GINA ALTAMURA is the best-dressed philosopher this side of Oz, and accordingly she is frequently mistaken for Dorothy Gale by elderly men with shopping carts in downtown Portland, Oregon. Her shiny red shoes and spotless blue baby doll dresses lead Cairn Terriers to follow her about in public parks, and maybe even around the stunning Lewis and Clark College campus, where she studies Philosophy with special interest in aesthetics/lit theory and political theory. There's no place like home (when your home is Portland), and there's no better feeling than writing sassy pop culture commentary for rock music venues and alternative papers, her other passion.

RANDALL E. AUXIER has been to Kansas. He was surprised to discover that Kansas is in color, but the Texas panhandle actually *is* in sepia-tones. Confused and troubled, he began to think. Decades later he thinks out loud, to the delight and consternation of students at Southern Illinois University in Carbondale (which has nice rainbows but is far, very far, from Oz). Sometimes Auxier writes down what he thinks and puts it in books like *Bruce Springsteen and Philosophy*, or *Monty Python and Philosophy*, or even *Pink Floyd and Philosophy*, among others. The Dean at SIUC is very impressed by the importance of Auxier's research, and wishes his whole faculty would be as serious.

JESSICA BELL teaches American History and Science at Casady School, in Oklahoma City, and **JASON BELL** is completing a dissertation on the philosopher Josiah Royce at Vanderbilt University. Jessica and Jason have recently delivered the prestigious (but unpaid) Professor H.M. Wogglebug, T.E. Lectures at the Royal Athletic College of Oz. Across the street from their alma mater, Oklahoma City University, they are building a little café on the once-Route 66. You can buy philosophy books there, too, like this book (which would go better with a cup of coffee, wouldn't it?) and Plato, and of course, Baum.

352 *Doctors of Thinkology*

STEVE BICKHAM was a philosophy teacher for thirty-three years and a department chair for over twenty. He is happily retired from Mansfield University. It is nice to report that the piles of freshman essays and the almost as numerous meetings threatening to dissolve one's department do come to an end. He now enjoys Oz-like activities—organizing APA sessions for the Society for Philosophy of Creativity, participating in community theater, and fishing with his grandson.

TOMMY J. CURRY never learned to dance like Lil Michael, but has recently taken up KRUMPIN after many failed attempts to imitate the dance style of Michael Jackson. After a failed rap career, Curry continues his work on culturalogics, Critical Race Theory and African American philosophy on a post-doctoral fellowship at Penn State University. As a renowned freestyle battle rapper, Curry has repeatedly brought the extemporaneous style of Hip-Hop culture to bear on popular culture projects like *The Wizard of Oz and Philosophy* and *Philosophy looks at Chess* published by Open Court. However, working on this project in particular and being inspired by the rhythmic beauty, and spectacles of dancing in *The Wiz*, Curry has vowed to take considerable time away from his projects on the American Negro Academy to learn the moonwalk.

LUKE DICK was raised in Cogar, Oklahoma, which has witnessed many a twister. He's seen the dank walls of various fraidy holes and has emerged virtually unscathed (due to red dirt wisdom and Oklahoma's superior radar systems). Luke's travels, toils, and studies have never led him much farther than the central time zone. Luke now resides in Nashville, Tennessee, with Dorothy, aka, his daughter, Emily, where they do their best to study and revel in the virtues and vices of the heart-ful, the high-minded, and the courageous.

GEORGE A. DUNN regularly teaches a course on "Philosophy through Pop Culture" at Indiana University–Purdue University at Indianapolis. His publications include essays on philosophical issues in *X-Men and Philosophy* and *Buffy the Vampire Slayer and Philosophy*. He's been a visiting lecturer at Purdue University, the University of Indianapolis and, as this volume goes to press, the Ningbo Institute of Technology in the People's Republic of China. Once he leaves China, he's heading straight to Oz, where he plans to ask the Wizard for something clever to say in his bioblurb.

KEVIN K. DURAND annoys his students regularly by humming along to Oz, even if it's only playing in his head. He read *The Wonderful Wizard of Oz* in 1974, sitting in a back room at his grandparents' house as Hurricane Carmen kicked up a bit of a ruckus outside. Having discovered Baum's book on the shelf, he was perplexed that the movie left out so many wondrous parts. Thus began a career of puzzling why. Why are things they way they are and not some other way entirely? Why are things left out when they should be in; why are they in when they should be out; and why should we pay attention to that man behind the curtain; and why isn't soccer the official sport of Oz? Durand's research is renowned for filling much-need gaps in the philosophic literature.

MATTHEW CALEB FLAMM is the Assistant Professor of Philosophy behind the curtain at Rockford College where he writes articles on the wizard George Santayana and American Philosophy while wondering if Oz really exists or if that Wicked Witch on the broom stick circling over the college quad is married.

AARON FORTUNE is from Oklahoma, which is like Kansas, except, well, hotter. And browner. Troubled by things he didn't understand (like the existence of rainbows, to say nothing of what lies over them), Aaron flew off to graduate school at Southern Illinois University Carbondale. There, he learned that he always already had everything that wise men have—except, of course, a diploma. Just to be safe, Aaron got two. Since the world seems to be out of wicked witches to slay, Aaron moved back to Oklahoma because there really is no place like home. He now spends his days as an adjunct instructor at the University of Central Oklahoma and his evenings at home with his wife, daughter, and cat.

J.M. FRITZMAN teaches ethics, aesthetics, philosophy of law, Indian philosophy, nineteenth-century philosophy, and recent continental philosophy at Lewis and Clark College. He often writes about the philosopher Georg Hegel. He's visited India several times. He hopes to take Hegel there someday and throw him in the Ganges. Fritzman brags that he's seen more than two hundred Bollywood movies, and he suspects that the makers of *The Wizard of Oz* watched nearly as many. He loves Indian food. He's fortunate to live in Portland, Oregon, which has Indian restaurants as good as those in India. Lately he's boasted about learning to cook dal makhani and pindi chana. He aspires to become the second best-dressed philosopher this side of Oz.

RICHARD GREENE would like you to believe that he is an Associate Professor of Philosophy at Weber State University who earned his Ph.D. at UC Santa Barbara and has published work in epistemology while co-editing *The Sopranos and Philosophy*, *The Undead and Philosophy*, and *Quentin Tarantino and Philosophy*. But, in fact, none of the above is true as he is merely a cleverly disguised Tik Tok machine.

COREY MCCALL teaches philosophy at Elmira College, a place that sometimes reminds him a little of Oz for reasons that he'll keep to himself. When he was young, he once told his sister that she would melt if she got wet, but she didn't believe him. These days he spends his time getting students to believe similar tall tales from the history of philosophy and trying to remember where he put his brain.

JAMES MCLACHLAN teaches munchkins, winkies, and a few winged monkeys at Western Carolina University, where he has no more brains than any of them but he does have one thing they haven't got, a diploma. It's in Thinkology from a school in Canada where he once followed the famous "only road" to Toronto hoping to find the Wizard. He writes about French existentialists, Mormons, and obscure American philosophers. The Wicked Witch of the East was one of the few to read his book, *The Desire to be God: Freedom and the Other in Sartre and Berdyaev,* but then a house fell on her. He desires only to meet the wizard and get home some day.

MICHAEL F. PATTON, JR. confidently reported that he could write a great essay about *The Wonderful Wizard of Oz* and then realized he'd never read it. Then he realized that he sort of hated the movie. Rather than pass up an opportunity to get a publication, he read the original book and found it full of things to poke philosophical fun at. His hobbies include writing silly articles, astronomy, and referring to himself in the third person. He lives in Montevallo, Alabama, where he teaches at the eponymous University and where he shares a house with his wife Cheryl and his five cats whose names he never gets right anyway.

JENNIFER A. REA is the Wicked Witch of Rhetoric at Rockford College where she uses the Golden Cap to magically summon a flock of flying green monkeys to persuade her students to write well. She is finishing up her dissertation on Irish children's literature and is positive that she will relocate to the Emerald City once she discovers who that man is behind the curtain.

PAM R. SAILORS has never owned a pair of ruby slippers. When she's not stitching wings onto the backs of monkeys, she teaches in the Philosophy Department at Missouri State University. Most of her research has been in applied ethics, particularly bioethics and sports ethics, but she teaches Feminist Philosophy and Theories of Ethics as well. She also holds the position of Department Head, but only because she couldn't get them to change the title to Wizard. Her career has been only slightly hampered by her inexplicable fear of girls in gingham dresses . . . and their little dogs, too.

PHILLIP S. SENG is from Nebraska, and that put him close enough to Kansas to know better than to run around outside during cyclones. He now lives in Washington, D.C., and sees many, many people made of straw there. Watching movies as a child, he found himself wondering how he could possibly make a living out of it. Now, he still watches movies and tells students at the University of Maryland, Baltimore County which movies they should watch (almost all of them) and why they should watch them. Seng earns enough to buy DVDs of the movies he likes so he can watch them over and over again; these take up less room than the books he reads about the movies he likes.

MARK DIETRICH TSCHAEPE is currently a post-doc research fellow at the Center for Inquiry in Amherst, New York, where he is attempting to argue how the Scarecrow can do deductive proofs without possessing a brain. So far all of his arguments contain a straw man.

Index